SELL

THIRD CANADIAN EDITION

Thomas N. Ingram
Colorado State University

Raymond W. LaForge
University of Louisville

Ramon A. Avila
Ball State University

Charles H. Schwepker Jr.
University of Central Missouri

Michael R. Williams
Oklahoma City University

Kirby Shannahan
Memorial University of Newfoundland

Rachelle Shannahan
Memorial University of Newfoundland

 CENGAGE

Australia • Brazil • Canada • Mexico • Singapore • United Kingdom • United States

SELL, Third Canadian Edition
Thomas N. Ingram, Raymond W. LaForge, Ramon A. Avila, Charles H. Schwepker Jr., Michael R. Williams, Kirby Shannahan, Rachelle Shannahan

Senior Director, Product: Jackie Wood

Senior Portfolio Manager: Leanna Maclean

Marketing Manager: Lindsay Shipman

Director, Content and Production: Toula Dileo

Content Development Manager: Dylan Schoenmakers

Senior Content Production Manager: Jennifer Hare

Production Service: MPS Limited

Copy Editor: Kelli Howey

Text Designer: Ken Cadinouche

Cover Designer: Courtney Hellam

For product information and technology assistance, contact us at **Canada Support, canadasupport.cengage.com.**

For permission to use material from this text or product, submit all requests online at **www.cengage.com/permissions.**

Library and Archives Canada Cataloguing in Publication:

Title: Sell / Thomas N. Ingram (Colorado State University), Raymond W. LaForge (University of Louisville), Ramon A. Avila (Ball State University), Charles H. Schwepker Jr. (University of Central Missouri), Michael R. Williams (Oklahoma City University), Kirby Shannahan (Memorial University of Newfoundland), Rachelle Shannahan (Memorial University of Newfoundland).

Names: Ingram, Thomas N., author. | LaForge, Raymond W., author. | Avila, Ramon A., 1955- author. | Schwepker, Charles H., Jr., author. | Williams, Michael R. (Professor of marketing), author. | Shannahan, Kirby, author. | Shannahan, Rachelle, author.

Description: Third Canadian edition. | Includes bibliographical references and index.

Identifiers: Canadiana 2020027757X | ISBN 9780176916015 (softcover)

Subjects: LCSH: Selling—Textbooks. | LCSH: Sales management—Textbooks. | LCGFT: Textbooks.

Classification: LCC HF5438.25 .I54 2020 | DDC 658.85—dc23

ISBN-13: 978-0-17-691601-5
ISBN-10: 0-17-691601-6

Cengage Canada
1120 Birchmount Road
Toronto, ON M1K 5G4
Canada

Cengage is a leading provider of customized learning solutions with employees residing in nearly 40 different countries and sales in more than 125 countries around the world. Find your local representative at **www.cengage.com.**

To learn more about Cengage platforms and services, register or access your online learning solution, or purchase materials for your course, visit **www.cengage.ca.**

Printed in Canada
Print Number: 01   Print Year: 2020

INGRAM / LAFORGE / AVILA / SCHWEPKER / WILLIAMS / SHANNAHAN / SHANNAHAN

SELL

BRIEF CONTENTS

CONTENTS

© wwing/iStock by Getty Images

© SimplyCreativePhotography/iStock

PREFACE

Created through a "student-tested, faculty-approved" review process with hundreds of students and faculty, *SELL* is an engaging and accessible solution to accommodate the diverse lifestyles of today's learners. This resource employs comprehensive coverage of contemporary professional selling in an interesting and challenging manner. Including relational consultative selling, the text is organized on a more contemporary relationship-selling process that the author team has tested in, and developed for, major selling organizations.

We are grateful to the many reviewers who offered suggestions and recommendations that have helped guide the third Canadian edition of *SELL*:

Gary Glatter, St. Clair College

Ludvik Jakopin, George Brown College

Alison MacCallum, Georgian College
    and Sheridan College

Ed J. McHugh, Nova Scotia Community College
    Leslie Pidcock, SAIT

Wendy Threader, Algonquin College

**Endorsed by the Canadian Professional
Sales Association**

This resource has been approved by the Canadian Professional Sales Association (CPSA) for students taking the Personal Selling Course across Canada, and features an overview of the CPSA Professional Sales Competency Framework, developed to indicate key areas that are essential to the success of selling professionals in today's complex, competitive marketplace. Concepts throughout the book have been aligned to CPSA competencies, helping students to get closer to the critical step of achieving CPSA Accreditation. The comprehensive version of the competency framework can be found at CPSA.com.

WHAT IS CPSA?

For as long as sales has existed in Canada, CPSA has been there to support and advance sales professionals with tools, sales training, and resources that accelerate their success.

CPSA has transformed the sales industry, bringing in rigorous standards, ethical guidelines, and recognition programs that have professionalized sales and set the bar for excellence.

Today, CPSA continues to shape the future of sales with innovative, forward-thinking programs that advance the profession and support sales professionals at every stage in achieving their goals.

Modern students require modern solutions. MindTap is a flexible all-in-one teaching and learning platform including the full ebook, a customizable learning path, and various course-specific activities that drive student engagement and critical thinking.

DOWNLOAD THE CENGAGE MOBILE APP

Get access to a full, interactive ebook, readable online or off, study tools that empower anytime, anywhere learning and 24/7 course access, the *Cengage Mobile App* keeps students focused and ready to study whenever it's convenient for them.

Download the Cengage Mobile App:

FEATURES

NEW FEATURES

We're excited to introduce a range of new features in *SELL*, Third Canadian Edition, that support the current needs of students while developing the next generation of sales professionals.

- The **CPSA Competency Framework Alignment** indicates concepts and examples that are directly aligned with the CPSA's core competencies for sales professionals. This framework has been developed by CPSA to indicate key areas that are essential to sales success. The comprehensive version of the competency framework can be found at CPSA.com.

- **Technology in Sales** boxes describe current innovations that are evolving sales practices and provide instruction on how to best incorporate them.

- **Selling in Action** boxes feature tips and practical considerations to improve sales skills, delivered through industry professional advice.

- **Every Business Sells** boxes highlight sales professionals from diverse Canadian companies to demonstrate how they rely on sales skills for success.

- Additional end-of-chapter **Integrative Cases**, which focus on current, Canadian topics, allow students to exercise their sales knowledge in real-life examples.

UPDATED FEATURES

In addition to new features, we have maintained and revised elements of *SELL*, Second Canadian Edition, that have proven critical to student learning and success.

- **An Ethical Dilemma** boxes guide students to think carefully about moral concerns and best practices when making sales decisions.

- End-of-chapter **Cases** help students to apply chapter concepts in practical business examples.

- End-of-chapter **Role Plays** encourage students to inhabit a range of sales situations and develop interpersonal skills.

- **Chapter Review Cards** summarize key chapter concepts and definitions.

- **Continuing Case Cards** provide further experience applying sales knowledge within a sustained, company-focused example.

SUPPLEMENTS FOR SUCCESS

INSTRUCTOR RESOURCES

The following instructor resources have been created for *SELL*, Third Canadian Edition. Access these ultimate tools for customizing lectures and presentations at login.cengage.com.

TEST BANK

The Test Bank for the third Canadian Edition of *SELL* is available in Cognero®, a secure online testing system that allows instructors to author, edit, and manage test bank content from anywhere Internet access is available. No special installations or downloads are needed, and the desktop-inspired interface, with its drop-down menus and familiar, intuitive tools, allows instructors to create and manage tests with ease. Multiple test versions can be created in an instant, and content can be imported or exported into other systems. Tests can be delivered from a learning management system, the classroom, or wherever an instructor chooses. Cognero for *SELL*, Third Canadian Edition, can be accessed through login.cengage.com.

POWERPOINT

Microsoft® PowerPoint® lecture slides are available for every chapter and feature key figures, tables, and photographs from *SELL*, Third Canadian Edition. Principles of clear design and engaging content have been incorporated throughout, making it simple for instructors to customize the deck for their courses.

IMAGE LIBRARY

This resource consists of digital copies of figures, short tables, and photographs used in the book. Instructors may use these jpegs to customize the PowerPoint or create their own PowerPoint presentations.

INSTRUCTOR GUIDE

This resource is organized according to the chapters and addresses key educational concerns. Included are activities and cases and their suggested responses from both the book and the MindTap.

ABOUT THE AUTHORS

THOMAS N. INGRAM, COLORADO STATE UNIVERSITY

Thomas N. Ingram (Ph.D., Georgia State University) is professor emeritus of marketing and department chair at Colorado State University. Before commencing his academic career, he worked in sales, product management, and sales management with Exxon and Mobil. Tom is a recipient of the Marketing Educator of the Year Award given by Sales and Marketing Executives International (SMEI). He was honoured as the first recipient of the Mu Kappa Tau National Marketing Honor Society recognition award for Outstanding Scholarly Contributions to the Sales Discipline. The University Sales Center Alliance has designated Professor Ingram as a Distinguished Sales Educator for his long-term contributions to sales education. Tom has served as the editor of the JOURNAL OF PERSONAL SELLING & SALES MANAGEMENT, chair of the SMEI Accreditation Institute, and as a member of the Board of Directors of SMEI. He is the former editor of the JOURNAL OF MARKETING THEORY & PRACTICE. Tom's primary research is in personal selling and sales management. His work has appeared in the JOURNAL OF MARKETING, JOURNAL OF MARKETING RESEARCH, JOURNAL OF PERSONAL SELLING & SALES MANAGEMENT, and the JOURNAL OF THE ACADEMY OF MARKETING SCIENCE, among others. He is the coauthor of one of the "Ten Most Influential Articles of the 20th Century" as designated by the Sales and Sales Management Special Interest Group of the American Marketing Association.

RAYMOND W. LAFORGE, UNIVERSITY OF LOUISVILLE

Raymond W. LaForge is the Brown-Forman Professor of Marketing at the University of Louisville. His research is published in many journals, including the JOURNAL OF MARKETING, JOURNAL OF MARKETING RESEARCH, JOURNAL OF THE ACDEMY OF MARKETING SCIENCE, among others. He has coauthored MARKETING; PRICIPLES & PERSEPCTIVES 5E, SALES MANAGEMENT: ANALYSIS AND DECISION MAKING 9E, PROFESSIONAL SELLING: A TRUST-BASED APPROACH 4E, STRATEGIC LEADERSHIP: BREAKTHROUGH THINKING FOR BREAKTHROUGH RESULTS, and THE PROFESSIONAL SELLING SKILLS WORKBOOK. LaForge has served on the board of many organizations, including as Vice President/Marketing for the Academy of Business Education; Vice President of Marketing, Teaching, and Conferences for the American Marketing Association Academic Council; and as Chair and Vice Chair for Awards and Recognition for the American Marketing Association Sales Interest Group. Buddy has received a number of awards that include the Outstanding Sales Scholar Award from Mu Kappa Tau, Special Recognition Award from the American Marketing Association Sales SIG, Top Thirteen Faculty Favorites at the University of Louisville, Distinguished Scholar Award from the Research Symposium on Marketing and Entrepreneurship, Distinguished Sales Educator Award from the University Sales Center Alliance, Undergraduate Teaching Award from the College of Business, Faculty Favorite Award from REACH Ambassadors, Beta Alpha Psi Outstanding College of Business Faculty Award, James M. Comer Award from the Journal of Personal Selling and Sales Management, Gerald E. Hills Best Paper Award from the American Marketing Association Entrepreneurial Marketing SIG, Sales Excellence Award from Louisville Sales Leaders, College of Business Student Council Faculty-of-the Year Award, Lifetime Achievement Award from the American Marketing Association Sales SIG, and Lifetime Achievement Award from the Global Research Symposium on Marketing and Entrepreneurship.

RAMON A. AVILA, BALL STATE UNIVERSITY

Ramon A. Avila (Ph.D., Virginia Tech University) is the George and Frances Ball Distinguished Professor of Marketing at Ball State University. Before coming to Ball State, he worked in sales with the Burroughs Corporation. He has held two visiting professorships at the University of Hawaii and another at the Kelley School of Business at Indiana University. Dr. Avila was awarded the 2009 University Sales Center Alliance Distinguished Sales Educator. In 2003, Avila earned Ball State's Outstanding Faculty Award. In April 2002, he received a Leavey Award. This award was given for innovation in the classroom with his advanced selling class. Avila was presented the 1999 Mu Kappa Tau's Outstanding Contributor to the Sales Profession. He is only the third recipient of this award. He has also received the University's Outstanding Service award, the University's Outstanding Junior Faculty Award, the College of Business Professor of the Year, and the Dean's Teaching Award every year since its inception in 1987. Avila also sits on five editorial review boards. His primary research is in personal selling and sales management. His work has appeared in the JOURNAL OF MARKETING RESEARCH, JOURNAL OF PERSONAL SELLING & SALES MANAGEMENT, THE JOURNAL OF MANAGEMENT, INDUSTRIAL MARKETING MANAGEMENT, THE MARKETING MANAGEMENT JOURNAL, and the JOURNAL OF MARKETING THEORY & PRACTICE, among others. He is the coauthor of THE PROFESSIONAL SELLING SKILLS WORKBOOK and SALES MANAGEMENT: ANALYSIS AND DECISION MAKING.

CHARLES H. SCHWEPKER JR., UNIVERSITY OF CENTRAL MISSOURI

Charles H. Schwepker, Jr. (Ph.D., University of Memphis), is the Mike and Patti Davidson Distinguished Marketing Professor at the University of Central Missouri. He has experience in wholesale and retail sales. His primary research interests are in sales management, personal selling, and marketing ethics. Dr. Schwepker's articles have been published in the JOURNAL OF THE ACADEMY OF MARKETING SCIENCE, JOURNAL OF BUSINESS RESEARCH, JOURNAL OF PUBLIC POLICY AND MARKETING, JOURNAL OF PERSONAL SELLING & SALES MANAGEMENT, JOURNAL OF SERVICE RESEARCH, and JOURNAL OF BUSINESS ETHICS, among other journals; various national and regional proceedings; and books, including MARKETING COMMUNICATIONS CLASSICS and ENVIRONMENTAL MARKETING. He has received several honours for both teaching and advising, including the Hormel Teaching Excellence award and the Alumni Foundation Harmon College of Business Administration Distinguished Professor Award. Dr. Schwepker received the James Comer Award for best contribution to selling and sales management theory awarded by the JOURNAL OF PERSONAL SELLING & SALES MANAGEMENT and two "Outstanding Paper" awards at the National Conference in Sales Management, among others. He is on the editorial review boards of the JOURNAL OF PERSONAL

SELLING & SALES MANAGEMENT, JOURNAL OF MARKETING THEORY & PRACTICE, JOURNAL OF BUSINESS & INDUSTRIAL MARKETING, JOURNAL OF RELATIONSHIP MARKETING, JOURNAL OF SELLING AND MAJOR ACCOUNT MANAGEMENT, and SOUTHERN BUSINESS REVIEW, and has five times won awards for outstanding reviewer. He is a coauthor of SALES MANAGEMENT: ANALYSIS AND DECISION MAKING.

MICHAEL R. WILLIAMS, OKLAHOMA CITY UNIVERSITY

Michael R. Williams (Ph.D., Oklahoma State University) is professor of marketing and director of the Academy of Customer Excellence and Sales at Oklahoma City University. Prior to his academic career, Williams established a successful 30-plus year career in industrial sales, market research, and sales management and continues to consult and work with a wide range of business organizations. He has coauthored THE PROFESSIONAL SELLING SKILLS WORKBOOK, SALES MANAGEMENT: ANALYSIS AND DECISION MAKING, and a variety of executive monographs and white papers on sales performance topics. Williams's research has been published in many different national and international journals, including the JOURNAL OF PERSONAL SELLING & SALES MANAGEMENT, INTERNATIONAL JOURNAL OF PURCHASING AND MATERIALS MANAGEMENT, JOURNAL OF BUSINESS AND INDUSTRIAL MARKETING, QUALITY MANAGEMENT JOURNAL, and JOURNAL OF BUSINESS-TO-BUSINESS MARKETING. His work has also received numerous honours, including Outstanding Article for the Year in Journal of Business and Industrial Marketing, the AACSB's Leadership in Innovative Business Education Award, and the Marketing Science Institute's Alden G. Clayton Competition. In 2004, Williams was honored with the Mu Kappa Tau Marketing Society recognition award for Outstanding Scholarly Contributor to the Sales Discipline. He has also been honored with numerous university, college, and corporate teaching and research awards, including Old Republic Research Scholar, the presentation of a seminar at Oxford's Braesnose College, Who's Who in American Education, and Who's Who in America. Williams has and continues to serve in leadership roles as an advisor and board member for sales and sales management associations and organizations, including the University Sales Center Alliance, National Conference in Sales and Sales Management, and Vector Marketing.

KIRBY SHANNAHAN, MEMORIAL UNIVERSITY OF NEWFOUNDLAND

Dr. Kirby Shannahan is a Professor of Marketing at Memorial University of Newfoundland, Newfoundland and Labrador, Canada. He holds a Doctor of Philosophy (Ph.D.) in Business Administration (Marketing and Supply Chain Management) from the Fogelman College of Business and Economics, University of Memphis. His research interests include salesforce management, marketing research, customer relationship management, and integrated marketing communications. His main interest is in helping sales organizations identify, recruit, and retain effective salesforce members. His research has been published in such outlets as the JOURNAL OF THE ACADEMY OF MARKETING SCIENCE, JOURNAL OF PERSONAL SELLING AND SALES MANAGEMENT, and JOURNAL OF BUSINESS AND INDUSTRIAL MARKETING. In 2006, Kirby was a winner of the American Marketing Association's Direct Selling Education Foundation dissertation grant. More recently, he and his research team were the winners of the James M. Comer Award for Best Contribution to Selling and Sales Management Theory, 2013, for their article "Making Sense of the Customer's Role in the Personal Selling Process: A Theory of Organizing and Sensemaking Perspective," published in JOURNAL OF PERSONAL SELLING AND SALES MANAGEMENT. Kirby has been an active member of the Society for Marketing Advances (SMA), the American Marketing Association (AMA), and Academy of Marketing Science (AMS) since 2004.

RACHELLE SHANNAHAN, MEMORIAL UNIVERSITY OF NEWFOUNDLAND

Dr. Rachelle Shannahan is an Associate Dean (Academic Programs) and an Associate Professor of Marketing in the Faculty of Business Administration at Memorial University of Newfoundland, Newfoundland and Labrador, Canada. She holds a Ph.D. in Business Administration (marketing and supply chain management) from the Fogelman College of Business and Economics, University of Memphis. Her primary research interest is in studying customer influence on the personal selling process and on salesperson performance in a relational, business-to-business context. She is also interested in customer participation in service delivery and how this participation impacts customer satisfaction. Her research has been published in such outlets as the JOURNAL OF THE ACADEMY OF MARKETING SCIENCE, JOURNAL OF PERSONAL SELLING AND SALES MANAGEMENT, JOURNAL OF BUSINESS AND INDUSTRIAL MARKETING, INDUSTRIAL MARKETING MANAGEMENT, and the JOURNAL OF MARKETING THEORY AND PRACTICE. In 2007, Rachelle was a winner of the American Marketing Association's Direct Selling Education Foundation dissertation grant and she was part of the research team that was awarded the James M. Comer Award for Best Contribution to Selling and Sales Management Theory for 2013. Rachelle is an active member of the American Marketing Association (AMA) and the Society for Marketing Advances (SMA). Her industry experience includes several years with a major sales and marketing organization.

ACKNOWLEDGMENTS

DEDICATION

For Simon and Adrienne.

—KS and RS

This project could not have been completed without the assistance, support, guidance, mentorship, and friendship of many people. First, we would like to thank Drs. Thomas Ingram and Raymond Laforge for their initial support and faith in us as we embarked on this project. We would also like to thank our research assistants, Courtney Sacuta and Holly Hill. Your hard work and dedication allowed this project to succeed, and for that, we thank you. Thank you also to Dr. Alan Bush, whose ongoing support has guided us through our careers.

Our thanks also to Alexis Hood, Portfolio Manager; Dylan Schoenmakers, Content Manager; Jennifer Hare, Senior Content Manager; and our detailed and thorough copyeditor, Kelli Howey. Their guidance throughout the development and production of the Third Canadian Edition has been invaluable.

CPSA COMPETENCY FRAMEWORK

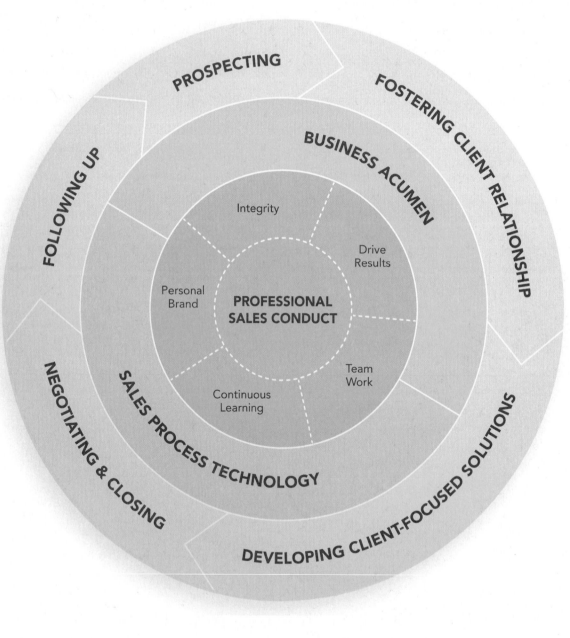

PROSPECTING

FOSTERING CLIENT RELATIONSHIP

FOLLOWING UP

BUSINESS ACUMEN

Integrity

Drive Results

Personal Brand

PROFESSIONAL SALES CONDUCT

Team Work

Continuous Learning

SALES PROCESS TECHNOLOGY

NEGOTIATING & CLOSING

DEVELOPING CLIENT-FOCUSED SOLUTIONS

PROSPECTING

Description: Understanding one's own company and its offerings, the client's business challenges and the characteristics of the market in which it operates (e.g., strengths, weaknesses, competition, trends) ensures that sales professionals work efficiently and participate in client conversions productively. This requires skills related to gathering and synthesizing client market intelligence, aligning one's own company's strengths and weaknesses toward solution creation, as well as developing and implementing an action plan.

1.1 Understand the Market

1.2 Conduct Sales Planning

1.3 Develop Client Intelligence

Learn about the specific performance skills and knowledge statements that indicate proficiency in Prospecting at cpsa.com/professional-certification/competency-framework.

To help students gain critical skill sets and get closer to achieving CPSA accreditation, concepts throughout the book have been aligned to CPSA competencies. Look for the following icons to see where *SELL* addresses the competency of Prospecting.

 1.1 Understand the Market   1.3 Develop Client Intelligence

 1.2 Conduct Sales Planning

FOSTERING CLIENT RELATIONSHIPS

Description: A major component of the sales cycle involves creating lasting relationships with new or existing clients. The essence related to developing and maintaining those relationships is rooted in fundamental skills applicable to a number of industries. These include: establishing rapport, various forms of communication, and being able to conduct a meeting.

2.1 Develop Client Relationships

2.2 Practice Active Listening

2.3 Communicate Verbally

2.4 Communicate in Writing

2.5 Conduct Meetings

Learn about the specific performance skills and knowledge statements that indicate proficiency in Fostering Client Relationships at cpsa.com/professional-certification/competency-framework.

To help students gain critical skill sets and get closer to achieving CPSA accreditation, concepts throughout the book have been aligned to CPSA competencies. Look for the following icons to see where *SELL* addresses the competency of Fostering Client Relationships.

 2.1 Develop Client Relationships   2.4 Communicate in Writing

 2.2 Practice Active Listening   2.5 Conduct Meetings

 2.3 Communicate Verbally

DEVELOPING CLIENT-FOCUSED SOLUTIONS

Description: The aim of every sales professional in the field rests in providing solutions that meet the needs and expectations of their clients. This requires a thorough understanding of client challenges and goals before presenting your organizations products or services. Being adaptable, understanding trends, handling objections and thinking on the spot are a few examples of the skills pertinent to delivering of client-focused solutions.

3.1 Develop Solutions

3.2 Conduct Sales Presentations

Learn about the specific performance skills and knowledge statements that indicate proficiency in Developing Client-Focused Solutions at cpsa.com/professional-certification/competency-framework.

To help students gain critical skill sets and get closer to achieving CPSA accreditation, concepts throughout the book have been aligned to CPSA competencies. Look for the following icons to see where *SELL* addresses the competency of Developing Client-Focused Solutions.

 3.1 Develop Solutions   3.2 Conduct Sales Presentations

NEGOTIATING AND CLOSING

Description: To consolidate a sale, the ability to work with unforeseen changes and situations is mandatory. When a sale becomes stalled in negotiations, it is a signal that skills in earlier stages of the sales cycle were not exercised. Understanding various facets of financial and legal matters, and terms of sale helps sales professionals navigate this critical component of the sales cycle.

4.1 Close the Sale

4.2 Negotiate Terms of Sale

4.3 Identify Third-Party Strategic Relationships

Learn about the specific performance skills and knowledge statements that indicate proficiency in Negotiating and Closing at cpsa.com/professional-certification/competency-framework.

To help students gain critical skill sets and get closer to achieving CPSA accreditation, concepts throughout the book have been aligned to CPSA competencies. Look for the following icons to see where *SELL* addresses the competency of Negotiating and Closing.

 4.1 Close the Sale   4.3 Identify Third-Party Strategic Relationships

 4.2 Negotiate Terms of Sale

FOLLOWING UP

Description: Following-up is a component of the sales cycle wherein client expectations, project milestones and timelines are referenced for completion and satisfaction, and the client relationship is strengthened toward future expansion of services and offerings that may be sold to the client. Competent sales professionals focus their efforts in this competency toward offering assurance to clients that key aspects of the agreed-upon sale are being achieved. Similarly, being adaptable and flexible toward the likelihood of changes and unforeseen circumstances is encouraged.

5.1 Follow-Up on the Sale

Learn about the specific performance skills and knowledge statements that indicate proficiency in Following Up at cpsa.com/professional-certification/competency-framework.

To help students gain critical skill sets and get closer to achieving CPSA accreditation, concepts throughout the book have been aligned to CPSA competencies. Look for the following icons to see where *SELL* addresses the competency of Following Up.

 5.1 Follow-Up on the Sale

BUSINESS ACUMEN

Description: Competent sales professionals should possess general business skills to be effective in certain stages of the sales cycle. Understanding the basics of financial and legal terms as well as having general knowledge of your own business, in terms of products and services offered, allows professionals to remain nimble in many sales-related industries.

6.1 Understand Your Company

6.2 Demonstrate Financial Literacy

6.3 Demonstrate Legal Literacy

Learn about the specific performance skills and knowledge statements that indicate proficiency in Business Acumen at cpsa.com/professional-certification/competency-framework.

To help students gain critical skill sets and get closer to achieving CPSA accreditation, concepts throughout the book have been aligned to CPSA competencies. Look for the following icons to see where *SELL* addresses the competency of Business Acumen.

 6.1 Understand Your Company

 6.3 Demonstrate Legal Literacy

 6.2 Demonstrate Financial Literacy

SALES PROCESS TECHNOLOGY

Description: The sales industry contains many forms of technology which can be leveraged at various stages of the sales cycle. Being familiar with available and appropriate technologies allows professionals to remain current with trends shaping the industry, engage in the sales process more efficiently, and promotes an identity that is willing to learn and implement new skills.

7.1 Leverage Sales Technology

7.2 Implement Social Selling

Learn about the specific performance skills and knowledge statements that indicate proficiency in Sales Process Technology at cpsa.com/professional-certification/competency-framework.

To help students gain critical skill sets and get closer to achieving CPSA accreditation, concepts throughout the book have been aligned to CPSA competencies. Look for the following icons to see where *SELL* addresses the competency of Sales Process Technology.

 7.1 Leverage Sales Technology   7.2 Implement Social Selling

PROFESSIONAL SALES CONDUCT

Description: Developing skills related to professional conduct in any industry is of the utmost importance. Serving as a model practitioner, who acts with integrity, bodes well in terms of one's professional image and the image of the company one represents. Similarly, having the ability to adapt and shape one's personal brand and selling style on a regular basis ensures continued relevance in quickly evolving markets.

8.1 Act with Integrity

8.2 Drive Results

8.3 Work as Part of a Team

8.4 Engage in Continuous Learning

8.5 Develop Personal Brand

Learn about the specific performance skills and knowledge statements that indicate proficiency in Professional Sales Conduct at cpsa.com/professional-certification/competency-framework.

To help students gain critical skill sets and get closer to achieving CPSA accreditation, concepts throughout the book have been aligned to CPSA competencies. Look for the following icons to see where *SELL* addresses the competency of Professional Sales Conduct.

 8.1 Act with Integrity   8.4 Engage in Continuous Learning

 8.2 Drive Results   8.5 Develop Personal Brand

 8.3 Work as Part of a Team

1 | Overview of Personal Selling

After completing this chapter, you should be able to

LO 1 | Define personal selling and describe its unique characteristics as a marketing communications tool.

LO 2 | Distinguish between transaction-focused traditional selling and trust-based relationship selling, with the latter focusing on customer value and sales dialogue.

LO 3 | Describe the emphasis on sales professionalism.

LO 4 | Explain the contributions of personal selling to society, business firms, and customers.

LO 5 | Discuss five alternative approaches to personal selling.

LO 6 | Understand the sales process as a series of interrelated steps.

LO 7 | Understand the characteristics of sales careers and the skills and qualifications necessary for success in sales careers.

AFTER FINISHING THIS CHAPTER GO TO THE BACK OF THE BOOK FOR CHAPTER REVIEW CARDS, AND VISIT MINDTAP FOR ACCESS TO STUDY TOOLS.

Founded in Montreal in 1865, Sun Life Financial is one of the largest life insurance companies in the world. Starting with insurance, the company has grown and expanded its sales offerings to provide wealth solutions and customized health programs to millions of individuals across Canada, and millions more around the world. With 37,000 employees, the company's corporate values are focused on building trust with customers.[1] The company has achieved this through the development of products and services that consider the client's needs first and embrace a culture of listening to customers to provide the best value.[2] For the first time in Sun Life's history the company's Canadian annuity sales increased to over $3 billion in 2017, from $1.2 billion in 2007. Sun Life attributes this increase in annuity sales to the growth of average deal sizes within the market. In just one year from 2016 to 2017 the company successfully grew its average deal size by 60 percent.[3] Sun Life's success is due in part to its deep understanding of the personal selling process.

Introduction

In the current business environment, buyers are under intense pressure to solve problems, realize opportunities, and cut costs. They are cautious, risk-averse, and have an abundant amount of information about potential suppliers for the products they purchase. Further, they hate to waste time in unproductive meetings with salespeople. This means that successful salespeople must discard high-pressure sales "pitches" in favour of a customer-oriented sales approach. Salespeople must be capable of establishing dialogue with customers to focus on the customer's needs and situation before making a purchase recommendation. According to a leading sales consulting firm, customers have little interest in meeting with "talking brochures," or salespeople who merely dispense information. Salespeople must adapt to customers' level of knowledge and information-gathering

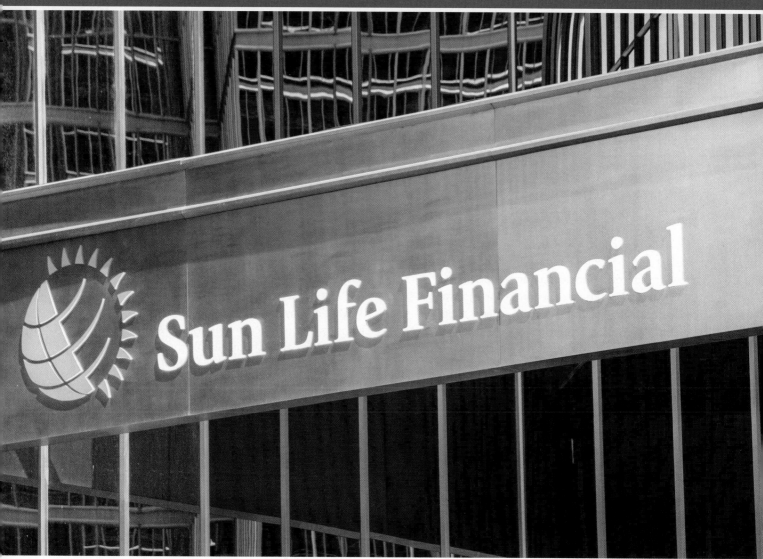

preferences. In some cases, prospective customers are experts and may value interactions with salespeople only later in the buying process. In other cases, less-expert customers rely heavily on salespeople for critical tasks in understanding how to solve problems, define alternatives, and choose a solution. Increasingly, today's successful salesperson will use a mix of personal interactions along with sales technologies such as e-mail, video conferencing, and social media to ensure that customers receive timely, useful information.[4]

A productive sales approach first defines customer needs, then illustrates how the sales organization can deliver the value the customer is seeking, and ultimately leads to customer acknowledgment of the value to be gained. This results in a mutually beneficial joint decision between the buyer and seller. With this approach, the sales process is much more about "selling with" customers rather than "selling to" customers.

LO 1 | PERSONAL SELLING DEFINED

 CPSA   2.1 Develop client relationships

The successful professional salesperson is likely a better listener than a talker; is oriented more toward developing long-term relationships with customers than using high-pressure, short-term sales techniques; and has the skills and patience to endure lengthy, complex sales processes. As portrayed in the chapter introduction, today's salesperson strives to furnish valuable information based on unique customer needs. Meeting those customer needs requires teamwork between salespeople and others in the organization. For more on teamwork, see Selling in Action: The Importance of Teamwork in Sales.

Selling in Action

The Importance of Teamwork in Sales

Christine Corelli, a corporate trainer whose clients include Honda, Century 21, Pepsi, and Caterpillar, addresses the importance of teamwork in sales:

The customer rules. If your entire team, including all sales and service employees, does not excel in providing an excellent customer experience, buyers will take their business elsewhere. To provide excellent customer experiences, it is crucial that sales and service personnel share goals and communicate efficiently and effectively. In terms of goals, Ms. Corelli urges companies to go beyond customer satisfaction, noting that satisfaction is not enough and that customer loyalty should be the primary goal of sales and service personnel. With customer loyalty as the goal, customers are more likely to become advocates within their companies for deserving sales organizations. Further, loyal customers frequently furnish referrals to other prospective customers and provide favourable word mouth communications to industry counterparts. Loyal customers are also more likely to endorse loyalty-focused sales organizations on LinkedIn and other business-centred social media sites.

To foster teamwork between sales and service personnel, Ms. Corelli cites the importance of eliminating barriers to great teamwork. Barriers include unproductive and negative employees who place blame when problems arise or are overly competitive with other employees. Another barrier to teamwork is a sense of territorialism, or "us versus them" attitudes that can exist between business areas. This can lead to an "it's not my job" stance that compromises the all-important goal of customer loyalty. Ms. Corelli also says that companies should enable their employees through training on topics ranging from how to connect with customers to how to handle difficult customers and service challenges. She also suggests cultivating and sharing best practices in building customer loyalty throughout the company as part of a continuous improvement initiative. Clearly, Ms. Corelli knows that superior teamwork does not happen simply because it is a good idea. Teamwork requires a coordinated effort, but the payoff is well worth the effort.

Source: Christie Corelli, "Teamwork Essential for Increased Productivity and Profitability," from www.christinespeaks. com (August 13, 2016).

Personal selling, an important part of marketing, relies heavily on interpersonal interactions between buyers and sellers to initiate, develop, and enhance customer relationships. The interpersonal communications dimension sets personal selling apart from other marketing communications such as advertising and sales promotion, which are directed at mass markets. Personal selling is also distinguished from direct marketing and electronic marketing in that salespeople are talking with buyers before, during, and after the sale. This contact allows for a high degree of immediate customer feedback, which becomes a strong advantage of personal selling over most other forms of marketing communications.

personal selling An important part of marketing that relies heavily on interpersonal interactions between buyers and sellers to initiate, develop, and enhance customer relationships.

trust-based relationship selling A form of personal selling that requires that salespeople earn customer trust and that their selling strategy meets customer needs and contributes to the creation, communication, and delivery of customer value.

Although advertising is a far more visible activity, personal selling is the most important part of marketing communications for most businesses. This is particularly true in business-to-business marketing, in which more is spent on personal selling than on advertising, sales promotion, publicity, or public relations. In this book, we typically describe personal selling in this business-to-business context, in which a salesperson or sales team interacts with one or more individuals from another organization.

LO 2 | TRUST-BASED RELATIONSHIP SELLING

Trust-based relationship selling (a form of personal selling) requires that salespeople earn customer trust and that their selling strategy meets customer needs and contributes to the creation, communication, and delivery of customer value. As illustrated in Exhibit 1.1, trust-based relationship

Exhibit 1.1

Comparison of Transaction-Focused Traditional Selling with Trust-Based Relationship Selling

	Transaction-Focused Traditional Selling	Trust-Based Relationship Selling
Typical skills required	Selling skills, e.g., finding prospects, making sales presentations	Selling skills Information gathering Listening and questioning Strategic problem solving Creating and demonstrating unique, value-added solutions Teambuilding and teamwork
Primary focus	The salesperson and the selling firm	The customer and the customer's customers
Desired outcomes	Closed sales, order volume	Trust, joint planning, mutual benefits, enhanced profits
Role of salesperson	Make calls and close sales	Business consultant and long-term ally Key player in the customer's business
Nature of communications with customers	One-way, from salesperson to customer Pushing products	Two-way and collaborative Strive for dialogue with the customer
Degree of salesperson's involvement in customer's decision-making process	Isolated from customer's decision-making process	Actively involved in customer's decision-making process
Knowledge required	Product knowledge Competitive knowledge Identifying opportunities Account strategies	Product knowledge Selling company resources Competitive knowledge Identifying opportunities General business and industry knowledge and insight Customer's products, competition, and customers Account strategies Costs
Postsale follow-up	Little or none: move on to conquer next customer	Continued follow-through to • ensure customer satisfaction • keep customer informed • add customer value • manage opportunities

selling is quite different from traditional selling. Rather than trying to maximize sales in the short run (also called a transaction focus), trust-based relationship selling focuses on solving customer problems, providing opportunities, and adding value to the customer's business over an extended period. Chapter 2 will provide detailed coverage of how salespeople can earn buyers' trust.

Importance of Customer Value

CPSA | 2.1 Develop client relationships

As personal selling continues to evolve, it is more important than ever that salespeople focus on delivering customer value while initiating, developing, and enhancing customer relationships. What constitutes value will likely vary from one customer to the next depending on the customer's situation, needs, and priorities, but **customer value** will always be determined by customers' perception of what they get in exchange for what they have to give up. In the simplest situations, customers buy a product in exchange for money. In most situations, however, customers define value in a more complex manner, by addressing such questions as follows:

- Does the salesperson do a good job in helping me make or save money?

- Is this salesperson dependable?

- Does this salesperson help me achieve my strategic priorities?

- Is the salesperson's company easy to work with (i.e., hassle-free)?

- Does the salesperson enlist others in their organization when needed to create value for me?

- Does the sales representative understand my business and my industry?

Successful salespeople must be able to make sales calls and build relationships at the same time.

Personal selling also recognizes that customers would like to be heard when expressing what they want suppliers and salespeople to provide for them. In days gone by, personal selling often consisted of delivering a message or making a pitch. That approach was typically associated with a "product push" strategy in which customers were pressured to buy without much appreciation for their real needs. Today, the most progressive sales organizations are far more interested in establishing a productive dialogue with customers than in simply pitching products that customers may or may not want or need. In our highly competitive world, professional buyers have little tolerance for aggressive, pushy salespeople.

> Customers want to be heard loud and clear when expressing what they want from suppliers and salespeople.

Importance of Sales Dialogue

CPSA | 2.1 Develop client relationships

Sales dialogue refers to the series of conversations between buyers and sellers that take place over time in an attempt to build relationships. The purposes of these conversations are to

- determine whether a prospective customer should be targeted for further sales attention

- clarify the prospective customer's situation and buying processes

- discover the prospective customer's unique needs and requirements

customer value Customers' perception of what they get for what they have to give up; for example, benefits from buying a product in exchange for money paid.

sales dialogue Business conversations between buyers and sellers that occur as salespeople attempt to initiate, develop, and enhance customer relationships. Sales dialogue should be customer focused and have a clear purpose.

- determine the prospective customer's strategic priorities
- communicate how the sales organization can create and deliver customer value
- negotiate a business deal and earn a commitment from the customer
- make the customer aware of additional opportunities to increase the value received
- assess sales organization and salesperson performance so that customer value is continually improved

As you can see, sales dialogue is far more than idle chitchat. The business conversations that constitute the dialogue are customer-focused and have a clear purpose; otherwise, there would be a high probability of wasting both the customer's and the salesperson's time, which no one can afford in today's business environment. Whether the sales dialogue features a question-and-answer format, a conversation dominated by the buyer conveying information and requirements, or a formal sales presentation in which the salesperson responds to buyer feedback throughout, the key idea is that both parties participate in and benefit from the process.

Throughout this course, you will learn about new technologies and techniques that have contributed to the evolution of the practice of personal selling. This chapter provides an overview of personal selling, affording insight into the operating rationale of today's salespeople and sales managers. It also describes different approaches to personal selling and presents the sales process as a series of interrelated steps. The chapter concludes with a discussion of several important aspects of sales careers, including types of selling jobs and characteristics and skills needed for sales success. In the highly competitive, complex international business community, personal selling and sales management have never played more critical roles.

LO 3 | EVOLUTION OF PROFESSIONAL SELLING

8.1 Act with integrity

For the past several decades, there has been a steady increase in the complexity of the business world, the level of competitive activity, and buyer expectations. These developments have driven an increased focus on **sales professionalism** by the most progressive sales organizations. Sales professionalism requires a customer-oriented sales approach that uses truthful,

Sales is becoming more professional, as indicated by a growing number of publications and a market for Web sites with professional development materials and reviews.

nonmanipulative tactics to satisfy the long-term needs of both the customer and the selling firm.

In examining the status of sales as a true profession, one study found that sales meets four of the six criteria that define professions, and that progress is still needed on the other two dimensions.[5] This study concluded that sales meets the criterion of operating from a substantial knowledge base that has been developed by academics, corporate trainers and executives, and professional organizations. Second, sales meets the criterion of making a significant contribution to society, which is discussed in the next section of this chapter. Third, through professional organizations such as the Canadian Professional Sales Association (CPSA) and through a common sales vocabulary such as that found in textbooks and training materials, sales meets the professional criterion of having a defined culture and organization of colleagues. Fourth, sales does have a unique set of professional skills, although these skills vary depending on the specific nature of a given sales position.

Two areas in the study indicated that sales needs additional progress to be viewed as a profession on a par with law, medicine, and other long-recognized professions. The first area has to do with how much autonomy salespeople have to make decisions and the amount of public trust granted to salespeople. Although many business-to-business salespeople have considerable decision-making autonomy, others have very little. Public trust could be improved by a widely accepted certification program such as the Chartered Professional Accountant (CPA) designation for accountants. At present, however, very few salespeople have

sales professionalism A customer-oriented approach that uses truthful, nonmanipulative tactics to satisfy the long-term needs of both the customer and the selling firm.

Exhibit 1.2

Continued Evolution of Personal Selling

Change	Salesforce Response
Intensified competition	More emphasis on developing and maintaining trust-based, long-term customer relationships
	More focus on creating and delivering customer value
More emphasis on improving sales productivity	Increased use of technology (e.g., laptop computers, electronic mail, databases, customer relationship management software)
	Increased use of lower-cost-per-contact methods (e.g., telemarketing for some customers)
	More emphasis on profitability (e.g., gross margin) objectives
Fragmentation of traditional customer bases	Sales specialists for specific customer types
	Multiple sales channels (e.g., major accounts programs, telemarketing, electronic networks)
	Globalization of sales efforts
Customers dictating quality standards and inventory/ shipping procedures to be met by vendors	Team selling
	Salesforce compensation sometimes based on customer satisfaction and team performance
	More emphasis on sales dialogues rather than on sales pitches
Demand for in-depth, specialized knowledge as an input to purchase decisions	Team selling
	More emphasis on customer-oriented sales training

professional certification credentials. Although many salespeople do have considerable autonomy, public trust in certification programs is modest; thus, the results are mixed as to whether the sales profession meets this professional criterion. Currently in Canada, the CPSA was created to support and advance sales professionals with training and resources to help salespeople advance their careers. This organization has designed a competency framework for individuals to pursue the CPSA Institute designations of Certified Sales Associate (CSA), Certified Sales Professional (CSP), and Certified Sales Leader (CSL).

The final area where sales needs to improve is adherence to a uniform ethical code. Many companies have employee codes of conduct and some professional organizations have ethical codes for salespeople. In Canada, the CPSA created its own Sales Institute Code of Ethics. This code is present for all current members of the CPSA and must be followed in order to keep your designations. However, there is no universal code of ethics with a mechanism for dealing with violators. Until such a code is developed and widely accepted in business, some members of society will not view sales as a true profession.

Whether or not sales is viewed as a true profession comparable to law and medicine, salespeople can benefit tremendously by embracing high ethical standards, participating in professional organizations, and working from a continually evolving knowledge base. In so doing, they not only will be more effective but also will help advance sales as a true profession.

Future evolution is inevitable as tomorrow's professional salesperson responds to a more complex and dynamic environment. Increased sophistication of buyers and of new technologies will also demand more from the next generation of salespeople. Exhibit 1.2 summarizes some of the likely events of the future.[6] For a discussion of how salespeople are using sales technology tools, see Technology in Sales: Top Salespeople Reach Customers with Techno-Tools.

Technology in Sales

Top Salespeople Reach Customers with Techno-Tools

According to a LinkedIn study, the technology tools that a salesperson uses is highly correlated to their sales performance, with top salespeople 24 percent more likely to attribute their success to sales technology than lower-performing salespeople. Popular tools include social media, e-mail tracking, sales intelligence software, and customer relationship management (CRM) systems. Salespeople are increasingly using social selling software that helps salespeople initiate and establish relationships with buyers on social media sites such as Twitter, Facebook, LinkedIn, Snapchat, and Instagram. LinkedIn's Sales Navigator is a popular tool for creating prospect lists and contacting prospective customers. E-mail tracking alerts the seller when a recipient opens an e-mail or clicks on a link in an e-mail. Sales intelligence software provides contact and company information to help build prospect profiles and prioritize sale opportunities.

Popular intelligence providers include DiscoverOrg, which provides organizational charts to companies that target information technology, finance, and marketing departments. CRM software is one of the more mature products in the sales technology space, yet less than one-third of large companies use CRM to bolster and manage sales. This is surprising given that 80 percent of the top salespeople in the LinkedIn study report that CRM is "critical" or "extremely critical" to their success.

As the use of sales technology spreads, some experts are concerned about potential abuses by overly aggressive salespeople who use technology to deploy pushy sales tactics. This could sour buyers on the new technology and the salespeople who use it. If abuses make social media sites less relevant over time, more private sites such as Kik, WeChat, Facebook Messenger, and Slack will likely become more important for salespeople.

Source: Pete Caputa, "Top Salespeople Are More Likely to Use These Tools Than the Rest of You," from HubSpot's Sales Blog, online at https://blog.hubspot.com, June 15, 2016.

LO 4 | CONTRIBUTIONS OF PERSONAL SELLING

As mentioned earlier in this chapter, more money is spent on personal selling than on any other form of marketing communications. Salespeople are usually well compensated, and salesforces of major companies often number in the thousands. For example, in North America PepsiCo has 17,200 salespeople, RBC Wealth Management has 5,800, AVON products has 6.1 million, and Apple has 16,000.[7]

We now take a look at how this investment is justified by reviewing the contributions of personal selling to society in general, to the employing firm, and to customers.

Salespeople and Society

Salespeople contribute to their nation's economic growth in two basic ways: They stimulate economic transactions and further the diffusion of innovation.

SALESPEOPLE AS ECONOMIC STIMULI Salespeople are expected to stimulate action in the business world—hence the term **economic stimuli**. In a fluctuating economy, salespeople make valuable contributions by assisting in recovery cycles and helping to sustain periods of relative prosperity. As the world economic system deals with such issues as increased globalization of business, more emphasis on customer satisfaction, and building competitiveness through quality improvement programs, it is expected that salespeople will be recognized as a key force in executing the appropriate strategies and tactics necessary for survival and growth.

SALESPEOPLE AND DIFFUSION OF INNOVATION Salespeople play a critical role in the **diffusion of innovation**, the process whereby new products, services, and ideas are distributed to the members of society. Consumers who are likely to be early adopters of an

economic stimuli Something that stimulates or incites activity in the economy.

diffusion of innovation The process whereby new products, services, and ideas are distributed to the members of society.

innovation often rely on salespeople as a primary source of information. Frequently, well-informed, specialized salespeople provide useful information to potential customers. Sometimes those customers ultimately purchase the new product from a lower-cost outlet; nonetheless, the information provided by the original well-informed salesperson contributes critically to the adoption of the innovation and more widespread popularity of the new product. The role of salespeople in the diffusion of industrial products and services is particularly crucial. Imagine trying to purchase a companywide computer system without the assistance of a competent salesperson or sales team!

While acting as an agent of innovation, the salesperson invariably encounters a strong resistance to change in the later stages of the diffusion process. The status quo seems to be extremely satisfactory to many parties, even though, in the long run, change is necessary for continued progress or survival. By encouraging the adoption of innovative products and services, salespeople may indeed be making a positive contribution to society.

Salespeople and the Employing Firm

Because salespeople are in direct contact with the all-important customer, they can make valuable contributions to their employers. Salespeople contribute to their firms as revenue producers, as sources of market research and feedback, and as candidates for management positions.

SALESPEOPLE AS REVENUE PRODUCERS

6.2 Demonstrate financial literacy

Salespeople occupy the somewhat unique role of **revenue producers** in their firms. Consequently, they usually feel the brunt of that pressure along with the managers in the firm. Although accountants and financial staff are concerned with profitability in bottom-line terms, salespeople are constantly reminded of their responsibility to achieve a healthy "top

> **revenue producers** A role fulfilled by salespeople that brings in revenue or income to a firm or company.

> Along with the management of a firm, salespeople occupy the somewhat unique role of revenue producers in their firms.

line" on the profit and loss statement. This should not suggest that salespeople are concerned only with sales revenue and not with overall profitability. Indeed, salespeople are increasingly responsible for improving profitability, not only by producing sales revenues but also by improving the productivity of their actions.

MARKET RESEARCH AND FEEDBACK

1.1 Understand the market

Because salespeople spend so much time in direct contact with their customers, it is only logical that they would play an important role in market research and in providing feedback to their firms. For example, Xerox uses a system called SCOOP to store customer information gathered by the salesforce. This information fully describes each sales territory in terms of Xerox and competitive products currently in use, machine types, age, and potential replacement dates. Marketing executives use this information to develop market forecasts and to help develop marketing and sales strategies for various customer segments.[8]

The emergence of communications technologies gives salespeople and their organizations more opportunities to gather customer feedback. For example, retailers and service providers routinely use Facebook to solicit customer feedback. In the business-to-business sector, buyers are increasingly sharing their opinions, identifying problems, and asking for vendor recommendations via Twitter and LinkedIn. Customer relationship management programs such as Chatter by Salesforce.com are incorporating social media to improve collaboration between customers and the sales organization.

Some would argue that salespeople are not trained as market researchers, or that salespeople's time could be better used than in research and feedback activities. Many firms, however, refute this argument by finding

numerous ways to capitalize on the salesforce as a reservoir of ideas. It is not an exaggeration to say that many firms have concluded they cannot afford to operate in the absence of salesforce feedback and research.

SALESPEOPLE AS FUTURE MANAGERS In recent years, marketing and sales personnel have been in strong demand for upper management positions. Recognizing the need for a top management trained in sales, many firms use the sales job as an entry-level position that provides a foundation for future assignments. As progressive firms continue to emphasize customer orientation as a basic operating concept, it is only natural that salespeople who have learned how to meet customer needs will be good candidates for management jobs.

Salespeople and the Customer

Given the increasing importance of building trust with customers and an emphasis on establishing and maintaining long-term relationships, it is imperative that salespeople are honest and candid with customers. Salespeople must also be able to demonstrate knowledge of their products and services, especially as they compare competitive offerings. Customers also expect salespeople to be knowledgeable about market opportunities and relevant business trends that may affect a customer's business. There has been a longstanding expectation that salespeople need to be the key contact for the buyer, who expects that they will coordinate activities within the selling firm to deliver maximum value to the customer.

The overall conclusion is that buyers expect salespeople to contribute to the success of the buyer's firm. Buyers value the information furnished by salespeople, and they expect salespeople to act in a highly professional manner.[9]

As salespeople serve their customers, they simultaneously serve their employers and society. When the interests of these two groups conflict, the salesperson can be caught in the middle. By learning to resolve these conflicts as a routine part of their jobs, salespeople further contribute to developing a business system based on progress through problem solving. Sales ethics will be discussed in detail in Chapter 2.

LO 5 | ALTERNATIVE PERSONAL SELLING APPROACHES

In this section, we take a closer look at alternative approaches to personal selling that professionals may choose from to best interact with their customers. Some of these approaches are simple; others are more sophisticated and require that the salesperson play a strategic role to use them successfully. Five basic approaches to personal selling have been in use for decades: stimulus response, mental states, need satisfaction, problem solving, and consultative selling.[10] All five approaches to selling are practised today. Furthermore, many salespeople use elements of more than one approach in their own hybrids of personal selling.

Recall from earlier in the chapter that personal selling differs from other forms of marketing communications because it is personal communication delivered by employees or agents of the sales organization. Because the personal element is present, salespeople have the opportunity to alter their sales messages and behaviours during a sales presentation or as they encounter unique situations and customers. This method is referred to as **adaptive selling**. Because salespeople often encounter buyers with different personalities, communication styles, needs, and goals, adaptive selling is an important concept. Adaptive selling is prevalent with the need satisfaction, problem-solving, and consultative approaches. It is less prevalent with mental states selling and essentially nonexistent with stimulus-response selling.

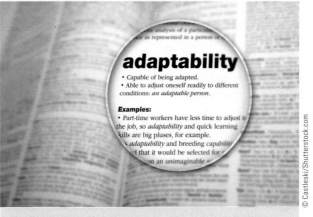

Salespeople who figure out that all customers are different and can adapt will be the most successful.

© Castleski/Shutterstock.com

adaptive selling The ability of salespeople to alter their sales messages and behaviours during a sales presentation or as they encounter different sales situations and different customers.

FIG. 1.1 STIMULUS-RESPONSE APPROACH TO SELLING

Salesperson Provides Stimuli:
Statements
Questions
Actions
Audio/Visual Aids
Demonstrations

Buyer Responses Sought:
Favourable Reactions and Eventual Purchase

Continue Process Until Purchase Decision

The salesperson attempts to gain favourable responses from the customer by providing stimuli, or cues, to influence the buyer. After the customer has been properly conditioned, the salesperson tries to secure a positive purchase decision.

Stimulus-Response Selling

 CPSA 3.2 Conduct sales presentations

Of the five views of personal selling, **stimulus-response selling** is the simplest. The theoretical background for this approach originated in early experiments with animal behaviour. The key idea is that various stimuli can elicit predictable responses. Salespeople furnish the stimuli from a repertoire of words and actions designed to produce the desired response. This approach to selling is illustrated in Figure 1.1.

An example of the stimulus-response view of selling would be **continued affirmation**, a method in which a series of questions or statements furnished by the salesperson is designed to condition the prospective buyer to answering yes time after time—until, it is hoped, they will be inclined to say yes to the entire sales proposition. This method is often used by telemarketing personnel, who rely on comprehensive sales scripts read or delivered from memory.

Stimulus-response sales strategies, particularly when implemented with a canned sales presentation, have some advantages for the seller. The sales message can be structured in a logical order. Questions and objections from the buyer can usually be anticipated and addressed before they are magnified during buyer–seller interaction. Inexperienced salespeople can rely on stimulus-response sales methods in some settings, and this may eventually contribute to sales expertise.

The limitations of stimulus-response methods, however, can be severe, especially if the salesperson is dealing with a professional buyer. Most buyers like to take an active role in sales dialogue, and the stimulus-response approach calls for the salesperson to dominate the flow of conversation. The lack of flexibility in this approach is also a disadvantage, as buyer responses and unforeseen interruptions may neutralize or damage the effectiveness of the stimuli.

Considering the net effects of this method's advantages and disadvantages, it appears most suitable for relatively unimportant purchase decisions, when time is severely constrained and when professional buyers are not the prospects. As consumers in general become more sophisticated, this approach will become more problematic.

Mental States Selling

 CPSA 3.2 Conduct sales presentations

Mental states selling, or the *formula approach* to personal selling, assumes that the buying process for most buyers is essentially identical and that buyers can be led through certain mental states, or steps, in the buying process. These mental states are typically referred to as AIDA (attention, interest, desire, and action). Appropriate sales messages provide a transition from one mental state to the next. The mental states method is illustrated in Exhibit 1.3.

stimulus-response selling An approach to selling in which the key idea is that various stimuli can elicit predictable responses from customers. Salespeople furnish the stimuli from a repertoire of words and actions designed to produce the desired response.

continued affirmation An example of stimulus-response selling in which a series of questions or statements furnished by the salesperson is designed to condition the prospective buyer to answering yes time after time, until, it is hoped, they will be inclined to say yes to the entire sales proposition.

mental states selling An approach to personal selling that assumes that the buying process for most buyers is essentially identical and that buyers can be led through certain mental states, or steps, in the buying process; also called the formula approach.

Exhibit 1.3

Mental States View of Selling

Buyer's Mental State	Common Sales Tactics
Attention	Build rapport with the prospect, ask questions to generate excitement for the sales offering
Interest	Discover buyer needs; uncover purchase decision process; gain precommitment to consider purchase of seller's product
Desire	Build a sense of urgency; demonstrate the product; persuade the buyer to try the product, for example, a test drive or hands-on involvement with the product
Action	Overcome buyer resistance and make the sale; multiple attempts to close the sale are sometimes used

As with stimulus-response selling, the mental states approach relies on a highly structured sales presentation. The salesperson does most of the talking, as feedback from the prospect could be disruptive to the flow of the presentation.

A positive feature of this method is that it forces the salesperson to plan the sales presentation before calling on the customer. It also helps the salesperson recognize that timing is an important element in the purchase decision process and that careful listening is necessary to determine which stage the buyer is in at any given point.

A problem with the mental states method is that it is difficult to determine which state a prospect is in. Sometimes a prospect is spanning two mental states or moving back and forth between two states during the sales presentation. Consequently, the heavy guidance structure the salesperson implements may be inappropriate, confusing, and even counterproductive to sales effectiveness. We should also note that this method is not customer-oriented. Although the salesperson tailors the presentation to each customer somewhat, this is done by noting customer mental states rather than needs.

Need Satisfaction Selling

 1.3 Develop client intelligence

Need satisfaction selling is based on the notion that the customer is buying to satisfy a particular need or set of needs. This approach is shown in Figure 1.2. It is the salesperson's task to identify the need to be met and then help the buyer meet that need. Unlike the mental states and stimulus-response methods, this method focuses on the customer rather than on the salesperson. The salesperson uses a questioning, probing tactic to uncover important buyer needs. Customer

> **need satisfaction selling** An approach to selling based on the notion that the customer is buying to satisfy a particular need or set of needs.

FIG. 1.2   NEED SATISFACTION APPROACH TO SELLING

Uncover and Confirm Buyer Needs → Present Offering to Satisfy Buyer Needs → Continue Selling Until Purchase Decision

The salesperson attempts to uncover customer needs that are related to the product or service they are offering. This may require extensive questioning in the early stages of the sales process. After confirming the buyer's needs, the salesperson proceeds with a presentation based on how the offering can meet those needs.

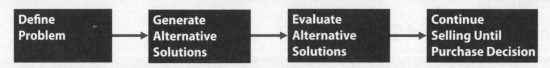

FIG. 1.3 PROBLEM-SOLVING APPROACH TO SELLING

Define Problem → Generate Alternative Solutions → Evaluate Alternative Solutions → Continue Selling Until Purchase Decision

The salesperson defines a customer problem that may be solved by various alternatives. Then an offering is made that represents at least one of these alternatives. All alternatives are carefully evaluated before a purchase decision is made.

responses dominate the early portion of the sales interaction, and only after relevant needs have been established does the salesperson begin to relate how their offering can satisfy these needs.

Customers seem to appreciate this selling method and are often willing to spend considerable time in preliminary meetings to define needs before a sales presentation or written sales proposal. Also, this method avoids the defensiveness that arises in some prospects when a salesperson rushes to the persuasive part of the sales message without adequate attention to the buyer's needs.

problem-solving selling An extension of need satisfaction selling that goes beyond identifying needs to developing alternative solutions for satisfying these needs.

Problem-Solving Selling

 3.1 Develop solutions

Problem-solving selling is an extension of need satisfaction selling. It goes beyond identifying needs to developing alternative solutions for satisfying these needs. The problem-solving approach to selling is depicted in Figure 1.3. Sometimes even competitors' offerings are included as alternatives in the purchase decision.

The problem-solving approach typically requires educating the customer about the full impact of the existing problem and clearly communicating how the solution delivers significant customer value. This is true in cases where the customer does not perceive a problem

An Ethical Dilemma

 8.1 Act with integrity

Bill Jackson is a sales representative for BestBags, a supplier of custom-print shopping bags in Kitchener, Ontario. His customers are upscale retailers who see the value of colourful shopping bags not only as a convenience for customers, but also as "walking billboards" that help advertise for the retailer. BestBags offers a variety of sizes and colours. Pricing to the retailers depends on the size of the bag ordered, quantities ordered, and how many colours are used in custom-print designs. Bill has been successful in this market for two years, but a recent economic slump has had a slight negative impact on his performance. His retail customers are cutting costs by ordering less expensive bags or by using generic shopping bags instead of the more expensive options from BestBags. Jeffrey Bergeron, the sales manager at BestBags, recently told Bill, "You have slipped a bit over the past couple of months. I would hate to see you miss out on your year-end

bonus if you don't make your quota this year. You have to find a way to get your customers into the more expensive bags. Tell them that the best time to advertise is when things are slow. When the upturn comes, tell them they will be glad they invested more in their business." Bill tried to sell the more expensive items for a couple of weeks without any results. Customers pushed back hard, saying now was simply not the time to spend more. What should Bill do?

(a) Keep trying to follow Jeffrey's directive—after all, he is the boss.

(b) Try to convince Jeffrey that a customer-oriented approach will work best over the long run.

(c) Tell Jeffrey that he is working on selling the more expensive bags, but don't push expensive bags to the customers.

or even when the solution seems to be an obviously beneficial course of action for the buyer. According to The Brooks Group, a leading sales training firm, problem-solving selling is not so much about convincing someone to buy, but rather it is about offering a logical solution to a problem faced by the client. Of course, the salesperson is trying to make the sale as soon as possible, but first they must learn exactly what the problem is and determine the best solution from the customer's perspective.[11] To be successful in problem-solution selling, salespeople must be able to get the buyer to agree that a problem exists and that solving it is worth the time and effort required. The problem-solving approach to selling can take a lot of time. In some cases, the selling company cannot afford this much time with each prospective customer. In other cases, the customers may be unwilling to spend the time. Insurance salespeople, for example, report this customer response. The problem-solving approach appears to be most successful in technical industrial sales situations, in which the parties involved are usually oriented toward scientific reasoning and processes and thus find this approach to sales amenable.

Consultative Selling

3.1 Develop solutions

Consultative selling is the process of helping customers reach their strategic goals by using the products, services, and expertise of the sales organization.[12] This approach is shown in Figure 1.4. Notice that this method focuses on achieving strategic goals of customers, not just meeting needs or solving problems. Salespeople confirm their customers' strategic goals, and then work collaboratively with customers to achieve those goals.

In consultative selling, salespeople fulfill three primary roles: strategic orchestrator, business consultant, and long-term ally. As a **strategic orchestrator**, the salesperson arranges the use of the sales organization's resources in an effort to satisfy the customer. This usually calls for involving other individuals in the sales organization. For example, the salesperson may need expert advice from production or logistics personnel to address a customer problem or opportunity fully. In the **business consultant** role, the salesperson uses internal and external (outside the sales organization) sources to become an expert on the customer's business. This role also includes an educational element—that is, salespeople educate their customers on products they offer and how these products compare with competitive offerings. As a **long-term ally**, the salesperson supports the customer, even when an immediate sale is not expected.

Yellow Pages Group (YPG), Canada's leading local commercial search provider and largest directory publisher, uses consultative selling to satisfy the needs of a wide variety of small businesses. Nearly all of YPG's revenues are derived from the sale of Yellow Pages directory advertising to businesses,

consultative selling The process of helping customers reach their strategic goals by using the products, services, and expertise of the sales organization.

strategic orchestrator A role the salesperson plays in consultative selling in which they arrange the use of the sales organization's resources in an effort to satisfy the customer.

business consultant A role the salesperson plays in consultative selling in which they use internal and external (outside the sales organization) sources to become an expert on the customer's business. This role also involves educating customers on the sales firm's products and how these products compare with competitive offerings.

long-term ally A role the salesperson plays in consultative selling in which they support the customer, even when an immediate sale is not expected.

FIG. 1.4 THE CONSULTATIVE SELLING PROCESS

The process of helping customers reach their strategic goals by using the products, services, and expertise of the selling organization

Business Consultant

Strategic Orchestrator

Long-Term Ally

The salesperson helps customers reach their strategic goals by fulfilling three roles with customers.

In consultative selling, the salesperson is a lot like an orchestra conductor. The salesperson must involve all parts of the selling firm.

© Igor Bulgarin/Shutterstock.com

strategy and be able to provide details of the expected and actual return on investment. Accordingly, YPG incorporates these topics into its sales training program.[13]

LO 6 | THE TRUST-BASED SALES PROCESS

CPSA   2.1 Develop client relationships

The nonselling activities on which most salespeople spend a majority of their time are essential for the successful execution of the most important part of the salesperson's job: the **sales process**. The sales process has traditionally been described as a series of interrelated steps beginning with locating qualified prospective customers. From there, the salesperson plans the sales presentation, makes an appointment to see the customer, completes the sale, and performs postsale activities.

As you should recall from the earlier discussion of the continued evolution of personal selling (refer to Exhibit 1.2), the sales process is increasingly being viewed as a relationship management process, as depicted in Figure 1.5.

sales process A series of interrelated steps beginning with locating qualified prospective customers. From there, the salesperson plans the sales presentation, makes an appointment to see the customer, completes the sale, and performs postsale activities.

mostly small- and medium-sized enterprises (SME). To be successful, YPG salespeople must be able to understand and explain the value of their products in the context of the customer's overall business

FIG. 1.5   TRUST-BASED SALES PROCESS

Selling Foundations
- Trust and Ethics
- Understanding Buyers
- Communication Skills

Selling Strategy Based on Customer Needs and Value
- Sales Territory
- Each Customer
- Each Sales Call

Initiating Customer Relationships
- Strategic prospecting
- Assessing the prospect's situation
- Discovering the prospect's needs
- Planning value-based sales dialogue and presentations

Developing Customer Relationships
- Engaging prospects and customers through sales dialogue and presentations
- Co-creating and validating customer value
- Earning customer commitment

Enhancing Customer Relationships
- Building value through postsale follow-up
- Assessing value and relationship performance
- Creating new value opportunities
- Increasing customer value through self-leadership and teamwork

Understanding Customer Value → Creating and Communicating Customer Value → Delivering and Increasing Customer Value

The three major phases of the sales process are initiating, developing, and enhancing customer relationships. Salespeople must possess certain attributes to earn the trust of their customers and be able to adapt their selling strategies to different situations. Throughout the sales process, salespeople should focus on customer value, first by understanding what it is and then by working with customers to create value, communicate value, and continually increase customer value.

Every Business Sells

Justin LeGrow is a sales and marketing coordinator at Cal LeGrow Insurance & Financial Group, where he's worked for six years (five of those years have been in sales). His company's industry is in insurance brokerage and financial services. Justin sells business insurance, financial planning, mortgages, commercial property insurance, commercial auto insurance, business group insurance, investments, and life insurance. He is responsible for over 4,000 clients across Newfoundland and Labrador (St. John's, Bay Roberts, Gander, Corner Brook, Labrador City) and Nova Scotia (Halifax).

As a salesperson, how do you provide value to your customers?

By researching competitive products by identifying and evaluating product characteristics, market share, pricing, and advertising, all while maintaining research databases. In addition, actualizing marketing strategies, handling contracts, and maintaining business communications with clients before, during, and after a sale.

As a salesperson, how do you provide value to your organization?

I provide value by assisting the sales team to manage monthly, annual quotas and by preparing sales meetings and presentations required for those meetings. Also, by integrating and maintaining new computer programs to help aid the sales process, and preparing marketing reports by collecting, analyzing, and summarizing sales data.

What is your greatest challenge you face today as a salesperson?

Selling in an ever-changing world is difficult to overcome. The tactics you used one year may be considered obsolete or a way of the past by next year. Technology is constantly changing and a lot of selling is completed online now instead of face-to-face. Making sure you stay educated and aware of all the different options to sell is crucial if you don't want to be left behind.

How do you try to overcome this challenge?

By being able to reach the client and sell to them in a number of different ways. Every client is unique with a different process of purchasing products and services. So we make sure we are able to accommodate any and all clients' needs and wants. Whether that's by phone, text, e-mail, in-person, online account, app, Web site, or social media, we need to be able to reach our clients how they want to be reached in order to sell effectively.

What advice do you have for someone starting out in sales?

Put yourself in the shoes of your client: the buyer. Think of those times when you needed to purchase products or services and how you went about completing the transaction. Was it convenient? Was it completed promptly? Did the purchase require any extra work from you that could have been easily bypassed by a simpler solution? Did you deal with a person or robot during the transaction? By applying your own purchasing experiences you will be more aware of what needs to be addressed within your own organization in order to sell successfully, frequently, and efficiently.

In this conceptualization of the sales process, salespeople strive to attain lasting relationships with their customers. The basis for such relationships may vary, but the element of trust between the customer and the salesperson is an essential part of enduring relationships. To earn the trust of customers, salespeople should be customer-oriented, honest, and dependable. They must also be competent and able to display an appropriate level of expertise to their customers. Finally, the trust-building process is facilitated if salespeople are compatible with their customers—that is, if they get along with and work well with each other.[14]

Another important element of achieving sound relationships with customers is to recognize that individual

Every Business Sells

William Hickey is a commercial insurance broker at Steers Insurance Limited. He's worked at Steers Insurance for three years, and has been in sales for six. He sells commercial property and casualty insurance across Newfoundland.

As a salesperson, how do you provide value to your customers?

1. Properly assessing the needs of commercial insurance clients based on their assets and operations.

2. Recommending the appropriate coverages to protect against the risks to which each client is exposed, with the best possible premium available.

3. Ensuring the customer understands what they have purchased and how it will help them.

4. Communication and responsiveness throughout the relationship.

As a salesperson, how do you provide value to your organization?

1. By delivering clients and ensuring client risks exposures are protected.

2. By effectively representing the organization's brand in all interactions, internal and external.

What is your greatest challenge you face today as a salesperson?

1. The economy. A poor economy results in more business closures than start-ups and deters customers from adding property or expanding operations.

2. A poor economy significantly reduces opportunity to sell additional but important coverages.

3. Market conditions limiting choice and increasing rates.

How do you try to overcome this challenge?

1. To work with my clients and continually explain the need to keep coverages current in relation to their operations.

2. Work to build the reputation of being a reliable insurance broker, ready to work with new and potential customers when conditions improve.

3. Leave no stone unturned when it comes to finding product options and markets for my clients.

What advice do you have for someone starting out in sales?

1. Know the products you are selling.

2. Provide expertise and authenticity; educate your customer through the process.

3. Responsiveness: get back to clients as soon as you possibly can.

4. Communicate: keep your customer apprised throughout the sales cycle

5. Live up to your commitments.

customers and their particular needs must be addressed with the appropriate selling strategies and tactics. In selling, we discuss strategy at four levels: corporate, business unit, marketing department, and the overall sales function. An individual salesperson is strongly guided by strategy at these higher levels in the organization but must also develop selling strategies and tactics to fit the sales territory, each customer, and, ultimately, each sales call. Our coverage in this text focuses on developing sales strategies for individual customers and specific sales calls.

When studying the sales process, we should note that there are countless versions of the process in terms of number and names of steps. If, however, you were to examine popular trade books on selling and training manuals used by corporations, you would find that the various depictions of the sales process are actually more alike than different. The sales process shown in Figure 1.5 is comparable to most versions of the sales process, with the exception of those versions that advocate high-pressure methods focusing on getting the customer to say yes rather than focusing on meeting the customer's true needs. Our version of the sales process suggests that salespeople must have certain attributes to inspire trust in their customers and that salespeople should adapt their selling strategy to fit the situation.

Another point that should be stressed is that the sales process is broken into steps to facilitate discussion and sales training, not to suggest discrete lines between the steps. The steps are actually highly interrelated and, in some instances, may overlap. Further, the stepwise flow of Figure 1.5 does not imply a strict sequence of events. Salespeople may move back and forth in the process with a given customer, sometimes shifting from step to step several times in the same sales encounter. Finally, claiming a new customer typically will require multiple sales calls.

LO 7 | SALES CAREERS

In this section, we first discuss various aspects of sales careers, and then describe several different types of personal selling jobs. The chapter concludes with a discussion of the skills and qualifications necessary for success in sales careers. For some advice on how to achieve success in a sales career, see From the Classroom to the Field: Building a Successful Career in Sales.

Characteristics of Sales Careers

Although individual opinions will vary, the ideal career for most individuals offers a bright future, including good opportunities for financial rewards and job advancement. As you read the following sections on the characteristics of sales careers, you might think about what you expect from a career and whether your expectations could be met in a sales career. The following characteristics are discussed:

- Occupational outlook
- Advancement opportunities
- Immediate feedback
- Prestige
- Job variety
- Independence
- Compensation

OCCUPATIONAL OUTLOOK Salespeople are revenue producers and thus enjoy relatively good job security compared with other occupational groups. Certainly, individual job security depends on individual performance,

but in general salespeople are usually the last group to be negatively affected by personnel cutbacks.

Competent salespeople also have some degree of job security based on the universality of their basic sales skills. In many cases, salespeople are able to move successfully to another employer, maybe even change industries, because sales skills are largely transferable. For salespeople working in declining or stagnant industries, this is heartening news.

ADVANCEMENT OPPORTUNITIES As the business world continues to become more competitive, the advancement opportunities for salespeople will continue to be an attractive dimension of sales careers. One reason why many successful salespeople ultimately find their way into top management is that they display some of the key attributes required for success in executive positions. Top executives must have highly developed personal skills, be able to communicate clearly and persuasively, and have high levels of self-confidence, motivation, business judgment, and determination.

IMMEDIATE FEEDBACK Salespeople receive constant, immediate feedback on their job performance. Usually, the results of their efforts can be plainly observed by both salespeople and their sales managers—a source of motivation and job satisfaction. On a daily basis, salespeople receive direct feedback from their customers, and this can be stimulating, challenging, and productive. The opportunity to react immediately to customer feedback during sales presentations is a strong benefit of adaptive selling, and it distinguishes selling from other forms of marketing communications, such as advertising and public relations. The spontaneity and creativity involved in reacting to immediate feedback is one dimension of selling that makes it such an interesting job.

PRESTIGE Traditionally, sales has not been a prestigious occupation in the eyes of the general public. There is some evidence that as the general public learns more about the activities and qualifications of professional salespeople, the image of salespeople, and thus the prestige of selling, is improving. An analysis of the popular press (excluding business publications) reveals that there are more positive than negative mentions of news-making salespeople. In a positive light, salespeople are frequently seen as knowledgeable, well-trained, educated, and capable of solving customer problems. The negative aspects of salespeople's image often centre on deception and high-pressure techniques.[15]

Another study indicates that salespeople historically have been depicted in movies and television programs more often than not in a negative light.[16] Even so, the struggling, down-and-out huckster as depicted by Willy Loman in Arthur Miller's 1949 classic *Death of a Salesman* is hardly typical of the professional salesperson of today and the future. Professional salespeople destroy such unfavourable stereotypes, and they would not jeopardize customer relationships by using high-pressure sales techniques to force a premature sale.[17] These perceptions are especially true in the business world, where encounters with professional salespeople are commonplace.

JOB VARIETY   Salespeople rarely vegetate due to boredom. Their jobs are multifaceted and dynamic. Multicultural diversity is increasing in most customer segments, and selling into global markets is on the rise. For a person seeking the comfort of a well-established routine, sales might not be a good career choice. For those who dislike office jobs, sales can be an especially good fit. In sales, day-to-day variation on the job is the norm. Customers change, new products and services are developed, and competition introduces new elements at a rapid pace. In addition to interacting with customers, many salespeople spend a considerable amount of time on such activities as training, attending trade shows, working with other salespeople at the distributor and retail levels to stimulate demand, and completing administrative tasks.

INDEPENDENCE   Independence of action and freedom to make decisions are usually presented as advantages that sales positions have over tightly supervised jobs. This independence is frequently a byproduct of decentralized sales operations in which salespeople live and work away from headquarters, therefore working from their homes and making their own plans for extensive travel.

Salespeople work in a dynamic environment with a wide variety of job activities, including prospecting, planning and making sales calls, attending training sessions, participating in trade shows, and completing administrative tasks.

Despite its appeal, however, independence does present some problems. New recruits working from their homes may find the lack of a company office somewhat disorienting. They may need an office environment to relate to, especially if their past work experience provided regular contact in an office environment.

The independence of action traditionally enjoyed by salespeople is being scrutinized by sales managers more heavily now than in the past. The emphasis on sales productivity, accomplished in part through cost containment, is encouraging sales managers to take a more active role in dictating travel plans and sales call schedules.

COMPENSATION   Compensation is generally thought to be a strong advantage of sales careers. Pay is closely tied to performance, especially if commissions and bonuses are part of the pay package. Starting salaries for inexperienced salespeople with a degree typically average $45,000 to $50,000, with opportunities to earn more through bonuses and commissions. Between the extremes of the highly experienced salesperson and the inexperienced recruit, the average salesperson earns approximately $65,000 to $75,000 per year. More experienced salespeople, including those who deal with large customers, often earn in the $90,000 to $150,000 range. The potential for higher earnings is based on performance and the complexity of the job.

Classification of Personal Selling Jobs

Because there are so many unique sales jobs, the term *salesperson* is not by itself very descriptive. A salesperson could be a flower vendor at a busy downtown intersection or the sales executive negotiating the sale of Boeing aircraft to a major airline.

We briefly discuss six types of personal selling jobs:

- Sales support
- New business
- Existing business
- Inside sales (nonretail)
- Direct-to-consumer sales
- Combination sales jobs

SALES SUPPORT   Sales support personnel are not usually involved in the direct solicitation of purchase orders. Rather, their primary responsibility is dissemination of information and performance of other activities designed to stimulate sales. They might concentrate at the end-user level or another level in the channel of distribution to support the overall sales effort. They may report to another salesperson who is responsible for direct handling of purchase orders, or to the sales manager. There are two well-known categories of support salespeople: missionary or detail salespeople and technical support salespeople.

Missionary salespeople usually work for a manufacturer but may also work for brokers and manufacturing representatives, especially in the grocery industry. There are strong similarities between sales missionaries and religious missionaries. As with their counterparts, sales missionaries are expected to "spread the word" with the purpose of conversion—to customer status. Once converted, the customer receives reinforcing messages, new information, and the benefit of the missionary's activities to strengthen the relationship between buyer and seller.

In the pharmaceutical industry, the **detailer** is a fixture. Detailers working at the physician level furnish valuable information regarding the capabilities and limitations of medications in an attempt to get the physician to prescribe their product. Another sales representative from the same pharmaceutical company will sell the medication to the wholesaler or pharmacist, but it is the detailer's job to support the direct sales effort by calling on physicians.

Technical specialists are sometimes considered to be sales support personnel. These **technical support salespeople** may assist in design and specification processes, installation of equipment, training of the customer's employees, and follow-up service of a technical nature. They are sometimes part of a sales team that includes another salesperson who specializes in identifying and satisfying customer needs by recommending the appropriate product or service.

NEW BUSINESS   New business is generated for the selling firm by adding new customers or introducing new products to the marketplace. Two types of new-business salespeople are pioneers and order-getters.

Pioneers, as the term suggests, are constantly involved with new products, new customers, or both. Their task requires creative selling and the ability to counter the resistance to change that will likely be present in prospective customers. Pioneers are well represented in the sale of business franchises, in which the sales representatives travel from city to city seeking new franchisees.

Order-getters, also called **hunters**, are salespeople who actively seek orders, usually in a highly competitive environment. Although all pioneers are also order-getters, the reverse is not true. An order-getter may serve existing customers on an ongoing basis, whereas the pioneer moves on to new customers as soon as possible. Order-getters may seek new business by selling an existing customer additional items from the product line. A well-known tactic is to establish a relationship with a

customer by selling a single product from the line, then to follow up with subsequent sales calls for other items from the product line.

Most corporations emphasize sales growth, and salespeople operating as pioneers and order-getters are at the heart of sales growth objectives. The pressure to perform in these roles is fairly intense; the results are highly visible. For these reasons, the new-business salesperson is often among the elite in any company's salesforce.

EXISTING BUSINESS   In direct contrast to new-business salespeople, other salespeople's primary responsibility is to maintain and further cultivate relationships with existing customers. Salespeople who specialize in maintaining existing business include **order-takers** or **farmers**. These salespeople frequently work for wholesalers and, as the term *order-taker* implies, they are not too involved in creative selling. Route salespeople who work an established customer base, taking routine reorders of stock items, are order-takers. They sometimes follow a pioneer salesperson and take over the account after the pioneer has made the initial sale.

These salespeople are no less valuable to their firms than the new-business salespeople, but creative selling skills are less important to this category of sales personnel. Their strengths tend to be reliability and competence in ensuring customer convenience. Customers grow to depend on the services provided by this type of salesperson. As most markets are becoming more competitive, the role of existing-business salespeople is sometimes critical to prevent erosion of the customer base.

missionary salespeople A category of sales support personnel who are not typically involved in the direct solicitation of purchase orders. Their primary roles are disseminating information, stimulating the sales effort to convert prospects into customers, and reinforcing customer relationships.

detailer A category of sales support personnel in the pharmaceutical industry working at the physician level to furnish information regarding the capabilities and limitations of medications in an attempt to get the physician to prescribe their product.

technical support salespeople Technical specialists who may assist in the design and specification process, installation of equipment, training of customer's employees, and follow-up technical service.

pioneers Salespeople who are constantly involved with either new products, new customers, or both. Their task requires creative selling and the ability to counter the resistance to change that will likely be present in prospective customers.

order-getters Also called **hunters,** these salespeople actively seek orders, usually in a highly competitive environment.

order-takers Also called **farmers,** these salespeople specialize in maintaining current business.

Many firms, believing that it is easier to protect and maintain profitable customers than it is to find replacement customers, are reinforcing sales efforts to existing customers. For example, Frito-Lay uses 18,000 route service salespeople to call on retail customers at least three times weekly. Larger customers see their Frito-Lay representative on a daily basis. These salespeople spend a lot of their time educating customers about the profitability of Frito-Lay's snack foods, which leads to increased sales both for the retailer and for Frito-Lay.

INSIDE SALES In this text, **inside sales** refers to nonretail salespeople who remain in their employer's place of business while dealing with customers. The inside-sales operation has received considerable attention in recent years not only as a supplementary sales tactic but also as an alternative to field selling.

Inside sales can be conducted on an active or a passive sales basis. Active inside sales include the solicitation of entire orders, either as part of a telemarketing operation or when customers walk into the seller's facilities. Passive inside sales imply the acceptance, rather than solicitation, of customer orders, although it is common practice for these transactions to include add-on sales attempts. We should note that customer service personnel sometimes function as inside-sales personnel as an ongoing part of their jobs.

DIRECT-TO-CONSUMER SALES Direct-to-consumer salespeople are the most numerous type of salespeople. There are approximately 1.6 million retail salespeople in Canada, with another 570,000 selling real estate, insurance, and securities. Not included in these numbers are the many sales representatives selling directly to the consumer for such companies as AVON, Mary Kay, and Tupperware.

This diverse category of salespeople ranges from the part-time, often temporary salesperson in a retail store to the highly educated, professionally trained stockbroker on Bay Street. As a general statement, the more challenging direct-to-consumer sales positions are those involving the sale of intangible services, such as insurance and financial services.

COMBINATION SALES JOBS Now that we have reviewed some of the basic types of sales jobs, let us consider the salesperson who performs multiple types of sales jobs within the framework of a single

position. We use the case of the territory manager's position with GlaxoSmithKline Consumer Healthcare (GSK) to illustrate the **combination sales job** concept. GSK, whose products include Aqua-Fresh toothpaste, markets a wide range of consumer healthcare goods to food, drug, variety, and mass merchandisers. The territory manager's job blends responsibilities for developing new business, maintaining and stimulating existing business, and performing sales support activities.

During a typical day in the field, the GSK territory manager is involved in sales support activities, such as merchandising and in-store promotion at the individual retail store level. Maintaining contact and goodwill with store personnel is another routine sales support activity. The territory manager also makes sales calls on chain headquarters personnel to handle existing business and to seek new business. And it is the territory manager who introduces new GSK products in the marketplace.

Qualifications and Skills Required for Success by Salespeople

Because there are so many different types of jobs in sales, it is rather difficult to generalize about the qualifications and skills needed for success. This list would have to vary according to the details of a given job. Even then, it is reasonable to believe that for any given job, different people with different skills could be successful. These conclusions have been reached after decades of research that has tried to correlate sales performance with physical traits, mental abilities, personality characteristics, and the experience and background of the salesperson.

Success in sales is increasingly being thought of in terms of a strategic team effort, rather than the characteristics of individual salespersons. For example, three studies of more than 200 companies that employ 25,000 salespeople found that being customer-oriented and cooperating as team players were critical to salespeople's success.[18]

Being careful not to suggest that sales success is solely a function of individual traits, let us consider some of the skills and qualifications that are thought to be especially critical for success in most sales jobs. Five factors that seem to be particularly important for success in sales are empathy, ego drive, ego strength, verbal communication skills, and enthusiasm. These factors have been selected after reviewing three primary sources of information:

- A study of more than 750,000 salespeople in 15,000 companies[19]

- Two reviews of four decades of research on factors related to sales success[20]

- Surveys of sales executives[21]

inside sales Nonretail salespeople who remain in their employer's place of business while dealing with customers.

combination sales job A sales job in which the salesperson performs multiple types of sales jobs within the framework of a single position.

EMPATHY

2.1 Develop client relationships

In a sales context, **empathy** (the ability to see things as others would see them) includes being able to read cues furnished by the customer to better determine the customer's viewpoint. According to Spiro and Weitz, empathy is crucial for successful interaction between a buyer and a seller.[22] An empathetic salesperson is presumably in a better position to tailor the sales presentation to the customer during the planning stages. More important, empathetic salespeople can adjust to feedback during the presentation.

The research of Greenberg and Greenberg found empathy to be a significant predictor of sales success. This finding was partially supported in the review by Comer and Dubinsky, who found empathy to be an important factor in consumer and insurance sales but not in retail or industrial sales. Supporting the importance of empathy in sales success is a multi-industry study of 215 sales managers by Marshall, Goebel, and Moncrief.[23] These researchers found empathy to be among the top 25 percent of skills and personal attributes thought to be important determinants of sales success. Even though some studies do not find direct links between salesperson empathy and success, empathy is generally accepted as an important trait for successful salespeople. As relationship selling grows in importance, empathy logically will become even more important for sales success.

EGO DRIVE

8.2 Drive results

In a sales context, **ego drive** (an indication of the degree of determination a person has to achieve goals and overcome obstacles in striving for success) is manifested as an inner need to persuade others in order to achieve personal gratification. Greenberg and Greenberg point out the complementary relationship between empathy and ego drive that is necessary for sales success. The salesperson who is extremely empathetic but lacks ego drive may have problems in taking active steps to confirm a sale. However, a salesperson with more ego drive than empathy may ignore the customer's viewpoint in an ill-advised, overly anxious attempt to gain commitment from the customer.

EGO STRENGTH The degree to which a person is able to achieve an approximation of inner drives is **ego strength**. Salespeople with high levels of ego strength are likely to be self-assured and self-accepting. Salespeople with healthy egos are better equipped to deal with the possibility of rejection throughout the sales process. They are probably less likely to experience sales call reluctance and are resilient enough to overcome the disappointment of inevitable lost sales.

Salespeople with strong ego drives who are well-equipped to do their jobs will likely be high in **self-efficacy**; that is, they will strongly believe that they can be successful on the job. In situations in which their initial efforts meet resistance, rejection, or failure, salespeople high in self-efficacy are likely to persist in pursuing their goals. In complex sales involving large dollar amounts and a long sales cycle (the time from first customer contact to eventual sale), it is crucial to continue working toward a distant goal despite the very real possibility of setbacks along the way. For example, airplane manufacturers hoping to land contracts with the airlines typically pursue such contracts for several years before a buying decision is made. For those who persevere, however, the payoff can be well worth the extended effort.

INTERPERSONAL COMMUNICATION SKILLS **Interpersonal communication skills**, including listening and questioning, are essential for sales success. An in-depth study of 300 sales executives, salespeople, and customers of 24 major sales companies in North America, Europe, and Japan found that effective salespeople are constantly seeking ways to improve communication skills that enable them to develop, explain, and implement customer solutions. The companies in the study are some of the best in the world at professional selling: Sony, Xerox, American Airlines, Fuji, and Scott paper.[24]

Another major study across several industries found that three communications skills in particular were among the top 10 percent of success factors for professional salespeople.[25] The highest-rated success factor in this study was listening skills, with ability to adapt presentations according to the situation and verbal communications skills following close behind.

To meet customer needs, salespeople must be able to solicit opinions, listen effectively, and confirm customer needs and concerns. They must be capable of probing customer expectations with

> **empathy** The ability to see things as others would see them; salespeople with empathy are better able to adapt to various sales situations and adjust to customer feedback.
>
> **ego drive** An indication of the degree of determination a person has to achieve goals and overcome obstacles in striving for success.
>
> **ego strength** The degree to which a person is able to achieve an approximation of inner drives.
>
> **self-efficacy** The strong belief that success will occur on the job.
>
> **interpersonal communication skills** Skills that include listening and questioning.

open- and closed-ended questions and responding in a flexible manner to individual personalities and different business cultures in ways that demonstrate respect for differences.[26] This requires adaptable, socially intelligent salespeople, especially when dealing with multicultural customers.[27]

The importance of communication skills has been recognized by sales managers, recruiters, and sales researchers. These skills can be continually refined throughout a sales career, a positive factor from both a personal and a career development perspective.

ENTHUSIASM When sales executives and recruiters discuss qualifications for sales positions, they invariably include **enthusiasm**. They are usually referring to dual dimensions of enthusiasm—an enthusiastic attitude in a general sense and a special enthusiasm for selling. On-campus recruiters have mentioned that they seek students who are well beyond "interested in sales" to the point of truly being enthusiastic about career opportunities in sales. Recruiters are somewhat weary of "selling sales" as a viable career, and they welcome the job applicant who displays genuine enthusiasm for the field.

COMMENTS ON QUALIFICATIONS AND SKILLS The qualifications and skills needed for sales success are different today from those required for success two decades ago. As the popularity of relationship selling grows, the skills necessary for sales success will evolve to meet the needs of the marketplace. For example, Greenberg and Greenberg's research has identified what they call an "emerging factor" for sales success, a strong motivation to provide service to the customer. They contrast this **service motivation** with ego drive by noting that although ego drive relates to persuading others, service motivation comes from desiring the approval of others. For example, a salesperson may be extremely gratified to please a customer through superior postsale service. Greenberg and Greenberg conclude that most salespeople will need both service motivation and ego drive to succeed, although they note that extremely high levels of both attributes are not likely to exist in the same individual. Nonetheless, there is a growing interest in bringing service concepts and practices into the world of professional selling. Whereas it may be difficult to recruit salespeople who are high on the service dimension, it is certainly feasible to provide appropriate training and to reinforce the desired service behaviours through sales management practices. Without significant emphasis on servicing existing customers, a company is not truly practising relationship selling.[28]

These five key skills aren't the only ones needed to succeed in a sales career. According to the O*NET Resource Center, salespeople in a wide variety of industries need these attributes to be successful.[29]

- Active listening—to include asking appropriate questions, and not interrupting at inappropriate times
- Service orientation—actively seeking ways to help customers
- Oral communication skills—including persuasive communications
- Coordination and problem solving—to include bringing others together and reconciling differences
- Written communication skills—including computer and other technologically facilitated communications
- Logical reasoning resulting in rational reasons to take action
- Strategic and organizational skills so work can be planned and executed efficiently
- Dependability and attention to detail
- Motivation and persistence in the face of obstacles
- Integrity—honest and ethical
- Initiative—willing to take on responsibilities and challenges
- Adaptability—open to change and devoted to continual learning

Our discussion of factors related to sales success is necessarily brief, as a fully descriptive treatment of the topic must be tied to a given sales position. Veteran sales managers and recruiters can often specify with amazing precision what qualifications and skills are needed to succeed in a given sales job. These assessments are usually based on a mixture of objective and subjective judgments.

Professional selling offers virtually unlimited career opportunities for the right person. Many of the skills and qualifications necessary for success in selling are also important for success as an entrepreneur or as a leader in a corporate setting. For those interested in learning more about sales careers, consult *Selling Power* magazine

enthusiasm A strong feeling of excitement. Salespeople should have an enthusiastic attitude in a general sense and a specific enthusiasm for selling.

service motivation A strong desire to provide service to the customer. Service motivation comes from desiring the approval of others.

at sellingpower.com and the Sales Management Association at salesmanagement.org.

The remainder of this book explores the sales process shown in Figure 1.5. Chapters 2 to 4 comprise the foundations of personal selling. Chapter 2 discusses the important topics of building trust and sales ethics. Chapter 3 provides in-depth coverage of buyer behaviour, and Chapter 4 focuses on the communication skills necessary for sales success. Chapters 5 and 6 are about initiating customer relationships, starting with strategic prospecting in Chapter 5. Chapter 6 covers planning value-based sales dialogue and presentations as well as initiating contact with the customer. Developing customer relationships is next, with Chapter 7 discussing issues that arise during sales dialogues and presentations, and Chapter 8 discussing how salespeople can validate customer value and earn customer commitment. Enhancing customer relationships is presented in Chapters 9 and 10, and focuses on how salespeople add customer value through follow-up (Chapter 9) and through self-leadership and teamwork (Chapter 10).

STUDY TOOLS

At the back of the textbook, use tear-out cards to review key chapter information.
Visit cengage.ca to purchase digital tools to help you succeed.

Personal Computer

☐ Gain unique perspectives on key concepts through a variety of videos and cases

☐ Increase your comprehension with online quizzes

☐ Study with existing flashcards and make your own

Mobile

☐ Stay focused and ready to study whenever it's convenient for you!

☐ Access a full, interactive ebook: online or offline

☐ Study tools that empower anytime, anywhere learning and 24/7 course access

LOEXPOSURE OUTERWARE

BACKGROUND

LoExposure Outerware, a Calgary-based company, sells two primary product lines to specialty outdoor stores throughout North America. One product line, called No-Sun, protects consumers from exposure to sunshine, and the other (No-Cold) is functional in cold temperatures. LoExposure has been in business for eight years, and has become a favourite of outdoor enthusiasts who value quality over price. Accordingly, LoExposure is among the higher-priced suppliers in the market. LoExposure promotes it brands through social media, with avid followers on Facebook and Instagram. Occasionally the company will use extreme athletes to promote its brands at specific events, but does not believe in hiring celebrity spokespersons on a longer-term basis. LoExposure does no formal advertising or sales promotion, preferring word-of-mouth and social media to spread the word about its product lines.

CURRENT SITUATION

Kelly Kinard recently joined LoExposure as a sales representative in southwestern Ontario. Kelly's primary customers are outdoor specialty stores, the university towns of Guelph and Waterloo, and nearby ski areas such as Glen Eden and Blue Mountain. With the No-Cold and No-Sun product lines available, Kelly's potential for year-round sales is excellent. Kelly is a recent graduate with a degree in marketing. He had several part-time jobs as he worked his way through university. He also did an internship with LoExposure during his senior year and was excited to land a full-time sales position upon graduation. During his internship with LoExposure, Kelly became totally sold on the quality of the products. By the time he finished his initial product knowledge and sales training with the company, Kelly was genuinely enthusiastic about representing LoExposure in his sales territory. After a few months in the field, Kelly was doing well with existing customers and had added several new accounts. After a great week in the field ended with adding a new retail account, Kelly told a friend, "This is a great job. The products are so good, they practically sell themselves!"

Despite his success, Kelly had run into an obstacle with UpMountain Gear Shop, a small chain with four stores in his territory. When Kelly first began pursuing UpMountain, he did some Web-based research on the company. Kelly found that UpMountain was proud of its sales growth in recent years and that the company attributed a lot its success to providing the highest-quality products at competitive prices. Its customers seemed very pleased according to posts on UpMountain's Web site and in social media. According to Kelly's research, UpMountain seemed concerned about the environment, taking an especially strong stance against the "throwaway society." Kelly was pleased to learn these things about UpMountain, as his company had similar views. LoExposure also attributed its success to providing the best customer experience possible. In addition, LoExposure made extremely durable products backed by a generous repair warranty that kept its products in use well beyond the typical life span for outdoor clothing.

When Kelly first approached Amanda Wilson, the lead clothing buyer for UpMountain, things went well. Amanda was impressed that Kelly had done his homework on UpMountain and pleased that the two companies shared core values related to the customer experience and environmentally friendly practices. In their first meeting, Kelly had provided Amanda with an overview of his two product lines and tried to determine what would be important to Amanda if she were to further consider adding LoExposure as a supplier. Amanda was open with Kelly and indicated that she was impressed with the products, but not sure they would fit in her stores. Near the end of their first meeting, the following conversation took place:

Kelly: Amanda, I hope you will agree that our products fit the bill in terms of high quality at a competitive price.

Amanda: I agree on the high-quality piece, but am not sure about the pricing. Our customers want high quality, but they also want really good value.

Kelly: I understand completely and we have thousands of customers who tell us that our products are worth the price. And of course you know that a higher retail price means more profits for UpMountain.

Amanda: Well, yes that's obvious if it is something we can sustain in the long run. But if we get greedy, we can lose those loyal customers.

Kelly: We both know that customers vote with their dollars and we have a great record of pleasing our customers. In my opinion, your customers will see the value and price will not be a major concern. Sure you have some customers who won't buy our products, but those who are seeking long-term value will gladly pay the price.

Amanda: They may, but I am not convinced just yet.

Kelly: I know we are running out of time before your next meeting, so could I summarize where we are for now?

Amanda: Sure, go ahead.

Kelly: You like our products, but you are not sure the price point fits your customer base. You like the durability of our products and the fact that we don't sell throwaway items. Am I right about those two things?

Amanda: No arguments from me.

Kelly: I think the only way to answer the price-point issue is for you to give our products a try. I am sure they will sell without any problem—let the market decide.

Amanda: Well, I am not prepared to make that decision today and I really do need to get to my next meeting.

Kelly: Is there anything other than the price-point issue that we need to discuss before you make a decision?

Amanda: Well, yes there is. I ask all of our suppliers to give me a plan for how they would help drive consumer traffic to my stores and then, through merchandising and personal selling, help convert that traffic to sales in the store. I have to run now, but I would be willing to meet again if you have some concrete ideas on those topics.

Kelly: That works for me. Would 2 p.m. next Thursday work for you?

Amanda: I will put it on my calendar, see you then.

Kelly left Amanda's office with mixed feelings. It was clear that Amanda did not think LoExposure's products would "sell themselves" as Kelly believed. Further, Kelly was concerned that Amanda wanted marketing ideas for driving consumer traffic to the UpMountain stores. LoExposure did not use traditional advertising or sales promotion. Kelly thought, "Well I am a salesperson, and I could definitely train UpMountain's salespeople on how to sell the products in the store. Maybe I can come up with something on driving consumer traffic to the stores and merchandising our products in the store." Later that day, Kelly scheduled a meeting with his sales manager, Shannon Morin, to plan his upcoming meeting with Amanda.

QUESTIONS

1. How would you evaluate Kelly's performance in the situation? Include any positive and negative aspects of Kelly's performance.

2. What recommendations can you make for Kelly's next meeting with Amanda?

ROLE PLAY

Characters: LoExposure sales representative Kelly Kinard and his sales manager, Shannon Morin.

Scene:

Location—Shannon Morin's office

Action—Shannon has directed Kelly to plan for his next sales call with Amanda at UpMountain. One step in the planning will be to role-play with Shannon playing the role of Amanda. In setting up the role play, Shannon told Kelly, "Decide how you want to proceed. You should come in with some ideas for marketing, merchandising, and in-store selling. But there might also be some questions for Amanda to set the stage for the rest of the sales call. I just want to critique your first few minutes of how you plan to approach Amanda the next time you see her." Following the role play, Shannon will provide Kelly with feedback.

1 INTEGRATIVE CASE

IT SALES EDUCATION

BACKGROUND

As Canada slowly moves away from being a resource-based economy, much is made about what industry will fill this significant gap. The most likely answer is the information technology (IT) industry.

However, filling such a sizable gap comes with significant challenges. There needs to be enough investment and funding to set up the necessary infrastructure for IT companies. This does not just include technology resources like hardware and software; equally important are the human resources that go along with it.

And this is precisely the problem in Canada: a shortage of tech talent. Everything from a lack of education programs to immigration policies are cited as problems relating to building and sustaining talented professionals. For example, average salaries for IT workers in San Francisco and New York are more than double the Canadian average.[30]

But what seems to be overlooked is the importance of sales positions in the IT marketplace. "Sales sometimes doesn't get the spotlight it deserves … mention 'tech jobs' and thoughts typically turn to developers—the programmers and engineers who translate great ideas into working technology and keep the tools we all use humming along. But the reality is that it's impossible to scale and sustain most software platforms today without a highly capable, highly trained sales team."[31]

A study out of Wilfrid Laurier University found that 7 out of 10 high-tech firms in Canada have significant challenges attracting executive-level sales staff.[32] Clearly, the issue of recruiting talented and motivated salespeople has become a major impediment to diversifying Canada's economic engine.

CURRENT SITUATION

You are graduating from your post-secondary institution, and you have a great idea for a new software program: something along the lines of Salesforce. But your idea is a bit different, and it reflects your knowledge of sales and selling from your education.

You realize that Salesforce is a bit of a misnomer, as that SaaS platform is focused more on marketing analytics and CRM, which are connected to sales but not truly representative of the complex nature of selling. There is a need to understand and respect the sales function, especially in the world of IT.

Your idea, therefore, is to create a software program that trains everyone in the IT industry on the importance of sales. The goal is primarily to educate technology firms in understanding and respecting the place of sales in an organization. Your goal is to develop a tool that will make everyone in an organization a salesperson.

Upon speaking with a friend who is an angel investor, they recommend you create a pitch deck for your idea. You decide to draw up the slides and overall content for your proposal. Be prepared to put your best effort into this: it's time you made selling personal.

QUESTIONS

1. In your slide deck, you mention the importance of building relationships by creating a series of conversations over time between buyer and seller. What aspect of trust-based selling are you describing?

   a. customer value

   b. conversation building

   c. sales dialogue

   d. relationship building

2. To provide a well-rounded overview, you feel it's important your slide deck include different sales approaches. One approach that you find compelling is revising a message or behaviour during a presentation, depending on the response from the potential buyer. What type of selling is this?

   a. stimulus selling

   b. response selling

   c. differential selling

   d. adaptive selling

3. You feel that in the IT industry, salespeople will need to perform multiple sales tasks within the framework of a single job. What trend in selling careers is this?

   a. combination sales job

   b. synergistic career pathing

   c. framework synergy job

   d. job sharing

CHAPTER ROLE PLAY 1
Interviewing for a Sales Position

BACKGROUND

Assume you are seeking a job as a sales representative with a company you want to work for after graduation from college. The recruiter has told you that you should come prepared to talk about five of your attributes that would make you a good candidate for the position. The recruiter told you that you could pick five of your strengths from the following list of attributes:

1. Active listening—to include asking appropriate questions, and not interrupting at inappropriate times

2. Service orientation—actively seeking ways to help customers

3. Oral communication skills—including persuasive communications

4. Coordination and problem solving—to include bringing others together and reconciling differences

5. Written communication skills—including computer and other technologically facilitated communications

6. Logical reasoning resulting in rational reasons to take action

7. Strategic and organizational skills so work can be planned and executed efficiently

8. Dependability and attention to detail

9. Motivation and persistence in the face of obstacles

10. Integrity—honest and ethical

11. Initiative—willing to take on responsibilities and challenges

12. Adaptability—open to change, and devoted to continual learning

The recruiter told you that you will discuss your five strengths, with one minute allowed for each strength. After you discuss each strength, the recruiter may have questions before you move on to the next strength until all five of your chosen strengths have been covered.

ROLE PLAY

Situation: Before the role play, all students choose five attributes from the list of twelve above and prepare to briefly explain (one minute per attribute) why these attributes are strengths for you.

Characters: There are three characters: a sales recruiter; a student applying for a sales position; and an assistant to the recruiter who will take notes and evaluate the job applicant's performance.

Scene: Commence with the exercise and, upon conclusion, provide feedback to the job applicant. For example, did the applicant make a convincing case? What did they do well? What could they have done better?

Repeat the exercise until all three students have played the role of the applicant, the recruiter, and the assistant to the recruiter.

2 | Building Trust and Sales Ethics: Developing Trust and Mutual Respect with Clients

LEARNING OBJECTIVES

After completing this chapter, you should be able to

LO 1 | Explain what trust is.

LO 2 | Understand why trust is important.

LO 3 | Understand how to earn trust.

LO 4 | Explain how knowledge bases help build trust and relationships.

LO 5 | Understand sales ethics and legal implications.

AFTER FINISHING THIS CHAPTER GO TO THE BACK OF THE BOOK FOR CHAPTER REVIEW CARDS, AND VISIT MINDTAP FOR ACCESS TO STUDY TOOLS.

Proudly family-owned and operated since 1957 in Florenceville, New Brunswick, McCain Foods is celebrating over 60 years of business and partnership with Canadian farmers.[1] The business began with four entrepreneurial brothers using their family knowledge of agriculture and thirst for innovation to open a production facility for frozen french fries, which is their signature product to this day. The company now produces a wide range of potato products, appetizers, pizzas, and desserts and has also expanded into other segments such as potato seed cultivation and transportation. With global headquarters in Florenceville McCain has operations in six continents, plant sites across the world, sales in over 160 countries, and a global team of 22,000 people.[2] McCain has been recognized as one of Canada's Best Managed Companies for seven years in a

> **trust** The extent of the buyer's confidence that they can rely on the salesperson's integrity.

row.[3] They strive to source local, work with partners that support their vision on quality and ethics, and embrace innovation. Their business is driven by five main values that include family, authenticity, commitment, trust, and a motto of "Be Good. Do Good." The McCain sales team has built strong and meaningful customer relationships through these values and the company has achieved global annual sales of $10 billion CAD as a result.[4] McCain's success is due in part to their ability to build trust and relationships that support the selling process.

Introduction

The extent of the buyer's confidence in the salesperson's integrity is known as **trust**. But trust can mean different things to different people. According to John Newman,[5] vice president of the Integrated Supply Chains Segment at A. T. Kearney, trust is defined in many ways. Buyers

define trust with such terms as **openness**, dependability, candour, **honesty**, **confidentiality**, **security**, **reliability**, **fairness**, and predictability.[6] For example, in a Kearney study, one manufacturer related trust to credibility: "What trust boils down to, in a nutshell, is credibility, and when you say you are going to do something, you do it, and the whole organization has to be behind that decision."

Another manufacturer related trust to confidentiality in that "they were afraid that the sales guys were going around and telling account B what account A is doing," which was identified as a violation of trust. Another company related trust to openness, claiming "we have to share information that traditionally is not shared." One president told how his engineers were sharing manufacturing secrets with their suppliers that would have cost the engineers their jobs five years earlier.[7]

Research reveals that little is known about what ongoing behaviours (i.e., service behaviours) salespeople can employ to satisfy and build trust with customers.[8] Recent research shows that consultative tasks and personal relationship behaviours play a vital role in influencing buyer perceptions, trust, and relationship loyalty.[9] A salesperson has to determine what trust means to each of their buyers, as shown in Figure 2.1. If it is confidentiality, then the salesperson must demonstrate how their company handles sensitive information. If credibility is the concern, then the salesperson must demonstrate that all promises will be kept.

openness Completely free from concealment; exposed to general view or knowledge.

honesty Fairness and straightforward conduct.

confidentiality The state of being entrusted with information from a buyer that cannot be shared.

security The quality of being free from danger.

reliability Consistency of a salesperson over time to do what is right.

fairness Impartiality and honesty.

FIG. 2.1 TRUST BUILDERS

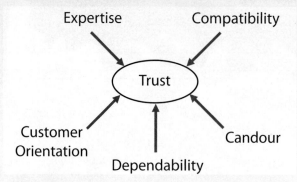

Trust means different things to different people. Trust can be developed by using any of the trust builders. It is the salesperson's job, through questioning, to determine what trust attributes are critical to relationship building for a specific buyer.

Therefore, the buyer defines trust; it is the salesperson's job through questioning to determine what trust attributes are critical to relationship building for a specific buyer.

In this chapter, we first discuss the meaning of trust in the sales context. Next, we explore the importance of trust to salespeople. This is followed by a discussion of how to earn trust and what knowledge bases a salesperson can use to build trust in buyer–seller relationships. Finally, we review the importance of sales ethics in building trust.

Every Business Sells

Stuart Baird is Vice President, Sales and Operations at Country Ribbon Inc., a chicken processing organization that sells fresh and frozen chicken products. Stuart oversees all of Country Ribbon's sales, which is approximately 300 customers. Most of their product is sold in Newfoundland, with the remainder sold to customers in the Maritimes, Quebec, and Ontario. He's been with Country Ribbon for 13 years and has had a 30-year-long career in sales.

As a salesperson, how do you provide value to your customers?

By providing expertise on the market in which their operations are located, and by being experts in the categories where our products are sold. Using this expertise helps our customers with the strategies they need to maximize sales and profits.

As a salesperson, how do you provide value to your organization?

You must have a vast understating of your customers and must be able to convey their strategies and objectives to your organization. If your organization understands, they will help your customer succeed and your organization will succeed too.

What is your greatest challenge you face today as a salesperson?

The centralization of head offices, moving decision making from regional offices with local market understating to national offices that look at the entire country under the same lens. This starts to eliminate unique products that sell in specific markets.

How do you try to overcome this challenge?

Being a market expert and providing that knowledge to the national head offices, and providing recommendations to grow regional sales.

What advice do you have for someone starting out in sales?

Know your customers intimately and then work to figure out how your products or services benefit their strategy.

LO 1 | WHAT IS TRUST?

2.1 Develop client relationships

Trust is earned when an industrial buyer believes and can rely on a salesperson's claims or promises when the buyer is dependent on the salesperson's honesty and reliability.[10] One of the keys to a long-term relationship with any client is to create a basis of trust between the sales representative and the client organization.[11]

Thus, gaining trust is essential to being seen as a reliable salesperson. Long-term sales success in any industry will generally be built on the concept of referral, in which trust plays an important role. Others argue that truthfulness is valuable for its own sake and instrumental to other goals, such as improved long-term relationships.[12] Clients obviously seek a salesperson they can trust. The problem is, depending on the industry and the situation, previous bad experiences might make them wary of future partners. Consultative salespeople are in a unique position to capitalize on building credibility with customers who place a high value on trust. Customers are looking for trustworthy business partners but may have difficulty trusting most salespeople; the salesperson should recognize this as an opportunity.

> Trust is an integral part of the relationship between customers and suppliers.

Every Business Sells

David Noftall is a business development manager who sells executive health, occupational health, and virtual care and wellness to over 75 accounts in Atlantic Canada. He's worked at his current organization for three years and has a 20-year-long sales career.

As a salesperson, how do you provide value to your customers?

- Provide constant communication.
- Be consistent.
- Always follow up with your clients within 24 hours, whether you have an answer or not.
- Always have your client's financial value in mind.

As a salesperson, how do you provide value to your organization?

- Be reliable
- Show professionalism at all times
- Develop strong client relationships

What is your greatest challenge you face today as a salesperson?

I believe competition will always be your greatest challenge. You and your organization have to learn how to differentiate your services from your competitors. Whether it's by the breadth or width of services you offer to customizing for your client.

How do you try to overcome this challenge?

It's easy to go into a potential client meeting and talk about all the great services you offer—99 percent of the time you are selling a solution to improve their efficiency and not a widget!

Before your meeting you want to research your client, their leadership and decision makers, the industry they're in, industry regulation, federal, provincial, and municipal regulations, and their competition. Only then can you really understand a client and their needs. By researching it will allow you as a salesperson to show competency and that you fully understand what they do.

When you land that first meeting, then you can go in and talk about them, their potential needs, and how you see your company becoming a member of their team in improving their business.

What advice do you have for someone starting out in sales?

Honesty and integrity. You have to earn your potential client's trust.

Be prepared to hear "No, thanks" more than "Yes, let's do business!"

The "trust" described here is beyond the typical transaction-oriented trust schema. Many issues—Will the product arrive as promised? Will the right product actually be in stock and be shipped on time? Will the invoice contain the agreed-on price? Can the salesperson be found if something goes wrong?—are only preliminary concerns. In relationship selling, trust is based on a larger set of factors because of the expanded intimacy and long-term nature of the relationship. The intimacy of this relationship will result in both parties sharing information that could be damaging if leaked or used against the other partner.

Trust answers these questions:

1. **Do you know what you are talking about? (competence, expertise)**
2. **Will you recommend what is best for me? (customer orientation)**
3. **Are you truthful? (honesty, candour)**
4. **Can you and your company back up your promises? (dependability)**
5. **Will you safeguard confidential information that I share with you? (customer orientation, dependability)**

Trust is an integral part of the relationship between customers and suppliers and results in increased long-term revenues and profits.[13] In addition, a salesperson's ethical behaviours have an impact on their performance.[14]

LO 2 | WHY IS TRUST IMPORTANT?

 CPSA 3.1 Develop solutions

In today's increasingly competitive marketplace, buyers typically find themselves inundated with choices regarding both products and suppliers. In this virtual buyers' market, traditional selling methods that focused on closing the sale have been inefficient and often counterproductive to the organization's larger, longer-term marketing strategy. In this new competitive environment buyers are demanding unique solutions to their problems—product solutions that are customized on the basis of their particular problems and needs. Additionally, the adversarial win-lose characteristics so customary in traditional selling are fading fast. In their place, long-term buyer–seller relationships are evolving as the preferred form of doing business. Although buyers are finding it more effective and efficient to do *more* business with *fewer* suppliers, sellers are finding it more effective to develop a continuing stream of business from the right customers. Such long-term relationships develop mutually beneficial outcomes and are characterized by trust, open communication, common goals, commitment to mutual gain, and organizational support.[15] Additionally, recent research has shown perceived ethical treatment has been positively related to trust in a salesperson and purchase intentions, and trust has been positively related to purchase intentions.[16]

This shift toward relationship selling has altered both the roles salespeople play and the activities and skills they exercise in carrying out these roles—the selling process itself. Today's more contemporary selling process is embedded within the relationship marketing paradigm. As such, it emphasizes the initiation and nurturing of long-term buyer–seller relationships based on mutual trust and value-added benefits. It is difficult for a salesperson to build a relationship or sustain trust with a prospect or client if they are misrepresenting themselves or their company by answering a question they don't know the answer to. The level of problem-solving activity common to relationship selling requires deliberate and purposeful collaboration between both parties. These joint efforts are directed at creating unique solutions based on an enhanced knowledge and understanding of the customer's needs and the supplier's capabilities so that both parties derive mutual benefits. The nature of this integrative, win-win, and collaborative negotiation relies on augmented communication and interpersonal skills that nurture and sustain the reciprocal trust that allows all parties to share information fully and work together as a strategic problem-solving team.

The skills and activities inherent to relationship selling can be classified according to their purpose as (1) initiation of the relationship (Chapters 5 and 6), (2) development of the relationship (Chapters 7 and 8), and (3) enhancement of the relationship (Chapters 9 and 10). As the activities comprising the selling process have changed, so too have the relative importance and degree of selling effort devoted to each stage of the process.

LO 3 | HOW TO EARN TRUST

Trust is important to any relationship. Several critical variables help salespeople earn a buyer's trust, such as **expertise**, dependability, candour, customer orientation, and compatibility. The importance of each is briefly discussed.

expertise The ability, knowledge, and resources to meet customer expectations.

A salesperson can build trust by demonstrating dependability when assisting in an order delivery.

Expertise

CPSA **1.1 Understand the market**

Inexperience is a difficult thing for a young salesperson to overcome. Most recent university graduates will not have the expertise to be immediately successful, especially in industrial sales. Companies spend billions of dollars to train new recruits in the hope of speeding up the expertise variable. Training to gain knowledge on company products and programs, industry, competition, and general market conditions are typical subjects covered in most sales training programs. Young salespeople can shadow more experienced salespeople to learn what it takes to be successful. They must also go the extra distance to prove to their customers their dedication to service. For example, Karl Decker, a sales rep for Stryker Neuro/Spine for five years, has witnessed over four hundred hip replacements. Karl is in the operating room to answer the orthopedic surgeons' questions and to assist in the fitting of the hip. Sizing the titanium rod that goes into the femur and the polyurethane ball that goes into the socket are critical for success in a hip replacement. Karl must be available for emergency surgeries and several of these have taken place at 3 or 4 a.m.

Another factor to consider is that many organizations have recently been downsized, thus dramatically cutting the purchasing area in terms of both personnel and support resources. As a result, buyers have to do more with less and, as such, are thirsty for expertise, be it current insights into their own operations, financial situation, industry trends, or tactical skills in effectively identifying emerging cost-cutting and revenue opportunities in their business. Of course, expertise will be even more critical with certain buyers who are technical, detail-driven, and/ or just uninformed in a certain area.

Salespeople should strive to help clients meet their goals. As an example, individuals or business owners can go online and trade stocks for themselves, but if they think a financial planner or securities company is more knowledgeable and brings more expertise to the table, then they will employ him or her.

Today's buyers will respond positively to any attempts to assist them in their efforts to reach bottom-line objectives, be it revenue growth, profitability, or financial or strategic objectives. Thus, "expertise" will take on an even more important role in the customer's assessment of the seller's credibility. For some buyers, especially those with economic or financial responsibilities (e.g., CFO, treasurer, owner-manager), a representative's ability to contribute to the bottom line will dominate the perception of a seller's credibility. This is a very important consideration for salespeople given their pivotal strategy of penetrating accounts at the economic buyer level. Salespeople are seeking to convince clients that they are (1) actively dedicated to the task of positively influencing their bottom-line objectives and (2) capable of providing assistance, counsel, and advice that will positively affect the ability to reach objectives.[17] This is easier said than done because salespeople frequently do not understand the long-term financial objectives of their client.[18]

Buyers today want recommendations and solutions, not just options. Salespeople must be prepared to help their clients meet their goals by adding value.

Buyers are continually asking themselves whether or not the salesperson has the ability, knowledge, and resources to meet their prospective customers' expectations. Salespeople are selling not only their knowledge, but also their entire organization and the support they bring to the buyer. Does the salesperson display a technical command of products and applications (i.e., are they accurate, complete, objective)? During one sales call, a buyer asked about a specific new product that the company was promoting in its advertising. The salesperson responded that the product was launched before he was trained on it. This casts doubt not only on the salesperson's ability but also on the company for failing to train the salesperson.

Expertise also deals with the salesperson's skill, knowledge, time, and resources to do what is promised and what the buyer wants. Customers from small accounts must think that they are being treated as well as customers from large accounts and have access to the same resources.

Salespeople must exhibit knowledge generally exceeding that of their customer, not just in terms of the

Salespeople must be prepared to update their customers on product upgrades or industry trends.

products and services they are selling but in terms of the full scope of the customer's financial and business operations (e.g., products, programs, competitors, customers, vendors). They must bring skills to the table, be it discovery, problem solving, program and systems development, financial management, or planning. These skills must complement those of the customer and offer insight into the best practices in the customer's industry. It is not enough to be an expert. This expertise must translate into observable results and **contributions** for the buyer.

Dependability

CPSA | **8.2 Drive results**

Dependability centres on the **predictability** of the salesperson's actions. Buyers have been heard to say, "I can always depend on her. She always does what she says she is going to do." Salespeople must remember the promises they make to a customer or prospect. Once a promise is made, the buyer expects that promise to be honoured. The buyer should not have to call the salesperson to remind him or her of the promise. The salesperson should take notes during all sales calls for later review. It is harder to forget to do something if it is written down. A salesperson is trying to establish that their actions fit a pattern of prior dependable behaviour. That is, the salesperson refuses to promise what they cannot deliver. The salesperson must also demonstrate an ability to handle confidential information. Buyers and sellers depend on each other to guard secrets carefully and keep confidential information confidential.

Candour

CPSA | **8.1 Act with integrity**

Candour deals with the honesty of the spoken word. A sales manager was overheard telling his salesforce to do "whatever it takes to get the order." One of the salespeople replied, "Are you telling us to stretch the truth if it helps us get the order?" The manager replied, "Of course!" The trustworthy salesperson understands doing "anything to get an order" will ultimately damage the buyer–seller relationship.

Salespeople have more than words to win over the support of the buyer; they have other sales aids, such as testimonials, third-party endorsements, trade publications, and consumer reports. The salesperson must be just as careful to guarantee that the proof is credible. It takes only one misleading event to lose all credibility. Nathan Schmidt, Senior Sales Representative for PCE Insurance, talks about the importance of "intent" and how he uses it to build trust and long-term relationships. (See Selling in Action: The Importance of Intent.)

Customer Orientation

CPSA | **2.1 Develop client relationships**

Customer orientation means placing as much emphasis on the customer's interests as you would on your own. An important facet of customer orientation is that salespeople work to satisfy the long-term needs of their customers rather than their own short-term goals.

A salesperson who has a customer orientation gives fair and balanced presentations. This includes covering both the pros and the cons of the recommended product. The pharmaceutical industry has done a good job understanding this principle, as many firms require their salespeople to describe at least one side effect of their drug for each benefit given. This is done not only because of the legal consideration but also to demonstrate expertise and trustworthiness to the physician. Traditional salespeople often ignored negative aspects of a product, which can turn off many buyers. A customer orientation should also include clear statements of benefits and not overpower the buyer with information overload.

---

contributions Something given to improve a situation or state for a buyer.

dependability Predictability of a person's actions.

predictability A salesperson's behaviour that can be foretold on the basis of observation or experience by a buyer.

candour Honesty of the spoken word.

customer orientation The act of salespeople placing as much emphasis on the customer's interests as their own.

Selling in Action

The Importance of Intent

Nathan Smith, Senior Sales Representative for PCE Insurance in Winnipeg, talks about the importance of building long-term relationships. Nathan says, "it is critically important for me to build trust with each client and transform this trust into long-term partnerships. My goal must be to not only build trust but also long-term relationships. It is important that I have a customer orientation. I think sales has everything to do with 'intent.'

If my clients think my intent is to sell them something on each sales call, then it will be difficult for me to grow the relationship. If my client believes my intent is to help them reduce their stress with their insurance needs, then I will have an opportunity to enhance the relationship. Then if I have a strong customer orientation and my intent is to help, then my chances of success will have gone up dramatically."

Salespeople must truly care about the partnership, and they must be willing to "go to bat" for the client when the need arises. A warehouse fire left one company without any space to store inventory. The salesperson worked out same-day delivery until the warehouse was rebuilt. This left a lasting impression on the buyer. They knew that if they ever needed any help, their salesperson would come through for them.

Salespeople must be fully committed to representing the customer's interests. Although most salespeople are quick to "talk the talk" about their absolute allegiance to their customer's interests, when it comes to "walking the walk" for their customer on such issues as pricing, production flexibility, and design changes, many lack the commitment and/or skills necessary to support the interests of their clients.

To be an effective salesperson and gain access to a customer's business at a partnership level, the client must feel comfortable with the idea that the salesperson is motivated and capable of representing their interests. Exhibit 2.1 looks at some of the questions salespeople need to answer satisfactorily to gain the buyer's trust and confidence.

Compatibility/Likeability

 2.1 Develop client relationships

Customers generally like to deal with sales representatives whom they know and like, and with whom they can feel a bond. Gary Schliessman of Gary Schliessman and Associates states that his best friends are his clients. He takes an annual trip to walk the Appalachian Trail

---

Exhibit 2.1

Questions That Salespeople Need to Answer Satisfactorily to Gain a Buyer's Trust

Expertise: Does the salesperson know what they need to know? Does the salesperson and their company have the ability and resources to get the job done right?

Dependability: Can I rely on the salesperson? Does the salesperson keep promises?

Candour: Is the salesperson honest in their spoken word? Is the salesperson's presentation fair and balanced?

Customer orientation: Does the salesperson truly care about the partnership? Will the salesperson go to bat for the customer (e.g., wrong order, late delivery)?

Compatibility: Will the buyer like doing business with the salesperson? Will the buyer like doing business with the salesperson's company?

with one of his clients. Another favourite activity is to take biking trips with his customers that like to ride. He enjoys these activities and learns something new about his clients on each trip. He goes on to state, "Not all of my clients have the same interests that I do, but the ones that do are especially fun to do business with. I believe that compatibility does play a big role in my success."[19]

Some salespeople are too quick to minimize the importance of rapport building in this era of the economic buyer. It also may be true that today's buyers are not as prone to spending time discussing personal issues in sales calls as they might have been 10 or 15 years ago. Salespeople today have to be more creative and resourceful when attempting to build rapport. It is not unusual for a pharmaceutical salesperson to take a

> Good salespeople are never in a hurry to earn commitment!

lunch for the entire staff into a physician's office. These lunches can be for as many as 20 to 40 people. The salesperson now has time to discuss their products over lunch with a captive audience.

Salespeople have to be aware that their buyers are under considerable time pressure and that some will find it difficult to dedicate time to issues outside of the business. However, remember that buyers are human and do value compatibility—some more, some less.

Compatibility and likeability are important to establishing a relationship with key gatekeepers (e.g., receptionists and secretaries). First impressions are important, and a salesperson's ability to find commonalities with these individuals can go a long way in creating much-needed allies within the buying organization. Likeability is admittedly an emotional factor that is difficult to pin down, yet it is a powerful force in some buyer–seller relationships. An Ethical Dilemma demonstrates the challenges salespeople

compatibility and likeability A salesperson's commonalities with other individuals.

An Ethical Dilemma

 CPSA **8.1 Act with Integrity**

Jane Staten was in her first year as a sales rep for a large medical supply company, and her area included a number of physicians' offices in the Ottawa area. One of these accounts had been particularly troublesome; she had been calling on the gatekeeper and was having quite a bit of trouble getting her foot in the door to see the doctors. An industry practice suggests that serving lunch for the doctors, nurses, and staff is a good way to meet everyone and to get an opportunity to present key product information. The receptionist told Jane that lunches were booked for the rest of the year and she would have to inquire again in three to four months. Just as Jane was about to leave, the receptionist made an interesting proposition. If Jane was willing to cater from Christine's, a fancy restaurant that had just opened, the receptionist could work her in within two to three weeks. Jane really wanted to get in front of this group of doctors, but she knew that if she catered from this restaurant she'd use all of her budget for lunches for the rest of the year. Jane already had three lunches scheduled with other offices that must be paid for out of this budget. Jane also worried

that other offices would hear she catered from Christine's and expect the same. What should Jane do?

(a) Go ahead and schedule the lunch. She needs to get in to see these doctors.

(b) Politely tell the receptionist she'll be back in three months.

(c) Talk to her boss about the situation and see if more money is available to pay for all the scheduled lunches.

© Siri Stafford/Iconica/Getty

FIG. 2.2 | KNOWLEDGE BASES

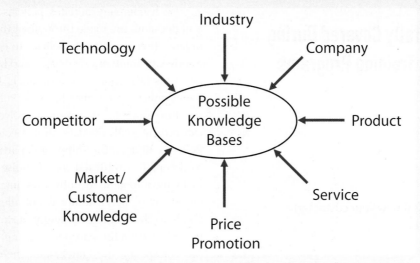

The more the salesperson knows, the easier it is to build trust and gain the confidence of the buyer. Buyers have certain expectations of the salesperson and the knowledge that they bring to the table. Most knowledge is gained from the sales training programs and on-the-job training.

might face when trying to build key relationships with potential clients.

If a salesperson has done a good job of demonstrating the other trust-building characteristics, then compatibility can be used to enhance trust building. Buyers do not necessarily trust everyone they like. However, it is difficult for them to trust someone they do not like.

LO 4 | KNOWLEDGE BASES HELP BUILD TRUST AND RELATIONSHIPS

The more the salesperson knows, the easier it is to build trust and gain the confidence of the buyer. Buyers have certain expectations of the salesperson and the knowledge that they bring to the table. As outlined in Figure 2.2, salespeople may draw from several knowledge bases. Most knowledge is gained from the sales training program and on-the-job training.

Sales training will generally concentrate on knowledge of the industry and company history, company

> Companies provide extensive training to be sure they send knowledgeable sales representatives into the field.

policies, products, promotion, prices, market knowledge of customers, **competitor knowledge**, and basic selling techniques. Exhibit 2.2 summarizes topics generally covered during initial sales training programs.

Industry and Company Knowledge

 CPSA 6.1 Understand your company

Salespeople may be asked what they know about their company and industry. Every industry and company has a history. The personal computer industry has a short history of 35 years; fax technology, even shorter. Other industries have been around for centuries. Some industries change so quickly, such as the pharmaceutical industry through multiple mergers, that it is critical for the salesperson to know their industry to keep physicians informed on new companies, drugs, and procedures. Many buyers are too busy to stay informed and count on their salespeople to help them make sound decisions.

competitor knowledge
Knowledge of a competitor's strengths and weaknesses in the market.

product knowledge
Detailed information on the manufacture of a product and knowing whether the company has up-to-date production methods.

service issues Concerns of the buyer that the salesperson should address.

Salespeople should be familiar with their own company's operation and policies. Buyers may ask the salesperson such questions as: How long has your company been in the market? How many people does the company employ? Does the company have a local, a regional, a national, or an international customer base? Who started the company? Who is the president? the CEO? What is the company's market share? What is the market share on this particular product? Salespeople who could not answer such questions would not inspire the trust of the buyer.

Each company initiates policies to ensure consistent decisions are made throughout the organization. An organization implements policies to control such factors as price, guarantees, warranties, and how much to spend per week taking clients out to lunch. Knowing the company's policies prevents a misunderstanding.

For example, if a representative says a customer can return goods 60 days after receipt when company policy is 30 days, the shipping department might refuse to accept the returned merchandise. The salesperson looks incompetent to both sales management and the customer. If the customer is not allowed to return the goods to the factory, the angry customer probably will never buy from the salesperson again.

Salespeople must understand their company policies. This includes being familiar with the company's formal structure and key personnel. It is important to work as a team with all company personnel. This helps build team spirit and a willingness to cooperate when a salesperson needs help in meeting a customer's need. It is difficult to provide outstanding service when the sales department is not on good terms with shipping and delivery.

Product Knowledge

 6.1 Understand your company

Product knowledge includes detailed information on the manufacture of a product and knowing whether the company has up-to-date production methods. What materials are used when making the products? What quality control procedures are involved? Who are the design engineers?

Salespeople representing their company are expected to be experts on the products they sell. The fastest way to win the respect of a buyer is to be perceived as an expert. If the buyer truly feels the salesperson knows what they are talking about, then the buyer will be more willing to discuss the salesperson's solution to the buyer's problems or opportunities.

Service

 6.1 Understand your company

The effective salesperson must be ready to address **service issues** such as:

- Does the company service its products or does the company send them to a third party?

Exhibit 2.3

Service Superiority

Dimension	Potential Superiority
1. Delivery	Can our company demonstrate speed? Deliver more often?
2. Inventory	Can we meet the demands of our customers at all times?
3. Training	Do we offer training? At our site? At our customer's?
4. Field maintenance	Do we go to the field to fix our products? Do our customers have to bring their equipment to us to fix?
5. Credit and financial consideration	Do we grant credit? Do we help finance?
6. Installation	Do we send a team to your site for start-up?
7. Guarantees and warranties	What are our guarantees? How long? What do we cover?
8. Others	Do we offer anything unique that our competition does not?

- Does the company service its products locally or send them off to another city for service?

- Does the price include service or will there be a service charge when service is needed?

- What does the service agreement include? Shipping? Labour? Or neither of these?

- How long does the service generally take? Same day? Within a week? Will a loaner be provided until the product is fixed?

- Are there any conditions that make service not available? After five years? Damage from flood? Fire?

Buyers need to be comfortable answering these questions, and a good salesperson will make sure they are answered appropriately.

Paul Gibbons from Rocket Systems in St. John's, Newfoundland, spends quite a bit of time discussing service with each of his prospects. His company sells collection software (i.e., receivables) that requires support from his field engineers. Rocket Systems also has a support group that takes calls 24 hours a day, seven days a week. Why is this important to Gibbons? One of his major competitors also has a support group, but only 8 a.m. to 5 p.m., Monday through Friday. Gibbons knows that he has service superiority. Salespeople who can offer the better service have an advantage for generating new business and taking away business from the competition. The salesperson's service mission is to provide added value for the customer. It is important for the salesperson to understand what service dimensions concern the buyer.

For instance, delivery, installation, training, field maintenance, and investing are all issues that a salesperson may be prepared to talk about. Buyers, however, may be concerned only with inventory, because their present supplier runs out of stock frequently.

Exhibit 2.3 reviews service dimensions in which a salesperson could demonstrate service superiority. Additions may be made depending on specific customer demands.

Promotion and Price

Promotion knowledge and **price knowledge** are other knowledge tools that the salesperson must understand. The ability to use this knowledge often makes the difference between a well-informed buyer who is ready to

promotion knowledge Knowledge tools salespeople must possess to explain their firm's promotional programs.

price knowledge Knowledge tools salespeople must have about pricing policies in order to quote prices and offer discounts on products.

Promotional programs must be explained properly so the buyer can place the correct order size during the promotion.

make a decision and another buyer who is reluctant to move the sales process forward. Hershey Foods Corporation supports its retailers with heavy promotions during Halloween, Christmas, and Easter. The promotional programs must be explained properly so the buyer can place the correct order size during the promotion. How many dollars are to be spent? Is it a national program? Is this a co-op program? What will it cost the buyer? If these questions are answered properly, the buyer will be more at ease and ready to make a purchase.

Price can be another area that makes a buyer hesitant if not properly explained. Knowledge of pricing policies is important because the salesperson often is responsible for quoting price and offering discounts. As a representative of the selling firm, the salesperson's quotes legally bind a company to their completion.

Salespeople need complete understanding of their company's pricing policies. Does the company sell its products for a set price or can the salesperson negotiate? Can the salesperson give additional discounts to get a potential client whom the company has been after for years? Does the company allow trade-ins?

market knowledge
Information salespeople must have if larger companies break their customers into distinct markets; salespeople must be familiar with these markets to tailor their sales presentations.

customer knowledge
Information about customers that is gathered over time and from very different sources that helps the salesperson determine customer needs to better serve them.

Market and Customer Knowledge

CPSA | 1.3 Develop client intelligence

Market knowledge and **customer knowledge** are critical to the success of today's salesperson.

Some companies today, because of their size, send their salesforce out to call on all customer types. Larger companies typically break their customers into distinct markets. Computer manufacturers may break out their customer types by markets (i.e., salespeople sell to a particular line of business). For instance, the salesperson may sell only to manufacturers, wholesalers, financial institutions, government, education, or medical companies. This allows the salesperson to become an expert in a line of business. For a salesperson to be effective, the salesperson must learn what the client needs, what benefits the client is seeking, and how the salesperson's products satisfy the buyer's specific needs. Buyers are not interested in factual knowledge unless it relates to fulfilling their specific needs. Having the salesforce learn one line of business well allows the salesperson to concentrate on the needs of a specific market. The salesperson can become an expert in one line of business more quickly than if they have to know how the entire marketplace uses the salesperson's products.

Information about customers is gathered over time and from very different sources. A salesperson can use trade associations, credit agencies, trade magazines, trade directories, newspapers, and the World Wide Web as valuable resources. Canada 411, owned by Yellow Pages Group, has directories on people, businesses, and Web sites. Using the Web to do an initial search on a company can tell a salesperson about what products a company makes, what markets they serve, and so on. A salesperson must use their time wisely when gathering information. Gabe Jones, COO, Ash & Company, states, "I have to thoroughly know my industry and my customer's business. I must know where to find this information."

Competitor Knowledge

CPSA | 1.1 Understand the market

Salespeople will probably be asked how their product stands up against the competition. The buyer may ask— Who are your competitors in our marketplace? How big are you compared with your competitors? How do your company's prices compare with others in your industry? How does your product quality compare with the industry norm? These are important questions that

Exhibit 2.4

Using Technology to Build Bridges to Customers

Technology	Bridge
World Wide	Price updates can be placed on the Web for customers to access. New product information can be made available to customers and prospects.
E-mail	Buyer and salesperson can communicate 24 hours a day. Mass communications can be sent out to all customers and prospects.
Facsimile	Non-electronic documents can be transmitted 24 hours a day. Fax on demand.
Cell phones	Buyer and seller have immediate access to each other.
Voice mail	Salesperson and buyer can leave messages for each other and save time and effort.

> Salespeople must be well versed in technology tools and how to use them effectively to build a bridge to the buyer.

every salesperson must be prepared to answer. Salespeople must have knowledge of their competitors' strengths and weaknesses to better understand their own product's position when comparing. A good salesperson must adjust their selling strategy depending on the competition.

Salespeople must be able to deliver complete comparative product information in a sales presentation. Comparisons of competitors' products for a customer's decision are critical, especially when your features and benefits are superior to those of the competition.

It is important that salespeople distinguish their products from the competition. The ultimate question a buyer asks is—Why should I use your product over the one I am currently using? A salesperson must have competitive knowledge to answer this question. What are the competitor's relative strengths and weaknesses? What weaknesses make this competitor vulnerable? Once the salesperson can determine the competitor's limitations, the salesperson can demonstrate the superiority of their product. A salesperson must answer these questions: How

are you different from the competition? How are you better than the competition? A salesperson must be able to determine their differential competitive advantage.

Technology Knowledge

 CPSA   7.1 Leverage sales technology

Salespeople must use **technology knowledge** to their advantage. Twenty-five years ago, salespeople had to know where a reliable pay phone was located in each city they visited. Many opportunities were missed because salespeople could not reach prospects while they were in the field. Today's salesperson has the luxury of smartphones, facsimile technology, the World Wide Web, voice mail, and e-mail. Salespeople should communicate in the manner their prospects and clients prefer. Some clients use e-mail extensively and want to use e-mail over phone conversations. Some buyers like to fax in their orders and would rather not meet the salesperson face to face. A good salesperson must recognize these preferences and act accordingly. Each of these can either be a bridge to the customer or an obstacle. Salespeople should be building bridges to all their prospects and customers by using technology appropriately (see Exhibit 2.4). If a buyer likes to e-mail requests to a salesperson, then the salesperson must not use e-mail to screen buyers. Likewise, if a facsimile number is given to prospects, then

technology knowledge
Information salespeople must have about the latest technology.

Technology in Sales

GPS Tracking Systems

Global Positioning System (GPS) tracking systems are intended for tracking both automobiles and salespeople. Employed as part of a sales fleet's management strategy, GPS can improve salesforce effectiveness and minimize costs, allowing a company to monitor its salespeople wherever they may be.

The benefits to a company using GPS to track its salesforce are numerous: recovering stolen vehicles quickly (keeping insurance costs down); helping salespeople plan their routes effectively; ensuring the salesforce is taking the most effective routes; and alerting the company and emergency responders if a salesperson's automobile is involved in a road traffic incident.

Modern technologies like GPS are designed to make a salesperson's driving more efficient and much safer.

© Andrey_Popov/Shutterstock.com

---

the fax machine must be turned on at all times and working properly.

Probably the most oversold form of technology is voice mail. Many companies have gone to this method of communication hoping to free up secretaries and make it easier to leave messages for the salesperson. The difficulty arises when a customer wants to talk to a salesperson and can only get a recording. Sometimes, the voice mailbox is full and it is impossible to leave a message. It is also possible to use voice mail to screen calls, and many buyers and salespeople complain that it is virtually impossible to make contact when their counterpart refuses to return their call. Salespeople can use GPS technology to better serve their clients. Coverage in a territory can be improved with the implementation of a GPS system in each salesperson's car. See Technology in Sales: GPS Tracking Systems to learn about the benefits of GPS tracking systems.

Technology can be a friend or foe to a salesperson. If used properly, technology can build bridges to prospects and clients and develop relationships. If technology is *not* used properly, a salesperson

ethics The right and wrong conduct of individuals and institutions of which they are a part.

can alienate customers and turn a potential resource into a reason for a prospect not to do business with the salesperson.

LO 5 | SALES ETHICS AND LEGAL IMPLICATIONS

 CPSA **8.1 Act with integrity**

Ethics refers to right and wrong conduct of individuals and the institutions of which they are a part. Personal ethics and formal codes of conduct provide a basis for deciding what is right or wrong in a given situation. Ethical standards for a profession are based on society's standards, and most industries have developed a code of behaviours that are compatible with society's standards. Many professions in North America owe much of their public regard to standards of conduct established by professional organizations. Reflecting this, both the Canadian Marketing Association (CMA) and the Canadian Professional Sales Association (CPSA) have adopted their own codes of ethics. The CPSA code of ethics is provided later in the chapter in Exhibit 2.7.

Salespeople are constantly involved with ethical issues. In fact, salespeople are exposed to greater ethical pressures than individuals in many other occupations.[20] A sales manager might encourage their salesforce to pad their expense accounts in lieu of a raise, or ask a rep to withhold information from a prospect.[21] A salesperson might sell a product or service to a customer that the buyer does not need. A salesperson might exaggerate the benefits of a product to get a sale. The list can go on and on.

Recall that sales professionalism requires a truthful, customer-oriented approach. Customers are increasingly intolerant of nonprofessional, unethical practices. Sales ethics is closely related to trust. Deceptive practices, illegal activities, and noncustomer-oriented behaviour have to be attempted only once for a buyer to lose trust in their salesperson. Research has identified some of the sales practices deemed unethical, as shown in Exhibit 2.5.[22]

Image of Salespeople and Sales Executives

Sales and Marketing Executives International (SMEI) has been concerned with the image of salespeople and has developed a code of ethics as a set of principles that outline the minimum requirements for professional conduct. SMEI has developed a 20- to 30-hour certification process that declares a salesperson shall support and preserve the highest standards of professional conduct in all areas of sales and in all relationships in the sales process. Exhibit 2.6[23] is the SMEI Code of Ethics that pledges a salesperson will adhere to these standards. Like SMEI, the CPSA has a professional development program that allows individuals to become a Certified Sales Professional. Once certified a salesperson must abide by the CPSA code of ethics as outlined in Exhibit 2.7.

A sales professional deserves and receives a high level of respect on the job. Buyers who do not interact with professional salespeople on a regular basis may believe in the negative stereotype of the salesperson as pushy, shifty, and untrustworthy. Where does this stereotype come from? Some salespeople are not professional in their approach and contribute to the negative stereotype. In the past, television programs, movies, and theatre productions have fostered the negative image of salespeople. During the 1960s and 1970s, the popular press also contributed to this negative image. A study of how salespeople are portrayed in the popular press found that salespeople are often associated with deceptive, illegal, and noncustomer-oriented behaviour.[24] Dilemmas exist also for sales

---

Exhibit 2.5

What Types of Sales Behaviours Are Unethical?

According to a survey of 327 customers, salespeople are acting unethically if they do any of the following:

- Show concern for their own interest, not their clients'
- Pass the blame for something they did wrong
- Take advantage of poor or uneducated buyers
- Accept favours from customers so the seller feels obliged to bend policies
- Sell products/services that people do not need
- Give answers when they do not really know if they are correct or not.
- Pose as a market researcher when doing phone sales
- Sell dangerous or hazardous products
- Withhold information
- Exaggerate benefits of product
- Lie about product availability to make sale
- Lie about competitors
- Falsify product testimonials

Reprinted by permission of Sales & Marketing Executives International, Inc. (http://www.smei .org). "SMEI Certified Professional Salesperson" and "SCPS" are registered trademarks of Sales & Marketing Executives International, Inc.

---

executives implementing strategic account relationships regarding such issues as information sharing, trust, and hidden incentives for unethical behaviours.[25] Three of the more important areas of unethical behaviour—deceptive practices, legal implications and illegal activities, and noncustomer-oriented behaviour—are discussed.

Deceptive Practices

Buyers have been turned off by all salespeople because of experience with only a few unscrupulous salespeople. All salespeople (good and bad) pay the price for this behaviour. Unfortunately, some salespeople do use quota pressure as an excuse to be deceptive. The salesperson has the choice to either ignore the trust-building approach and persuade the customer

Exhibit 2.6

SMEI Certified Professional Salesperson Code of Ethics

The SMEI Certified Professional Salesperson (SCPS) Code of Ethics is a set of principles that outline minimum requirements for professional conduct. Those who attain SCPS status should consider these principles as more than just rules to follow. They are guiding standards above which the salesperson should rise.

An SCPS shall support and preserve the highest standards of professional conduct in all areas of sales and in all relationships in the sales process. Toward this end an SCPS pledges and commits to these standards in all activities under this code.

As an SCPS I pledge to the following individuals and parties:

I. With respect to **The Customer, I** will: Maintain honesty and integrity in my relationship with all customers and prospective customers.

Accurately represent my product or service in order to place the customer or prospective customer in a position to make a decision consistent with the principle of mutuality of benefit and profit to the buyer and seller. Continually keep abreast and increase the knowledge of my product(s), service(s), and industry in which I work. This is necessary to better serve those who place their trust in me.

II. With respect to **The Company** and other parties whom I represent, I will: Use their resources that are at my disposal and will be utilized only for legitimate business purposes.

Respect and protect proprietary and confidential information entrusted to me by my company.

Not engage in any activities that will either jeopardize or conflict with the interests of my company. Activities that may be or which may appear to be illegal or unethical will be strictly avoided. To this effect I will not participate in activities that are illegal or unethical.

III. With respect to **The Competition**, regarding those organizations and individuals that I compete with in the marketplace, I will:

Only obtain competitive information through legal and ethical methods.

Only portray my competitors, and their products and services in a manner which is honest, truthful, and based on accurate information that can or has been substantiated.

VI. With respect to **The Community** and society which provide me with my livelihood, I will: Engage in business and selling practices which contribute to a positive relationship with the communities in which I and my company have presence.

Support public policy objectives consistent with maintaining and protecting the environment and community.

Participate in community activities and associations which provide for the betterment of the community and society.

I AM COMMITTED to the letter and spirit of this code. The reputation of salespeople depends upon me as well as others who engage in the profession of selling. My adherence to these standards will strengthen the reputation and integrity for which we strive as professional salespeople.

I understand that failure to consistently act according to the above standards and principles could result in the forfeiture of the privilege of using the SCPS designation.

Candidate's Name (Please Print) _____

Signature _____

Date _____

Exhibit 2.7

CPSA Member Code of Ethics

The CPSA Member Code of Ethics is the set of principles and standards that a Member agrees to adhere to with customers, organizations, competitors, communities, and colleagues.

The CPSA Member commits to uphold these standards always. As a CPSA Member I will:

1. Maintain honesty and integrity in all relationships with customers, prospective customers, and colleagues and continually work to earn their trust and respect.

2. Accurately represent my products or services to the best of my ability in a manner that places my customer or prospective customer and my company in a position that benefits both.

3. Respect and protect the proprietary and confidential information entrusted to me by my company and my customers and not engage in activities that may conflict with the best interest of my customers or my company.

4. Continually upgrade my knowledge of my products/services, skills, and my industry.

5. Use the time and resources available to me only for legitimate business purposes. I will only participate in activities that are ethical and legal, and when in doubt, I will seek counsel.

6. Respect my competitors and their products and services by representing them in a manner which is honest, truthful and based on accurate information that has been substantiated.

7. Endeavour to engage in business and selling practices which contribute to a positive relationship with the community.

8. Assist and counsel my fellow sales professionals where possible in the performance of their duties.

9. Treat fellow members with special consideration, be a part of the sales community, collaborate for coaching, guidance and information.

10. Abide by and encourage others to adhere to this Member Code of Ethics.

As a CPSA Member, I understand that the reputation and professionalism of all salespeople depends on me as well as others engaged in the sales profession, and I will adhere to these standards to strengthen the reputation and integrity for which we all strive. I understand that failure to consistently act according to this Member Code of Ethics may result in the loss of my CPSA membership and its associated benefits.

to buy, or go to the next sales meeting and catch the wrath of their sales manager for being under quota. Salespeople giving unfounded answers, exaggerating product benefits, and withholding information might appear only to shade the truth, but when it causes harm to the buyers, such salespeople have jeopardized future dealings with the buyer.

Legal Implications and Illegal Activities

 6.3 Demonstrate legal literacy

LEGAL IMPLICATIONS When considering the legal implications involved in professional selling, it is important to consider the federal and provincial/territorial legislation that is in place to regulate these activities.

The *Competition Act* is the major federal legislation in Canada that defines illegal practices, including **price fixing**, **bid rigging**, **price discrimination**, **predatory pricing**, **bait and switch selling**, and **pyramid selling**.

All Canadian provinces and territories have established a *cooling off* period during which the consumer may void a contract to purchase goods or services. These cooling off laws vary across jurisdictions, but their primary purpose is to give customers an opportunity to reconsider a buying decision made under a salesperson's persuasive influence. In most places, this legislation is referred to as the *Direct Sellers Act* or the *Consumer Protection Act*. For more information about the legislation involved with professional selling, please visit the Competition Bureau's Web site at www .competitionbureau .gc.ca.

It is also important to remember that sales representatives often have to engage in a contract with an individual or a firm to secure the sale. A *contract* is a promise or promises that the courts can enforce. Oral contracts are enforceable, but written contracts are preferable as they reduce the possibility of disagreement. Courts give written contracts greater weight in a lawsuit. A written contract may consist of a sales slip, a notation on a cheque, or any other writing that offers evidence of the promises the party made.

When a salesperson is hired, they may be asked to sign an employment contract. Most of these agreements include a *noncompete clause*. This prohibits salespeople from working for a competing firm for a set time (often a year) after they leave the position. Most clauses are legally binding even when an employee's position is cut.

ILLEGAL ACTIVITIES Misusing company assets has been a longstanding problem for many sales organizations. Using the company car for personal use, charging expenses that did not occur, and selling samples for income are examples of misusing company assets. Some of these violations of company property also constitute violations of Canada Revenue Agency (CRA) regulations and are offences that could lead to jail or heavy fines.

Bribery is another area that causes some salespeople to run afoul of the law. A competitor might offer bribes; this, in turn, puts pressure on the salesperson's company to respond with bribes of its own. It is difficult for a salesperson to see potential sales going to the competition. Salespeople offering bribes on their own can be punished. Companies that engage in bribery could find themselves being prosecuted and fined. In some cultures, giving bribes is perceived to be acceptable business practice. However, bribes or payoffs may violate federal government legislation. Canada has the *Corruption of Foreign Public Officials Act*, and for Canadian salespeople working with U.S. companies, the U.S. *Foreign Corrupt Practices Act (FCPA)* exists.

Another area of legal concern that involves the salesforce is product liability. Salespeople can create product liabilities for a company in three ways: **express warranty**, **misrepresentation**, and **negligence**. A salesperson can create a product warranty or guarantee that obligates the selling organization even if they do not intend to give the warranty. Express warranties are created by any affirmation of fact or promise, any description, or any sample or model that a salesperson uses, which is made part of the basis of the bargain.

Basis of the bargain is taken to mean that the buyer relied on the seller's statements in making the purchase decision. If a salesperson tells a prospect that a machine will turn out 50 units per hour, a legal obligation has been created for the firm to supply a machine that will accomplish this. A salesperson's misrepresentation can also lead to product liability even if the salesperson makes a false claim thinking it is true. The burden of accuracy is on the seller. Salespeople are required by law to exercise "reasonable care" in formulating claims. If a salesperson asserts that a given drug is safe without

price fixing Agreements between sellers to prevent or unduly lessen competition or to unreasonably enhance the price of a product by selling at a fixed price.

bid rigging An agreement in which competitors agree in advance who will win a bid based on the tenders submitted.

price discrimination Knowingly and systematically selling the same goods or services at different prices to different buyers.

predatory pricing A firm or an individual deliberately sets prices to incur losses for a long time to eliminate a competitor or to inhibit competition in the expectation that the firm or individual will later be able to recoup its losses by charging prices above competitive levels.

bait and switch selling Firms or individuals advertise products at bargain prices that they do not have available in reasonable quantities and try to sell more expensive products instead.

pyramid selling Fees or commissions paid not on the basis of product sales but on the recruitment of others to make sales.

express warranty A way a salesperson can create product liabilities by giving a product warranty or guarantee that obligates the selling organization even if the salesperson does not intend to give the warranty.

misrepresentation False claim(s) made by a salesperson.

negligence False claim(s) made by a salesperson about the product or service they are trying to sell.

basis of the bargain When a buyer relies on the seller's statements in making a purchase decision.

Exhibit 2.8

Areas of Unethical Behaviour

Deceptive Practices	Illegal Activities
Deceive	Defraud
Hustle	Con
Scam	Misuse company assets
Exaggerate	
Withhold information/bluff	

Noncustomer-Oriented Behaviour

Pushy

Hard sell

Fast talking

High pressure

exercising reasonable care to see that this claim is accurate, the salesperson has been negligent. Negligence is a basis for product liability on the part of the seller.

Although these tactics might increase sales in the short run, salespeople ruin their trust relationship with their customer and company. Given the legal restrictions that relate to selling practices, a salesperson, as well as the selling organization, should exercise care in developing sales presentations.

Noncustomer-Oriented Behaviour

Most of today's sales organizations emphasize trust-building behaviours and are customer-oriented. Unfortunately, there are a few salespeople and companies today that concentrate on short-term goals and allow outmoded sales tactics to be practised. Most buyers will not buy from salespeople who are pushy and practise the hard sell. Too much is at stake to fall for the fast-talking, high-pressure salesperson. Buyers have been through their own training, and they understand the importance of developing a long-term relationship with their suppliers. Exhibit 2.8 summarizes these practices.

How Are Companies Dealing with Sales Ethics?

CPSA 8.1 Act with integrity

Many companies spend time covering ethics in their training programs. These programs should cover such topics as the appropriateness of gift giving, the use of expense accounts, and dealing with a prospect's unethical demands. Each company will have its own policies on gift

giving. John Huff of Shering-Plough states, "Just a few years ago, I could spend my expense account on Indiana Pacers tickets or a golf outing with doctors. That is not the case today. There is a lot of grey area concerning gift giving by salespeople to their business clients and prospects. The pharmaceutical industry has policed itself so now gift giving has all but been eliminated. I must know the rules of my company and industry."[26] Some buyers are not allowed to accept gifts from salespeople.

Another important training area is the use of expense accounts. Salespeople should be trained in how to fill out the expense account form and what is acceptable for submission. Some companies allow personal travel kilometres to be included; others do not. If guidelines are established, there is less chance for salesperson misunderstanding.

Sometimes unethical behaviour is initiated not by the salesperson but by the buyer.[27] Salespeople must be trained in dealing with prospects who make unethical demands. Buyers can be under pressure from their company to stay within budget or to move up the timetable on an order. A buyer may ask a salesperson to move him or her up on the order list in exchange for more business down the road. One pharmacist set up a deal with a salesperson to buy samples illegally. The trust-based salesperson has to shut down any short-term gain for long-term success. A salesperson's career is over if the word circulates that they cannot be trusted.

A salesperson must also be concerned with our legal system and those of other countries. It cannot be an excuse for today's well-trained salesperson to say they did not know that a law was being broken. When in doubt,

Exhibit 2.9

Legal Reminders

For salespeople

1. Use factual data rather than general statements of praise during the sales presentation. Avoid misrepresentation.
2. Thoroughly educate customers before the sale on the product's specifications, capabilities, and limitations.
3. Do not overstep your authority, as the salesperson's actions can be binding to the selling firm.
4. Avoid discussing these topics with competitors: prices, profit margins, discounts, terms of sale, bids or intent to bid, sales territories or markets to be served, rejection or termination of customers.
5. Do not use one product as bait for selling another product.
6. Do not try to force the customer to buy only from your organization.
7. Offer the same price and support to buyers who purchase under the same set of circumstances.
8. Do not tamper with a competitor's product.
9. Do not disparage a competitor's product without specific evidence of your contentions.
10. Avoid promises that will be difficult or impossible to honour.

For the sales organization

1. Review sales presentations and claims for possible legal problems.
2. Make the salesforce aware of potential conflicts with the law.
3. Carefully screen any independent sales agents the organization uses.
4. With technical products and services make sure the sales presentation fully explains the capabilities and dangers of products and service.

the salesperson must check out all provincial/territorial and local laws. In addition, there are industry-specific rules and regulations to be considered. Exhibit 2.9 covers a number of legal reminders.

A salesperson has their reputation to tarnish only once. In this day and age of mass communication (phone, e-mail, Web sites), it is easy for a buyer to get the word out that a salesperson is acting unethically, possibly ending that salesperson's career.

STUDY TOOLS

At the back of the textbook, use tear-out cards to review key chapter information. Visit cengage.ca to purchase digital tools to help you succeed.

CENGAGE | MINDTAP

Personal Computer

☐ Gain unique perspectives on key concepts through a variety of videos and cases
☐ Increase your comprehension with online quizzes
☐ Study with existing flashcards and make your own

Mobile

☐ Stay focused and ready to study whenever it's convenient for you!
☐ Access a full, interactive ebook: online or offline
☐ Study tools that empower anytime, anywhere learning and 24/7 course access

CINDY RANGER'S DILEMMA

BACKGROUND

Cindy Ranger has spent the past three months trying to gather all the information she needs to submit a bid on an order that is very important to her company. Bids are due tomorrow and the decision will be made within a week. She has made a great impression on the purchasing agent, Janet Williams, and she has just ended a conversation with her sales manager who believes Cindy needs to make one more call on Cindy to see if she can find out any additional information that might help her prepare the bid. Cindy's boss specifically wants to know who the other bidders are.

CURRENT SITUATION

Later that day, Cindy visited with Janet Williams. During the course of the conversation with Williams, Cindy asked who the other bidders were. Williams beat around the bush for a while, but she did not reveal the other bidders. She did mention the other bids were in and pulled the folder out of the filing cabinet where they were kept. Janet opened the file and looked over the bids in front of Cindy.

There was a knock on the door and Janet's boss asked if he could see her for a minute and she walked down the hall with her boss. Cindy realized all the bids were left out in front of her. There was a summary sheet of all of the bids on top and she could easily see all the bids. When Williams returned she returned the folder to the file and the two made some small talk and ended their conversation.

Cindy returned to her office and completed her bid and turned it in to Janet Williams the next morning. Cindy knew her bid would be the lowest by $500. One week later Cindy learned she won the bid.

QUESTIONS

1. What are the ethical issues involved in this situation?

2. If you were Cindy Ranger, do you think Janet Williams intended for you to see the competitive bids? What would you have done, given this situation? Why?

TRUST AT THE CAR DEALERSHIP

BACKGROUND

Sales has a trust problem. Not necessarily with itself or its best practices, but with general public perception. A recent survey found that "people believe those who lie more would be better at sales jobs."[28] In a separate HubSpot survey, only 3 percent of respondents considered salespeople to be trustworthy.[29]

There were only a few professions below salesperson on the list, and not surprisingly they included stockbrokers and politicians. But near the very bottom of the list, who only 1 percent of people would consider trustworthy, is unfortunately not surprising: the car salesperson.

Much has been said about the negative experience of sales at a car dealership: the in-your-face pressure, the promises, the unnecessary add-ons. However, given a recent meeting of Canadian auto executives, the days of the car dealership salesperson might be coming to an end. Calling the many challenges to the traditional car selling models "barbarians at the gate," Hyundai Canada's CEO noted that there were many different business models, like Tesla's direct selling approach, that could significantly impact the traditional dealership.[30]

One intriguing option for the car selling industry is with companies like car sharing firm Turo. Infiniti Canada's Managing Director Adam Paterson describes his company's interest in this area: "[Infiniti] is examining launching an extended test-drive program with the car-sharing company Turo that would allow customers to drive a vehicle they are interested in for a matter of days."[31]

CURRENT SITUATION

AutoCanada is a large dealership group that operates all across North America. However, the company has had to shut down locations in Chicago, and recently sold a dealership in Calgary.[32] In light of these closures, the company is eager to make changes to its approach to the car selling business model.

Having heard car companies like Infiniti are investigating the efficacy of using car sharing services like Turo, executives are intrigued at further investigating the possibility of having mobile car salespeople. The hope is that by removing salespeople from the physical dealership, which is often interpreted as a space that lacks trustworthiness, the company can reinvent the car selling approach.

The company is considering creating a mobile car selling team that will focus entirely on bringing cars to people where they are, at work or home. The company is considering using the existing infrastructure of a car share service like Turo, but is thus far noncommittal on making a final selection on a partner. It believes it needs to iron out some wrinkles in its existing approach to sales, given the most recent closures and accompanying uncertainty of the car sales model.

But this mobile car sales approach requires a re-think toward trust in sales. Consumers are highly skeptical of car sales teams, and much needs to be done to overcome this significant challenge. The company is thinking of hiring a new sales manager to oversee this process, and it creates a job posting. On the posting it asks potential candidates to prepare an extensive cover letter that provides a brief overview on the importance of creating trust in the car selling process.

You have decided to apply to this position, and now you have to create your cover letter. You realize it will have to cover everything you know about sales trust, and you will have to refer to your learnings from sales class in school. As you open up a new file on your computer, you reflect back on trust and begin to type. You don't want to stall out, so get in gear and put together a great cover letter.

QUESTIONS

1. The extent of the buyer's confidence in the salesperson's integrity is known as trust. But trust can mean different things to different people. Which of the following terms is NOT associated with trust?

   a. openness
   b. unpredictability
   c. confidentiality
   d. reliability

2. In your cover letter you provide an example of how a mobile car salesforce must ensure that the "do whatever it takes" sales mentality will end. You are suggesting an emphasis on which aspect of trust?

   a. dependability
   b. truthfulness
   c. candour
   d. clarity

3. You feel that you should discuss deceptive practices, noncustomer-oriented behaviour, and illegal activities in your cover letter. Which of the following does NOT align with those unethical descriptions?

   a. exaggerate
   b. pushy
   c. high pressure
   d. predictability

CHAPTER ROLE PLAY 2

Building Trust and Sales Ethics: Reef Uniform Company

BACKGROUND

Reef Uniform Company (RUC) specializes in providing uniforms to hotels and restaurants. RUC is a new company from Australia trying to break into the Canadian market. They have had trouble breaking into larger accounts (Marriott, Delta, Sheraton) because as a new company they don't have the name recognition in Canada.

As the account exec in the area, you have been working on a new Sheraton hotel with over 5,000 rooms and 500 employees. You recently submitted a proposal and the buyer, Anthony Norman, has told you he is leaning your way with the order. He also told you that this order must come off without a hitch as his hide is on the line if things go wrong.

You know there could be a problem down the road as one of your unions has been negotiating a contract that is about to expire. The last time this contract came up, there was a strike and orders were backlogged for weeks. The hotel has many customized uniforms and has to have these for their grand opening in three months. What is your obligation to the hotel having this information? This order will make your year and probably send you on a trip to Rome for exceeding quota.

ROLE PLAY

Location: Anthony Norman's office

Action: Role-play a sales call with Anthony Norman, addressing the issues in the case.

3 | Understanding Buyers

LEARNING OBJECTIVES

After completing this chapter, you should be able to

LO 1 | Categorize the primary types of buyers.

LO 2 | Discuss the distinguishing characteristics of business markets.

LO 3 | List the different steps in the business-to-business buying process.

LO 4 | Discuss the different types of buyer needs.

LO 5 | Describe how buyers evaluate suppliers and alternative sales offerings by using the multiattribute model of evaluation.

LO 6 | Explain the two-factor model that buyers use to evaluate the performance of sales offerings and develop satisfaction.

LO 7 | Explain the different types of purchasing decisions.

LO 8 | Describe the four communication styles and how salespeople must adapt their own styles to maximize communication.

LO 9 | Explain the concept of buying teams and specify the different member roles.

LO 10 | Understand means for engaging customers.

AFTER FINISHING THIS CHAPTER GO TO THE BACK OF THE BOOK FOR CHAPTER REVIEW CARDS, AND VISIT MINDTAP FOR ACCESS TO STUDY TOOLS.

Empire Company Limited is a Canadian company with headquarters in Stellarton, Nova Scotia. Its key businesses are food retailing and related real estate, and it owns Sobeys Inc. as a subsidiary. Annualized sales for Empire are approximately $25.6 billion, with $13.8 billion in assets, and the company and its subsidiaries, franchisees, and affiliates employ approximately 123,000 people.[1] Since Sobeys' start in 1907, the company has grown to more than 1,500 stores across Canada. Understanding customers and placing them at the core of their existence has helped Sobeys achieve its success. This growth stemmed from considering its customers' needs. Sobeys' purpose as it continues to grow has also evolved. In 2018, the company's purpose changed to "We are a family nurturing families." Maintaining its success, Sobeys will continue to foster a caring family culture built on trust and respect for themselves, their company, and most of all, their customers.[2] The company continues to stay true to its core, ensuring it always offers the best products and services for each market. Adding services such as online delivery or developing new products under the "Compliments" private label are just a few examples of growth that would provide Sobeys' customers with the best combination of price, quality, and experience. Through a number of acquisitions and new developments, the company currently operates the retail brands Safeway, IGA, Foodland, FreshCo, Thrifty Foods, Lawtons Drugs, and more than 350 retail and fuel locations.[3] In addition, Sobeys Wholesale is also in the Empire family. This national food wholesaler supports its own stores and serves over 4,700 other independent retailers across Canada.

Introduction

Understanding customers is necessary to succeed in today's highly competitive marketplace. Empire Company Limited's sustained success is due in part to its ability to understand its retail and business customer bases. Understanding the unique needs of each customer allows salespeople to tailor specific solutions for those needs. In doing so, salespeople are able to bring about value for these customers.

This chapter focuses on preparing you to better understand buyers. Following a discussion on different types of buyers, this chapter develops a model of the buying process and the corresponding roles of the salesperson. Buyer activities characteristic of each step of the purchase decision process are explained and related to salesperson activities for effectively interacting with buyers. This is followed by an explanation of different types of purchasing decisions to which salespeople must respond. The influence

of individual communication styles on selling effectiveness is also discussed. The growing incidence of multiple buying influences and buying teams is then demonstrated, along with their impact on selling strategy. Finally, means for engaging buyers—such as focusing on the customer experience, making relevant information easily accessible to buyers, and adding value demanded by buyers—are discussed from the perspective of the salesperson.

LO 1 | TYPES OF BUYERS

Salespeople work and interact with many different types of buyers. These buyer types range from heavy industry and manufacturing operations to consumers making a purchase for their own use. These variants of customer types arise out of the unique buying situations they occupy. As a result, one type of buyer will have needs, motivations, and buying behaviour that are very different from another type of buyer. Consider the different buying situations and the resulting needs of a corporate buyer for Foot Locker compared with the athletic equipment buyer for a major university or with Joe Smith, attorney at law and weekend warrior in the local YMCA's basketball league. As illustrated in Exhibit 3.1, each of these buyers may be looking for athletic shoes, but their buying needs are very different. To maximize selling effectiveness, salespeople must understand the type of buyer with whom they are working and respond to their specific needs, wants, and expectations.

The most common categorization of buyers splits them into either the (1) **consumer market** or (2) **business market**. Consumers purchase goods and services for their own use or consumption and are highly influenced by peer group behaviour, aesthetics, and personal taste. Business markets are composed of firms, institutions, and governments. These members of the business market acquire goods and services to use as inputs into their own manufacturing process (e.g., raw materials, component parts, and capital equipment), for use in their day-to-day operations (e.g., office supplies, professional services, insurance), or for resale to their own customers. Business customers tend to stress overall value as the cornerstone for purchase decisions.

LO 2 | DISTINGUISHING CHARACTERISTICS OF BUSINESS MARKETS

CPSA 1.1 Understand the market

consumer market A market in which consumers purchase goods and services for their use or consumption.

business market A market composed of firms, institutions, and governments who acquire goods and services to use as inputs into their own manufacturing process, for use in their day-to-day operations, or for resale to their own customers.

derived demand Demand in business markets that is closely associated with the demand for consumer goods.

acceleration principle When demand increases (or decreases) in the consumer market, the business market reacts by accelerating the buildup (or reduction) of inventories and increasing (or decreasing) plant capacity.

Although there are similarities between consumer and business buying behaviours, business markets tend to be much more complex and possess several characteristics that are in sharp contrast to those of the consumer market. These distinguishing characteristics are described in the following sections.

Concentrated Demand

Business markets typically exhibit high levels of concentration in which a small number of large buyers account for most of the purchases. The fact that business buyers tend to be larger in size but fewer in numbers can greatly affect a salesperson's selling plans and performance. For example, a salesperson selling grade industrial silicon for use in manufacturing computer chips will find that their fate rests on acquiring and nurturing the business of one or more of the four or five dominant chip makers around the world.

Derived Demand

Derived demand denotes that the demand in business markets is closely associated with the demand for consumer goods. When the consumer demand for new cars and trucks increases, the demand for rolled steel also goes up. Of course, when the demand for consumer products goes down, so goes the related demand in business markets. The most effective salespeople identify and monitor the consumer markets that are related to their business customers so they can better anticipate shifts in demand and assist their buyers in staying ahead of the demand shifts rather than being caught with too much, too little, or even the wrong inventory. Republic Gypsum's salespeople were able to accurately forecast a boom in residential construction and the pressure it would put on the supply of sheetrock wallboard. Working closely with their key customers, order quantities and shipping dates were revised to prevent those customers from being caught with inadequate inventories to supply the expanded demand. This gave those customers a significant advantage over their competitors, who were surprised and suddenly out of stock.

Higher Levels of Demand Fluctuation

Closely related to the derived demand characteristic, the demand for goods and services in the business market is more volatile than that of the consumer market. In economics, this is referred to as the **acceleration principle**. As demand increases (or decreases) in the consumer market, the business market reacts by accelerating the buildup (or reduction) of inventories and increasing (or decreasing) plant capacity. A good example would be the rapidly growing demand for smartphones with advanced capabilities such as inductive wireless charging, dual SD cards, water resistance, and larger screens. In response to higher consumer demand, wholesalers and retailers are increasing their inventories of these advanced phones while decreasing the number of less technologically advanced devices they carry. In response, manufacturers have shifted their

Exhibit 3.1

Different Needs of Different Athletic Shoe Buyers

	Buyer for Foot Locker Shoe Stores	University Athletic Equipment Buyer	Joe Smith—YMCA Weekend Warrior
Functional needs	• Has the features customers want • Well constructed—minimizes returns • Offers point-of-sale displays for store use • Competitive pricing	• Individualized sole texture for different player performance needs • Perfect fit and size for each team member • Custom match with university colours • Size of supplier's payment to coach and school for using their shoes	• Cutting-edge shoe features • Prominent brand logo • Highest-priced shoes in the store
Situational needs	• Can supply stores across North America • Ability to ship to individual stores on a just-in-time basis • Offers 90-day trade credit	• Ability to deliver on time • Provide supplier personnel for team fittings • Make contract payments to university and coach at beginning of season	• Right size in stock, ready to carry out • Takes Visa and MasterCard
Social needs	• Invitation for buying team to attend trade show and supplier-sponsored reception	• Sponsor and distribute shoes at annual team shoe night to build enthusiasm • Include team and athletes in supplier brand promotions	• Offers user-group newsletter to upscale customers • Periodic mailings for new products and incentives to purchase
Psychological needs	• Assurance that shoes will sell at retail • Brand name with strong market appeal • Option to return unsold goods for credit	• Brand name consistent with players' self-images • Entire team will accept and be enthusiastic toward product decision • Belief that the overall contract is best for the university, team, and coaches	• Reinforces customer's self-image as an innovator • Product will deliver the promised performance • Customer wants to be one of only a few people purchasing this style of shoe
Knowledge needs	• Level of quality—how the shoe is constructed • How the new features affect performance • What makes the shoe unique and superior to competitive offerings • Product training and materials for sales staff	• What makes the shoe unique and superior to competitive offerings • Supporting information and assurance that the contracted payments to university and coaches are superior to competitive offerings	• What makes the shoe unique and superior to competitive offerings • Assurance that everybody on the court will not be wearing the same shoe

Salespeople in retail businesses work closely with buyers to satisfy their needs.

© Syda Productions/Shutterstock.com

production toward these improved models. Salespeople are the source of valuable information and knowledge, enabling their customers to anticipate these fluctuations and assisting them in developing more effective marketing strategies. As a result, both the buying and selling organizations realize mutual positive benefits.

Purchasing Professionals

Buyers in the business markets are trained as purchasing agents. The process of identifying suppliers and sourcing goods and services is their job. This results in a more professional and rational approach to purchasing. As a result, salespeople must possess increased levels of knowledge and expertise to provide customers with a richer and more detailed assortment of application, performance, and technical data.

Multiple Buying Influences

Reflecting the increased complexity of many business purchases, groups of individuals within the buying firm often work together as a buying team or centre. As a result, salespeople often work simultaneously with several individuals during a sales call and even different sets of

supply chain management
The strategic coordination and integration of purchasing with other functions within the buying organization as well as external organizations.

> Salespeople in business markets work closely with buyers to satisfy various needs aimed at improving their business performance.

buyers during different sales calls. Buying team members come from different areas of expertise and play different roles in the purchasing process. To be effective, the salesperson must first identify, and then understand and respond to, the role and key buying motives of each member.

Collaborative Buyer–Seller Relationships

 CPSA **3.1 Develop solutions**

The smaller customer base and increased usage of **supply chain management**, characterized by the strategic coordination and integration of purchasing with other functions within the buying organization as well as external organizations, has resulted in buyers and sellers becoming much more interdependent than ever before. This increased interdependence and desire to reduce risk of the unknown has led to an emphasis on developing long-term buyer–seller relationships characterized by increased levels of buyer–seller interaction and higher levels of service expectations by buyers.

Rather than competing to win benefits at the expense of one another, leading organizations recognize that it is possible for all parties to reduce their risk and increase the level of benefits each receives by sharing information and coordinating activities, resources, and capabilities.[4] For instance, Walmart and Sam's Club stores share information with suppliers on the products they supply. Procter & Gamble synchronizes its product data with Walmart, allowing the two companies to simultaneously reduce inventory levels by as much as 70 percent, improve service levels to 99 percent, and save an estimated $1 million annually.[5] These longer-term buyer–seller relationships are based on the mutual benefits received by and the interdependence between all parties in this value network. In addition to being keenly aware of changing customer needs, collaborative relationships require salespeople to work closely with buyers to foster honest and open two-way communication and develop the mutual understanding required to create the desired solutions. This suggests that salespeople understand the buyer's customers to determine how to help the buyer succeed by better serving their customers. Such understanding provides insights to challenges facing the buyer, enhances the salesperson's credibility, and helps establish a strong business partnership.[6] Further, salespeople must consistently demonstrate that they are dependable and acting in the buyer's best interests.

LO 3 | THE BUYING PROCESS

Although not always the case in the consumer marketplace, buyers in the business marketplace typically undergo a conscious and logical process in making purchase decisions. As depicted in Figure 3.1, the sequential and interrelated phases of the business buyer's purchase process has eight phases: (1) recognition of the problem or need, (2) determination of the characteristics of the item and the quantity needed, (3) description of the characteristics of the item and quantity needed, (4) search for and qualification of potential sources, (5) acquisition and analysis of proposals, (6) evaluation of proposals and selection of suppliers, (7) selection of an order routine, and (8) performance feedback and evaluation.

> Business buyers typically undergo a conscious and logical process in making purchase decisions.

Depending on the nature of the buying organization and the buying situation, the buying process may be highly formalized or simply a rough approximation of what actually occurs. The decision process General Motors (GM) employs for the acquisition of a new organization-wide computer system will be highly formalized and purposefully reflect each of the previously described decision phases. Compared with GM, the decision process of Bloomington Bookkeeping, a single office and four-person operation, could be expected to be less formalized. In the decision to replenish stock office supplies, both organizations are likely to use a much less formalized routine—but still, the routine will reflect the different decision phases.

As Figure 3.1 further illustrates, there is a close correspondence between the phases of the buyer's decision process and the selling activities of the salesperson. It is important that salespeople understand and make use of the interrelationships between the phases of the buying process and selling activities. Effective use of these interrelationships offers salespeople numerous opportunities to interact with buyers in a way that shapes product specifications and the selection of sources while facilitating the purchase decision.

Phase One—Recognition of the Problem or Need: The Needs Gap

Needs are the result of a gap between buyers' **desired states** and their **actual states**. Consequently, need recognition results from an individual cognitively and emotionally processing information relevant to their actual state of being and comparing it with the desired state of being. As illustrated in Figure 3.2, any perceived difference, or **needs gap**, between these two states activates the motivation or drive to fill the gap and reach the desired state. For example, the SnowRunner Company's daily production capacity is limited to 1,000 moulded skimobile body housings. Their research indicates that increasing capacity to 1,250 units per day would result in significant reductions in per-unit costs and allow them to enter additional geographic markets—both moves that would have significant and positive impacts on financial performance. The perceived need to expand production activates a corresponding motivation to search for information regarding alternative solutions and acquire the capability to increase production by 250 units.

However, if there is no gap, then there is no need and no active buying motive. It is common for salespeople to find themselves working with buyers who, for one reason or another, do not perceive a needs gap to be present. It is possible that they do not have the right information or lack a full understanding of the situation and the existence of options better than their current state. It is also possible that their understanding of the actual state might be incomplete or mistaken. For example, SnowRunner's buyers might not understand the cost-reduction possibilities and increased market potential that could result from increased capacity. As a result, they perceive no need to increase production—the desired state is the same as their actual state. Similarly, the buyers might be functioning with incomplete information regarding the company's actual state of reduced production capacity because of SnowRunner's existing moulding machines requiring increased downtime for maintenance. Properly realized, this lowering of the actual state would result in a needs gap. Successful salespeople

desired states A state of being based on what the buyer desires.

actual states A buyer's actual state of being.

needs gap A perceived difference between a buyer's desired and actual state of being.

FIG. 3.1

COMPARISON OF BUYING DECISION PROCESS PHASES AND CORRESPONDING STEPS IN THE SELLING PROCESS

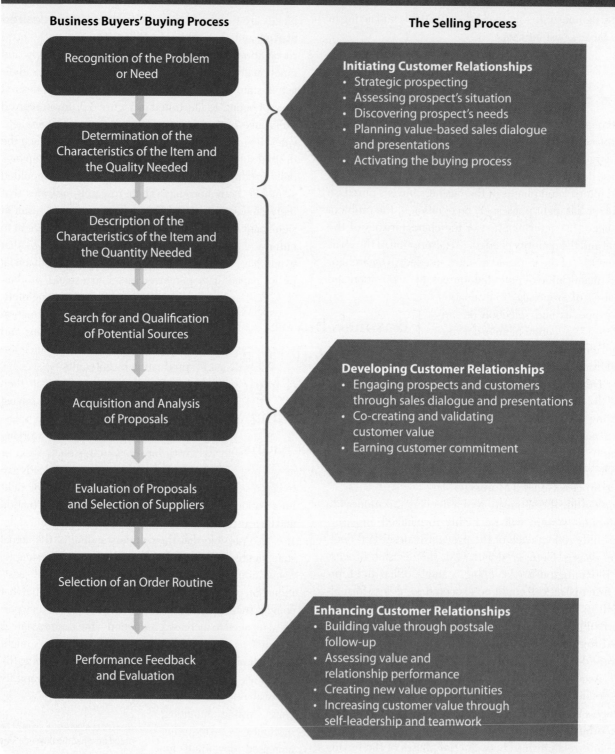

Business Buyers' Buying Process

- Recognition of the Problem or Need
- Determination of the Characteristics of the Item and the Quality Needed
- Description of the Characteristics of the Item and the Quantity Needed
- Search for and Qualification of Potential Sources
- Acquisition and Analysis of Proposals
- Evaluation of Proposals and Selection of Suppliers
- Selection of an Order Routine
- Performance Feedback and Evaluation

The Selling Process

Initiating Customer Relationships
- Strategic prospecting
- Assessing prospect's situation
- Discovering prospect's needs
- Planning value-based sales dialogue and presentations
- Activating the buying process

Developing Customer Relationships
- Engaging prospects and customers through sales dialogue and presentations
- Co-creating and validating customer value
- Earning customer commitment

Enhancing Customer Relationships
- Building value through postsale follow-up
- Assessing value and relationship performance
- Creating new value opportunities
- Increasing customer value through self-leadership and teamwork

position themselves to assist buyers in identifying and understanding needs as a result of their broader expertise and knowledge regarding product use and application. Salespeople can also use sales conversations to present buyers with information and opportunities that effectively raise the desired state, generate a need, and trigger the purchase decision process. Top-performing salespeople understand the importance of assisting their buyers in

FIG. 3.2 THE NEEDS GAP

Desired State
Produce 1,250 units per day

The Gap or Need
250 units per day

Actual State
Produce 1,000 units per day

The needs gap is the difference between the buyer's perceived desired state and the buyer's perceived actual state.

An Ethical Dilemma

8.1 Act with Integrity

Bob Labels is a sales representative for a firm that manufactures and sells various packaging machines. Bob is meeting with a prospect, Andrew Ale, who is a purchaser for a midsized beer manufacturer looking to expand its business. Thus, the company is in need of an additional bottle labeller. The bottle labeller currently used by the company was bought at auction several years ago. Having found Bob's company on the Internet, Andrew contacted Bob and they set up a meeting at Andrew's office. Upon assessing Andrew's needs, Bob determined that Andrew was looking for a roll-fed bottle labeller capable of labelling up to 1,200 bottles per minute. This concerned Bob because the fastest bottle labeller he carried was capable of labelling only up to 1,000 bottles per minute. Currently, Andrew's company was not running at full capacity, but he felt he would need this capability in the near future to meet expected demand. While Bob knew his labeller would work fine for the near future, he also knew that given Andrew's future needs, a faster labeller would actually be the most beneficial purchase. Bob really wanted to make this sale as it would be instrumental in him achieving a bonus. The bonus would be particularly useful to help Bob pay for medication associated with his wife's cancer. Bob believes that he could work with Andrew to get him to reassess his needs and convince him that the machine he has to offer will be quick enough to meet production needs now and in the future, particularly given that there is no guarantee of an expected growth in sales. Bob surmises that if Andrew's company outgrew this labeller, they could always purchase an additional labeller from him down the road. What should Bob do?

(a) Try to convince Andrew that he does not need a labeller that does 1,200 labels per minute.

(b) Suggest an alternate label machine supplier and ask Andrew to keep him in mind for additional packaging machinery needs.

(c) Refer to his company's code of conduct and/or contact his sales manager and ask for advice.

© Shablon/Shutterstock.com

forming realistic perceptions of the actual state and the desired state. In this manner, the salesperson can continue to serve as a nonmanipulative consultant to the buyer while affecting buying motives that yield mutual benefits to all parties. However, it should be noted that the persuasive power of assisting the buyer in determining and comparing desired and actual states can also be misused and lead to unethical and manipulative selling behaviours, such as those exhibited in An Ethical Dilemma.

LO 4 | TYPES OF BUYER NEEDS

 CPSA | 1.3 Develop client intelligence

The total number of potential customer needs is infinite and sometimes difficult for salespeople to grasp and understand on a customer-by-customer basis. Consequently, many salespeople find it helpful to group customer needs into one of five basic types or categories that focus on the buying situation and the benefits to be provided by the product or service being chosen.[7] These five general types of buyer needs are described as follows:

- **Situational needs** are the specific needs that are contingent on, and often a result of, conditions related to the specific environment, time, and place (e.g., emergency car repair while travelling out of town, a piece of customized production equipment to fulfill a customer's specific situational requirements, or providing for quick initial shipment to meet a buyer's out-of-stock status).

- **Functional needs** represent the need for a specific core task or function to be performed—the functional purpose of a specific product or service. The need for a sales offering to do what it is supposed to do (e.g., alcohol disinfects, switches open and close to control some flow, the flow control valve is accurate and reliable).

- **Social needs** are the need for acceptance from

and association with others—a desire to belong to some reference group. For example, a product or service might be associated with some specific and desired affinity group or segment (e.g., Polo clothing is associated with upper-income, successful people; ISO 9000 Certification is associated with high-quality vendors; leading e-commerce Web sites include discussion groups to build a sense of community).

- **Psychological needs** reflect the desire for feelings of assurance and risk reduction, as well as positive emotions and feelings such as success, joy, excitement, and stimulation (e.g., a Mont Blanc pen generates a feeling of success; effective training programs create a sense of self-control and determination; selection and use of well-known, high-quality brands provides assurance to buyers and organizations alike).

- **Knowledge needs** represent the desire for personal development, information, and knowledge to increase thought and understanding as to how and why things happen (e.g., product information, newsletters, brochures, along with training and user support group meetings or conferences, provide current information on products and topics of interest).

Categorizing buyer needs by type can assist the salesperson in bringing order to what could otherwise be a confusing and endless mix of needs and expectations. Organizing the buyer's different needs into their basic types can help salespeople in several ways. First, as Exhibit 3.1 and the example worksheet in Exhibit 3.2 illustrate, the basic types can serve as a checklist or worksheet to ensure that no significant problems or needs have been overlooked in the process of needs discovery. Organizing what at first might appear to be different needs and problems into their common types also helps the salesperson better understand the nature of the buyer's needs along with the interrelationships and commonalities between them. In turn, this enhanced understanding and the framework of basic types combine to serve as a guide for salespeople in generating and then demonstrating value-added solutions in response to the specific needs of the buyer.

As previously discussed, the specific circumstances or types of solution benefits that a buyer is seeking should determine a salesperson's strategy for working with that buyer.

Consequently, it should be noted that the needs of business buyers tend to be more complex than consumers' needs. As with consumers, organizational buyers are influenced by the same functional, social, psychological, knowledge, and situational experiences and forces

situational needs The needs that are contingent on, and often a result of, conditions related to the specific environment, time, and place.

functional needs The need for a specific core task or function to be performed.

social needs The need for acceptance from and association with others.

psychological needs The desire for feelings of assurance and risk reduction, as well as positive emotions and feelings, such as success, joy, excitement, and stimulation.

knowledge needs The desire for personal development, information, and knowledge to increase thought and understanding as to how and why things happen.

Exhibit 3.2

Example Worksheet for Organizing Buyer Needs and Benefit-Based Solutions

Primary Buyer: Bart Waits
Buying Organization: SouthWest Metal Stampings
Primary Industry: Stamped Metal Parts and Subcomponents

Basic Type of Need	Buyer's Specific Needs
Buyer's situational needs	• Requires an 18 percent increase in production to meet increased sales • On-hand inventory will not meet production/delivery schedule • Tight cash flow pending initial deliveries and receipt of payment
Buyer's functional needs	• Equipment to provide effective and efficient increase in production • Expedited delivery and installation in six weeks or less • Equipment financing extending payments beyond initial receipts
Buyer's social needs	• Expansion in production transforms them into Top 10 in Industry • Belonging to user group of companies using this equipment • Feeling that they are an important customer of the supplier
Buyer's psychological needs	• Confidence that selected equipment will meet needs and do the job • Assurance that seller can complete installation in six weeks • Saving face—to believe borrowing for equipment is common
Buyer's knowledge needs	• Evidence that this is the right choice • Understanding new technology featured in the selected equipment • Training program for production employees and maintenance staff

that affect and shape individual needs. However, in addition to those individual needs, organizational buyers must also satisfy the needs and requirements of the organization for which they work. As Figure 3.3 depicts, these organizational needs overlay and interact with the needs of the individual. To maximize selling effectiveness in the organizational or business-to-business market, salespeople must generate solutions addressing both the individual and organizational needs of business buyers.

Phase Two—Determination of the Characteristics of the Item and the Quantity Needed

Coincident to recognizing a need or problem is the motivation and drive to resolve it by undertaking a search for additional information leading to possible solutions. This particular phase of the buying process involves the consideration and study of the overall situation to understand what is required in the form of a preferred solution. This begins to establish the general characteristics and quantities necessary to resolve the need or problem.

Through effective sales conversations, salespeople use their knowledge and expertise at this point to assist the buyer in analyzing and interpreting the problem situation and needs. Salespeople offer valuable knowledge of problem situations and solution options that buyers typically perceive as beneficial.

Phase Three—Description of the Characteristics of the Item and the Quantity Needed

Using the desired characteristics and quantities developed in the previous phase as a starting point, buyers translate that general information into detailed specifications describing exactly what is expected and required. The determination of detailed specifications serves several purposes. First, detailed specifications guide supplier firms in developing their proposals. Second, these specifications give the buyer a framework for evaluating, comparing, and choosing among the proposed solutions. Postpurchase specifications serve as a standard for evaluation to ensure that the

Every Business Sells

Barbara McGrath is a sales representative in a company that manufactures fast-moving consumer goods (FMCG). She has worked in sales for six years, and currently has roughly 170 accounts that cover Eastern Canada.

As a salesperson, how do you provide value to your customers?

We provide value by servicing our regular customers to the point where we become trusted business advisers, helping them increase their business all the while increasing our sales as well.

As a salesperson how do you provide value to your organization?

I provide value to the organization by consistently servicing my customers in an efficient and effective manner whereby we outpace the industry and gain market share.

What is your greatest challenge you face today as a salesperson?

The greatest challenge we face in our industry is the consistent decline of sales. This comes from multiple sources, such as anti-tobacco agencies, government regulations, changing consumer habits, and new reduced-risk products, to name a few. Overcoming these obstacles are the biggest challenges we face.

How do you try to overcome this challenge?

We try to overcome these challenges by trying to capture market share from our competitors. Essentially, we are all fighting for a piece of the pie, in which the pie decreases 1 to 2 percent per year. Therefore, we must provide more value to our customers through relationship selling to either increase sales and/or market share.

What advice do you have for someone starting out in sales?

The main piece of advice I would have for someone starting out in sales is to be likeable and honest. Once you get to know a customer and they trust you, it becomes more difficult for them to say no to you. Therefore, you should look to build a relationship first with the customer and try to stay away from the transactional selling.

FIG. 3.3   COMPLEX MIX OF BUSINESS BUYER NEEDS

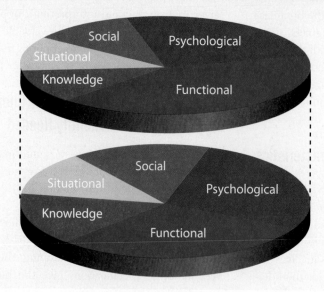

Business buyers' needs are a combination of the buyers' individual needs and the organization's needs.

Every Business Sells

Maren Stewart works as a district sales manager in alcohol manufacturing and distribution (beverage industry: retail and licensee sales). He sells spirits and alcoholic beverages to nearly 60 accounts across Eastern Canada (Ontario, Quebec, New Brunswick, PEI, Nova Scotia, and Newfoundland). He recently celebrated his one-year anniversary with his current company, and has worked in sales for four years.

As a salesperson, how do you provide value to your customers?

As the local market product specialist and brand liaison, there are many ways I can bring value to my customers. I work closely with account owners and managers to assess their needs and find brands within our product portfolio that would complement the brand of the licensee. By working with owners and finding products that align with account strategies, we can then attract the desired target demographic that accounts are trying to retain and that our brands cater to.

By being a consistent, reliable and hardworking liaison for our brands, account owners receive value from the work I do as I help facilitate current sales within accounts, but also assist in the investments necessary to achieve long term sustainable success. An example of one of these investments that I make is through education. I can help bring value and educate through product knowledge transfers; I prepare owners, managers, and sales staff by educating and training them on our products, which helps facilitate beverage sales for their account. I also educate by providing the latest in market trends and insights. Providing market insights and keeping accounts informed with the latest local, national, and international market trends helps our customers stay relevant and competitive within this industry.

As a salesperson, how do you provide value to your organization?

I provide value to the organization I work for by helping facilitate sales on the brands we own and represent. By servicing our key accounts and customers, I bring value to the front line of sales, which in turn helps push our brands and products to the general consumers. Since I've started my position, I have always tried to find ways to develop my day-to-day productivity to increase the value I can bring to our customers. In doing so, I have been able to strengthen the relationships my company has within the local market, which can help set ourselves apart from the competition or other suppliers.

What is your greatest challenge you face today as a salesperson?

The greatest challenge I face today as a salesperson is balancing the pursuit of new business ventures with existing or prior accounts I manage and work with. As the bar and restaurant service industry is continuously developing, there are always new accounts opening where business opportunities arise, but remaining available and keeping your existing clientele happy has to remain priority.

How do you try to overcome this challenge?

I work on overcoming this challenge by developing effective time-management skills, and routinely focusing on pre-planning and preparing my weeks, months, and quarters in advance. Utilizing a great pre-plan and a consumer-centric mindset leads to effective strategizing with key accounts that can occur weeks or months in advance of big selling periods. This strategizing leads to great execution and consistent sales growth with existing clientele. By keeping these existing accounts happy, time can then be allocated to pursuing new business ventures and exploring new accounts to partner with.

What advice do you have for someone starting out in sales?

I would advise somebody starting in sales to develop great organization skills. Although sales can be very relationship-based and relies on interpersonal or communicational skills, a strong sales professional needs to stay organized by keeping on top of their short-term and long-term planning as well as their administrative work. By staying organized, a sales professional allows themselves the time and opportunity to plan and strategize the best ways to bring value to their existing or potential customer base.

© Ian Hayes

Exhibit 3.3

Business-to-Business Content Marketing Tactics and Channels

B2B Marketers' Content Marketing Tactic Usage		Channels B2B Marketers Use to Distribute Content	
Tactic	Percent Using	Channel	Percent Using
Webinars/Webcasts	83%	Instagram	93%
Infographics	80%	SlideShare	89%
Video (pre-produced)	77%	Print	77%
Ebooks/White Papers	68%	Google+	76%
In-Person Events	65%	YouTube	59%
Email Newsletters	60%	Facebook	35%
Blogs	58%	Twitter	30%
Social Media Content	58%	LinkedIn	26%
		E-mail	26%

buying firm receives the required product features and quantities. Trust-based buyer–seller relationships allow salespeople to work closely with buyers and collaboratively assist them in establishing the detailed specifications of the preferred solutions.

Phase Four—Search for and Qualification of Potential Sources

Next, buyers must locate and qualify potential suppliers capable of providing the preferred solution. Although buyers certainly use information provided by salespeople to identify qualified suppliers, an abundance of information is available from other sources, such as trade associations, product source directories, trade shows, the Internet, advertising, and word of mouth. Sellers often use **content marketing** to enhance their opportunity of being considered as not only a viable supplier, but the preferred choice. Content marketing involves creating and distributing valuable, relevant, and consistent content to attract and retain buyers. As seen in Exhibit 3.3, sellers use a variety of tactics and several sources to deliver content to business customers.[8]

content marketing A form of marketing that involves creating and distributing valuable, relevant, and consistent content to attract and retain buyers.

Once identified, potential suppliers are qualified on their ability to perform and deliver consistently at the level of quality and quantity required. Because of the large number of information sources available to buyers researching potential suppliers, one of the most important tasks in personal selling is to win the position of one of those information sources and keep buyers informed about the salesperson's company, its new products, and solution capabilities.

© docstockmedia/Shutterstock.com

Buyers sometimes attend trade shows to find qualified suppliers.

Phase Five—Acquisition and Analysis of Proposals

 3.1 Develop solutions

Based on the detailed specifications developed in phase three, a **request for proposals** (known in the trade as an **RFP**) is developed and distributed to the qualified potential suppliers. Based on the RFP, qualified suppliers develop and submit proposals to provide the products as specified. Salespeople play a critical and influential role in this stage of the buying process by developing and presenting the proposed solution to the buyers. In this role, the salesperson is responsible for presenting the proposed features, advantages, and benefits in such a manner that the proposed solution is evaluated as providing higher levels of benefits and value to the buyer than other competing proposals. Consequently, it is imperative that salespeople understand the basic evaluation procedures used by buyers in comparing alternative and competitive proposals so they can be more proficient in demonstrating the superiority of their solution over the competition.

LO 5 | PROCEDURES FOR EVALUATING SUPPLIERS AND PRODUCTS

Purchase decisions are based on buyers' comparative evaluations of suppliers and the products and services they propose for satisfying buyers' needs. Some buyers may look for the sales offering that receives the highest rating on the one characteristic they perceive as being most important. Others may prefer the sales offering that achieves some acceptable assessment score across each and every attribute desired by the buyer. However, research into how purchase decisions are made suggests that most buyers use a compensatory, **multiattribute model** incorporating weighted averages across desired characteristics.[9] These weighted averages incorporate (1) assessments of how well the product or supplier performs in meeting each of the specified characteristics and (2) the relative importance of each specified characteristic.

Assessment of Product or Supplier Performance

The first step in applying the multiattribute model is to rate objectively how well each characteristic of the competing products or suppliers meets the buyers' needs. Let us use the example of GM evaluating adhesives for use in manufacturing. The buyers have narrowed the alternatives to products proposed by three suppliers: BondIt #302, AdCo #45, and StikFast #217. As illustrated in Exhibit 3.4, the GM buying team has assessed the competitive products according to how well they perform on certain important attributes. These assessments are converted to scores as depicted in Exhibit 3.5, with scores ranging from 1 (very poor performance) to 10 (excellent performance).

As illustrated, no single product is consistently outstanding across each of the eight identified characteristics. Although BondIt #302 is easy to apply and uses the buyer's current equipment, it is also more expensive and has the shortest durability time in the field. StikFast #217 also scores well for ease of application, and it has superior durability. However, it has the longest bonding time and could negatively influence production time.

Accounting for Relative Importance of Each Characteristic

 2.1 Develop client relationships

To compare these performance differences properly, each score must be weighted by the characteristic's perceived importance. In the adhesive example, importance weights are assigned on a scale of 1 (relatively unimportant) to 10 (very important). As illustrated

> **request for proposals (RFP)** A form created by firms and distributed to qualified potential suppliers that helps suppliers develop and submit proposals to provide products as specified by the firm.
>
> **multiattribute model** A procedure for evaluating suppliers and products that incorporates weighted averages across desired characteristics.

Exhibit 3.4

Important Product Information

Characteristics	BondIt #302	AdCo #45	StikFast #217
Ease of application	Excellent	Good	Very good
Bonding time	8 minutes	10 minutes	12 minutes
Durability	10 years	12 years	15 years
Reliability	Very good	Excellent	Good
Nontoxic	Very good	Excellent	Very good
Quoted price	$7 per L	$5.5 per L	$6.5 per L
Shelf-life in storage	6 months	4 months	4 months
Service factors	Good	Very good	Excellent

in Exhibit 3.6, multiplying each performance score by the corresponding attribute's importance weight results in a weighted average that can be totalled to calculate an overall rating for each product. Keep in mind that each alternative product generally must meet a minimum specification on each desired product characteristic for it to be considered. The product or supplier having the highest comparative rating is typically the product selected for purchase. In this example, AdCo has the highest overall evaluation, totalling 468 points, compared with BondIt's 430 points and StikFast's 438 points. In some cases, the buyer may be focusing on one characteristic as being the most important and will choose the seller that performs best on that characteristic, assuming that minimum performance specifications are met across all other criteria. In the GM example, if "durability" were the most important characteristic, with a minimum performance specification of 4 for all other criteria, then StikFast #217 would be chosen.

Exhibit 3.5

Product Performance Scores

Characteristics	BondIt #302	AdCo #45	StikFast#217
Ease of application	10	5	8
Bonding time	8	6	4
Durability	6	8	9
Reliability	8	10	5
Nontoxic	8	10	8
Quoted price	5	9	7
Shelf-life in storage	9	6	6
Service factors	5	8	10

Exhibit 3.6

Weighted Averages for Performance (P) Times Importance (I) and Overall Evaluation Scores

Characteristics	BondIt #302			AdCo #45			StikFast #217		
	P	I	P × I	P	I	P × I	P	I	P × I
Ease of application	10	8	80	5	8	40	8	8	64
Bonding time	8	6	48	6	6	36	4	6	24
Durability	6	9	54	8	9	72	9	9	81
Reliability	8	7	56	10	7	70	5	7	35
Nontoxic	8	6	48	10	6	60	8	6	48
Quoted price	5	10	50	9	10	90	7	10	70
Shelf-life in storage	9	6	54	6	6	36	6	6	36
Service factors	5	8	40	8	8	64	10	8	80
Overall evaluation score			430			468			438

Despite such extensive evaluation, it is important to keep in mind that buyers often find the biggest factor differentiating one supplier from another is the salesperson. They tend to find that one supplier's offering is not differentiated enough from another's to make a real difference. In this case, the buyer looks to the salesperson as the point of differentiation. In fact, a study of more than 80,000 business customers comprising 7,200 salesforces found that salesperson effectiveness is the most important decision factor in choosing a vendor, accounting for 39 percent of customers' buying decisions.[10]

Employing Buyer Evaluation Procedures to Enhance Selling Strategies

3.2 Conduct sales presentations

Understanding evaluation procedures and gaining insight as to how a specific buyer or team of buyers is evaluating suppliers and proposals is vital for the salesperson to be effective and requires the integration of several bases of knowledge. First, information gathered before the sales call must be combined with an effective needs-discovery dialogue with the buyer(s) to delineate the buyers' needs and the nature of the desired solution. This establishes the most likely criteria for evaluation. Further discussion between the buyer and seller can begin to establish the importance the buyers place on each of the different performance criteria and often yields information as to what suppliers and products are being considered.

Using this information and the salesperson's knowledge of how their products compare with competitors' offerings allows the salesperson to complete a likely facsimile of the buyers' evaluation. With this enhanced level of preparation and understanding, the salesperson can plan, create, and deliver a more effective presentation by using the five fundamental strategies that are inherent within the evaluation procedures buyers use.

- *Modify the Product Offering Being Proposed.* Often, in the course of preparing or delivering a presentation, it becomes apparent that the product offering will not maximize the buyer's evaluation score in comparison with a competitor's offering. In this case, the strategy would be to modify or change the product to one that better meets the buyer's overall needs and thus would receive a higher evaluation. For example, by developing a better understanding of the adhesive buyer's perceived importance of certain characteristics, the BondIt salesperson could offer a different adhesive formulation that is not as easy to apply (low perceived importance) but offers improved durability (high perceived importance) and more competitive price (high perceived importance).

- *Alter the Buyer's Beliefs about the Proposed Offering.* Provide information and support to alter the buyer's beliefs as to where the proposed product stands on certain attributes. This is a recommended strategy for cases in which the buyer underestimates the true qualities of the proposed product. However, if the buyer's perceptions are correct, this strategy would encourage the salesperson to exaggerate and overstate claims and, thus, should be avoided. In the instance of BondIt #302's low evaluation score, the salesperson could offer the buyer information and evidence that the product's durability and service factors actually perform much better than the buyer initially believed. By working with the buyer to develop a more realistic perception of the product's performance, BondIt #302 could become the buyer's preferred choice.

- *Alter the Buyer's Beliefs about the Competitor's Offering.* For a variety of reasons, buyers often mistakenly believe that a competitor's offering has higher-level attributes or qualities than it actually does. In such an instance, the salesperson can provide information to create a more accurate picture of the competitor's attributes. This has been referred to as **competitive depositioning** and is carried out by openly comparing (not simply degrading) the competing offering's attributes, advantages, and weaknesses. As an illustration, the BondIt salesperson might demonstrate the total cost for each of the three product alternatives, including a quoted price, ease of application, and bonding time. BondIt is much easier to apply and has a faster bonding time. Consequently, less of it needs to be applied for each application, which results in a significantly lower total cost and a much-improved evaluation score.

- *Alter the Importance Weights.* In this strategy, the salesperson uses information to emphasize and thus increase the importance of certain attributes on which the product offering is exceptionally strong. In the case of attributes on which the offering might be short, the strategy would be to deemphasize their importance. Continuing the adhesive purchase decision, BondIt's salesperson might offer

competitive depositioning
Providing information to create a more accurate picture of a competitor's attributes or qualities.

information to influence the buyer's importance rating for ease of application and storage shelf-life—two characteristics in which BondIt is much stronger than the two competitors.

- *Call Attention to Neglected Attributes.* In the case in which it becomes apparent that significant attributes may have been neglected or overlooked by the buyer, the salesperson can increase the buyer's evaluation of the proposed offering by pointing out the attribute that was missed. For instance, the BondIt #302 adhesive dries to an invisible, transparent, and semiflexible adhesive compared with the two competitors, which cure to a light grey that could detract from the final product if the adhesive flowed out of the joint. The appearance of the final product is a significant concern, and this neglected attribute could substantially influence the comparative evaluations.

Phase Six—Evaluation of Proposals and Selection of Suppliers

The buying decision is the outcome of the buyer's evaluation of the various proposals acquired from potential suppliers. Typically, further negotiations will be conducted with the selected supplier(s) for the purpose of establishing the final terms regarding product characteristics, pricing, and delivery. Salespeople play a central role in gaining the buyer's commitment to the purchase decision and in the subsequent negotiations of the final terms.

Phase Seven—Selection of an Order Routine

 4.2 Negotiate terms of sale

Once the supplier(s) has been selected, details associated with the purchase decision must be settled. These details include delivery quantities, locations, and times along with return policies and the routine for reorders associated with the purchase. For cases in which the purchase requires multiple deliveries over time, the routine for placing subsequent orders and making deliveries must be set out and understood. Is the order routine standardized on the basis of a prearranged time schedule, or is the salesperson expected to monitor usage and inventories to place orders and schedule shipments? Will orders be placed automatically through the use of electronic data interchange or the Internet? Regardless of the nature of the order routine, the salesperson plays a critical role in facilitating communication, completing ordering procedures, and settling the final details.

FIG. 3.4 | THE TWO-FACTOR MODEL OF BUYER EVALUATION

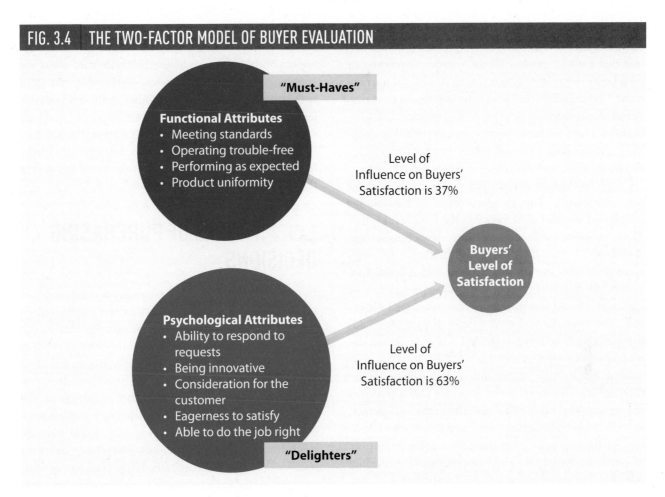

Buyers evaluate functional attributes and psychological attributes of a sales offering to assess overall performance and satisfaction.

Phase Eight—Performance Feedback and Evaluation

5.1 Follow-up on the sale

The final phase in the buying process is the evaluation of performance and feedback shared among all parties for the purpose of improving future performance and enhancing buyer–seller relationships. Research supports that salespeople's customer interaction activities and communication at this stage of the buying process become the primary determinants of customer satisfaction and buyer loyalty. Consequently, it is critical that salespeople continue working with buyers after the sale. The salesperson's follow-up activities provide the critical points of contact between the buyer and seller to ensure consistent performance, respond to and take care of problems, maximize customer satisfaction, create new value opportunities, and further enhance buyer–seller relationships.

LO 6 | UNDERSTANDING POSTPURCHASE EVALUATION AND THE FORMATION OF SATISFACTION

Research shows that buyers evaluate their experience with a product purchase on the basis of product characteristics that fall into a **two-factor model of evaluation,** as depicted in Figure 3.4.[11] The first category, **functional attributes**, refers to the features and characteristics that are related to what the product actually does or is expected to do—its functional characteristics. These functional characteristics have also been referred to as

two-factor model of evaluation A postpurchase evaluation process buyers use that evaluates a product purchase by using functional and psychological attributes.

functional attributes The features and characteristics that are related to what the product actually does or is expected to do.

must-have attributes, features of the core product that the customer takes for granted. These are the attributes that must be present for the supplier or product to even be included among those being considered for purchase. Consequently, they tend to be fairly common across the set of suppliers and products being considered for purchase by a buyer. Characteristics such as reliability, durability, conformance to specifications, competitive pricing, and performance are illustrative of functional attributes.

Psychological attributes make up the second general category. This category refers to how things are carried out and done between the buyer and seller. These supplier and market offering characteristics are described as the **delighter attributes**—the augmented features and characteristics included in the total market offering that go beyond buyer expectations and have a significant positive impact on customer satisfaction. The psychological or delighter characteristics are not perceived as being universal features across the evoked set of suppliers and market offerings being considered. Rather, these are the differentiators between the competitors. The competence, attitudes, and behaviours of supplier personnel with whom the buyer has contact, as well as the salesperson's trustworthiness, consideration for the customer, responsiveness, ability to recover when there is a problem, and innovativeness in providing solutions, are exemplary psychological attributes.

The Growing Importance of Salespeople in Buyers' Postpurchase Evaluation

2.1 Develop client relationships

Understanding the differential impact of functional (*must-haves*) and psychological (*delighters*) attributes is important for salespeople. Functional attributes possess a close correspondence to the technical and more tangible product attributes whereas the psychological attributes are similar to the interpersonal communication and behaviours of salespeople and other personnel having contact with customers. Numerous research studies across a variety of industries evidence psychological attributes as having up to two times as much influence on buyer satisfaction and loyalty as functional attributes. This observation underscores special implications for salespeople, as it is their interpersonal communication and behaviours—what they do—that make up the psychological attributes. Although both categories of product characteristics are important and have significant influences on buyer satisfaction, the activities and behaviours of the salesperson as they interact with the buyer have more impact on that buyer's evaluation than the features of the product or service itself.[12]

LO 7 | TYPES OF PURCHASING DECISIONS

Buyers are learners in that purchase decisions are not isolated behaviours. Buyer behaviour and purchase decisions are based on the relevant knowledge that buyers have accumulated from multiple sources to assist them in making the proper choice. Internally, buyers reflect on past experiences as guides for making purchase decisions. When sufficient knowledge from past experiences is not available, buyers access external sources of information: secondary sources of information (e.g., trade journals, product test reports, white papers, advertising) and other individuals (e.g., salespeople) the buyer perceives as being trustworthy and knowledgeable in a given area. For more information on how the type of purchasing decision can influence the purchasing process, see Selling in Action: The Influence of Purchasing Decision Type.

The level of relevant experience and knowledge a buyer or buying organization possesses in relation to a given purchasing decision is a primary determinant of the time and resources the buyer will allocate to that purchasing decision. The level of a buyer's existing experience and knowledge has been used to categorize buyer behaviour into three types of purchasing decisions: straight rebuys, modified rebuys, and new tasks. As summarized in Exhibit 3.7, selling strategies should reflect the differences in buyer behaviours and decision-making characteristics of each type of buying decision.

Straight Rebuys

5.1 Follow-up on the sale

If past experiences with a product resulted in high levels of satisfaction, buyers tend to purchase the same product from the same sources. Comparable with a routine repurchase in which nothing has changed, the **straight rebuy decision** is often the result of a long-term purchase agreement. Needs have been predetermined

---

must-have attributes Features of the core product that the customer takes for granted.

psychological attributes A category of product characteristics that refers to how things are carried out and done between the buyer and seller.

delighter attributes The augmented features included in the total market offering that go beyond the buyer's expectations and have a significant positive impact on customer satisfaction.

straight rebuy decision A purchase decision resulting from an ongoing purchasing relationship with a supplier.

Selling in Action

The Influence of Purchasing Decision Type

Andrea Young graduated from the University of Central Missouri in May 2016 and went to work as an account executive at Division D, offering innovative, evolving ad units to help advertisers thrive in the online advertising marketplace. Andrea discusses the influence of the type of purchasing decision in the purchasing process.

"Understanding the nature of the buyer and of the purchase itself, be it straight rebuy, new task, or modified rebuy, allows the salesperson to adapt the message. At Division D, it should be noted that there was a spectrum

within the new task buy situation where, as an account executive, you were required to figure out if the buyer had any familiarity with digital online marketing at all and adapt your message from there. The size of the buying agency or company, and how advanced they were in the development of their online marketing, changed the content and the depth of not only the information that was required for them to decide, but also the amount of continued communication required throughout the entire process."

Exhibit 3.7

Three Types of Buying Decisions

	Decision Type		
	Straight Rebuy	Modified Rebuy	New Task
Newness of problem or need	Low	Medium	High
Information requirements	Minimal	Moderate	Maximum
Information search	Minimal	Limited	Extensive
Consideration of new alternatives	None	Limited	Extensive
Multiple buying influences	Very small	Moderate	Large
Financial risk	Low	Moderate	High

with the corresponding specifications, pricing, and shipping requirements already established by a blanket purchase order or an annual purchase agreement. Ordering is automatic and often computerized using **electronic data interchange (EDI)** and e-commerce (Internet, intranet, and extranet). Walmart, for instance, uses EDI to link with one of the suppliers of its slacks, the Seminole Manufacturing Company. This has cut delivery time of the slacks by 50 percent on a product that is regularly purchased via straight rebuy decision making.[13]

Although no purchasing decision begins as a straight rebuy, once established buyers allocate little, if any, time and resources to this form of purchase decision. The primary emphasis is on receipt of the products and their continued satisfactory performance. With most of the purchasing process automated, straight rebuy decisions are little more than record keeping that clerical staff in the purchasing office often handles.

electronic data interchange (EDI) Transfer of data electronically between two computer systems.

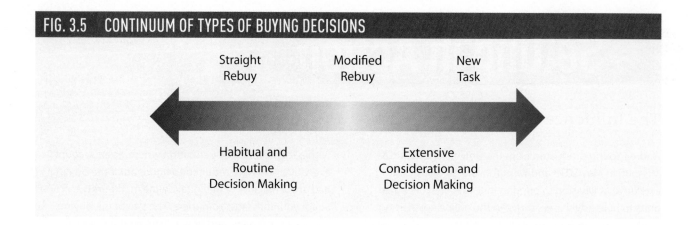

FIG. 3.5 CONTINUUM OF TYPES OF BUYING DECISIONS

Straight Rebuy   Modified Rebuy   New Task

Habitual and Routine Decision Making   Extensive Consideration and Decision Making

For the in-supplier (a current supplier), straight rebuys offer the advantage of reduced levels of potential competition. Rather than becoming complacent, however, in-salespeople must continually monitor the competitive environment for advances in product capabilities or changes in price structures. They should also follow up on deliveries and interact with users as well as decision makers to make sure that product and performance continue to receive strong and positive evaluations.

Straight rebuy decisions present a major challenge to the out-salesperson. Buyers are satisfied with the products and services from current suppliers and see no need to change. This is a classic case in which the buyer perceives no difference or needs gap between their actual and desired state. Consequently, there is no active buying motive to which the out-salesperson can respond. In this case, out-salespeople are typically presented with two strategy choices. First, they can continue to make contact with the buyer so that when there is a change in the buying situation, or if the current supplier makes a mistake, they are there to respond. Second, they can provide information and evidence relevant to either the desired or actual states so that the buyer will perceive a needs gap. For example, Seminole's competitors will find it most difficult to gain this portion of Walmart's business by offering similar or equal products and systems. However, a competitor might adopt future advances in technology that would enable them to offer significant added value over and beyond that which Seminole offers. Effectively communicating and demonstrating their advanced capabilities holds the potential for raising the desired state and thus producing a needs gap favouring their solution over Seminole's existing sales offering.

new task decision A purchase decision that occurs when a buyer is purchasing a product or service for the first time.

New Tasks

The purchase decision characterized as a **new task decision** occurs when the buyer is purchasing a product or service for the first time. As illustrated in Figure 3.5, new task purchase decisions are located at the opposite end of the continuum from the straight rebuy and typify situations in which buyers have no experience or knowledge on which to rely. Consequently, they undertake an extensive purchase decision and search for information designed to identify and compare alternative solutions. Reflecting the extensive nature of this type of purchase decision, multiple members of the buying team are usually involved. As a result, the salesperson will be working with several different individuals rather than a single buyer. Mitsubishi buyers and suppliers were presented with new task decisions when a new Mitsubishi four-wheel-drive sport utility vehicle was moving from design to production. Moving from their historical two-wheel-drive to four-wheel-drive power lines and transmissions presented a variety of new needs and problems.

Sea World worked with St. Charles-based Craftsmen Industries to develop a pod of six Shamu cruisers to meet its new task decision on a means for conducting a special Shamu promotion.

Relevant to a new task purchasing decision, there is no in- or out-supplier. Further, the buyer is aware of the existing needs gap. With no prior experience in dealing with this particular need, buyers are often eager for information and expertise that will assist them in effectively resolving the perceived needs gap. Selling strategies for new task decisions should include collaborating with the buyer in a number of ways. First, the salesperson can provide expertise in fully developing and understanding the need. The salesperson's extensive experience and base of knowledge is also valuable to the buyer in terms of specifying and evaluating potential solutions. Finally, top salespeople will assist the buyer in making a purchase decision and provide extensive follow-up to ensure long-term satisfaction. By implementing this type of consultative strategy, the salesperson establishes a relationship with the buyer and gains considerable competitive advantage.

Modified Rebuys

Modified rebuy decisions occupy a middle position on the continuum between straight rebuys and new tasks. In these cases, the buyer has experience in purchasing the product in the past but is interested in acquiring additional information regarding alternative products and suppliers. As there is more familiarity with the decision, there is less uncertainty and perceived risk than for new task decisions. The modified rebuy typically occurs as the result of changing conditions or needs. Perhaps the buyer wants to consider new suppliers for current purchase needs or new products existing suppliers offer. Continuing the example of buyer–seller experiences at Walmart, if the company decided to re-examine its sources for slacks this would correspond to the characteristics of a modified rebuy decision. Changing consumer styles, coupled with rising prices by their current supplier, may prompt them to consider alternative suppliers to provide them with slacks.

Often a buyer enters into a modified rebuy type of purchase decision simply to check the competitiveness of existing suppliers in terms of the product offering and pricing levels. Consequently, in-salespeople will emphasize how well their product has performed in resolving the needs gap. Out-salespeople will use strategies similar to those undertaken in the straight rebuy. These strategies are designed to alter the relative positions of the desired and actual states in a way that creates a perceived gap and influences buyers to rethink and re-evaluate their current buying patterns and suppliers.

Walmart is involved in straight rebuy, new task, and modified rebuy decisions.

LO 8 | UNDERSTANDING COMMUNICATION STYLES

CPSA   2.1 Develop client relationships

Verbal and nonverbal messages can also provide salespeople with important cues regarding buyers' personalities and communication styles. Experienced salespeople emphasize the importance of reading and responding to customer communication styles. Effectively sensing and interpreting customers' communication styles allows salespeople to adapt their own interaction behaviours in a way that facilitates buyer–seller communication and enhances relationship formation. Most sales training programs use a two-by-two matrix as a basis for categorizing communication styles into four primary types.[14] As Figure 3.6 illustrates, the four styles are based on two determinant dimensions: assertiveness and responsiveness.

- *Assertiveness*—**Assertiveness** refers to the degree to which a person holds opinions about issues and attempts to dominate or control situations by directing the thoughts and actions of others. Highly assertive individuals tend to be fast-paced, opinionated, and quick to speak out and take confrontational

> **modified rebuy decision** A purchase decision that occurs when a buyer has experience in purchasing a product in the past but is interested in acquiring additional information regarding alternative products and/ or suppliers.
>
> **assertiveness** The degree to which a person holds opinions about issues and attempts to dominate or control situations by directing the thoughts and actions of others.

Low Assertiveness

- Slow-Paced
- Cooperative
- Avoids Taking Risks
- Supportive
- Team Player
- Nondirective
- Easygoing
- Reserved in Expressing Opinions

High Assertiveness

- Fast-Paced
- Competitive
- Takes Risks
- Independent
- Directive
- Confrontational
- Forcefully Expresses Opinions

Low Responsiveness

- Task-Oriented
- Guarded and Cool
- Rational
- Meticulous Organizer
- Inflexible Regarding Time
- Controlled Gesturing
- Nondirective
- Formal

High Responsiveness

- Relationship-Oriented
- Open and Warm
- Emotional
- Unorganized
- Flexible Regarding Time
- Highly Animated
- Spontaneous
- Informal

Most sales training programs use a two-by-two matrix as a basis for categorizing communication styles into four primary types. The four styles are based on two dimensions: assertiveness and responsiveness.

positions. Low-assertive individuals tend to exhibit a slower pace. They typically hold back, let others take charge, and are slow and deliberate in their communication and actions.

- *Responsiveness*—**Responsiveness** points to the level of feelings and sociability an individual openly displays. Highly responsive individuals are relationship-oriented and openly emotional. They readily express their feelings and tend to be personable, friendly, and informal. However, low-responsive individuals tend to be task-oriented and very controlled in their display of emotions. They tend to be impersonal in dealing with others, with an emphasis on formality and self-discipline.

The actual levels of assertiveness and responsiveness will vary from one individual to another on a continuum ranging from high to low. An individual may be located anywhere along the particular continuum, and where the individual is located determines the degree to which they possess and demonstrate the particular behaviours associated with that dimension. Figure 3.6 illustrates the range of behaviours commonly associated with each dimension.

Overlaying the assertiveness and responsiveness dimensions produces a four-quadrant matrix as illustrated in Figure 3.7. The four quadrants characterize an individual as exhibiting one of four different communication styles on the basis of their demonstrated levels of assertiveness and responsiveness. *Amiables* are high on responsiveness but low on assertiveness. *Expressives* are defined as high on both responsiveness and assertiveness. *Drivers* are low on responsiveness but high on assertiveness. *Analyticals* are characterized as being low on assertiveness as well as responsiveness. A salesperson's skill in properly classifying customers can provide valuable cues regarding customer attitudes and behaviours. In turn, these cues allow the salesperson to be more effective by adapting their communication and responses to better fit the customer's style.

responsiveness The level of feelings and sociability an individual openly displays.

FIG. 3.7 COMMUNICATION STYLES MATRIX

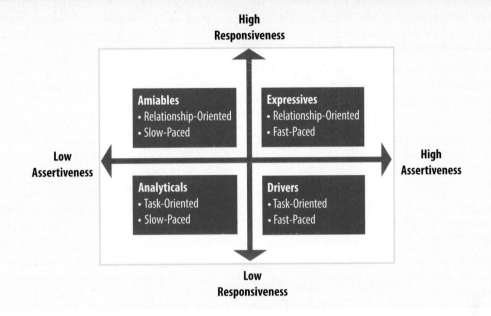

The four quadrants characterize an individual as having one of four different communication styles on the basis of their demonstrated levels of assertiveness and responsiveness. A salesperson's skill in properly classifying customers can provide valuable cues regarding customer attitudes and behaviours.

- *Amiables*—Developing and maintaining close personal relationships are important to **amiables**. Easygoing and cooperative, they are often characterized as friendly back-slappers because of their preference for belonging to groups and their sincere interest in other people—their hobbies, interests, families, and mutual friends. With a natural propensity for talking and socializing, they have little or no desire to control others but rather prefer building consensus. Amiables are not risk takers and need to feel safe in making a decision. Somewhat undisciplined with regard to time, amiables appear to be slow and deliberate in their actions. They avoid conflict and tend to be more concerned with opinions—what others think—than with details and facts. When confronted or attacked, amiables tend to submit. In working with an amiable customer, salespeople should remember that their "must-have" is to be liked and their fundamental "want" is for attention.

- *Expressives*—**Expressives** are animated and highly communicative. Although very competitive by nature, they also exhibit warm personalities and value building close relationships with others. In fact, they dislike being alone and readily seek out others. Expressives are extroverted and are highly uninhibited in their communication. When confronted or crossed, they

will attack. Enthusiastic and stimulating, they seem to talk in terms of people rather than things and have a ready opinion on everything. Yet they remain open-minded and changeable. Expressives are fast paced in their decision making and behaviour and prefer the big picture rather than getting bogged down in details. As a result, they are very spontaneous, unconcerned with time schedules, and not especially organized in their daily lives. They are creative, comfortable operating on intuition, and demonstrate a willingness to take risks. The two keys for expressives that salespeople must keep in mind are the "must-have" of never being hurt emotionally and their underlying "want" is attention.

- *Drivers*—Sometimes referred to as the director or dictator style, **drivers** are hard and detached from their relationships with others. Described as being cool, tough, and competitive in their relationships, drivers are independent and willing to run over

amiables Individuals who are high on responsiveness, low on assertiveness, prefer to belong to groups, and are interested in others.

expressives Individuals who are high on both responsiveness and assertiveness, are animated and communicative, and value building close relationships with others.

drivers Individuals who are low on responsiveness, high on assertiveness, and detached from relationships.

others to get their preferred results. As they seek out and openly demonstrate power and control over people and situations, they are difficult to get close to and appear to treat people as things. Drivers are extremely formal, businesslike, and impatient, with a penchant for time and organization. They are highly opinionated and quick to share those opinions with those around them. When attacked or confronted, drivers will dictate. Drivers exhibit a low tolerance for taking advice, tend to be risk takers, and favour making their own decisions. Although they are highly task oriented, drivers prefer to ignore facts and figures and instead rely on their own gut feelings in making decisions—after all, they do know it all. When working with drivers, salespeople should remember that this style's "must-have" is winning, and their fundamental "want" is results.

- *Analyticals*—The descriptive name for this style is derived from their penchant for gathering and analyzing facts and details before making a decision. **Analyticals** are meticulous and disciplined in everything they do. Logical and very controlled, they are systematic problem solvers and thus very deliberate and slower in pace. In stressful situations and confrontations, analyticals tend to withdraw. Many times, they appear to be nitpicky about everything around them. They do not readily let their feelings show nor are they spontaneous in their behaviours. As a result, they are often seen as being cool and aloof. Analyticals shy away from personal relationships and avoid taking risks. Time and personal schedules are close to being a religious ritual for the analytical. The two fundamentals that salespeople must keep in mind when working with this style are the "must-have" of being right and the underlying "want" is for analytical activities.

Mastering Communication Style Flexing

In addition to sensing and interpreting the customer's communication style, a salesperson must also be aware of their own personal style. Mismatched and possibly clashing styles can be dysfunctional and present significant barriers to communication and relationship building. To minimize possible negative effects stemming from mismatched styles, salespeople can flex their own style to facilitate effective communication.

analyticals Individuals who are low on responsiveness and assertiveness, and are analytical, meticulous, and disciplined in everything they do.

For example, an expressive salesperson calling on an analytical buyer would find considerable differences in both pace and relationship/task orientation that could hinder the selling process unless adjustments are made. Flexing their own style to better match that of the buyer enhances communication. In terms of our example, the salesperson would need to adjust by slowing down their natural pace, reining in the level of spontaneity and animation, and increasing task orientation by offering more detailed information and analysis.

Adapting to buyers by flexing their own communication style has been found to have a positive impact on salespeople's performance and the quality of buyer–seller relationships. Nevertheless, flexing should not be interpreted as meaning an exact match between a salesperson's style and that of a customer. Not only is it not required, but exact matches could even be detrimental. For example, a buyer and seller with matching expressive styles could easily discover that the entire sales call regressed to little more than a personal discussion with nothing of substance being accomplished. However, a buyer and seller matched as drivers could find it difficult, if not impossible, to reach a decision that was mutually beneficial. Rather than matching the buyer's style, flexing implies that the salesperson should adjust to the needs and preferences of the buyer to maximize effectiveness. Growmark, an international agricultural product and service organization, teaches its salespeople to flex throughout their interaction with a buyer by studying different behaviours a salesperson might demonstrate with each style of buyer. (See the Appendix to this chapter.[15])

Study and compare the flexing behaviours that Growmark recommends their salespeople demonstrate when working with each different buyer communication style. Note the differences in recommended salesperson behaviour and rationalize them in terms of the specific characteristics of each buyer's style. Note the differences in recommended salesperson behaviour and rationalize them in terms of the specific characteristics of each buyer's style. Overlaying and integrating these two sets of information will enhance the understanding of how to flex to different buyers and why that form of flexing is recommended.

It is not always possible to gain much information about a buyer's communication style, especially if the buyer is new. If this is the case, it may be more appropriate to assume that the buyer is an analytical-driver and prepare for this style. If the buyer proves to be close to an amiable-expressive, then the salesperson can easily adapt. It is much more difficult to prepare for the amiable-expressive and then switch to an analytical-driver style.

Complex buying decisions incorporate buying influences of people from different departments of an organization.

LO 9 | BUYING TEAMS

CPSA 7.2 Implement social selling

A single individual typically makes routine purchase decisions, such as straight rebuys and simpler modified rebuys. However, the more complex modified rebuy and new task purchase decisions often involve the joint decisions of multiple participants within a buying centre or team. **Buying teams** (also referred to as buying centres) use the expertise and multiple buying influences of people from different departments throughout the organization. As the object of the purchase decision changes, the makeup of the buying team may also change to maximize the relevant expertise of team members. The organization's size, as well as the nature and volume of the products being purchased, will influence the actual number and makeup of buying teams. The different members of a buying team will often have varied goals reflecting their individual needs and those of their different departments.

Buying team members are described in terms of their roles and responsibilities within the team.[16]

- *Initiators*—**Initiators** are individuals within the organization who identify a need or perhaps realize that the acquisition of a product might solve a need or problem.

- *Influencers*—Individuals who guide the decision process by making recommendations and expressing preferences are referred to as **influencers**. While they could be anyone, they are often technical or engineering personnel.

- *Users*—**Users** are the individuals within the organization who will actually use the product being purchased. They evaluate a product on the basis of how it will affect their own job performance. Users often serve as initiators and influencers.

- *Deciders*—The ultimate responsibility for determining which product or service will be purchased rests with the role of **deciders**. Although buyers may also be deciders, it is not unusual for different people to fill these roles.

- *Purchasers*—**Purchasers** have the responsibility for negotiating final terms of purchase with suppliers and executing the actual purchase or acquisition.

- *Gatekeepers*—Members who are in a position to control the flow of information to and between vendors and other buying centre members are referred to as **gatekeepers**. This often includes secretaries and administrative assistants.

Although each of these influencer types will not necessarily be present on all buying teams, the use of buying teams incorporating some or all of these multiple influences has increased in recent years. One example of multiple buying influences is offered in the recent experience of an Executive Jet International salesperson selling a Gulfstream V corporate jet to a Toronto-based pharmaceutical company. Stretching over a period of six months, the salesperson worked with a variety of individuals serving different roles within the buying organization:

- *Initiator:* The initiator of the purchase process was the chief operating officer of the corporation, who found that the recent corporate expansions had outgrown the effective service range of the organization's existing aircraft. Beyond pointing out the need and thus

buying teams Teams of individuals in organizations that use the expertise and multiple buying influences of people from different departments throughout the organization.

initiators Individuals within an organization who identify a need.

influencers Individuals within an organization who guide the decision process by making recommendations and expressing preferences.

users Individuals within an organization who will actually use the product being purchased.

deciders Individuals within an organization who have the ultimate responsibility of determining which product or service will be purchased.

purchasers Organizational members who negotiate final terms of the purchase and execute the actual purchase.

gatekeepers Members of an organization who are in a position to control the flow of information to and between vendors and other buying centre members.

initiating the search, this individual would also be highly involved in the final choice based on her personal experiences and the perceived needs of the company.

- *Influencers:* Two different employee groups acted as the primary influencers. First were the corporate pilots who contributed a readily available and extensive background of knowledge and experience with a variety of aircraft types. Also playing a key influencer role were members from the capital budgeting group in the finance department. Although concerned with documented performance capabilities, they also provided inputs and assessments of the different alternatives by using their capital investment models.

- *Users:* The users provided some of the most dynamic inputs, as they were anxious to make the transition to a higher performance aircraft to enhance their own efficiency and performance in working at marketing/sales offices and plants that now stretched over North and South America. Primary players in this group included the vice presidents for marketing and for production/operations in addition to the corporate pilots who would be flying the plane.

- *Deciders:* Based on the contribution and inputs of each member of the buying team, the chief executive officer would make the ultimate decision. Her role as decider was based more on her position within the firm rather than her use of the chosen alternative, given that she travelled primarily by commercial carriers. As the organization's highest operating officer, she was in a position to move freely among all members of the buying team and make the decision on overall merits rather than personal feelings or desires.

- *Purchaser:* The corporate purchasing department was responsible for making the actual purchase, negotiating the final terms, and completing all the required paperwork, with the director of purchasing actually assuming the immediate contact role. The purchasing office typically handles purchasing contracts and is staffed to draw up, complete, and file the related registrations and legal documents.

- *Gatekeepers:* This purchase decision involved two different gatekeepers within the customer organization: the executive assistant to the chief operating officer and an assistant purchasing officer. The positioning of these gatekeepers facilitated the salesperson's exchange of information and ability to keep in contact with the various members of the buying team. The COO's executive assistant moved easily among the various executives influencing the decision and was able to make appointments with the right people at the right times. However, the assistant purchasing officer was directly involved with the coordination of each member and bringing their various inputs into one summary document for the CEO. The salesperson's positive dealings and good relationships with each gatekeeper played a significant role in Executive Jet getting the sale.

A classic and all-too-common mistake among salespeople is to make repetitive calls on a purchasing manager over several months only to discover that a buying team exists and that someone other than the purchasing manager will make the ultimate decision. Salespeople must gather information to discover who is in the buying team, what their individual roles are, and which members are the most influential. This information might be collected from account history files, people inside the salesperson's organization who are familiar with the account sources within the client organization, and even other salespeople. A salesperson should work with all members of the buying team and be careful to address their varied needs and objectives properly. Nevertheless, circumstances sometimes prevent a salesperson from working with all members of the team, and it is important that the salesperson reaches those who are most influential.

It may be difficult, however, to get past the gatekeeper to reach those individuals most influential in the buying process. Brett Eiskina, Corporate Acquisition Account Executive at Sprint Nextel, has found that using social media allows him to bypass the gatekeeper and go directly to decision makers. As Brett explains, "In the past, effective gatekeepers have been a salesperson's worst nightmare. There is nothing worse than repeatedly calling on a client only to learn that they are always 'In a meeting' or 'Out of the office' EVERY time you call. Well, with the growing number of people using social media, it is becoming increasingly easier for salespeople to skip those gatekeepers and go straight to those decision makers. I have found LinkedIn to be particularly valuable. It gives me information and insight to buyers (e.g., college, field of study, groups they belong to) that I would never have known before contacting them. I've set many appointments simply by mentioning that I was an alum of the same college as the person I was trying to reach out to. LinkedIn will also show you if you have any mutual connections that you can query for information before reaching out for the appointment. Don't just stick to LinkedIn though; Hoovers, Data.com, Twitter, and even Facebook are all very powerful tools that can help you get an edge over the other salespeople reaching out to the same decision maker."°

LO 10 | ENGAGING CUSTOMERS

Today's business organizations are undergoing profound change in response to ever-increasing competition and rapid changes in the business environment. The worldwide spread of technology has resulted in intense and increasingly global competition that is highly dynamic in nature. Accelerating rates of change have fragmented what were once mass markets into more micro and niche markets composed of more knowledgeable and demanding customers with escalating expectations. In response, traditional purchasing practices are also rapidly changing.

Focusing on the Customer Experience

CPSA   **1.3 Develop client intelligence**

A study of customer experience professionals from large multinational business-to-business organizations representing an array of industries provides insight on what the business customer experience will look like moving forward.[17] According to the study, customers will expect companies to have a clear understanding of their needs and to proactively address their current and future needs with a personalized customer experience. Accessing the Internet to get the most current information on products, solutions, and best practices, customers will have a more informed base of understanding and will expect an equally informed salesperson. Consequently, salespeople must move beyond providing solutions to current needs and move toward "insight selling" by anticipating and fulfilling customer needs necessary for them to adeptly face the future. Salespeople must have access to customer intelligence and emphasize proactive and personalized customer support. According to the survey, 62 percent of respondents indicated that they are investing in understanding individual customer characteristics to better meet the changing needs of customers. To keep customers, salespeople will be required to anticipate needs along the stages of the customer lifecycle and proactively respond. This will entail the use of big data to generate customer intelligence that can be used to provide a comprehensive view of the customer. Customers

will expect sellers to keep them informed by interacting with them using the buyer's preferred method of communication. Exhibit 3.8 indicates communication channels most likely to be used often by business customers in 2020.[18]

The Role of Information Technology

CPSA   **7.1 Leverage sales technology**

Buyers and sellers alike are increasingly using technology to enhance the effectiveness and efficiency of the purchasing process. Business-to-business e-commerce is rapidly growing. Although EDI over private networks has been in use for some time, nearly all the current growth has been in Internet-based transactions.

Information technology electronically links buyers and sellers for direct and immediate communication and transmission of information and data. Transactional exchanges, such as straight rebuy decisions, can now be automated with Internet- and World Wide Web-enabled programs tracking sales at the point of purchase and capturing the data for real-time inventory control and order placing. By cutting order and shipping times, overall cycle times are reduced, mistakes are minimized, and working capital invested in inventories is made available for more productive applications. Further, the automation of these routine transactions allows buyers and salespeople to devote more time to new tasks, complex sales, and postsale service and relationship-building activities.

Customer relationship management (CRM) systems integrated with the Web allow reps to have a more informed conversation with prospects and customers by helping them to better understand customers. Sales organizations know keywords searched to find the seller's company, pages clicked on the company's Web site, and particular products and services buyers examined before asking for more information. Additionally, data collected on customer demographics, sales and customer service histories, and marketing preferences and customer feedback can be easily accumulated through a CRM system and used to better understand customers and provide customized offerings to best serve their needs. Dell supplements its CRM system with software provided by Lattice, which provides sales reps with comprehensive intelligence (e.g., past purchases, corporate activity, likely next purchase from Dell) obtained via LinkedIn announcements, Web site information, and other public statements or sources of information that allows them to participate in relevant and timely discussions with prospects and customers. Moreover,

Exhibit 3.8

Communication Channels Likely to Be Used Often in 2020

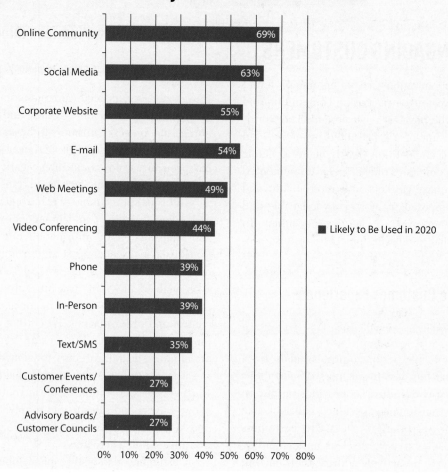

Channel	Likely to Be Used in 2020
Online Community	69%
Social Media	63%
Corporate Website	55%
E-mail	54%
Web Meetings	49%
Video Conferencing	44%
Phone	39%
In-Person	39%
Text/SMS	35%
Customer Events/Conferences	27%
Advisory Boards/Customer Councils	27%

the software looks for buying triggers and behaviour and converts them into mathematical algorithms that can predict the likelihood that a potential customer will buy a certain product.[19]

Social networking technologies are likely to play an important role in CRM systems, making it more convenient for customers to provide information that goes into product planning and development, as well as provide deeper insights into customer buying motives.

For instance, Microsoft offers its Sales Productivity CRM software that incorporates Outlook, Lync, Skype, and Yammer to allow for social collaboration between buyers and sellers. To see how Cisco Systems Inc. incorporates business analytics provided by FirstRain to gain a deeper understanding of its customers, see Technology in Sales: Understanding Customers from an Outside-In Perspective.[20]

In addition to facilitating exchange transactions, applications integrating the Internet are also being used to distribute product and company information along with training courses and materials. Several companies have begun publishing their product catalogues online as a replacement for the reams of product brochures salespeople have traditionally had to carry with them. The online catalogues can be easily updated without the expense of obsolete brochures and can be selectively downloaded by salespeople to create customized presentations and proposals.

Sellers are also turning to automation software to help them gather customer information. For instance, a software product called Amity Lifecycle uses flexible business rules to sense changes in customer rhythms to allow salespeople to deliver timely, tailored engagement that matches the needs of every customer.

Technology in Sales

 CPSA

7.1 Leverage sales technology

Understanding Customers from an Outside-In Perspective

Cisco Systems Inc., a leader in developing, manufacturing, and selling information technology, prides itself on understanding customers, which it credits as being a key element in creating long-term customer relationships. To ensure its customers' needs were met, Cisco determined that it needed to take an "outside-in" approach to understanding its customers. This involved listening to specific public conversations about customers, markets, and industries to better understand the challenges facing its customers. To accomplish this goal, Cisco sought a platform that would provide a holistic, comprehensive view to harness knowledge in a single repository. They found such a platform in FirstRain.

FirstRain technology platform captures the enormous amount of unstructured data available across the Web and applies layered algorithms to mine meaning, extract business developments and implicit relationships, and distribute an in-depth timely understanding of events unfolding in companies and markets. The salesforce at Cisco uses FirstRain to track every C-level discussion on any campaign or topic so that each of its salespeople can attend any customer meeting prepared with a real-time, unmatched view of the space in which they operate.

FirstRain streamlines the information-gathering process for Cisco salespeople by providing one source for the specific conversations about customer topics and campaigns on a daily basis. Salespeople can access this information via e-mail, portal, or a mobile device. The analytics provided by FirstRain offer insights that empower the sales team to provide the kind of highly focused conversations with customers that formerly were not possible. In sum, FirstRain allows the Cisco salesforce to continuously remain abreast of market, customer, and competitor news to improve their effectiveness with customers.

© Lucky Business,/Shutterstock.com

Buyers' Demand for Access to Relevant Information

 CPSA   7.1 Leverage sales technology

With ever-expanding information technology, buyers have easier access to information on vendors and are utilizing technology to become more informed buyers. This has shifted some of the power to buyers, who can accompany more bidders, making the landscape even more competitive. As buyers increasingly undertake a larger share of the purchase process on their own, they are demanding that sellers make available to them relevant content to help them justify their buying decisions. Buyers often do their own research rather than waiting for salespeople to contact them. As such, buyers are demanding that information be made available to them

via their laptops, desktops, iPads, and smartphones as they seek out more and more information prior to connecting with a salesperson. These buyers are looking for personalized dialogue that can help guide them through the decision process. For instance, content aimed at an economic buyer might include a return-on-investment (ROI) calculator. To help the analytical buyer understand the company's novel approach to solving a problem, a case study might prove valuable.

Blogs, white papers, webinars, videos, recorded interviews, product demos, and presentations—providing anything from expert analysis and advice to product announcements—should be offered to targeted customers through media such as a company Web site, Twitter stream, or LinkedIn discussion group. Logicalis, an integrated information and communication technologies provider, tries to gain attention as a thought leader by helping buyers understand cutting-edge IT topics by posting informative content on its own Web site and having a presence on Facebook and LinkedIn. Citrix Systems, a provider of virtualization and cloud-computing technologies, is using blogs to provide information to those searching for trends in cloud computing and virtualization, while LinkWare, a developer of electronic forms, posts relevant information on community sites that prospective customers visit.[21] The more streamlined and personalized the information the better, as buyers increasingly face information overload. Overwhelmingly, buyers are looking for information that proves how the seller's product will result in savings, enhance productivity, and positively affect profitability.

The Need for Adding Value

8.2 Drive results

The increased interdependence between buyer and seller organizations hinges on the salesperson's capabilities to serve as a problem solver in a dynamic and fast-changing business environment. Buyers expect value, and more and more sellers plan to provide it, as evidenced by research on 250 global B2B firms showing that 58 percent are focused on "value marketing."[22] According to a study of 80,000 business customers, buyers expect several things from salespeople.[23] For one, they expect salespeople to personally manage their business. In fact, many buying organizations **outsource** to a supplier certain activities that the buying organization previously performed. These activities are necessary for the day-to-day functioning of the buying organization but are not within the organization's core or distinct possibilities. Moreover, buyers depend on the salesperson to provide unique and value-added solutions to their changing problems and needs. To shape such innovative solutions, salespeople must have broad-based and comprehensive knowledge readily available and the ability to use that knowledge in creative ways. This includes knowledge of one's own products and capabilities, as well as the products and capabilities of competitors. More important, the salesperson must possess a thorough understanding of product applications and the needs of the customer to work with the buyer in generating innovative solutions. Finally, buyers expect salespeople to be easily accessible in order to respond to ongoing concerns and solve problems that may arise after the sale. By fulfilling these expectations, salespeople can add value to the customer buying experience and more fully engage the buyer.

outsource To give to a supplier certain activities that were previously performed by the buying organization.

STUDY TOOLS

At the back of the textbook, use tear-out cards to review key chapter information.
Visit cengage.ca to purchase digital tools to help you succeed.

CENGAGE | MINDTAP

Personal Computer

☐ Gain unique perspectives on key concepts through a variety of videos and cases

☐ Increase your comprehension with online quizzes

☐ Study with existing flashcards and make your own

Mobile

☐ Stay focused and ready to study whenever it's convenient for you!

☐ Access a full, interactive ebook: online or offline

☐ Study tools that empower anytime, anywhere learning and 24/7 course access

APPENDIX CHAPTER 3

Recommended Flexing Behaviour for Different Communication Styles

Selling Task or Objective

Setting an Appointment

Selling to the Analytical

- Send a business letter with details about yourself and the company.
- Follow the letter with a phone call to confirm expectations and set an appointment.

Selling to the Driver

- Drivers may not take time to read your letter.
- Contact them by phone first and follow up with a letter.
- Keep the call businesslike and to the point by identifying yourself, explaining the business problem addressed by your product, and asking for an appointment.
- The letter should simply confirm the time and date of appointment and include materials the driver might review before the meeting.

Selling to the Amiable

- Send a letter with a personal touch stating who you are and why you are contacting him or her.
- The letter should include your experience working with clients the prospect knows by reputation or experience, your reliability and follow-through, and the quality of your product or service.
- Follow the letter with a personal phone call.
- Take time to be friendly, open, and sincere, and to establish trust in the relationship.

Selling to the Expressive

- Generally, a phone call is most appropriate.
- Make your call open and friendly, stressing quick benefits, personal service, your experience, and your company's experience with its products and services.

- If you send a letter, make it short and personal, stressing who you are, how you know of him or her, and what you are interested in talking about.

Opening the Call

Selling to the Analytical

- Provide background information about you and the company.
- Approach in an advisory capacity, acknowledging buyer's expertise.
- Show evidence that you have done your homework on the buyer's situation.
- Offer evidence of having provided solutions in the past.
- Be conscious of how you are using the buyer's time.

Selling to the Driver

- Listen and focus on the driver's ideas and objectives.
- Provide knowledge and insight relevant to the driver's specific business problems.
- Be personable but reserved and relatively formal.
- Present factual evidence that establishes the business problem and resulting outcome.
- Maintain a quick pace. Drivers value punctuality and the efficient use of time.

Selling to the Amiable

- Engage in informal conversation before getting down to business.
- Demonstrate that you are personally interested in the amiable's work and personal goals.
- You will have to earn the right to learn more personally about the amiable.
- Demonstrate your product or service knowledge by referencing a common acquaintance with whom you've done business.

Selling to the Expressive

- Quickly describe the purpose of your call and establish credibility—you must earn the right to develop a business relationship with the expressive.

- Share stories about people you both know.

- Share information the expressive would perceive as exclusive.

- Share your feelings and enthusiasm for the expressive's ideas and goals.

- Once the expressive has confidence in your competence, take time to develop an open and trusting personal relationship.

Gathering Information

Selling to the Analytical

- Ask specific, fact-finding questions in a systematic manner.

- Establish a comprehensive exchange of information.

- Encourage the buyer to discuss ideas while focusing on factual information.

- Be thorough and unhurried—listen.

- Explain that you are in alignment with their thinking and can support their objectives.

Selling to the Driver

- Ask, don't tell. Ask fact-finding questions leading to what the driver values and rewards.

- Make your line of questioning consistent with your call objective.

- Follow up on requests for information immediately.

- Support the buyer's beliefs; indicate how you can positively affect goals.

- Clarify the driver's expectations.

Selling to the Amiable

- Create a cooperative atmosphere with an open exchange of information and feelings.

- Amiables tend to understate their objectives, so you may need to probe for details and specifics about their goals.

- Listen responsively. Give ample amounts of verbal and nonverbal feedback.

- Verify whether there are unresolved budget or cost justification issues.

- Find out who else will contribute to the buying decision.

- Summarize what you believe to be the amiable's key ideas and feelings.

Selling to the Expressive

- Begin by finding out the expressive's perception of the situation and vision of the ideal outcome.

- Identify other people who should contribute to analysis and planning.

- Listen and then respond with plenty of verbal and nonverbal feedback that supports the expressive's beliefs.

- Question carefully the critical data you'll need.

- Keep the discussion focused and moving toward a result.

- If the expressive shows limited interest in specifics, summarize what has been discussed and begin to suggest ways to move the vision toward reality.

Activating the Need to Change

Selling to the Analytical

- Use the buyer's records to supply information.

- Use a logical approach.

- Illustrate with dollars and cents.

Selling to the Driver

- Be fast paced and businesslike.

- Be sure of your figures.

- Show the driver the bottom line.

- Appeal to rational thinking and avoid appealing to emotions.

Selling to the Amiable

- Address emotional needs in line with safety and comfort needs.

- Use the amiable's figures rather than your own.

- Do not push!

Selling to the Expressive

- Support the expressive's ideas and goals.

- Work toward their esteem needs.

- Supply data from people seen as leaders by the expressive.

Engaging in the Sales Conversation

Selling to the Analytical

- Provide a detailed written proposal as part of your presentation.

- Include the strongest cost-benefit justifications

- Support with third-party data.

- Be reserved and decisive but not aggressive.
- Limit emotional or testimonial appeals.
- Recommend a specific course of action.
- Give the buyer chance to review all documents related to purchase and delivery.

Selling to the Driver

- Present your recommendation so that the driver can compare alternative solutions and probable outcomes.
- Provide documented options.
- Offer the best quality given the cost limitations.
- Be specific and factual without overwhelming the driver with details.
- Appeal to esteem and independence needs.
- Reinforce the driver's preference for acting in a forthright manner.
- Summarize content quickly, and then let the driver choose a course of action.

Selling to the Amiable

- Define clearly in writing and make sure the amiable understands the following:
    - What you can do to support the amiable's personal goals
    - What you will contribute and what the amiable needs to contribute
    - The support resources you intend to commit to the project
- Provide a clear solution to the amiable's problem with maximum assurances that this is the best solution and that there is no need to consider others.
- Ask the amiable to involve other decision makers.
- Satisfy needs by showing how your solution is best now and will be best in the future, and support it with references and third-party evidence.
- Use testimonials from perceived experts and others close to the amiable.

Selling to the Expressive

- Provide specific solutions to the expressive's ideas—in writing.
- Build confidence that you have the necessary facts, but do not overwhelm the expressive with details.
- Do not rush the discussion. Spend time developing ways to implement ideas.
- Appeal to personal esteem needs.
- Try to get commitments to action in writing.

Earning Commitment

Selling to the Analytical

- Ask for commitment in a low-key but direct manner.
- Expect to negotiate changes.
- Pay special attention to pricing issues.
- Work for commitment now to avoid the analytical's tendency to delay decisions.
- Cite data supporting your company's service records.
- Respond to objections by emphasizing the analytical's buying principles and objectivity.

Selling to the Driver

- Ask for the order directly.
- Put your offer in clear, factual terms.
- Offer options and alternatives.
- Be prepared to negotiate changes and concessions.
- Drivers sometimes attach conditions to a sale.
- Offer the driver time to consider the options.
- Anticipate objections in advance and come prepared with facts.
- Respond to objections based on the driver's values and priorities.

Selling to the Amiable

- Ask for the order indirectly—do not push.
- Emphasize the guarantees that offer protection to the amiable.
- Do not corner the amiable; they will want out if things go wrong.
- Guard against "buyer's remorse"—get a commitment even if you have to base it on a contingency.
- Stress your personal involvement after the sale.
- Encourage the amiable to involve others in the final purchase decision.
- Welcome objections and be patient and thorough in responding to them.
- When responding to objections,
    - Describe financial justification
    - Refer to experts or others the amiable respects
    - Keep in mind how the amiable feels about and will be affected by the purchase decision

Selling to the Expressive

- When you have enough information to understand the need and have tested the appropriateness of the recommendation, assume the sale and ask for the order in a casual and informal way.

- When the opportunity presents itself, offer incentives to encourage the purchase.

- Do not confuse the issue by presenting too many options or choices.

- Get a definite commitment. Be sure the expressive understands the decision to purchase.

- Save the details until after you have a firm buying decision. The expressive believes it is the salesperson's job to handle details.

- In handling objections,

    - Describe what others have done to get over that hurdle

    - Respond to the expressive's enthusiasm for their goals

    - Deal with how the recommendation meets with this buyer's options

    - Restate benefits that focus on the satisfaction a buying decision will bring

Providing Follow-Up

Selling to the Analytical

- Provide a detailed implementation plan.
- Maintain regular contact.
- Check to confirm satisfactory and on-schedule delivery.

Selling to the Driver

- Set up a communication process with the driver that encourages quick exchange of information about checkpoints and milestones.

- Make sure you have a contingency plan to responsively implement corrections and incorporate changes.

- Make sure there are no surprises.

Selling to the Amiable

- Immediately after the purchase decision is made, make a follow-up appointment.

- Initiate and maintain frequent contacts providing services, such as the following:

    - Periodic progress reports on installation

    - Arrangements for service and training

    - Introduction of new products and services

    - Listening carefully to concerns, even those that seem trivial

Selling to the Expressive

- As soon as the order is signed, reaffirm the schedule for delivery and your personal relationship with the buyer, and introduce the implementation person or team.

- A social situation, such as a lunch, can be a very effective opportunity for following up on business with this buyer.

- Work toward becoming an ongoing member of the buyer's team.

- In case of any complaints, handle them yourself. Never refer them to another in your organization without the buyer's consent.

CHAPTER CASE 3

SELLING FOR CUSTOMER-360 INC.: UNDERSTANDING YOUR PROSPECT

BACKGROUND

Customer-360 Inc. is a relatively new entrant in the cloud computing business management software industry, having been in existence for a little over four years. It specializes in providing Web-based customizable customer relationship management software solutions that support an entire company, from accounting to Web capabilities. Its software is constructed around an individual customer record so that accounting, sales, support, shipping, and billing all access identical information for each interaction. The company currently serves a variety of businesses across a number of industries. Customer satisfaction is the company's top priority and it acts with integrity to fulfill this mission.

Its technology is easy to learn and easy to use, and its information technology staff is extremely knowledgeable and customer friendly.

The company currently employs more than 125 salespeople who call directly on businesses and organizations throughout North America. Salespeople are trained to be customer-oriented problem solvers who seek to establish long-term relationships with customers. This approach has allowed Customer-360 to experience steady sales gains since its beginning and it hopes to continue its upward growth trajectory.

CURRENT SITUATION

Laura, a recent graduate who just completed the sales rep training program at Customer-360, is excited about her upcoming meeting with Lifestyle Furniture and Office Supply of Waterloo, Ontario. Privately owned, Lifestyle Furniture and Office Supply serves the furniture needs of its customers through its two large retail locations. Each location has a store manager, and several full- and part-time employees to assist with sales and operations. The company's owner serves as president and they also employ a director of marketing and sales, who among other things oversees its salesforce comprised of both inside and outside salespeople, a director of operations, a director of information technology (whose primary responsibility is to run the Web side of their business),

and a director of accounting and finance. The outside salesforce solicits commercial accounts and in large part is responsible for growing the non-retail business for Lifestyle Furniture and Office Supply.

A good friend of Laura's, Alex Goodneighbour, happens to be neighbours with Chris Style, Lifestyle Furniture and Office Supply's director of marketing and sales. In a recent conversation with Chris, Alex mentioned Laura and how she might be able to help him at Lifestyle Furniture and Office Supply. Chris suggested that Alex have Laura give him a call and subsequently Laura was able to secure a meeting with Chris Style the following Tuesday morning.

Laura was delighted that Alex provided her with this prospect and was confident that this would help her get off to a fast start at Customer-360. Laura has been friends with Alex since grade school. This is not unusual for Laura, who has many friends and close relationships, likely because she shows such a sincere interest in others, particularly in their hobbies, interests, family, and mutual friends. She enjoys listening to the opinions of others and seems to get along with most everyone, generally avoiding conflict rather than submitting to others. Laura credits her ability to communicate well orally (she loves to talk and socialize), get along well with others, and build a consensus, in part, for her landing a position in sales at Customer-360.

Prior to her meeting with Chris Style, Laura asked Alex if she could meet her for lunch to find out a little more about Chris and Lifestyle Furniture and Office Supply. When Laura finally arrived for lunch, late as usual, she wasn't able to learn as much about Lifestyle Furniture and Office Supply as she would have liked, but she did learn the following about Chris. Alex indicated that Chris was a good neighbour, but he certainly wasn't a friendly, outgoing relationship builder such as Laura. In fact, he tended to be rather cool, tough, and competitive when it came to relationships. He liked to be in charge of people and situations and was not willing to let others stand in the way of achieving his goals. Chris manages his time well, is impatient with others, and tends to be very businesslike. He likes extreme sports and appears to have a penchant for taking risks. According to Alex, at annual neighbourhood association meetings, Chris tends to be the most outspoken individual in attendance. While opinionated, Chris rarely takes advice from others and prefers to make his own decisions.

CHAPTER 3: Understanding Buyers   89

Although Laura believed she still had additional work to do before meeting with Chris, she was at least glad to know a little bit about the person she would be meeting. The more she knew about her buyer, she surmised, the better she could tailor her offering to meet his needs.

QUESTIONS

1. Based on your understanding of both Laura and Chris, how would you characterize the communication style of each?

2. What, if any, preparations and style flexing should Laura make to better relate to and communicate with Chris Style?

3. Who all might be involved in the buying decision for Lifestyle Furniture and Office Supply with regard to Laura's offering? For each, explain why and how.

4. Explain at least two needs that might be met by Lifestyle Furniture and Office Supply by purchasing the software offered by Customer-360.

ROLE PLAY

Situation: Read the case.

Characters: Laura, sales rep for Customer-360 Inc.; Chris Style, director of marketing and sales, Lifestyle Furniture and Office Supply.

Scene:

Location—Chris Style's office at Lifestyle Furniture and Office Supply.

Action—Laura meets with Chris to find out more about Lifestyle Furniture and Office Supply's operations and needs to see if she can help them. She is also trying to determine who else might be involved in the buying decision and what influence each might have. She has no plans to make a sale on this call.

INTEGRATIVE CASE

PLANT-BASED REVOLUTION

BACKGROUND

The battle for the non-meat market in the Canadian fast food industry is heating up. For every fast food restaurant that has successfully introduced meat alternative products like A&W, there are other retailers that have had to scale back plans, like Tim Hortons.

The alternative meat industry is rapidly growing. According to Statista, meat substitute sales are predicted to grow from $175 million in 2019 to $226 million in 2022.[24] In a recent study reported by *Canadian Grocer*, more than half (53%) of Canadians stated they eat meat alternatives. But most interestingly, this study asked Canadians the reasons why they chose to eat meat alternatives. They included wanting to eat less meat overall (35%), the price of meat (26%), watching weight (22%), easier to digest (22%), and finally environmental considerations (20%).[25]

The last reason is also a compelling one. Companies are finding that consumers are starting to make decisions based on the sustainability choices made by companies from which they buy products. Maple Leaf Foods, a Canadian-based manufacturer of prepared meats, announced in late 2019 that the company is now considered carbon neutral. This coincides with the Canadian company's increased focus on developing meat alternatives to its product lines.[26]

However, the company that tops the list for selling meat alternatives is Beyond Meat, a U.S.-based manufacturer. While first starting out working with fast food chains like A&W, the company has managed to move "beyond" these markets, developing a line of meatless burgers for grocery stores in 2019. With every company that signs up to create a new Beyond Meat burger, like Starbucks in early 2020, there is still some pushback from uncertain consumers and markets. Tim Hortons started selling Beyond Meat sausage patties in early 2019, then added burgers later that year. By January of 2020, the iconic Canadian retailer stopped selling all Beyond Meat products, due to what it deemed poor sales.[27]

So, it's clear that Canadians are interested and perhaps intrigued with meat substitutes, but it does not mean that interest will turn into action. With only a small percentage of Canadians that are vegetarian and vegan, that leaves much of the market to be convinced of going meatless.

CURRENT SITUATION

You have just started your job as a sales and marketing analyst for Wendy's Canada. The fast food retailer was relatively late in offering its meatless hamburger, only bringing its Plantiful Burger to Canadians in February 2020. What made the introduction of this product unique is that it was not created by partnering with Beyond Meat or other manufacturers.

Plantiful was designed in Canada and started out being offered only in Canadian-based Wendy's restaurants. The meat alternative burger was derived from peas and looks much like Wendy's meat-based offerings.

Your boss, Lisa Deletrotz, Senior Director of Marketing for Wendy's Canada, was quoted when the product was released: "Plant-based product offerings have become an expectation of Canadian consumers. We developed a flexitarian option the Wendy's Way—using high quality, flavorful ingredients—and this resulted in what we believe is the best plant-based burger available to Canadians."[28]

You have been handed this quote and tasked with putting together a short report on how Wendy's Canada can best manage the growth of this new product in the Canadian market. You remember from your sales class the importance of understanding buyers and their needs, and realize this should form the foundation of your report. A few models may also help in presenting your ideas.

QUESTIONS

1. When consumers are looking for healthy diets but have concerns about the environmental impact of some food sources like meat, they develop a difference between their actual state and a desired state. What is this difference called?
   a. desire gap
   b. needs gap
   c. demand gap
   d. needs difference

2. As eating habits change, customers may start to get concerned over how others will judge their food choices. Which of the general types of buyer needs does this relate to?

   a. situational
   b. psychological
   c. social
   d. knowledge

3. A new potential market for a product like Wendy's Plantiful meatless burger is a B2B one, specifically non-profit organizations. This group is looking for healthy options but is aware of the many challenges inherent with the existing food supply. They hold events where they serve food, and the event planners often hear about the need to supply food reflective of changing societal norms. These event planners form which part of the buying team?

   a. deciders
   b. purchasers
   c. gatekeepers
   d. initiators

CHAPTER ROLE PLAY 3

AT BAT INC.

BACKGROUND

You are a sales representative for At Bat Inc., a manufacturer and marketer of baseball and softball bats located in Vancouver. You are responsible for calling on a variety of accounts throughout western Canada, many of which are independently owned sporting goods retailers, often in small cities and towns.

CURRENT SITUATION

You recently scheduled a meeting with Casey Atthebat, owner of Benton Sporting Goods, an independent retail sporting goods store located in a small rural community in northern Alberta. Casey contacted you after finding your company on the Internet. She is in the process of evaluating several suppliers for her soon-to-be-opened store. Before meeting with Casey, you have decided to prepare a series of questions to ask Casey to identify her situational, functional, social, psychological, and knowledge needs. When meeting with Casey you want to ask her several questions so that you can fully understand her needs and then demonstrate to her how you and your company can best satisfy those needs.

ROLE PLAY

Location: Casey Atthebat's office at Benton Sporting Goods

Characters: You, At Bat Inc. sales representative; Casey Atthebat, owner of Benton Sporting Goods

Action: Using the questions you developed, have a conversation with Casey to assess her situational, functional, social, psychological, and knowledge needs (ask at least one to two questions to assess each need).

4 | Communication Skills

LEARNING OBJECTIVES

After completing this chapter, you should be able to

LO 1 | Explain the importance of collaborative, two-way communication in trust-based selling.

LO 2 | Explain the primary types of questions and how they are applied in selling.

LO 3 | Illustrate the diverse roles and uses of strategic questioning in trust-based selling.

LO 4 | Identify and describe the five steps of the ADAPT questioning sequence for effective fact finding and needs discovery.

LO 5 | Discuss the four sequential steps for effective active listening.

LO 6 | Discuss the superiority of pictures over words for explaining concepts and enhancing comprehension.

LO 7 | Describe and interpret the different forms of verbal and nonverbal communication.

AFTER FINISHING THIS CHAPTER GO TO THE BACK OF THE BOOK FOR CHAPTER REVIEW CARDS, AND VISIT MINDTAP FOR ACCESS TO STUDY TOOLS.

Alberta-based WestJet was formed in 1996 by Clive Beddoe and a team of partners looking to change the airline industry for the better. They began with three aircraft, five destinations, 220 employees, and a mission to enrich the lives of everyone in WestJet's world.[1] The airline currently flies to more than 100 destinations in North America, Central America, the Caribbean, and Europe. They have become one of Canada's most admired and respected corporate cultures and have a unique approach to customer service with a well-known friendly and customer-first attitude.[2] Passengers are called "guests" and their employees are referred to as "WestJetters." It is an airline where executives fly economy and the atmosphere is fun, positive, and open.[3] There are currently 14,000 WestJetters, more than 22 million guests a year, over 700 flights per day, and a fleet of over 150 aircraft.[4] The main corporate values include acting like an owner, caring from the heart, rising to the challenge, and working together to win. The company operates with a people-focused business model, which is the source of their approach to put guests and people first. WestJetters are highly valued and the company believes each and every one creates and is part of their success. WestJet has won numerous Trip Advisor awards, including their most recent awards in 2019 for Best Airline in Canada and Travellers' Choice Winner for Mid-Sized Airline in North America.[5] WestJet's success in growing its business is due in part to the company's ability to listen to and communicate with its internal and external stakeholders.

Introduction

Communication is an important aspect of the selling process not just for the airline industry. For example, as an accomplished sales trainer in the business-to-business marketplace, Al Simon identifies effective communication as the essential selling competency for successful selling performance.* Simon places particular emphasis on the concept of collaborative, active listening. "Prospects want salespeople to listen to them, to understand their business. This point was driven home for me one day when I was on a sales call with a client to observe her performance. She did what I thought was a good job, asking several excellent questions and the prospect responded with a lot of valuable information. As we were leaving, the salesperson excused herself to visit the restroom. Standing there at the elevator with the prospect, he said to me, 'That salesperson seems very sharp.' I had to chuckle to myself, as the salesperson had not said much else besides asking questions!"

Based on Simon's experience, there is a significant difference between the communication skills of highly successful salespeople and those who are not so successful, and he asserts that the biggest difference is the ability to utilize active listing. Collaborative, active listening is much more involved than simply listening to the other party's message. It involves two-way engagement: listening with your eyes, your mind, and your whole being—not just your ears. It requires a higher level of concentration on the total message being exchanged, maintaining effective eye contact without staring, considering and evaluating the message being received, and actively responding and participating by paraphrasing back what you heard the prospect say and asking related questions to clarify and gain additional information and detail.

*© Al Simon Source: sales.linkedin.com

An additional communication skill Simon stresses as being critical for salespeople to master is the ability to stay with the prospect's thought process and not think too far ahead or behind. If a salesperson allows their mind to get ahead or behind what the prospect is saying, concentration is broken, the full message will not be properly received and considered, and the salesperson will be unable to follow up on what the prospect has just said. "If you are unable to remember conversation from even a few minutes back, it will be painfully obvious to the prospect that you aren't listening and don't care about their issues. How much business do you suppose you will win that way? To be effective in today's business climate, really listen to the prospect and then help them solve the problem."[6]

The need to build mutual respect and trust through interactive, two-way communication emphasizes the critical and high-magnitude impact effective interpersonal communication has on selling success in today's business landscape. On the one hand, selling is basically interpersonal communication. The skill and effectiveness of a salesperson's interpersonal communication are fundamental determinants of selling performance. On the other hand, effective communication continues to be one of the least understood and understudied skills for successful selling.

This chapter addresses the need to better understand and master the art of collaborative, two-way communication. First, we will examine the basic nature of **trust-based sales communication**. Building on this preliminary understanding, the text breaks down trust-based sales communication into its component and subcomponent parts to facilitate study, application, and mastery. The verbal dimension of communication is examined first with an emphasis on three communication subcomponents: (1) developing effective questioning methods for use in uncovering and diagnosing buyers' needs and expectations, (2) using active listening skills to facilitate the interchange of ideas and information, and (3) maximizing the responsive sharing of information with buyers in a way that fully explains and brings to life the benefits of proposed solutions. Finally, the nonverbal dimension of interpersonal communication is examined with an emphasis on its application and meaningful interpretation.

trust-based sales communication Talking *with* rather than *at* the customer. A collaborative and two-way form of communication that allows buyers and sellers to develop a better understanding of the need situation and work together to co-create the best response for resolving the customer's needs.

LO 1 | SALES COMMUNICATION AS A COLLABORATIVE PROCESS

 2.1 Develop client relationships

Neither people nor organizations buy products. Rather, they seek out the satisfaction and benefits that certain product features provide. Although traditional selling has been described as "talking *at* the customer," trust-based selling has been referred to as "talking *with* the customer." Trust-based sales communication is a two-way and naturally collaborative interaction that allows buyers and sellers alike to develop a better understanding of the need situation and work together to generate the best response for solving the customer's needs. Although trust-based selling has become the preeminent model for contemporary selling, effectively engaging the buyer in collaborative conversations takes some thought and planning.

Trust-based sales communication is the sharing of meaning between buying and selling parties that results from the interactive process of exchanging information and ideas. It is important to note that the purpose of sales communication is not agreement but rather the maximization of common understanding among participants. With this emphasis on establishing understanding, communication is fundamental throughout each stage of the selling process. Effective communication skills are needed to identify buying needs and to demonstrate to buyers how a salesperson's proposed solution can satisfy those needs better than competitors. The critical capabilities for effective selling include questioning, listening, giving information, nonverbal communication, and written communication skills. Although each of these skills is pervasive in everyday life, they are literally the heart and soul of the interpersonal exchange that characterizes trust-based selling.

Verbal Communication: Questioning

 2.3 Communicate verbally

There are two ways to dominate or control a selling conversation. A salesperson can talk all the time, or can maintain a more subtle level of control by asking well-thought-out questions that guide the discussion and engage the customer. Salespeople should think like doctors—they ask relevant questions to methodically diagnose the situation and problems before presenting solutions. To present a cure to a patient before understanding the problem would be malpractice. In a similar fashion, salespeople must be masters at thinking through what they need to know, planning the questions they need to ask, and then asking those diagnostic questions in a sequential manner that builds understanding of the situation for themselves as well as for the customer. They should know exactly what information they need and which type of questions are best suited for eliciting that information from a prospective buyer.

Purposeful, carefully crafted questions can encourage thoughtful responses from a buyer and provide richly detailed information about the buyer's current situation, needs, and expectations. This additional detail and understanding is often as meaningful for the buyer as it is for the salesperson. That is, proper questioning can facilitate both the buyer's and the seller's understanding of a problem and its possible solutions. For example, questions can encourage meaningful feedback regarding the buyer's attitude and the logical progression through the purchase decision process. Questioning also shows interest in the buyer and their needs and actively involves the buyer in the selling process. Questions can also be used tactically to redirect, regain, or hold the buyer's attention should it begin to wander during the conversation. In a similar fashion, questions can provide a convenient and subtle transition to a different topic of discussion and provide a logical guide promoting sequential thought and decision making.

Questions are categorized by the results they are designed to accomplish. Does the salesperson want to receive a free flow of thoughts and ideas or a simple yes/ no confirmation? Is the salesperson seeking a general description of the overall situation or specific details regarding emergent needs or problematic experiences with current suppliers? To be effective, a salesperson must understand which type of question will best accomplish their desired outcome. In this manner, questions can be typed into two basic categories: (1) the amount of information and level of specificity desired and (2) the strategic purpose or intent.

> Successful salespeople are experts at considering what information they need to know and purposefully planning and asking the questions they need to ask.

LO 2 | TYPES OF QUESTIONS CLASSIFIED BY AMOUNT AND SPECIFICITY OF INFORMATION DESIRED

 2.3 Communicate verbally

Open-End Questions

Open-end questions, also called nondirective questions, are designed to let the customer respond freely. That is, the customer is not limited to one- or two-word answers but is encouraged to disclose personal business information. Open-end questions encourage buyers' thought processes and deliver richer and more expansive information than closed-end questions. Consequently, these questions are typically used to probe for descriptive information that allows the salesperson to better understand the specific needs and expectations of the customer. The secret to successfully using open-end questions lies in the first word used to form the question. Words often used to begin open-end questions include *what*, *how*, *where*, *when*, *tell*, *describe*, and *why*? Examples of open-end questions include:

- What happens when . . .?
- How do you feel . . .?
- Describe the . . .

Closed-End Questions

Closed-end questions are designed to limit the customer's response to one or two words. This type of question is typically used to confirm or clarify information gleaned from previous responses to open-end questions. Although the

open-end questions Questions designed to let the customer respond freely; the customer is not limited to one- or two-word answers but is encouraged to disclose personal or business information.

closed-end questions Questions designed to limit the customer's responses to one or two words.

Technology in Sales

Developing Account and Territory Action Plans with Salesforce.com

Morgan Rabas, a 2016 graduate of Illinois State University, is a Territory Manager for Michelin North America. As a Richmond, Virginia-based manufacturer's representative for Michelin's Truck Tire Division, Morgan is responsible for territory development and support of dealer and end-user accounts across the semi-truck, construction, and heavy equipment tire categories. During a recent conversation, Morgan explained how she uses technology to more effectively manage individual accounts and target her selling activities in a manner that maximizes both sales performance and account relationships. Her use of technology is clearly working, as Morgan has exceeded her sales numbers for each of the previous three quarters and is a candidate being considered for Rookie of the Year.

"With its emphasis on trust-based selling, the Illinois State selling program did a terrific job preparing me to be successful in Michelin's solutions-selling model and customer-oriented selling culture. Those diverse learning experiences provided me with the skills, abilities, and—most importantly—the self-confidence to work with and further develop the accounts in my territory. With a territory comprised of 150 plus accounts—including 75 major key accounts—across multiple business sectors, my challenge was keeping up with and effectively using all the industry and account-level data Michelin provides to its sales representatives."

"After considerable evaluation of leading CRM systems, Michelin selected Salesforce.com to become its enterprise-wide data platform for acquiring and organizing customer data in a manner that enables sales representatives to provide enhanced levels of support to each individual account. Well along in the three-year rollout of the system, I have immediate access to a complete catalogue of communication from and with individual accounts; automatic reminders to follow up on specific activities and engagements; and even coordinate sales team actions with Michelin representatives in other sales districts and territories where my accounts have overlapping operations. Nothing falls through the cracks! The system also provides call reports along with on- demand information about account purchasing patterns and trends. I recently used the purchase information to develop second quarter targeted selling opportunities for individual accounts. This same real-time information was then used to track progress toward achieving those opportunities through the period and to better inform my sales call plans and account communication. In a nutshell, the data inform me who is buying and who is not—it tells me where I need to be and prioritizes my selling time by individual account."

© Jerome Kundrotas/Shutterstock.com

most common form is the yes/no question, closed-end questions come in many forms—provided the response is limited to one or two words. Common closed-end questions include:

dichotomous questions A directive form of questioning; these questions ask the customer to choose from two or more options.

- Do you . . .?
- Are you . . . ?

- How many . . .?
- How often . . .?

Dichotomous/Multiple-Choice Questions

Dichotomous questions and multiple-choice questions are directive forms of questioning. This type of question asks a customer to choose from two or more options and is used in selling to discover customer preferences and move the purchase decision process forward. An example of this form of question would be, "Which do you prefer, the _____ or the _____?"

Types of Questions Classified by Strategic Purpose

PROBING QUESTIONS **Probing questions** are designed to penetrate below generalized or superficial information to elicit more articulate and precise details for use in needs discovery and solution identification. Rather than interrogating a buyer, probing questions are best used in a conversational style: (1) requesting clarification ("Can you share with me an example of that?" "How long has this been a problem?"), (2) encouraging elaboration ("How are you dealing with that situation now?" "What is your experience with _____?"), and (3) verifying information and responses ("That is interesting, could you tell me more?" "So, if I understand correctly, _____. Is that right?").

EVALUATIVE QUESTIONS **Evaluative questions** use open- and closed-end question formats to gain confirmation and to uncover attitudes, opinions, and preferences the prospect holds. These questions are designed to go beyond generalized fact finding and uncover prospects' perceptions and feelings regarding existing and desired circumstances as well as potential solutions. Exemplary evaluative questions include "How do you feel about _____?" "Do you see the merits of _____?" and "What do you think _____?"

TACTICAL QUESTIONS **Tactical questions** are used to shift or redirect the topic of discussion when the discussion gets off course or when a line of questioning proves to be of little interest or value. For example, the salesperson might be exploring the chances of plant expansion only to find that the prospect cannot provide that type of proprietary information at this early stage of the buyer–seller relationship. To avoid either embarrassing the prospect or himself or herself by proceeding on a forbidden or nonproductive line of questioning, the seller uses a tactical question designed to change topics. An example of such a tactical question might be expressed as "Earlier you mentioned that _____. Could you tell me more about how that might affect _____?"

REACTIVE QUESTIONS **Reactive questions** are questions that refer to or directly result from information the other party previously provided. Reactive questions are used to elicit additional information, explore for further detail, and keep the flow of information going. Illustrative reactive questions are "You mentioned that _____. Can you give me an example of what you mean?" and "That is interesting. Can you tell me how it happened?"

These different groupings of question types are not mutually exclusive. As depicted in the guidelines for combining question types in Exhibit 4.1, effective questions integrate elements from different question types. For example, "How do you feel about the current trend of sales in the industry?" is an open-end (classified by format) question and evaluative (classified by purpose) in nature.

Regardless of the types of questions one might combine in a sales dialogue, the natural tendency is to overuse closed-end questions. Monitor the types of questions you ask over the next several hours and see if you share the tendency to use more closed-end than open-end questions. It is not uncommon to find salespeople using an average of ten closed-end questions for every open-end question used in a sales conversation. This overuse of closed-end questions is dangerous in selling. The discovery and exploration of customer needs are fundamental to trust-based selling, and discovery and exploration are best done with open-end questions.

As previously discussed, closed-end questions certainly have their place in selling, but they are best used for clarification and confirmation, not discovery and exploration. An additional issue in overusing closed-end questions is that when they are used in a sequence, the resulting communication takes on the demeanour of interrogation rather than conversation.

probing questions Questions designed to penetrate below generalized or superficial information to elicit more articulate and precise details for use in needs discovery and solution identification.

evaluative questions Questions that use the open- and closed-end question formats to gain confirmation and to uncover attitudes, opinions, and preferences the prospect holds.

tactical questions Questions used to shift or redirect the topic of discussion when the discussion gets off course or when a line of questioning proves to be of little interest or value.

reactive questions Questions that refer to or directly result from information the other party previously provided.

Exhibit 4.1

Guidelines for Combining Types of Questions

Amount and Specificity of Information Desired	Strategic Objective or Purpose of Questioning			
	Explore and Dig for Details	Gain Confirmation and Discover Attitudes/ Opinions	Change Topics or Re-direct Buyer's Attention	Follow Up Previously Elicited Statements
Discussion and Interpretation	*Open-end* questions designed to be *probing in nature*	*Open-end* questions designed to be *evaluative* in nature	*Open-end* questions designed to be *tactical* in nature	*Open-end* questions designed to be *reactive* in nature
Confirmation and Agreement	*Closed-end* questions designed to be *probing* in nature	*Closed-end* questions designed to be *evaluative* in nature	*Closed-end* questions designed to be *tactical* in nature	*Closed-end* questions designed to be *reactive* in nature
Choosing from Alternatives	Dichotomous or multiple-choice questions designed to be probing in nature	Dichotomous or multiple-choice questions designed to be evaluative in nature	Dichotomous or multiple-choice questions designed to be tactical in nature	Dichotomous or multiple-choice questions designed to be reactive in nature

LO 3 | STRATEGIC APPLICATION OF QUESTIONING IN TRUST-BASED SELLING

 2.3 Communicate verbally

Effective questioning skills are indispensable in selling and are used to address critical issues throughout all stages of the selling process. In practice, salespeople combine the different types of questions discussed earlier to accomplish multiple and closely related sales objectives:

- *Generate buyer involvement.* Rather than the salesperson dominating the conversation and interaction, purposeful and planned questions are used to encourage prospective buyers to participate actively in a two-way collaborative discussion.

- *Provoke thinking.* Innovative and effective solutions require cognitive efforts and contributions from each participant. Strategic questions stimulate buyers and salespeople to think thoroughly and pragmatically about and consider all aspects of a given situation.

- *Gather information.* Good questions result from advance planning and should be directed toward gathering the information required to fill in the gap between "What do we need to know?" and "What do we already know?"

- *Clarification and emphasis.* Rather than assuming that the salesperson understands what a buyer has said, questions can be used to clarify meaning further and to emphasize the important points within a buyer–seller exchange further.

- *Show interest.* In response to statements from buyers, salespeople ask related questions and paraphrase what the buyer has said to demonstrate their interest in and understanding of what the buyer is saying.

- *Gain confirmation.* The use of simple and direct questions allows salespeople to check back with the prospective buyer to confirm the buyer's understanding or agreement and gain their commitment to move forward.

- *Advance the sale.* Effective questions are applied in a fashion that guides and moves the selling process forward in a logical progression from initiation through needs development and through needs resolution and follow-up.

With the aim of simultaneously targeting and achieving each of these objectives, several systems have been developed to guide salespeople in properly developing and using effective questions. Two of the more prominent questioning systems are SPIN and ADAPT. Both of these systems use a logical sequencing—a sort of funnelling effect—that begins with broad-based, non-threatening, general questions. Questioning progressively proceeds through more narrowly focused questions designed to clarify the buyer's needs and to propel the selling process logically toward the presentation and demonstration of solution features, advantages, and benefits.

SPIN Questioning System

 2.3 Communicate verbally

The **SPIN** system sequences four types of questions designed to uncover a buyer's current situation and inherent problems, enhance the buyer's understanding of the consequences and implications of those problems, and lead to the proposed solution.[7] SPIN is actually an acronym for the four types of questions making up the multiple question sequence: situation questions, problem questions, implication questions, and need-payoff questions.

- *Situation questions.* This type of question solicits data and facts in the form of general background information and descriptions of the buyer's existing situation. **Situation questions** are used early in the sales call and provide salespeople with leads to develop the buyer's needs and expectations fully. Situation questions might include "Who are your current suppliers?" "Do you typically purchase or lease?" and "Who is involved in purchasing decisions?" Situation questions are essential, but they should be used in moderation as too many general fact-finding questions can bore the buyer. Further, their interrogating nature can result in irritated buyers.

- *Problem questions.* **Problem questions** follow the more general situation questions to probe further for specific difficulties, developing problems, and areas of dissatisfaction that might be positively addressed by the salesperson's proposed sales offering. Some examples of problem questions include "How critical is this component for your production?" "What kinds of problems have you encountered with your current suppliers?" and "What types of reliability problems do you experience with your current system?" Problem questions actively involve the buyer and can assist the person in better understanding their own problems and needs. Nevertheless, inexperienced and unsuccessful salespeople generally do not ask enough problem questions.

- *Implication questions.* **Implication questions** follow and relate to the information flowing from problem questions. Their purpose is to assist the buyer in thinking about the potential consequences of the problem and understand the urgency of resolving the problem in a way that motivates him or her to seek a solution. Typical implication questions might include "How does this affect profitability?" "What impact does the slow response of your current supplier have on the productivity of your operation?" "How would a faster piece of equipment improve productivity and profits?" and "What happens when the supplier is late with a shipment?" Although implication questions are closely linked to success in selling, even experienced salespeople rarely use them effectively.

- *Need-payoff questions.* Based on the implications of a problem, salespeople use

SPIN A questioning system that sequences four types of questions designed to uncover a buyer's current situation and inherent problems, enhance the buyer's understanding of the consequences and implications of those problems, and lead to the proposed solution.

situation questions One of the four types of questions in the SPIN questioning system used early in the sales call that provides salespeople with leads to develop the buyer's needs and expectations fully.

problem questions One of the four types of questions in the SPIN questioning system that follows the more general situation questions to further probe for specific difficulties, developing problems, and areas of dissatisfaction that might be positively addressed by the salesperson's proposed sales offering.

implication questions One of the four types of questions in the SPIN questioning system that follows and is related to the information flowing from problem questions; they are used to assist the buyer in thinking about the potential consequences of the problem and understanding the urgency of resolving the problem in a way that motivates him or her to seek a solution.

FIG. 4.1   FUNNELLING SEQUENCE OF ADAPT TECHNIQUE FOR NEEDS DISCOVERY

Assessment Questions
- Broad-based and general facts describing situation
- Nonthreatening as no interpretation is requested
- Open-end questions for maximum information

Discovery Questions
- Questions probing information gained in assessment
- Seeking to uncover problems or dissatisfaction that could lead to suggested buyer needs
- Open-end questions for maximum information

Activation Questions
- Show the negative impact of a problem discovered in the discovery sequence
- Designed to activate buyer's interest in and desire to solve the problem

Projection Questions
- Projects what life would be like without the problems
- Buyer establishes the value of funding and implementing a solution

Transition Questions
- Confirms buyer's interest in solving problem
- Transitions to presentation of solution

The ADAPT questioning technique logically sequences questions from broad and general inquiries through increasingly detailed questions for effective needs discovery.

need-payoff questions to propose a solution and develop commitment from the buyer. These questions refocus the buyer's attention on solutions rather than problems and get the buyer to think about the positive benefits derived from solving the problems. Examples of need-payoff questions are "Would more frequent deliveries allow you to increase productivity?" "If we could provide you with increased reliability, would you be interested?" "If we could improve the quality of your purchased components, how would that help you?" and "Would you be interested in increasing productivity by 15 percent?" Top salespeople effectively incorporate a higher number of need-payoff questions into sales calls than do less successful salespeople.

need-payoff questions One of the four types of questions in the SPIN questioning system that is based on the implications of a problem; they are used to propose a solution and develop commitment from the buyer.

ADAPT A questioning system that uses a logic-based funnelling sequence of questions, beginning with broad and generalized inquiries designed to identify and assess the buyer's situation

LO 4 | ADAPT QUESTIONING SYSTEM

 CPSA   **2.3 Communicate verbally**

As Figure 4.1 illustrates, the **ADAPT** questioning system uses a logic-based funnelling sequence of questions, beginning with broad and generalized inquiries designed to identify and assess the buyer's situation. Based on information gained in this first phase, further questions are generated to probe and discover more details regarding the needs and expectations of the buyer. In turn, the resulting information is incorporated in further collaborative discussion in a way that activates the buyer's motivation to implement a solution and further establishes the buyer's perceived value of a possible solution. The last phase of ADAPT questioning transitions to the buyer's commitment to learning about the proposed solution and grants the salesperson permission to move forward into the presentation and demonstration

Exhibit 4.2

Assessment Questions

These questions are designed to elicit factual information about the customer's current situation. These questions do not seek conclusions; rather, they seek information that describes the customer and their business environment. The information sought should augment or confirm precall research.

Examples:

1. Question—"What types of operating arrangements do you have with your suppliers?"

   Answer—We use a just-in-time (JIT) system with our main suppliers.

2. Question—"Who is involved in the purchase decision-making process?"

   Answer—I make the decisions regarding supplies . . . .

   Assessment questions are generally open end; however, closed-end questions are used when seeking confirmation or basic descriptive information. For example, "So, you currently work with 10 different suppliers?" or "How many years have you been in business?" Assessment questions are necessary for drawing out information early in the sales cycle.

of the sales offering. ADAPT is an acronym for the five stages of strategic questioning and represents what the salesperson should be doing at each stage: assessment questions, discovery questions, activation questions, projection questions, and transition questions.[8]

- *Assessment questions.* This initial phase of questioning is designed to be nonthreatening and to spark conversation that elicits factual information about the customer's current situation that can provide a basis for further exploration and probing. As illustrated in Exhibit 4.2, **assessment questions** do not seek conclusions—rather, at a macro or 40,000-foot level of focus, these questions should address the buyer's company and operation, goals and objectives, market trends and customers, current suppliers, and even the buyer as an individual. The information sought should augment or confirm precall research. Examples would include "What is the current level of your production?" "How long has the current equipment been in place?" "How many suppliers are currently being used?" "What are the growth objectives of the company?" and "What individuals have input into purchase decisions?"

- *Discovery questions.* As portrayed in Exhibit 4.3, these questions follow up on the responses gained from the preceding assessment questions. At a more micro and ground-level focus, **discovery questions** should drill down and probe for further details needed to fully develop, clarify, and understand the nature of the buyer's problems. Facts

as well as the buyer's interpretations, perceptions, feelings, and opinions are sought about the buyer's needs, wants, dissatisfactions, and expectations relevant to product, delivery requirements, budget and financing issues, and desired service levels. The goal is to discover needs and dissatisfactions that the salesperson's sales offering can resolve. Examples of discovery questions might include "How often do these equipment failures occur?" "How well are your current suppliers performing?" "What disadvantages do you see in the current process?" "How satisfied are you with the quality of components you are currently purchasing?" and "How difficult are these for your operators to use?"

- *Activation questions.* The implied or suggested needs gained from discovery questions are not usually sufficient to gain the sale. Often, a buyer will believe that a particular problem does not cause any significant negative consequences; hence, the motivation to solve the problem will carry a low priority. Successful salespeople

assessment questions One of the five stages of questions in the ADAPT questioning system that do not seek conclusions but rather should address the buyer's company and operations, goals and objectives, market trends and customers, current suppliers, and even the buyer as an individual.

discovery questions One of the five stages of questions in the ADAPT questioning system that follows up on the assessment questions; they should drill down and probe for further details needed to develop, clarify, and understand the nature of the buyer's problems fully.

Exhibit 4.3

Discovery Questions

Discovery questions are used to uncover problems or dissatisfactions the customer is experiencing that the salesperson's product or company may be able to solve. Basically, these questions are used to distill or boil down the information gained from the preceding assessment questions and from precall research into suggested needs.

Examples:

1. Question—"I understand you prefer a JIT relationship with your suppliers—how have they been performing?"

   Answer—Pretty well . . . an occasional late delivery . . . but pretty well.

2. Question—"How do you feel about your current supplier occasionally being late with deliveries?"

   Answer—It is a real problem . . . for instance . . . .

The *suggested* needs gained from discovery questions are used as a foundation for the rest of the sales call. Yet a *suggested* need is usually not sufficient to close the sale. Often, a customer will believe that a particular problem does not cause any significant negative consequences. If this is the case, finding a solution to the problem will be a very low priority. The professional salesperson must then help the customer to reevaluate the impact of the *suggested* need by asking activation questions.

activation questions One of the five stages of questions in the ADAPT questioning system used to "activate" the customer's interest in solving discovered problems by helping him or her gain insight into the true ramifications of the problem and to realize that what may initially seem to be of little consequence is, in fact, of significant consequence.

help the customer realistically evaluate the full impact of the implied need through the use of **activation questions**. As detailed in Exhibit 4.4, the objective is to "activate" the customer's interest in solving discovered problems by helping him or her gain insight into the true ramifications of the problem and to realize that what may initially seem to be of little consequence is, in fact, of significant consequence. Examples include "What effects do these equipment breakdowns have on your business operations?" "To what extent are these increases in overtime expenses affecting profitability?" "How will the supplier's inability to deliver on time affect your planned expansion?" and "When

Exhibit 4.4

Activation Questions

Activation questions are used to show the impact of a problem, uncovered through discovery questions, on the customer's entire operation. The objective is to activate the customer's interest in solving the problem by helping him or her to gain insight into the true ramifications of the problem and realize that what may seem to be of little consequence is, in fact, of significant consequence.

Examples:

1. Question—"What effect does your supplier's late delivery have on your operation?"

   Answer—It slows production . . . . Operating costs go up.

2. Question—"If production drops off, how are your operating costs affected, and how does that affect your customers?"

   Answer—Customer orders are delayed . . . .

Potential to lose customers. Activation questions show the negative impact of a problem so that finding a solution to that problem is desirable. Now the salesperson can help the customer to discover the positive impact of solving the problems by using projection questions.

Exhibit 4.5

Projection Questions

Projection questions help the customer to project what life would be like without the problems or dissatisfactions uncovered through activation questions. This helps the customer to see value in finding solutions to the problems developed earlier in the sales call.

Examples:

1. Question—"If a supplier was never late with a delivery, what effects would that have on your JIT operating structure?"

   Answer—It would run more smoothly and at a lower cost.

2. Question—"If a supplier helped you meet the expectations of your customers, what impact would that have on your business?"

   Answer—Increased customer satisfaction would mean more business.

These questions are used to let the customer tell the salesperson the benefits of solving the problem. By doing so, the customer is reinforcing in their mind the importance of solving the problem and reducing the number of objections that might be raised.

components fail in the field, how does that failure influence customer satisfaction and repurchase?"

- *Projection questions.* As a natural extension of the activation questions, **projection questions** encourage and facilitate the buyer in "projecting" what it would be like without the problems that have been previously "discovered" and "activated." The use of good projection questions accomplishes several positive outcomes. First, the focus is switched from problems and their associated consequences to the upside—the benefits to be derived from solving the problems. What were initially perceived as costs and expenses are now logically structured as benefits to the buyer and their organization—the payoff for taking action and investing in a solution. Second—and equally important—the benefit payoff allows the buyer to establish the realistic value of implementing a solution. In this manner, the benefit payoff is perceived as a positive value received and serves as the foundation for demonstrating what the solution is worth—what the buyer would be willing to pay. As illustrated in Exhibit 4.5, projection questions encourage the buyer to think about how and why they should go about resolving a problem. In essence, projection questions assist the buyer by establishing the worth of the proposed solution. The customer, rather than the salesperson, establishes the benefits of solving the problem. This reinforces the importance of solving the problem and reduces the number of objections that might be

raised. Examples of projection questions include "If a supplier was never late with a delivery, what effects would that have on your overall operation?" "What would be the impact on profitability if you did not have problems with limited plant capacity and the resulting overtime expenses?" "How would a system that your operators found easier to use affect your business operations?" and "If component failures were minimized, what impact would the resulting improvement in customer satisfaction have on financial performance?"

- *Transition questions.* **Transition questions** are used to smooth the transition from needs discovery into the presentation and demonstration of the proposed solution's features, advantages, and benefits. As exemplified in Exhibit 4.6, transition questions are typically closed-end and evaluative in format. These questions confirm the buyer's desire to seek a solution and give consent for the salesperson to move forward with the selling process. Examples include "So, having suppliers that are consistently on time is important to you—if I could show you how

projection questions One of the five stages of questions in the ADAPT questioning system used to encourage and help the buyer project what it would be like without the problems that have been previously "discovered" and "activated".

transition questions One of the five stages of questions in the ADAPT questioning system used to smooth the transition from needs discovery into the presentation and demonstration of the proposed solution's features and benefits.

Exhibit 4.6

Transition Questions

Transition questions are simple closed-end questions that confirm the customer's desire to solve the problem(s) uncovered through the previous questions.

Examples:

1. Question—"So, having a supplier who is never late with deliveries is important to you?"

   Answer—Yes, it is.

2. Question—"If I can show you how our company ensures on-time delivery, would you be interested in exploring how it could work for your organization?"

   Answer—Yes, if I am convinced your company can guarantee on-time delivery.

The primary function of these questions is to make the transition from need confirmation into the sales presentation. In addition, these questions can lead to a customer commitment, provided the salesperson adequately presents how their company can solve the customer's problems.

Every Business Sells

Mark Rogers is a partner at Rogers Rogers Moyse, a personal injury firm that provides legal services. At his organization, each lawyer is responsible for their own individual practice (there are four partners and six associates). Mark's practice is long-term disability/injury claims and he carries anywhere from 125–200 clients in Newfoundland and Labrador at any given time. He's been with Rogers Rogers Moyse for 16 years, and has been a practising lawyer for 17.

As a salesperson, how do you provide value to your customers?

Value is provided in a number of ways, primary of which is high-quality service and expertise. We are a results-driven business. Good results for my clients invariably leads to referrals and new clients.

As a salesperson, how do you provide value to your organization?

Performance. Getting claims to closure, which means settlement and income for the firm. Good performance leads to future clients and future billings.

What is your greatest challenge you face oday as a salesperson?

High competition in the industry.

How do you try to overcome this challenge?

Setting myself apart from the competition by being the top in my field and providing a high level of service to all my clients. In addition, not sitting on files and achieving timely resolutions for clients.

What advice do you have for someone starting out in sales?

Good communication with clients is key. Always be the one pushing forward with your claims. Don't procrastinate or delay: be aggressive with files but be reasonable and know your case's limitations. Know what the claim is worth and achieve it.

Every Business Sells

Mark Wilkins is a general manager at BMW St. John's. He sells new and used vehicles, aftersales parts, and service and maintenance. While responsible for the greater St. John's area, he services coast to coast of Newfoundland and Canada depending on the transaction. He's worked in sales for 15 years, 10 of them at BMW St. John's.

As a salesperson, how do you provide value to your customers?

It's a simple formula in my opinion. Listen, identify your clients' needs, and work with them to find a solution that best fits them. Act with integrity at all times and execute on all commitments and promises made. This is what establishes strong relationships and generates long-term sustainability.

As a salesperson, how do you provide value to your organization?

Run it like you own it.

What is your greatest challenge you face today as a salesperson?

As a salesperson, one of the greatest challenges would have to be keeping up with the market and our industry as a whole. The vehicles we sell and the way we service them is changing overnight. Not to mention, our clients and the way they conduct business has also changed. Being a salesperson today requires you to be technologically savvy and grammatically correct as most transactions live on an e-mail or text message. Understanding how to sell in an age that demands less face time is the biggest challenge.

How do you try to overcome this challenge?

Focus on what I can control. Providing a client experience far greater than the competition. Being innovative and staying ahead of the curve. Not being afraid to step out of line and be a leader.

What advice do you have for someone starting out in sales?

It's not always about the product or service you sell. Sell yourself and what you have to offer. Sales is about building relationships; people do business with people they like. If you have the drive to be successful and keen ability to build relationships the rest will fall into place. And if you wake up on the wrong side of the bed—stay home!

---

our company ensures on-time delivery, would you be interested?" "It seems that increasing capacity is a key to reducing overtime and increasing profitability—would you be interested in a way to increase capacity by 20 percent through a simple addition to your production process?" and "Would you be interested in a system that is easier for your operators to use?"

Verbal Communication: Listening

 2.2 Practice active listening

Listening is the other half of effective questioning. Asking the customer for information is of little value if the salesperson does not listen. Effective listening is rated among the most critical skills for successful selling. Yet most of us share the common problem of being a lot better at sending messages than receiving them. Considerable research identifies effective listening as the number-one weakness of salespeople.[9]

Poor listening skills have been identified as one of the primary causes of salesperson failure.[10] To get the information needed to best serve, identify, and respond to needs, and nurture a collaborative buyer–seller relationship, salespeople must be able to listen to and understand what was said *and* what was meant. Nevertheless, situations similar to the one depicted in

> Effective listening requires more than just hearing what is being said.

Erin Sutton is an account manager for a large, Vancouver-based manufacturer of printing equipment and supplies. Erin feels that her 12 years of experience in the printing industry provide her with a level of expertise and knowledge much greater than most prospective buyers. This, combined with her unbridled impatience, often results in Erin interrupting buyers' statements, finishing their thoughts for them, and assuming she understands the buyers' needs better than the buyer does. Rather than allowing the buyer to fully describe what is going on and the nature of the buying organization's problems and needs, Erin often seems to be telling the buyer what their organization should be purchasing and using—solutions that have a closer correspondence with products Erin needs to sell than with the customer's actual needs. Erin continues to sell products; however, her customer retention level is below average and her sales revenues have peaked out. Erin recognizes something is wrong and is seeking to adopt a new and more effective selling process. She has recently completed a trust-based selling program and is contemplating changing the way she sells in order to enhance her selling performance. What should Erin do?

(a) Continue selling based on her experience and superior knowledge of what prospects need.

(b) Use the selling process she is comfortable with and simply call on more prospects to increase her sales performance.

(c) Learn to use effective questions to engage prospects; actively listen to gain understanding of a prospect's actual needs; develop unique solutions based on a prospect's specific needs.

An Ethical Dilemma are all too common. As Figure 4.2 illustrates, effective listening can be broken down into six primary facets:

1. *Pay attention*—Listen to understand, not to reply. Resist the urge to interrupt, and receive the full message the buyer is communicating.

2. *Monitor nonverbals*—Make effective eye contact and check to see if the buyer's body language and speech patterns match what is being said.

3. *Paraphrase and repeat*—Confirm your correct understanding of what the buyer is saying by paraphrasing and repeating what you have heard.

4. *Make no assumptions*—Ask questions to clarify the meaning of what the buyer is communicating.

5. *Encourage the buyer to talk*—Encourage the flow of information by giving positive feedback and help the buyer stay on track by asking purposeful, related questions.

6. *Visualize*—Maximize your attention and comprehension by thinking about and visualizing what the buyer is saying.

The practised listening skills of high-performance salespeople enable them to pick up, sort out, and interpret a greater number of buyers' verbal and nonverbal messages than lower-performing salespeople can. In addition to gaining information and understanding critical to the relational selling process, a salesperson's good listening behaviours provide the added benefits of positively influencing the formation and continuation of buyer–seller relationships. A salesperson's effective use and demonstration of good listening skills is positively associated with the customer's trust in the salesperson and the anticipation of having future interactions with the salesperson.[11] Clearly, effective listening is a critical component in trust-based, relational selling, and success requires continuous practice and improvement of our listening skills.

FIG. 4.2   SIX FACETS OF EFFECTIVE LISTENING

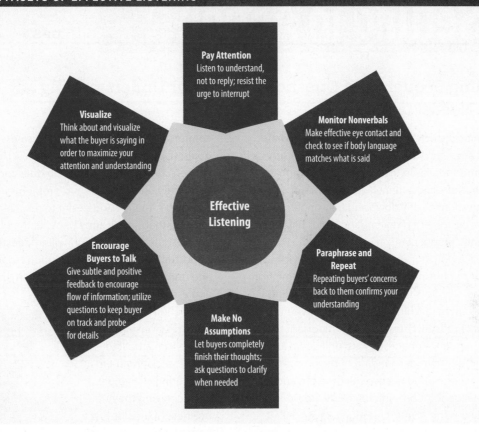

The six facets of effective listening enable salespeople to better pick up, sort out, and interpret buyers' verbal and nonverbal messages

Using Different Types of Listening

Communications research identifies two primary categories of listening: *social* and *serious*.[12] **Social listening** is an informal mode of listening that can be associated with day-to-day conversation and entertainment. Social listening is characterized by low levels of cognitive activity and concentration and is typically used in conversation with a friend or a store clerk or listening to music, a concert, a television program, or even a play. The received messages are taken at face value and do not require a high degree of concentration or thinking to sort through, interpret, and understand. However, **serious listening** is associated with events or topics in which it is important to sort through, interpret, understand, and respond to received messages. The serious form of listening is often referred to as *active listening*, as it requires high levels of concentration and cognition about the messages being received. *Concentration* is required to break through the distractions and other interference to facilitate receiving and remembering specific messages. *Cognition* is used to sort through and select the meaningful relevant messages and interpret them for meaning, information, and response.

LO 5 | ACTIVE LISTENING

CPSA   2.2 Practice active listening

In a selling context, **active listening** is defined as "the cognitive process of actively sensing, interpreting, evaluating, and responding to the verbal and nonverbal messages of present or potential customers."[13] This definition is very useful to those wanting to master active listening skills. First, it underscores the importance of receiving

social listening An informal mode of listening that can be associated with day-to-day conversation and entertainment.

serious listening A form of listening that is associated with events or topics in which it is important to sort through, interpret, understand, and respond to received messages

active listening The cognitive process of actively sensing, interpreting, evaluating, and responding to the verbal and nonverbal messages of present or potential customers.

Funnelling Sequence of Questions Is Key for Understanding Buyer's Needs

Steve O'Connor, district sales representative for Edward Don & Company—the leading distributor of food-service equipment and supplies in the United States, emphasizes the importance of using a funnelling sequence of open-end questions to drill down and fully understand a prospective customer's problems and needs before starting to pitch products.

"At Edward Don, our annual sales plan calls for 20 percent of our business during the year to come from new accounts. Needless to say, strategic prospecting is very important in reaching that objective. When meeting with a prospect, it is also very important to use a funnelling sequence of questions to drill down and develop an in-depth understanding of the prospect's situation, challenges, and needs, which we can address with added-value solutions unique to Edward Don. I consistently use the ADAPT Question Sequence I learned to use as a student in Illinois State University's professional selling classes. Using this sequence of questions allows me to engage the prospect in a

comfortable discussion of their business situation, goals, strategic plans, and challenges. This collaborative conversation leads to follow-up questions that begin to identify unmet needs and problems and activate the prospect's interest and desire to resolve the problems in a way that significantly benefits their business. The natural outcome of the funnelling questions is the opportunity to present my solutions to their problems and unmet needs, close the sale on an initial order, and establish a solid foundation for a buyer–seller relationship where I am a trusted adviser assisting them in meeting challenges and achieving their business goals. It is just a natural way to work with customers."

© Olivier Le Moal/Shutterstock.com

---

and interpreting both verbal and nonverbal cues and messages to better determine the full and correct meaning of the message. Second, it incorporates a well-accepted model of listening. As illustrated in Figure 4.3,[14] the **SIER** model depicts active listening as a hierarchical, four-step sequence of sensing, interpreting, evaluating, and responding.[15] Effective active listening requires each of these four hierarchical process activities to be carried out successfully and in proper succession.

- *Sensing.* Listening is much more than simply hearing. Nevertheless, the first activities in active listening are sensing (i.e., hearing and seeing) and receiving (i.e., paying attention to) the verbal and nonverbal components of the message being sent. Sensing does not occur without practice and should not be taken for granted. In fact,

research indicates that most of us listen at only 25 percent of our capacity. Think about yourself. How often have you had to ask someone to repeat what they said or perhaps assumed you knew what the sender was going to say before they could say it? Increased concentration and attention can improve sensing effectiveness. Taking notes, making eye contact with the sender, and not interrupting can improve sensing skills. Let the sender finish and provide the full content of the message. This not only improves the concentration of the receiver but also encourages the sender to provide more information and detail.

- *Interpreting.* After the message is received, it must be correctly interpreted. Interpreting addresses the question of "What meaning does the sender intend?" Both content and context are important. That is, in addition to the semantic meaning of the words and symbols, we must consider the experiences, knowledge, and attitudes of the sender

SIER A model that depicts active listening as a hierarchical, four-step sequence of sensing, interpreting, evaluating, and responding.

FIG. 4.3 SIER HIERARCHY OF ACTIVE LISTENING

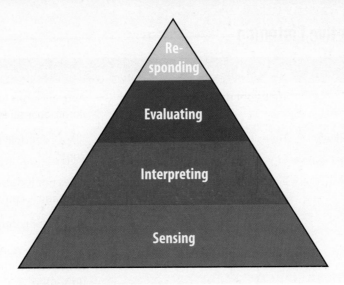

Active listening is a cognitive process of actively sensing, interpreting, evaluating, and responding to verbal and nonverbal messages from buyers and prospects.

to understand fully what was meant. Hold back the temptation to evaluate the message until the sender is through speaking. Note the nonverbal and verbal cues along with possible consistencies and inconsistencies between them. Incorporate knowledge of the sender's background and previous relevant statements and positions into the message interpretation.

- *Evaluating.* Active listening requires the receiver to decide whether they agree with the sender's message. The results from the interpretation stage are evaluated to sort fact from opinion and emotion. Too often, receivers complete this activity before receiving the full message, and on hearing something with which they disagree, the sender is effectively tuned out. As a result, communication is stifled. Evaluating can be improved through concentration and thoughtful consideration of the full message. Summarizing the key points as if they were going to be reported to others can further enhance evaluation skills. Searching for areas of interest rather than prejudging the message can also facilitate the evaluation process.

- *Responding.* Responding is both an expectation and a requirement for active listening to be effective. Collaborative, two-way communication requires that the listener respond to the sender. Responses provide feedback to the other party,

emphasize understanding, encourage further elaboration, and can serve as a beginning point for the receiver to transition into the role of sender for the next message sent. Responses can take many forms. Nonverbal cues, such as nodding and smiling, can indicate that the sender's message was received. Responses in the form of restating and paraphrasing the sender's message can provide strong signals of interest and understanding. Asking questions can elicit additional details and clarification.

The SIER model provides a useful framework for evaluating communication accuracy and pinpointing the sources of problems. Similarly, it can be effectively used for planning activities and behaviours designed to improve communication effectiveness. As the SIER model depicts, active listening is a hierarchical and sequential process. A person must sense the message before it can be interpreted. In turn, the message must be interpreted before it can be evaluated. Finally, it must be effectively evaluated before a proper response can be generated. When diagnosing a listening breakdown, look for the lowest level in the hierarchy where the breakdown could have originated and take proper action to remedy the problem. Exhibit 4.7[16] describes ten specific keys to effective listening that can be used in conjunction with the SIER model to pinpoint and improve listening problems.

Exhibit 4.7

Ten Keys to Effective Listening

The Key Practice	The Weak Listener	The Strong Listener
1. Find areas of interest	Tunes out dry subjects	Actively looks for opportunities of common interest
2. Judge content, not delivery	Tunes out if the delivery is poor	Skips over delivery errors and focuses on content
3. Hold your fire until full consideration	Evaluates and enters argument before completion of message	Does not judge or evaluate until message is complete
4. Listen for ideas	Listens for facts	Listens for central themes
5. Be flexible	Takes intensive and detailed notes	Takes fewer notes and limits the theme to the central theme and key ideas presented
6. Work at listening	Shows no energy output; attention is faked	Works hard at attending the message and exhibits active body state
7. Resist distractions	Is distracted easily	Resists distractions and knows how to concentrate
8. Exercise your mind	Resists difficult expository material in favour of light recreational materials	Uses complex and heavy material as exercise for the mind
9. Keep an open mind	Reacts to emotional words	Interprets colour words but does not get hung up on them
10. Capitalize on the fact that thought is faster than speech	Tends to daydream with slow speakers	Challenges, anticipates, mentally summarizes, weighs evidence, and listens between the lines

Verbal Communication: Giving Information

 2.3 Communicate verbally

Verbal information refers to statements of fact, opinion, and attitude that are encoded in the form of words, pictures, and numbers in such a way that they convey meaning to a receiver. However, many words and symbols mean different things to different people. Different industries, different cultures, and different types of training or work experience can result in the same word or phrase having multiple interpretations. For instance, to a design or production engineer, the word *quality* might mean "manufactured within design tolerance." However, to a customer it might be translated as "meeting or exceeding expectations." To maximize clarity and minimize misunderstandings, understand and use the vocabulary and terminology that corresponds with the perspective of the customer.

LO 6 | UNDERSTANDING THE SUPERIORITY OF PICTURES OVER WORDS

 2.3 Communicate verbally

Studies in cognitive psychology have found that pictures tend to be more memorable than their verbal counterparts.[17] The fact that pictures enhance understanding and are more easily recalled than abstract words and symbols has several implications for effective selling.

Sales aids such as samples, brochures, and charts reinforce the verbal message and enhance the receiver's understanding and recall.

- The verbal message should be constructed in a manner that generates a mental picture in the receiver's mind. For example, the phrase "Tropicana juices are bursting with flavour" is more visual than the more abstract version "Tropicana juices have more flavour." This can also be accomplished by providing a short and illustrative analogy or illustrative story to emphasize a key point and bring it alive in the buyer's mind.

- Rather than using abstract words that convey only a broad general understanding, use words and phrases that convey concrete and detailed meaning. Concrete expressions provide the receiver with greater information and are less likely to be misunderstood than their abstract counterparts. For example, "This Web transfer system will increase weekly production by 2,100 units" provides more detail than "This Web transfer system will increase production by 10 percent." Similarly, "This conveyor is faster than your existing system" does not deliver the same impact as "This conveyor system will move your product from production to shipping at 15 metres per second as compared with your current system's 6 metres per second."

- Integrate relevant visual sales aids into verbal communication. Sales support materials that explain and reinforce the verbal message will aid the receiver's understanding and enhance recall of the message. As an additional benefit, such sales aids as samples, brochures, graphs, and comparative charts can be left with the buyer to continue selling until the salesperson's next call on the buyer.

Impact of Grammar and Logical Sequencing

 2.3 Communicate verbally

Grammar and logical sequencing are also important in the process of giving information to others. The use of proper grammar is essential in business and social communication. In its absence, the receiver of the message tends to exhibit three closely related behaviours. First, the meaning and credibility of the message are significantly downgraded. Second, the receiver begins to focus on the sender rather than the message, which materially reduces the probability of effective communication. Last, the receiver dismisses the sender and the sender's organization as being unqualified to perform the role of an effective supplier and partner. The importance of proper grammar should not be overlooked.

Similarly, whether one is engaged in simply explaining details or making a formal proposal, logical sequencing of the material is critical. The facts and details must be organized and connected in a logical order. This is essential to clarity and assists the receiver in following the facts. A discussion or presentation that jumps around runs the risk of being inefficient and ineffective. At best, the receiver will have to ask many clarification questions. At worst, the receiver will dismiss the salesperson as incompetent and close off the sales negotiation. Advance planning and preparation can improve organization. Outline what needs to be covered and organize it into a logical flow. The outline becomes the agenda to be covered and can serve as an aid for staying on track.

LO 7 | NONVERBAL COMMUNICATION

 2.3 Communicate verbally

Nonverbal behaviours have been recognized as an important dimension of communication since medieval times. As early as 1605, Francis Bacon focused on the messages conveyed by *manual language*. Verbal communication deals with the semantic meaning of the message itself, whereas the nonverbal dimension consists of the more abstract message conveyed by how the message is delivered. **Nonverbal communication**

nonverbal communication The conscious and unconscious reactions, movements, and utterances that people use in addition to the words and symbols associated with language.

consists of the conscious and unconscious reactions, movements, and utterances that people use in addition to the words and symbols associated with language. This dimension of communication includes eye movements and facial expressions; placement and movements of hands, arms, head, and legs as well as body orientation; the amount of space maintained between individuals; and variations in vocal characteristics. Collectively, the various forms of nonverbal communication carry subtle and explicit meanings and feelings along with the linguistic message and are frequently more informative than the verbal content of a message.[18]

Research indicates that highly successful salespeople are capable of picking out and comprehending a higher number of behavioural cues from buyers than less successful salespeople are able to sense and interpret. In addition, evidence shows that 50 percent or more of the meaning conveyed within the communication process stems from nonverbal behaviour.[19] As the nonverbal components of a message carry as much or more meaning than the language portions, it is critical for salespeople to sense effectively, interpret accurately, and evaluate fully the nonverbal elements of a message as well as the verbal components. In addition to sensing verbal messages, learn to sense between the words for the thoughts and feelings not being conveyed verbally.

Facial Expressions

Possibly reflecting its central point of focus in interpersonal communication, the various elements of the face play a key role in giving off nonverbal messages. Frowning, pursed lips, and squinted eyes are common in moments of uncertainty, disagreement, and even outright skepticism. Suspicion and anger are typically accompanied by tightness along the jaw line. Smiles are indicative of agreement and interest, whereas biting of the lip can signal uncertainty. Raised eyebrows can signify surprise and are often found in moments of consideration and evaluation.

Eye Movements

In North America and Western Europe, avoiding eye contact results in a negative message and is often associated with deceit and dishonesty. However, a sender's increased eye contact infers honesty and self-confidence. Increased eye contact by the receiver of the message signals increasing levels of interest and concentration. However, when eye contact becomes a stare and continues unbroken, either by glances away or blinking, it is typically interpreted as a threat or inference of power. A blank

Fifty percent or more of the meaning conveyed in interpersonal communication comes through nonverbal behaviours. What nonverbal messages are being conveyed here?

stare or eye contact directed away from the conversation can show disinterest and boredom. Repeated glancing at a watch or possibly an exit door often indicate that the conversation is about to end.

Placement and Movements of Hands, Arms, Head, and Legs

Smooth and gradual movements denote calm and confidence, whereas jerky and hurried movements are associated with nervousness and stress. Uncrossed arms and legs signal openness, confidence, and cooperation. However, crossed arms and legs psychologically close out the other party and express disagreement and defensiveness. Increased movement of the head and limbs hints at increasing tension, as does the tight clasping of hands or fists. The placement of a hand on the chin or a tilted head suggests increased levels of evaluation, whereas nodding of the head expresses agreement. Growing impatience is associated with drumming of the fingers or tapping of a foot. Fingering the hair and rubbing the back of the neck signify increasing nervousness and apprehension.

Body Posture and Orientation

Fidgeting and shifting from side to side is generally considered to be a negative message associated with nervousness and apprehension. Leaning forward or sitting forward on the edge of a chair is a general sign of increasing interest and a positive disposition in regard to what is being discussed. Similarly, leaning away can indicate disinterest, boredom, or even distrust. Leaning back with both hands placed behind the head signifies

FIG. 4.4 PERSONAL SPACE AND INTERPERSONAL COMMUNICATION

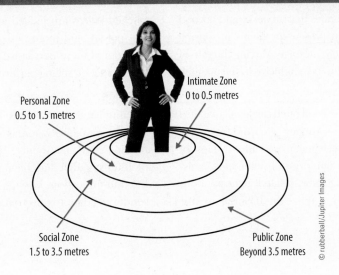

Personal Zone
0.5 to 1.5 metres

Intimate Zone
0 to 0.5 metres

Social Zone
1.5 to 3.5 metres

Public Zone
Beyond 3.5 metres

© rubberball/Jupiter Images

Individuals use four preferred spatial zones for interaction in different social and business situations.

a perceived sense of smugness and superiority. A rigid erect posture can convey inflexibility or even defensiveness, whereas sloppy posture suggests disinterest in the topic. Similar to sitting backward in a chair, sitting on the edge of the table or the arm of a chair is an expression of power and superiority.

Proxemics

Proxemics refers to the personal distance that individuals prefer to keep between themselves and other individuals and is an important element of nonverbal communication. The distance that a person places between himself or herself and others implies a meaningful message and affects the outcome of the selling process. If a salesperson pushes too close to a prospect who requires more distance, the prospect may perceive the salesperson to be manipulative, intimidating, and possibly threatening. However, salespeople who put too much distance between themselves and the customer risk being perceived as rigidly formal, aloof, or even apprehensive.

Proxemics differs across cultures and regions of the world. For example, in North Africa and Latin America business is conducted at a much closer distance than in North America. As depicted in Figure 4.4, North Americans generally recognize four distinct proxemic zones. The *intimate zone* is reserved for intimate relationships with immediate family and loved ones. The *personal zone* is for personal relationships with close friends and associates. The *social zone* is for business client relationships and is the zone in which most business is conducted. The

public zone is for the general public and group settings such as classrooms and presentations.

It is critical that salespeople understand proxemics and monitor the progression of their buyer–seller relationships so as to position themselves with different customers properly. Typically, salespeople begin working with a prospect at the far end of the social zone. As the salesperson–buyer relationship develops, the salesperson is in a position to move closer without violating the customer's space and causing him or her to become defensive.

Variations in Vocal Characteristics

Nonverbal vocal characteristics, such as speaking rates, pause duration, pitch or frequency, and intensity, have been linked to communication effectiveness and selling performance. These voice characteristics convey direct as well as subtle and implied meanings and feelings that can complement or accent the corresponding verbal message.

SPEAKING RATES AND PAUSE DURATION Within normal speaking rates, faster speakers are generally evaluated more favourably than slower speakers. Contrary to the often-cited fast-talking salesperson being perceived as high pressure, faster rates of speech and shorter pause duration are actually associated with higher levels of

> **proxemics** The personal distance that individuals prefer to keep between themselves and other individuals; an important element of nonverbal communication.

intelligence, credibility, and knowledge. Slower speakers are perceived as being less competent as well as less benevolent. However, speech rates that are jerky and beyond normal rates of speech can present problems in sensing and interpreting the complete message. Varying the rate of speech has also been found to be conducive to maintaining interest.

PITCH OR FREQUENCY Vocal pitch carries a great deal of information to the receiver. Varying pitch and frequency during the course of a message encourages attentiveness of the listener and accents certain forms of statements. A rising pitch during the message is associated with questions and can often be perceived as reflecting uncertainty. Just the opposite, a falling pitch is associated with declarative statements and completion of the message. Overall, high-pitched voices are judged as less truthful, less emphatic, less potent, and more nervous. Lower-pitched voices are considered more persuasive and truthful and have a positive impact on selling performance.

INTENSITY AND LOUDNESS Dominance, superiority, intensity, and aggression are commonly associated with loud voices, whereas soft voices characterize submission and uncertainty. However, it is the variability of intensity that has been found to be most effective in communication. Varying levels of loudness allow the sender to adapt to different situations and environments.

Exhibit 4.8

Common Nonverbal Clusters

Cluster Name	Cluster Meaning	Body Posture and Orientation	Movement of Hands, Arms, and Legs	Eyes and Facial Expressions
Openness	Openness, flexibility, and sincerity	• Moving closer • Leaning forward	• Open hands • Removing coat • Unbuttoning collar • Uncrossing arms and legs	• Slight smile • Good eye contact
Defensiveness	Defensiveness, skepticism, and apprehension	• Rigid body	• Crossed arms and legs • Clenched fists	• Minimal eye contact • Sideways glances • Pursed lips
Evaluation	Evaluation and consideration of message	• Leaning forward	• Hand on cheek • Stroking of chin • Chin in palm of hand	• Tilted head • Glasses dropping to tip of nose
Deception	Dishonesty and secretiveness	• Patterns of rocking	• Fidgeting with objects • Increasing leg movements	• Increased eye movement • Frequent gazes elsewhere • Forced smile
Readiness	Dedication or commitment	• Sitting forward	• Hands on hips • Legs uncrossed • Feet flat on floor	• Increased eye contact
Boredom	Lack of interest and impatience	• Leaning head in palm of hands • Slouching	• Drumming fingers • Swinging a foot • Brushing and picking at items • Tapping feet	• Poor eye contact • Glances at watch • Blank stares

Variation also increases the receiver's attention and can provide additional information inputs by accenting key points of a message.

Using Nonverbal Clusters

Nonverbal clusters are groups of related expressions, gestures, and movements. Similar to a one-word expression, a single isolated gesture or movement should not be taken as a reliable indication of the true intent or meaning of a message. Sensing and interpreting groups or clusters of nonverbal cues provides a more reliable indicator of the message and intent. When the individual behaviours and gestures begin to fit together, they form a common and unified message that the salesperson should consider. Common nonverbal clusters applicable to selling communication are described in Exhibit 4.8.[20]

Just as salespeople can interpret nonverbal messages to better understand communication with prospects and buyers, those same prospects and buyers can also sense and interpret the nonverbal messages the salesperson is sending. Consequently, it is important that salespeople monitor the nonverbal cues they are sending to ensure consistency with and reinforcement of the intended message.

nonverbal clusters Groups of related nonverbal expressions, gestures, and movements that can be interpreted to better understand the true message being communicated.

STUDY TOOLS

At the back of the textbook, use tear-out cards to review key chapter information. Visit cengage.ca to purchase digital tools to help you succeed.

CENGAGE | MINDTAP

Personal Computer

☐ Gain unique perspectives on key concepts through a variety of videos and cases

☐ Increase your comprehension with online quizzes

☐ Study with existing flashcards and make your own

Mobile

☐ Stay focused and ready to study whenever it's convenient for you!

☐ Access a full, interactive ebook: online or offline

☐ Study tools that empower anytime, anywhere learning and 24/7 course access

4 CHAPTER CASE

ISLAND VIEW TECH SOLUTIONS AND QUARTER & ASSOCIATES

BACKGROUND

This case involves you, as a salesperson representing the institutional sales division of Island View Tech Solutions, a leading reseller of technology hardware and software, and Dalton Genge, Director of Technology for Quarter & Associates, a prominent St. John's–based law firm specializing in corporate litigation. Quarter & Associates is preparing to move to larger facilities and wants to update its computer technology in the new facilities. Corner Brook-based Island View Tech Solutions has established itself as a major competitor in the technology marketplace specializing in value-added systems solutions for business institutions and government entities nationwide. This past year, Island View Tech Solutions has added sales and distribution centres in Burlington, Ontario, Halifax, Nova Scotia, and St. John's, Newfoundland and Labrador.

CURRENT SITUATION

As an integral part of their move to new and larger facilities, Quarter & Associates want to replace their computers and information technology systems including laptop/desktop combinations for each of their 21 attorneys, desktop systems for their 10 staff members, along with archive and e-mail servers. Island View Tech Solutions specializes in this type of systems selling and uses their network of hardware and software providers in combination with their own in-house engineering, programming, and systems group to consistently provide higher value solutions than the competition.

In preparation for an initial meeting with Dalton Genge, the Island View Tech Solutions sales representative is outlining their information needs and developing a draft set of needs

discovery questions. These needs discovery questions will be the focus of the meeting with Dalton Genge and enable Island View Tech Solutions to better identify and confirm the actual needs, desires, and expectations of Quarter & Associates in relation to new and expanded computer and information technology capabilities.

QUESTIONS

1. What information does the Island View Tech Solutions salesperson need in order to fully understand the technology needs of Quarter & Associates?

2. Following the ADAPT methodology for needs discovery questioning, develop a series of salesperson questions and anticipated buyer responses that might apply to this selling situation.

ROLE PLAY

Situation: Review the above Island View Tech Solutions–Quarter & Associates case and the ADAPT questions you developed in response to the questions associated with this case.

Characters: Yourself, salesperson for Island View Tech Solutions; Dalton Genge, Director of Technology for Quarter & Associates

Scene:

Location—Dalton Genge's office at Quarter & Associates

Action—As a salesperson for Island View Tech Solutions, you are making an initial sales call to Dalton Genge for the purpose of identifying and detailing the specific needs and expectations Quarter & Associates has for new and expanded computers and information technology. Role-play this needs discovery sales call and demonstrate how you might utilize SPIN or ADAPT questioning sequences to identify the technology needs.

INTEGRATIVE CASE | 4

QUESTION EVERYTHING

BACKGROUND

On October 18, 2018, the Federal Government of Canada and the Canadian Professional Sales Association (CPSA) announced an initiative to address the challenge of recruiting and incentivizing those interested in a career in personal selling.[21] The goal of the program is to address the shortage in sales talent by providing funding to the CPSA to build bridges with educators, employers, and sales professionals.

The government department Employment and Social Development Canada (ESDC) provided funding through an initiative called the Sectoral Initiatives Program (SIP), which is specifically geared toward helping industries create new employment opportunities. As part of the news release, the program's goals were laid out: "This SIP contribution will enable CPSA, and its industry partners, to accelerate the mission to raise the profile of sales as a professional career and the adoption of professional designations for sales."[22]

One of the aims of this program was to find a way to track skill development and to encourage those skills to become part of varying sales designations for the industry. The CPSA announced at the same time of the initial press release that it had tangible projects which would emerge from the SIP. One in particular was of great importance, a new competency framework for aspiring sales professionals.

The competencies included familiar sales aptitudes: Prospecting, Fostering Client Relationships, Developing Client-Focused Solutions, Negotiating and Closing, Following Up, Business Acumen, Sales Process Technology, and Professional Sales Conduct.[23] The skills developed in this list were identified by CPSA members as being the most pertinent and relevant to sales career success.

Under the Fostering Client Relationships competency, there are two subheadings that describe a vital characteristic of salespeople: communicate verbally and communicate in writing.[24] The focus provided is on best practices as they relate to both oral and written communication in addition to nonverbal communication. There is also a discussion of the importance of active listening and the characteristics related to engaging in true two-way communication. However, one aspect of communication that could be expanded upon is asking questions. The CPSA Competency Framework currently includes it by discussing how to "answer client questions" and "anticipate questions."[25]

CURRENT SITUATION

You have been hired by ESDC, partly due to your experience with business and sales principles from your educational background. You have spent time looking over the CPSA Competency Framework and realize that there could be additional development with regards to the importance of asking questions and developing a questioning policy—important aspects of training future sales professionals and meeting the goals of this SIP.

You meet with your superiors, and it's agreed that more could be developed in this area. You have been asked to create a briefing document that your department supervisor could use in their next meeting with CPSA about the SIP. Your task is to create something that is readable and understandable for many audiences, but also a document that shows that your government department understands the important skills that are vital for any sales professional.

You recall an important part of the sales class you took involved discussing varying ways in which to ask questions and develop protocols. You begin going back through your notes (both mental and physical) to figure out the best way to represent your perspective. You want to put your own SPIN on this document, but you know you should ADAPT it to fit the audience. There should be no question from this process that you have the skills to excel at your new position.

4 INTEGRATIVE CASE

QUESTIONS

1. One aspect of asking questions is to avoid interrogation and ask questions that are trying to elicit greater insights and information. What is this strategic type of question called?
   a. evaluative questioning
   b. tactical questioning
   c. reactive questioning
   d. probing questioning

2. You feel an important model for CPSA to include in its competency framework is the SPIN model. You believe the last stage of this model is most important, as it relates to proposing a solution to the problem. What is this stage called?

   a. needs assessment questions
   b. need-payoff questions
   c. need-solution questions
   d. non-tactical questions

3. Another important model to provide is the ADAPT questioning system. You want to emphasize a part of the model that could apply to the CPSA Competency Framework, which helps customers truly understand the impact of implied need. What does the second "A" in the ADAPT acronym represent?
   a. amplification
   b. actor
   c. activation
   d. ancillary

CHAPTER ROLE PLAY 4

Communication Skills: Port Wireless Inc.

BACKGROUND

Port Wireless Inc. specializes in providing wireless information technology for businesses having 10 to 500 employees and needs for wireless communication, information processing, and digital data transmittal. The company offers a full range of services ranging from the one-time design of applications for smartphones and digital devices to the design and building out of full enterprise systems. As a business development specialist for Port Wireless, you are making an initial sales call to Wally Stevens, technology manager for Island Claims & Adjusters, LLC. As a preferred provider for inspection and adjusting insurance claims across Atlantic Canada, Island Claims serves as an outsource provider of claims and adjusting services to many of the top 25 property and casualty insurance companies and has experienced rapid growth over the last five years. The company currently employs 65 people: 50 adjusters out in the field, 10 assistants located at company headquarters in Summerside, PEI, and 5 administrative and executive staff members.

The purpose of this initial call is to assess Island Claim's current use and needs for wireless communication and data services. According to the initial information you gained from a short phone conversation with Stevens, Island Claims is currently using a variety of different smartphones on Sprint's cellular and data service. However, they are exploring a combination of custom-designed apps for the iPad 4 for use by their adjusters in the field. This combination would enable adjusters to complete and submit data forms complete with pictures and eliminate the added processing required in their current use of paper-based forms and records. During the phone conversation, Stevens mentioned that some of the benefits are obvious. Nevertheless, they have concerns about the custom apps and transitioning to a fully digital system.

ROLE PLAY

Location: Wally Stevens' office at Island Claims & Adjusters

Action: Role-play this needs discovery sales call and demonstrate how you might utilize SPIN or ADAPT questioning sequences to identify the needs and concerns of the prospect.

5 | Strategic Prospecting and Preparing for Sales Dialogue

LEARNING OBJECTIVES

After completing this chapter, you should be able to

LO 1 | Discuss why prospecting is an important and challenging task for salespeople.

LO 2 | Explain strategic prospecting and each stage in the strategic prospecting process.

LO 3 | Describe the major prospecting methods and give examples of each method.

LO 4 | Explain the important components of a strategic prospecting plan.

LO 5 | Discuss the types of information salespeople need to prepare for sales dialogue.

AFTER FINISHING THIS CHAPTER GO TO THE BACK OF THE BOOK FOR CHAPTER REVIEW CARDS, AND VISIT MINDTAP FOR ACCESS TO STUDY TOOLS.

Established in 1999, True North Sports & Entertainment Limited was created with the goal of developing a multipurpose sports and entertainment facility in downtown Winnipeg. The company's mission has always been to provide superior facility experiences, develop championship-calibre hockey teams, and continue to contribute to the community. In 2004, with support from private partners and government, the company opened a 15,000-seat arena, the MTS Centre, which would become home to the AHL's Manitoba Moose hockey team. From there the MTS Centre continued to gain traction as it hosted a series of events including the Juno Awards in 2005 and the 2007 International Ice Hockey Federation Women's Word Championship, where Canada beat the United States 5–1 for the gold medal. After two years of development, in 2010 True North Sports expanded to open the MTS iceplex, which added four NHL regulation-size rinks to the arena.

Eventually True North Sports acquired the Atlanta Thrashers NHL franchise club, relocating the team to Winnipeg and renaming it the Winnipeg Jets. The Jets went on to play their first NHL game in the MTS Centre against the Montreal Canadiens in 2011.[1] The Winnipeg Jets are now worth $420 million, with $127 million in revenue.[2] Today, with 400 employees, True North Sports is continuing its mission to provide a consistent contribution to the community and has launched the True North Youth Foundation, a non-profit helping underserved youth in Manitoba fulfill their potential.[3]

Introduction

True North Sports & Entertainment's success in growing its business is due in part to its ability to strategically prospect and engage in meaningful

conversations with existing and prospective customers. Most salespeople have to spend time prospecting to generate business from new customers and to increase sales from existing customers. In fact, for many the time spent prospecting is on the rise. Although some salespeople are responsible for most of the strategic prospecting process, many firms are integrating the marketing and sales function with the latest technology to generate leads, qualify and prioritize prospects, and set appointments for sales dialogue.

Successful salespeople employ an effective strategic prospecting process that employs the most appropriate technology at each stage. Significant revenue increases have been achieved from effective sales and marketing alignment with the integration of various types of technology. Studies have reported promising results when sales and marketing work closely together: 36 percent fewer leads were lost, sales efforts at closing deals were improved

by 67 percent, and marketing generated 209 percent more value from marketing programs.[4] Consider how sales and marketing teamwork using different technologies produced improved prospecting in the following company example.

CAN Financial sells financial and marketing products to independent financial advisers. The company CEO was identifying potential customers at different events and assigning them to salespeople. Most of these leads were not good sales opportunities and the company did not have a process for tracking the leads once assigned to a salesperson. This approach was not very effective and salespeople were not happy with the leads they were receiving.

The company decided to develop a strategic prospecting process that integrated the marketing function with the latest technology. E-mail marketing campaigns were created to generate and nurture leads from a database of 50,000 independent financial advisers. The financial advisers that responded to an e-mail message were sent to a Web site to answer five questions to determine if they were qualified prospects. The questions addressed the length of time in business, income level, regulatory requirements, licences held, and range of financial services offered. Those scoring above 190 were assigned to a salesperson. The salesperson contacted the qualified sales lead and invited the financial adviser for an office visit. This approach increased the number of office visits by 43 percent and almost half of those visiting the office became new clients.

The entire strategic prospecting process is tracked using GreyMS lead management software and on the firm's CRM system. CAN Financial is very pleased with its new process. Salespeople are able to focus on the best sales opportunities with more qualified prospects being converted into new customers. The company plans to continue improving its strategic prospecting process in the future.[5]

Most salespeople have to cultivate new business if they are to sustain the sales growth objectives their company establishes. However, many sales organizations give almost total responsibility for all prospecting activities to the salesperson. In between these two extremes, there are many approaches that involve different strategic prospecting activities that are shared between marketing and sales in various ways. The discussion in this chapter is oriented toward situations in which salespeople are involved actively in all or most of the prospecting activities. Regardless of the strategic prospecting approach used by a firm, most salespeople have to cultivate new business if they are to sustain the sales growth objectives their company establishes. However, salespeople typically achieve sales growth objectives by finding the right balance between getting new customers and generating additional business from existing customers. Various prospecting approaches are available, with each having advantages and disadvantages. New technological advances are increasing the number of tools salespeople can use to determine the best sales opportunities. The purpose of this chapter is to examine the importance and challenges of prospecting, introduce the strategic prospecting process, present different prospecting methods, and discuss preparation for sales dialogue.

> The most productive salespeople pursue the best sales opportunities and translate a larger percentage of these opportunities into sales than less productive salespeople do.

LO 1 | THE IMPORTANCE AND CHALLENGES OF PROSPECTING

Prospecting is extremely important to most salespeople. Salespeople who do not regularly prospect are operating under the assumption that the current business with existing customers will be sufficient to generate the desired level of future revenue. This is a shaky assumption in good times, but it is especially questionable in the tough economic environment of recent years. As market conditions change, existing customers may buy less. Or customers may go out of business. Some customers might be acquired by another firm, with the buying decisions now being made outside the salesperson's territory. The salesperson could also simply lose customers because of competitive activity or dissatisfaction with the product, the salesperson, or the selling firm. Because there is typically a considerable time lag between the commencement of prospecting and the conversion of prospects to customer status, salespeople should spend time prospecting on a regular basis. Otherwise, lost sales volume cannot be regained quickly enough to satisfy the large majority of sales organizations—those that are growth-oriented.

Despite its importance, salespeople often find prospecting to be a daunting task. Many salespeople do not like to prospect because of their fear of rejection. Additionally, and quite simply, because today's buyers are often very knowledgeable and almost always pressed for time, many current and prospective customers are reluctant to see salespeople. Because many buyers complete most of their pre-purchase research online they often do not want to engage with a salesperson until the process is more than 50 percent complete.

Without doubt, changes in buying behaviour are making prospecting more difficult. Studies indicate that more people from different functions, positions, and locations are involved in the buying process than ever before, with the average number increasing from 5.4 to 6.8. This number is expected to increase in the future. The larger number of people involved in the buying process, the expanding number of purchasing options, and the enormous amount of available information are also making purchasing harder for some firms. This situation is one reason that 60 percent of qualified prospects do not end up making a purchasing decision, as found in one study.[6] Therefore, salespeople must try to identify and qualify prospects sooner, and determine the members of the buying centre and the stage in the buying process for these prospects to be able to have more of an impact on the purchasing decision.

Salespeople can overcome the challenges of prospecting and become more effective in determining the best sales opportunities by following a strategic sales prospecting process, using a variety of prospecting methods, developing a strategic prospecting plan, and preparing for sales dialogue with prospects.

LO 2 | THE STRATEGIC PROSPECTING PROCESS

 1.3 Develop client intelligence

The first step in the trust-based sales process presented in Chapter 1 is strategic prospecting. **Strategic prospecting** is a process designed to identify, qualify, and prioritize sales opportunities, whether they represent potential new customers or opportunities to generate additional business from existing customers. The basic purpose of strategic prospecting is to help salespeople determine the best sales opportunities in the most efficient way. Effective strategic prospecting helps salespeople spend their valuable selling time in the most productive manner.

The strategic prospecting process (illustrated in Figure 5.1) is often viewed as a **sales funnel** or **sales pipeline** because it presents the entire trust-based sales process and the strategic prospecting process in the form of a funnel. The funnel is very wide at the top, as salespeople typically have a large number of potential sales opportunities. As salespeople move through the strategic prospecting process and the other stages in the trust-based sales process, the funnel narrows because only the best sales opportunities are pursued and not all sale opportunities result in a sale or new customer relationship. For the most productive salespeople, the sales funnel is normally much wider at the bottom than it is for less productive salespeople. The most productive salespeople pursue the best sales opportunities and translate a larger percentage of these opportunities into actual sales than less productive salespeople do. The most successful salespeople are able to be more productive because they devote time to understanding their buyers, developing their communication

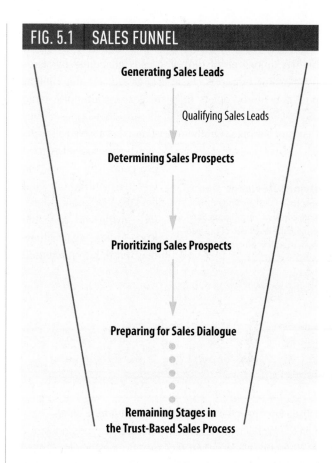

FIG. 5.1 SALES FUNNEL

Generating Sales Leads

Qualifying Sales Leads

Determining Sales Prospects

Prioritizing Sales Prospects

Preparing for Sales Dialogue

Remaining Stages in the Trust-Based Sales Process

The sales funnel presents the trust-based sales process and highlights the major steps of the strategic prospecting process.

skills, and strategizing when it comes to prospecting for new business. We will now discuss each step in the strategic prospecting process by considering each stage of the sales funnel (see Figure 5.1).

Generating Sales Leads

The first step in the strategic prospecting process is to identify sales leads. **Sales leads** or **suspects** are organizations or individuals who might possibly purchase the product or service a salesperson offers. This represents the realm of sales opportunities for a salesperson. For example, if a salesperson sells copiers in business markets, any organization that might need a copier would be a sales lead.

strategic prospecting A process designed to identify, qualify, and prioritize sales opportunities, whether they represent potential new customers or opportunities to generate additional business from existing customers.

sales funnel or **pipeline** A representation of the trust-based sales process and strategic sales prospecting process in the form of a funnel.

sales leads or **suspects** Organizations or individuals who might possibly purchase the product or service a salesperson offers.

Although more sales leads are usually better than fewer leads, there are normally large differences in sales opportunities among all of the sales leads generated by salespeople. For example, because large organizations might purchase more copiers than smaller organizations, large organizations might represent better sales opportunities than smaller ones. On the other hand, because small firms may be overlooked as good prospects, they may be less frequently contacted by salespeople and therefore might be a viable lead. Other organizations may have just purchased copiers or are very satisfied with their current copiers, which would mean they do not represent good sales opportunities. If salespeople merely generate leads and pursue most of them without fully qualifying them, they are likely to be spending a great deal of their time on leads that are not actually good sales opportunities.

qualifying sales leads The salesperson's act of searching out, collecting, and analyzing information to determine the likelihood of the lead being a good candidate for making a sale.

Determining Sales Prospects

The most productive salespeople evaluate sales leads to determine which ones are true prospects for their product or service. This evaluation process is usually called **qualifying sales leads**. Salespeople search for, collect, analyze, and use various types of screening

Every Business Sells

Dustin Eisenhaur is a territory manager at Arterra Wines Canada. Working in the consumer packaged goods industry, he is responsible for selling wine to all businesses with licences to sell alcohol (both on- and off-premise) within his territory, which is approximately 100 regular customers across New Brunswick and Prince Edward Island. He has worked in sales for 10 years, four of them with Arterra Wines Canada.

As a salesperson, how do you provide value to your customers?

Through working as a partner and an advocate for their business, and being a resource for industry/market knowledge and advice. I work closely with customers to understand their true needs and objectives, and then deliver solutions to help satisfy those needs and objectives.

As a salesperson, how do you provide value to your organization?

By having a deep understanding of my customers and my market, I'm able to be an expert on my territory, allowing me to know the best way to deliver results and contribute to our company's objectives.

What is your greatest challenge you face today as a salesperson?

Adjusting to rapidly changing consumer preferences and demand. Demographics and the digital age play a major role in this, but at the end of the day, consumer taste preferences are shifting faster than they used to, and on a much more regular basis. As such, the needs of our customers are changing just as rapidly.

How do you try to overcome this challenge?

By closely watching market trends in my territory and keeping an open dialogue with customers on what they're noticing. This allows me to deliver feedback to the Management and Innovation team, allowing them to evolve our product offerings so we keep up with trends, and meet and exceed the demands of our customers.

What advice do you have for someone starting out in sales?

Find a mentor and learn everything you can from them. Someone whose career you admire or who has accomplished what you aspire to accomplish. If you're lucky, you'll find someone within your organization, and you'll have the opportunity to work closely with them. Ask as many questions as you can, and closely observe their behaviours and actions. The skills you'll learn, the advice you'll receive, will prove to be incredibly valuable throughout your career.

© Dustin Eisenhaur

Every Business Sells

Allie Guerra is a retail and licensee sales representative at Devonian Coast Wineries. She sells wine to over 30 retail stores and 50 licensees in Nova Scotia. She has worked in sales for two years, and has been at Devonian Coast Wineries for one year.

As a salesperson, how do you provide value to your customers?

I think it is really important to understand what your customer is facing in their day-to-day business and to respect the times that they are going to be busy. In understanding this, you are creating a working relationship that does not hinder or interfere with their work. I think of this especially when building new relationships with customers. For example, in the service industry, it is not a good idea to show up during lunch or dinner service, expecting to speak to a manager when the restaurant is at its peak busyness.

Another example in the service industry is not just selling a product but being able to help educate staff members. Breaking down a bottle of wine in simple, relatable terms for management and wait staff is integral to help staff sell the wine and for them to feel comfortable discussing and answering guests' questions.

As a salesperson, how do you provide value to your organization?

Because of my background in the service industry, I am able to connect with management and staff and truly understand the challenges they face every day. I recognized that management has plenty of work outside of purchasing wine and I also sympathize with servers for having to learn about different products. Having these small insights lets me connect better with the accounts and lets them know that I am working hard to make their job easier.

What is your greatest challenge you face today as a salesperson?

There is so much happening today that it can be hard to get people to pay attention. I am working in an industry where there are new products on shelves every day and only a limited amount of space to sell them. You must be able to cut through the noise and educate customers.

How do you try to overcome this challenge?

Build strong mutually beneficial relationships. Make sure that you know the ins and outs of your product/services so you are able to promptly answer questions or concerns. It is hard to know everything, of course, but following up in a timely manner is crucial in letting your customer know they are valued and keeping you brand relevant.

What advice do you have for someone starting out in sales?

Be honest and genuine. If you truly believe in the product/service and you care about what you are doing, it will be obvious. Make sure to do your homework before meeting with a customer and try to gather as much information as possible before the meeting so you are prepared to provide answers to their questions. It is important to ask the right questions in meetings to gain insight on what exactly the customer is looking for or what they may be having issues with. By asking questions you are better able to understand the situation they are in and provide a solution they may not have thought about.

---

procedures to determine if the sales lead is really a good sales prospect. Although specific companies define sales prospects in different ways, a **sales prospect** is typically an individual or organization that

- has a need for the product or service
- has the budget or financial resources to purchase the product or service
- has the authority to make the purchase decision

Those that meet these criteria move down the sales funnel (see Figure 5.1) into the sales prospect category, while those that do not are set aside. In the CAN Financial process, those scoring above 190 on five key questions were considered to be qualified

> **sales prospect** An individual or organization that has a need for the product or service, has the budget or financial resources to purchase the product or service, and has the authority to make the purchase decision.

prospects. Interestingly, only 14 percent of the financial advisers who responded to a marketing e-mail were found to be qualified prospects. Salespeople who spend the time and effort qualifying their leads limit the time wasted on making calls with a low probability of success and focus their efforts on the more fruitful opportunities.

Prioritizing Sales Prospects

Even though the qualifying process has culled out the least promising sales leads, the remaining prospects do not all represent the same sales opportunity. The most productive salespeople prioritize their sales prospects to ensure that they spend most of their time on the best opportunities. One approach is to create an **ideal customer profile** and then analyze sales prospects by comparing them with this ideal customer profile. Those that most closely fit the profile are deemed to be the best sales prospects. Another approach is to identify one or more criteria, evaluate sales prospects against these criteria, and either rank all of the sales prospects based on this evaluation or place the sales prospects into A, B, and C categories, with A sales prospects representing the best sales opportunities. The CAN Financial salespeople prioritized their sales prospects according to their score on the five qualifying questions. Financial advisers with the highest scores were the best sales prospects. The net result is that their salespeople are spending their valuable time with the best sales opportunities.

ideal customer profile The characteristics of a firm's best customers or the perfect customer.

Preparing for Sales Dialogue

The final step in the strategic prospecting process is to prepare for the initial contact with a sales prospect by planning the sales dialogue. The information accumulated to this point in the process is helpful, but additional information is usually required to increase the chances of success in the initial sales dialogue. The types of additional information required are discussed later in this chapter.

LO 3 | PROSPECTING METHODS

 CPSA   7.2 Implement social selling

Many different sources and methods for effective strategic prospecting have been developed for use in different selling situations. A good selling organization and successful salespeople will have a number of ongoing prospecting methods in place at any given time. The salesperson must continually evaluate prospecting methods to determine which methods are bringing in the best results. New methods must also be evaluated and tested for their effectiveness. Many popular prospecting methods are presented in Exhibit 5.1. Some of the typical prospecting methods used in the past are becoming less effective in some selling situations. A recent study found that it takes 18 or more phone calls to connect with a prospect, call back rates are less than 1 percent, and only 24 percent of sales e-mails are ever opened.[7] More buyers are actively using social media as indicated by a study reporting that 75 percent of buyers are using

Exhibit 5.1
Prospecting Methods

Cold Canvassing	Networking	Company Sources	Commercial Sources
• Cold calling	• Centres of influence	• Company records	• Directories
• Referrals	• Noncompeting salespeople	• Advertising inquiries	• Lead management sources
• Introductions	• Social media	• Telephone inquiries	
		• Trade shows	
		• Seminars	

Social selling is an increasingly effective sales method.

social media in different ways throughout their purchasing process.[8] As suggested by Salesforce Vice President Wendy Johnstone: "Everyone is now connected and our customers are on multiple channels—mobile, social, and digital."[9]

This situation has led many sales people to engage in social selling as an important element of their strategic selling process. **Social selling** is leveraging social media to identify, understand, engage, and network with prospects to develop relationships.[10] Although often combined with other prospecting methods, social selling permeates much of the strategic prospecting process for many salespeople. It has been reported that more than 70 percent are involved in social selling activities.[11] And, the use of social selling has produced favourable results. For example, studies indicate that 72 percent of salespeople using social selling outperformed their peers, and 90 percent of top performing salespeople focused on social selling.[12] More specifics about social selling are presented in the discussion of social media as a prospecting method.

Cold Canvassing

CPSA   1.3 Develop client intelligence

Cold canvassing occurs when salespeople contact a sales lead unannounced with little if any information about the lead. **Cold calling** is the most extreme form of cold canvassing because salespeople merely knock on doors or make telephone calls to organizations or individuals. This is a very inefficient prospecting method. Typically, a very small percentage of cold calls produce, or lead to future sales dialogue with, qualified prospects. Because there is so much rejection, many salespeople do not like to cold call sales leads.

Using referrals or introductions can improve the success of cold calling. A **referral** is a sales lead a customer or some other influential person provides. Salespeople are often trained to ask customers and others for the names and contact information of potential prospects. Sometimes salespeople can also obtain sufficient information to qualify the lead as a good sales prospect. Additionally, salespeople can get permission to use the person's name when contacting the prospect. Social selling can be an effective way to get referrals. For example, an adviser for Guardian Life obtained 35 referrals from a client's professional network on LinkedIn. This is a much larger number of referrals than from more typical personal methods. This adviser's sales have almost doubled since engaging in social selling for prospecting.[13] In some cases, the person might agree to provide an **introduction** by writing a letter or making a phone call to introduce the salesperson to the prospect. This referral approach can work well but ethical issues might arise, as depicted in An Ethical Dilemma.

Networking

CPSA   1.3 Develop client intelligence

Salespeople can use various types of networking as effective methods for prospecting. Many salespeople join civic and professional organizations, country clubs, or fraternal organizations, and these memberships provide the opportunity for them to build relationships with other members. Sometimes these relationships yield prospects. Some members might be influential people in the community or other organizations, making them **centres of influence** for the salesperson and potentially providing help in locating prospects. Accountants, bankers, attorneys, teachers, business owners, politicians, and government workers are often good centres of influence.

social selling Leveraging social media to identify, understand, engage, and network with prospects to develop relationships

cold calling Contacting a sales lead unannounced and with little or no information about the lead.

referral A name of a company or person given to the salesperson as a lead by a customer or even a prospect who did not buy at this time.

introduction A variation of a referral in which, in addition to requesting the names of prospects, the salesperson asks the prospect or customer to prepare a note or letter of introduction that can be sent to the potential customer.

centres of influence Well-known and influential people who can help a salesperson prospect and gain leads.

Salespeople can network for prospects electronically.

Meg Hagan is a sales representative for United Office Furniture. She sells all types of office furniture to professional firms. Meg has been especially successful in using referrals to get appointments with the decision makers at prospect firms. For example, she used a referral to set up a meeting with Max Pursell, managing partner at an accounting firm, and ended up making her largest sale. Max is very satisfied with the office furniture he purchased for a satellite office. During a recent Chamber of Commerce event, Meg was talking with Max, and Max told a story about a fishing trip with his friend, Patrick Bassett. Meg knows that Patrick is the managing partner at a small but growing law firm. She recently saw in the business news that his law firm was going to open a new office in the suburbs and would announce the exact location in the next two weeks. Meg asked Max if he would be willing to refer her to Patrick and send an e-mail to Patrick introducing her. Max said he normally does not like to make referrals, but he might make an exception in her case. He said he would think about it and let her know within a week whether he would send a referral e-mail. Meg was excited and began to gather information about Patrick and his firm. After a week went by, Meg had not heard from Max, so she called his office and found out that he was on a three-week vacation in Europe. Meg knows that it is extremely important that she talk with Patrick as soon as possible to have the best chance for the office equipment at the new office location. A sale to Patrick's firm would lead to a hefty bonus for her. But, she does not have the referral approval from Max. Without the referral e-mail, Meg knows it will be harder to get a meeting with Patrick, and she will not have the favourable comments from Max about the satisfied experience he had working with her.

What should Meg do?

(a) Contact Patrick by phone, mention the positive experience she had working with Max, and try to set up an appointment without a direct referral and e-mail from Max.

(b) Contact Patrick by phone and indicate that Max had referred her to him for his office equipment needs and try to set up a meeting.

(c) Wait until Max is back at work and call to see if Max would write the referral e-mail to Patrick. Once the e-mail is sent, contact Patrick by phone to set up an appointment.

Networking with salespeople from noncompeting firms can also be a good source of prospects. Business Networking International (BNI), which has several active chapters throughout Canada, is a formal organization with each local group consisting of **noncompeting salespeople**. The basic purpose of this organization is for the members to generate prospects for each other. There are other sales and marketing organizations that salespeople can join to create the opportunity to identify prospects by networking with members.

It is important for salespeople to strike up conversations with other sales representatives while waiting to see buyers. Noncompeting salespeople can be found everywhere and can help in getting valuable information about prospects. An example of how noncompeting salespeople can help each other was demonstrated when a Hershey Chocolate salesperson went out of his way to tell a noncompeting sales representative from Hormel Foods about a new grocery store going into his territory. Hormel Foods is a manufacturer of food and meat products for consumers throughout the world. The Hormel representative was the first of his competitors to meet with the new grocery store management team and was given valuable shelf space that his competitors could not get. A few months later, the Hormel sales representative returned the favour when he found out that an independent convenience store was changing hands. The Hershey salesperson was able to get into the new owner's store early and added valuable shelf space for his products. The operating principle of "you scratch my back and I scratch yours" works when information flows in both directions.[14]

noncompeting salespeople
Salespeople selling noncompeting products.

Electronic Networking

New developments in technology have produced a variety of Web sites that allow salespeople to engage in **electronic networking**. Some of the sites are free, but others charge fees for some or all services provided. The specifics of each site differ, but all make it possible for salespeople to network online for prospects and obtain various types of information about the prospects. As presented earlier, the increasing use of social selling means that salespeople are actively involved with different media tools. LinkedIn is most often used, followed by Twitter. However, Facebook, Instagram, Snapchat, and industry-specific online communities can be effective in selling situations where prospects use them. The social media tools can help salespeople identify more leads and better prospects earlier in the buying process, and provide them with the opportunity to share valuable content in conversations with them.[15]

Consider one suggested approach for using LinkedIn. A salesperson can identify leads from the networks of their LinkedIn connections and from the "Who's Viewed Your Profile" on their LinkedIn screen. They can then send a connection request to the lead. Once connected to the lead, the salesperson can e-mail a message with meaningful content as a way to start a conversation with the lead and to determine whether the lead is a qualified prospect. If so, the salesperson can continue the conversation and try to move into the remainder of the sales process at the appropriate time. If not, the salesperson can still share relevant content, because the lead might become a qualified prospect in the future.

In addition to the basic LinkedIn product (linkedin.com), many salespeople use their Sales Navigator product. Sales Navigator (sales.linkedin.com) provides expanded and enhanced features not available in basic LinkedIn. Many salespeople have used Sales Navigator effectively, as evidenced in the example presented in Technology in Sales: Social Media and Social Selling.

> **electronic networking** Using Web sites designed to help salespeople identify and gather information about prospects.

Technology in Sales

Social Media and Social Selling

SAP introduced social selling in its sales organization in 2012 with the purchase of 50 Sales Navigator licences. The company now has more than 15,000 licences worldwide. Account executives use Sales Navigator as well as Twitter, Grapevine6, and the SAP Jam Collaboration tool to generate leads, identify the best prospects, and win business.

Sales Navigator helps account executives identify and follow leads and listen for opportunities to identify problems buyers are having. Leads with problems SAP can solve are engaged through InMail in Sales Navigator or a direct message on Twitter, WeChat, or Xing. The Jam Collaboration tool and Grapevine6 are used for sales and marketing to work together to determine the content most needed by the lead. This content is shared with the lead in the form of a video business card or video demonstration of a solution. Continued engagement identifies the best prospects for account executives to pursue as sales opportunities. This process of listening, learning, and engaging with potential buyers over social media helps to build trust and credibility early in the buying process and increases the likelihood of a sale in the future.

The social selling approach used by SAP has contributed to large sales increases. The highest-performing account executives are usually the best social sellers. These results are also encouraging SAP to increase its social selling efforts around the world. The SAP social selling philosophy is the focus of training programs called "Social Selling All Hands" that are conducted on a regular basis. More attention is also being given to develop benchmarks for social selling performance and business results.[16]

Personal Selling and Social Media

Various forms of social media, such as Facebook, Instagram, Twitter, and blogs, have become mainstream forms of communication for individuals and businesses alike. Since social media is top of mind for most businesses, and with sales organizations' emphasis on external communications, the pressure to stay current is high. However, sales experts agree that sale reps and managers must apply some type of filter so that social media remains a sales tool and not a distraction to the sales rep.[17]

"Social networking is a strategy for marketing promotions and relationship management. It is not a prospecting tool. A lot of the maintenance functions involved with social media tools are going to slide down to the lowest paid person who is competent to do them."[18] In other words, sales reps should not be focusing on daily tweets and Facebook updates. Some experts believe that these new communication tools are doing a disservice to salespeople; they are tools of communication and not meant to replace the sales process.

Company Sources

7.1 Leverage sales technology

Many companies have resources or are engaged in activities that can help their own salespeople with strategic prospecting. **Company records** can be a useful source of prospects. Salespeople can also review company records to identify previous customers who have not placed an order recently. Contacting previous customers to determine why they have stopped ordering could provide opportunities to win back business. Examining the purchasing behaviour of existing customers can also help in identifying opportunities to sell additional products to specific customers.

Advertising inquiries are potentially a good source of prospects. For example, one manufacturer's rep in the natural gas industry speaks highly of his company's advertising plan. The company advertises only in trade magazines that it believes buyers read. The salesperson's territory includes Alberta, Manitoba, and Saskatchewan. The advertising message is simply "If we can help you with any of your natural gas needs (e.g., flow meters, odourizers), please give us a call." These leads are then turned over to the salesperson who calls on that territory. One salesperson cannot cover territories of this size. The advertising program qualifies the prospect (with the help of the telephone) before the salesperson is sent out on the call.

The CAN Financial strategic prospecting process used e-mail marketing campaigns to identify sales leads and potential prospects. More companies are using online advertising as a way to generate sales leads. Expenditures for online advertising to obtain sales leads increased from $12.5 billion in 2005 to over $22.7 billion in 2009, with additional growth since 2009.[19] AP Under Inc. is one company that has used Web-based marketing effectively. The company redesigned its Web site to include interactive features that created a dialogue with visitors. It worked on the site's search engine optimization to get into the top five listings for healthcare audit-related terms and started a company blog. These efforts increased traffic to its Web site from 10 to 15 visits per week to 1,500 to 2,000, generated qualified sales prospects, and increased new business by $2 million. This Web-based marketing approach has replaced cold calling as the major source of new customers.[20]

> Online directories provide salespeople with useful information for prospecting.

Many organizations today use both inbound (prospect calls the company) and outbound (salesperson contacts the prospect) telemarketing. **Inbound telemarketing** involves a telephone number (usually a toll-free number) that prospects or customers can call for information. Companies distribute toll-free numbers by direct mail pieces (brochures), advertising campaigns, and their **outbound telemarketing** program. Some companies use both inbound and outbound telemarketing to serve their market. They use outbound telemarketing to generate and then qualify leads for their salesforce. Qualified leads are turned over to experienced salespeople. Usually, interns do all the outbound telemarketing. Inbound telemarketing is used to resolve problems, answer questions from prospects, and take orders from existing customers.

company records Information about customers in a company database.

advertising inquiries Sales leads generated from company advertising efforts.

inbound telemarketing A way to locate prospects in which the prospect calls the company to get information.

outbound telemarketing A way to locate prospects in which the salesperson contacts the prospect by telephone.

Participating in trade shows is an effective prospecting method.

Attending conventions and **trade shows** presents salespeople with excellent opportunities to collect leads. Generally, the company purchases booth space and sets up a stand that clearly identifies the company and its offerings. Salespeople are available at the booth to demonstrate their products or answer questions. Potential customers walk by and are asked to fill out information cards indicating an interest in the company or one of its products. The completed information card provides leads for the salesperson. Trade shows can stimulate interest in products and provide

trade shows Events at which companies purchase space and set up booths that clearly identify each company and its offerings and that are staffed with salespeople who demonstrate the products and answer questions.

Exhibit 5.2

List of Secondary Lead Sources

1. *Canadian Business Resource*, published by Canadian Newspaper Services International, maintains a database of 6,200 of Canada's largest firms and all firms listed on the TSX and TSX Venture exchanges. It also maintains more than 40,000 contact names that are downloadable to subscribers' contact management software from www.cbr.ca.

2. *Moody's Industrial Directory* is an annual publication with a wide range of statistical information about particular firms that might be prospects for a specific product or service. Names of executives, description of the company business, and a brief financial statement for more than 10,000 publicly held firms are available at www.moodys.com.

3. *Standard & Poor's Register of Corporations, Directors, and Executives* is an excellent source of personal information about individuals in companies. Such information can be used for qualifying prospects and for learning enough about them to plan an effective approach and presentation. This annual publication lists names, titles, and addresses for 50,000 firms. See www.standardandpoors.com.

4. *Canadian Trade Index*, published by Canadian Manufacturers and Exporters, is available in print, on CD-ROM, and online at www.ctidirectory.com. It lists more than 30,000 manufacturers, distributors, and industrial service companies and features nearly 100,000 product listings under 20,000 headings.

5. *Polk City Directory* supplies detailed information on individuals living in specific communities. Polk publishes more than 1,100 directories covering 6,500 communities throughout Canada and the United States. The local chamber of commerce should have access to this directory. See polkcitydirectories.com.

6. *Hoover's Business Directory*, available from Dun & Bradstreet Canada in print form or on CD, lists and profiles more than 20,000 of Canada's largest companies and maintains more than 60,000 key contact names. See www.dnb.ca/salesmarketing/keybusinessdir.html.

7. *World Scope: Industrial Company Profiles* (Wright Investors' Service) provides extensive coverage of 5,000 companies from 25 countries, within 27 major industry groupings. See wrightinvestorsservice.com.

8. Frasers.com provides a comprehensive online directory and search tool for Canadian manufacturers and industrial distributors and their products and services. It also lists international companies that sell in the Canadian marketplace. A separate Web site lists trade shows in Canada and the United States. See frasersdirectory.com.

9. Scott's Directories publishes separate directories for many sectors: corporate (140,000 manufacturers, distributors, banks, construction companies, etc.), medical (100,000 doctors, dentists, hospitals, etc.), government (federal, provincial/territorial, municipal), associations (10,000 listings), schools (various types), and residential (12 million listings, available by segment). Directories are available in print, on CD-ROM, or online. See www.scottsinfo.com.

leads. For example, bank loan officers attend home improvement trade shows and can offer the homeowner immediate credit to begin a project. Those who sign immediately may be offered a lower interest rate.

Firms can use **seminars** to generate leads and provide information to prospective customers. For example, a financial planner will set up a seminar at a local hotel to give a presentation on retirement planning, inviting prospects by direct mail, word of mouth, or advertising on local television and radio. The financial consultant discusses a technique or investment opportunities that will prepare the audience for retirement. Those present will be asked to fill out a card expressing their interest for follow-up discussions. The financial consultant hopes this free seminar will reward him or her with a few qualified prospects.

Commercial Sources

A variety of sources in print and electronic form can be very useful in prospecting. **Directories** offer an inexpensive, convenient means of identifying leads. Telephone books today contain a business section that lists all the community's businesses. This list is usually broken down further by business type. Manufacturers, medical facilities, pharmacies, and grocery stores, to name a few, can be easily identified by using the business pages of the phone book. Many other directories exist, such as Board of Trade directories, chamber of commerce directories, trade association lists, *Moody's Industrial Directory*, and *Standard & Poor's Register of Corporations, Directors, and Executives*. The online versions of these directories are especially valuable because they are updated regularly and usually have search capabilities to facilitate the identification of targeted leads. Directories are a wealth of information if used correctly. A salesperson must remember that when these lists are published they become obsolete. Companies change their names, merge with others, and even change addresses. Salespeople must verify information from published sources before using it. Exhibit 5.2 lists some of the directories that salespeople have at their disposal.

A growing number of companies are providing a variety of **lead management services**, such as lists of targeted businesses or individuals with detailed contact and other information, as well as e-mail, direct mail, telephone, and Web-based marketing services to connect with the targeted leads. Examples of companies providing different types of lead management services include infoCanada (www.infocanada.ca), Scott's Directories (www.scottsdirectories.com), and Innovation, Science and Economic Development Canada (www.ic.gc.ca). An interesting example of using artificial intelligence to manage sales leads is presented in Selling in Action: Smart Automation for Managing Leads.

seminars A presentation salespeople give to generate leads and provide information to prospective customers who are invited to the seminar by direct mail, word of mouth, or advertising on local television or radio.

directories Electronic or print sources that provide contact and other information about many different companies or individuals.

lead management services Lists of targeted businesses or individuals with detailed contact and other information, as well as e-mail, direct mail, telephone, and Web-based marketing services to connect with targeted leads.

Selling in Action

 CPSA

7.1 Leverage sales technology

Smart Automation for Managing Leads

Conversica (conversica.com) performed a study of how well firms responded to Web site leads. The study found that about 33 percent did not respond to these Web site inquiries and most only made one to two attempts to contact the lead. Only 2 percent of the firms could be considered top performers. The top performers provided prompt, personalized responses that mentioned the inquiry and asked for specific contact information for future follow up.

Conversica offers a virtual Sales Assistant that addresses many of the problems found in their study. The Sales Assistant responds promptly to Web site inquiries, personalizes every message, and keeps making attempts until it gets in contact with the lead. The messages from the Sales Assistant ask questions to qualify the lead and try to set up a phone call from a salesperson to qualified prospects. If successful, a salesperson is notified and provided with the phone number and time for the phone call. The salesperson speaks with the prospect and moves through the sales process. Based on experiences with 16,000 salespeople, 1,000 companies, and 180 million messages, the Sales Assistant gets a 35 percent response rate, with more than 30 percent engaging with a salesperson, and 13 percent turning into priority prospects.[21]

LO 4 | DEVELOPING A STRATEGIC PROSPECTING PLAN

CPSA   1.2 Conduct sales planning

The most productive salespeople use a variety of prospecting methods and follow the strategic prospecting process by generating leads, qualifying them to identify true prospects, and then prioritizing these prospects so that they pursue the best sales opportunities. The use of a strategic prospecting plan can help salespeople continually improve their prospecting effectiveness.

An example of an effective strategic prospecting plan is exhibited by Northwestern Mutual (NM). Salespeople use a referred lead prospecting approach to reach weekly prospecting goals. Their tracking system indicated that prospecting goals were not being met because clients were not providing enough referrals and were often not making the promised favourable introductions to these referrals. NM addressed these issues by having salespeople use LinkedIn, Facebook, or other social media to identify five to six people that the client knows and are likely to be qualified prospects. The client now selects referrals from this feeder list and gives reasons why those selected are good prospects. The salesperson also asks the

client to e-mail or text each referral introducing the salesperson and providing some favourable comments, and to copy the salesperson. This new approach has generated more qualified prospects, more favourable introductions, and has led to a higher success rate in securing appointments with the referred prospects.[22]

A **strategic prospecting plan** should fit the individual needs of the salesperson. As illustrated in Figure 5.2, the focal point of a prospecting plan should be the goal stating the number of qualified prospects to be generated. Formalized goals serve as guides to what is to be accomplished and help to keep a salesperson on track. The plan should also allocate an adequate and specific daily or weekly time period for prospecting. Having specific times set aside exclusively for prospecting helps to prevent other activities from creeping in and displacing prospecting activities. A good **tracking system** should also be a part of the prospecting plan. A tracking system can be as low-tech as a set of index cards or employ one of the many computerized and online contact

> **strategic prospecting plan** A salesperson's plan for gathering qualified prospects.
>
> **tracking system** Part of the strategic prospecting plan that records comprehensive information about the prospect, traces the prospecting methods used, and chronologically archives outcomes from any contacts with the prospect.

FIG. 5.2   PROSPECTING PLANS ARE THE FOUNDATION FOR EFFECTIVE PROSPECTING

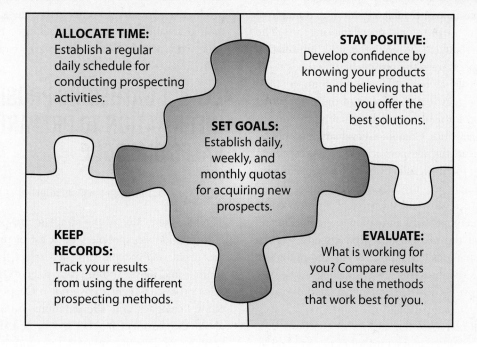

The strategic prospecting plan sets goals, allocates specific times to be used for prospecting, and continuously evaluates results to maximize the effectiveness of prospecting time and effort.

Exhibit 5.3

Personal Prospecting Log

PERSONAL PROSPECTING LOG						

Name: Tom Jenkins

Team: Charlottetown Commercial   Date 4/16

Organization	Contact Person	Source of Lead	Phone	Date of Appointment	Outcome of Call	Follow-Up Activity
Cummins Engine	Tyler Huston	Personal contact	902-444-1234	4/11 8:30 a.m.	Need info on printer	Send in mail
Ontario Systems	Darrell Beaty	Referral	902-223-4117	4/19 4 p.m.		
Shoppers Drug Mart	Isabelle Chen	Direct mail sent back 6/02	905-663-2214	4/16 Lunch	Didn't seem impressed, need more work	Need more contact with Alice HOCKEY GAME?
Thomson Consumer Electronics	Doug Lyon	Phone	905-212-4111	4/15 3 p.m.	Had bad experience with us several years ago	This one will take time

management or customer relationship management software applications (apps). Exhibit 5.3 shows an example of a simple but effective paper-and-pencil tracking form. The tracking system should record comprehensive information about the prospect, trace the prospecting methods used, and chronologically archive outcomes from any contacts with the prospect. A fourth element of the prospecting plan is a system for analyzing and evaluating the results of prospecting activities. Continuous evaluation should be employed to ensure the salesperson is meeting prospecting goals and using the most effective prospecting methods. The fifth and final element of a prospecting plan should be a program to review and stay up-to-date on product knowledge and competitor information to emphasize and underscore that the salesperson's products and services offer the best solutions to customer needs and problems. Self-confidence is critical to success in selling, and a base of comprehensive knowledge and understanding is the key to believing in one's self.

As with all phases of the sales process, salespeople must exercise judgment and set priorities in prospecting. There is a limited amount of time for prospecting, and a better understanding of the concepts and practices illustrated in this chapter can help a salesperson be more productive. An added bonus is that the sales process is more enjoyable for salespeople calling on bona fide prospects who can benefit from the salesperson's offering.

LO 5 | GATHERING PROSPECT INFORMATION TO PREPARE FOR SALES DIALOGUE

 1.3 Develop client intelligence

The basic objective of the strategic prospecting process is to provide salespeople with a list of prioritized sales prospects. Salespeople can then select the best opportunities and move into the next stage of the trust-based sales process, which is covered in Chapter 6, Planning Sales Dialogues and Presentations. Some information about the prospect has been collected throughout the strategic prospecting process, but more is needed to be effective at each stage of the trust-based sales process. In many cases, the next step is for the salesperson to contact the prospect by telephone. Although the purpose of this call is usually to set up an appointment, salespeople are often able to collect additional useful information. All of the information collected prior to meeting with a prospect provides a foundation for completing the Sales Dialogue Template addressed in Chapter 6.

> The most effective salespeople set prospecting priorities.

The more information a salesperson has about a prospect, the better chance the salesperson has to make a sale. Thus, gathering relevant information is an ongoing activity throughout the trust-based sales process, but is especially important prior to the initial sales dialogue with a prospect. The information needed varies depending on the product or service being sold and the specific buyer's situation. We will examine the types of basic information about the prospect and information about the selling situation. Then, sources of this information will be discussed. Assembling prospecting information before meeting with current customers to generate more business is also very important. An example from a salesperson with an electrical distribution company offers an effective approach. She accesses company records to create a gap analysis. This report indicates the products the customer is and is not buying from her firm. Her next step is to focus on the products the customer is not buying. Then, she reviews her firm's customer database to determine which of the products the customer is not buying would represent the best sales opportunities for her and selects one product to emphasize during the next meeting with the customer. This type of prospecting preparation has not only helped her emphasize the best sales opportunity with the customer, but also allows her to address other products if the customer indicates more interest in them.[23]

Basic Information about the Prospect

Usually there is a great deal of basic information about the prospective buyer and company that can be obtained and evaluated prior to the initial sales dialogue with a prospect. Examples of the most valuable information are presented in Exhibit 5.4. It is very important for salespeople to do their homework and obtain as much of this information as possible before meeting with a prospect. The basic information about the buyer helps the salesperson understand the buyer from a personal perspective. This knowledge will be useful in establishing rapport with the buyer, which is extremely important early in the trust-based sales process. The basic information about the company provides

Exhibit 5.4

Basic Information about the Prospect

About the Buyer	About the Company
• Buyer's name, title, and contact information	• Type of business
• Educational and work background	• History of business
• Community and organizational involvement	• Number of employees
• Hobbies and interests	• Target market served
• Communication style	• Products and services offered
	• Key competitors
	• Current strategy and performance

the salesperson with an understanding of the prospect company that will help the salesperson determine the best questions to ask during sales dialogue. Some companies are employing the latest technology to provide salespeople with useful prospect information. For example, Cintas has created a virtual office of various types of prospect information. Salespeople can access this information electronically and obtain valuable information before contacting a prospect. Prospects are typically impressed with salespeople who are prepared and know a lot about them and their company before the first meeting.[24]

Information about the Selling Situation

Specific information about the selling situation is extremely valuable to salespeople. Although much of the basic information about the prospect can normally be gathered prior to meeting with a prospect, much of the information about the selling situation will be obtained from the prospect during sales dialogues. However, salespeople should try to obtain this information as soon as possible, because it is useful during each stage of the trust-based sales process.

Specific types of selling situation information are presented in Exhibit 5.5. Most of this information helps the salesperson understand all aspects of the prospect's buying process and was discussed in Chapter 3, Understanding Buyers, and is part of the Sales Dialogue Template prepared in Chapter 6. Several pharmaceutical firms are using smartphone apps so that salespeople can get the latest information about a physician's situation

Exhibit 5.5

Information about the Selling Situation

- Type of purchase
- Motivation for buying
- Current supplier
- Buying centre members and roles
- Buying process
- Available budget
- Competitors involved

Exhibit 5.6

Sources of Information

- Online searches
- Online and print directories
- Prospect Web site
- Social media
- Annual reports
- Trade and business press
- Professional organizations
- Company databases
- Contact with prospect

before a sales call. A few clicks on the app and the salesperson is alerted to any changes in the physician's patient population or prescribing habit, as well as any physician engagements with digital media. Selling situation information that cannot be obtained prior to meeting with a prospect becomes a key focus during the sales dialogue.[25]

> The more a salesperson knows about a prospect, the better chance a salesperson has to make a sale.

Sources of Information

CPSA   **7.1 Leverage sales technology**

Salespeople have a variety of sources for the information they need. Examples of useful sources are presented in Exhibit 5.6. The use of social media as a valuable information source for salespeople has been increasing in recent years. Facebook, LinkedIn, and blogs are especially useful information sources. Many companies are also accumulating information about prospects and making it readily available to salespeople using the latest technology. Two examples are illustrative:

- Cintas has created a virtual office of various types of prospect information. Salespeople can access this

information electronically and get useful information before contacting a prospect.[26]

- Several pharmaceutical firms are pilot testing the use of smartphone apps. Salespeople can make a few clicks on a smartphone and get information about whether or not a physician has had any changes in patient population or prescribing habits, and even any physician engagements with digital media.[27]

The use of new and emerging technologies will certainly improve the availability of prospect information for salespeople in the future.

Even the most thorough preparation usually will not provide salespeople with all of the desired prospect information. The additional information is typically collected through questioning the prospect during sales dialogues. The information salespeople collect about prospects prior to the first meeting and throughout the trust-based sales process should be accumulated and updated on a regular basis. Although some salespeople do this manually with paper files, as illustrated in Exhibit 5.7, the use of contact management, salesforce automation (SFA), and customer relationship management (CRM) systems is increasing. These technologies are being improved continuously and are valuable tools for salespeople. For instance, BDC, the only bank dedicated to supporting entrepreneurs, has on its Web site a helpful list of free or low-cost customer relationship management solutions providers. This listing includes the service providers' ability to provide solutions and support in both of Canada's official languages.[28] In addition, Salesforce, Canada's most popular CRM provider, allows

Exhibit 5.7

Customer Profile

1. Name of Business _____
2. Address _____
3. Phone _____
4. Name of Buyer(s) _____ Title _____
   Personality, Hobbies, Interests _____
   _____
   _____
   _____
5. Source of Prospect (i.e., referral, cold call) _____
6. Other Key People _____
   Receptionists _____
   Personality, Hobbies, Interests _____
   Secretaries _____
   Personality, Hobbies, Interests _____
   Department Heads _____
   Personality, Hobbies, Interests _____
   Other Influencers—Who? _____
   Personality, Hobbies, Interests _____
7. What products does the company produce?
   _____
8. History and current standing in the industry
   _____
9. How many employees? _____
10. Extent of operations—local, regional, national, international _____
11. Is buying done by individuals or committee?
    _____
12. Does the company buy from single or multiple sources? _____

more than 6,000 Canadian companies—including Air Canada, Husky Energy, Loblaws, Manulife, Roots, TD Bank, and TELUS—new ways of connecting with customers across sales, service, marketing, and commerce.[29]

Determining Other Buyers' Influences

As products become more complex, we often see an increase in the number of buying influencers and decision makers involved in the purchase. The salesperson should attempt to determine the various buying influencers. For example, if a salesperson concentrates on the purchasing agent in an organization and ignores other key players (e.g.,

department head, data processing) in the decision-making process, the salesperson risks selling to the wrong person.

The salesperson must use observation and questioning to determine the role of each member of the buying team and the amount of influence each exerts; each member's needs should be determined before or during the presentation. Department heads may be interested in how the product will benefit their department, whereas the CFO may care only about the price. During group presentations, all the members of the buying party must feel involved. The salesperson must be sure to direct questions and comments to all potential decision makers in the group.

If a salesperson has only one contact (e.g., purchasing agent) in an organization, they run the risk that the key contact could die, get fired, change jobs, be transferred, or retire. By having contact with many influencers in an organization, the salesperson will always have a number of people who have had previous experiences to pass on to the new purchasing agent or team member. In the first instance, the salesperson must start the entire relationship process again; in the second, the salesperson will have help keeping the relationship in place.

STUDY TOOLS

At the back of the textbook, use tear-out cards to review key chapter information. Visit cengage.ca to purchase digital tools to help you succeed.

CENGAGE | MINDTAP

Personal Computer

☐ Gain unique perspectives on key concepts through a variety of videos and cases

☐ Increase your comprehension with online quizzes

☐ Study with existing flashcards and make your own

Mobile

☐ Stay focused and ready to study whenever it's convenient for you!

☐ Access a full, interactive ebook: online or offline

☐ Study tools that empower anytime, anywhere learning and 24/7 course access

DEVELOPING A STRATEGIC PROSPECTING PLAN

BACKGROUND

Colleen King graduated from Memorial University and was hired as a sales representative for the Connector Company. The Connector Company is a transportation broker that links companies needing products shipped with trucking firms to carry the shipments. After an initial training program, Colleen was given a couple of existing company customers and a small list of leads to get her started. She began by serving the shipment needs of the existing customers. This gave her some confidence, but she realized that for her to be successful, she must begin prospecting and try to identify the best sales opportunities. The Connector Company provides an ongoing list of leads that can be accessed by all salespeople. Once a salesperson contacts one of these leads, no other salesperson can contact them. Colleen started her prospecting by contacting these leads.

CURRENT SITUATION

Colleen has been calling a number of leads each day, but has not been very successful in generating much business. She feels like she is wasting much of her time on leads that are not good sales opportunities. The leads provided by her company are not qualified in any way and the training program she attended focused on cold calling as the basic prospecting method. Colleen took a professional selling class in university and remembered that the chapter on prospecting emphasized the need to follow the strategic prospecting process to identify the best sales opportunities. She found her professional selling textbook, went to the chapter on prospecting, and decided to create a strategic prospecting plan.

QUESTIONS

1. What methods should Colleen use to generate sales leads beyond those provided by her company?

2. How should Colleen qualify the leads provided by her company and those she generates herself? What is the profile of an ideal prospect?

3. How should Colleen prioritize her qualified prospects?

4. What information should Colleen collect to prepare for sales dialogue with a prospect?

5. Colleen used LinkedIn during university and wanted to employ it in her strategic prospecting process. How can she best use LinkedIn?

ROLE PLAY

Situation: Read case and prepare a strategic prospecting plan.

Characters: Colleen and her sales manager.

Scene: Colleen has implemented her strategic prospecting plan and been very successful. She has been the top seller in her office for the past two months. Her sales manager is impressed and he asks her what she is doing to be so successful. She indicates that her success is due to spending most of her time with the best sales opportunities. He wants to talk to her about her strategic prospecting plan and sets up a meeting.

Location—Sales manager's office.

Action—Role-play the meeting between Colleen and her sales manager. The sales manager should ask many questions and Colleen will respond to these questions. The use of LinkedIn has been valuable to Colleen and no other salespeople at the Connector Company are using LinkedIn, so make sure the role of LinkedIn is included in the role play.

PROSPECTIVE OPINION

BACKGROUND

In late August 2019, Canadian newspaper *The Globe and Mail* published an article by journalist Ellie Flynn that investigated the multilevel sales model. The article was titled "Multilevel Marketing Sells a Dream: Don't Buy It."[30]

The article provides a view on the multilevel marketing (MLM) model for sales that is not flattering. In describing the MLM environment, it mentions how the focus is on individuals often taking the role of distributor and salesperson. But the article follows with this: "delve a little deeper, and you will often find a murky underworld of predatory tactics that have led to allegations of pyramid-scheme business structures and psychological manipulations that mirror those used in cults."[31]

Harsh words indeed. The article does present a history of MLM, from the early days of Amway and Tupperware, to the modern times and use of Facebook and social media groups to generate leads. However, in the end the MLM world was summarized as a place where a handful of people can make a lot of money, but where many individuals who invest in an MLM program end up losing money.

The article goes on to include that being recruited seems to be a constant occurrence, and one that people need to guard against. "Any time I see the words 'exciting opportunity,' 'work from home' or 'message me for info,' alarm bells go off. Perhaps I've become cynical, but I can't help but wonder what the intent behind those messages is."[32]

One week later, on September 7, 2019, the Direct Sellers Association (DSA) of Canada published a response in *The Globe and Mail* to respond to the claims made in the August 31 article. Peter Maddox, the president of DSA, described the MLM in terms of it being part of the direct selling world, and highlighted the various actions that have been taken to ensure the veracity of the MLM model. Maddox noted: "DSA's member companies work diligently to help participants succeed, and it is in their best interests to promote personal success. For consultants, the barriers to starting their own business are minimal compared to other entrepreneurial opportunities, and it is easy to exit if it's not for them."[33]

One aspect of Flynn's article that Maddox and the DSA did not address was issues around prospecting. In her article, Flynn details how in one undercover investigation she conducted with an MLM company, new distributors were encouraged to target people based on their "vulnerabilities… to find people's 'weak points,' and use them as reasons they should join the company."[34]

She goes on to suggest some changes that are needed to the rules around MLMs: "Tighter regulations are needed, which force companies to publish realistic earning potential to any new recruits…There should also be rules on how much emphasis can be placed on recruitment. If the companies are encouraged to focus primarily on sales, I believe there would be less room for exploitation."[35]

CURRENT SITUATION

As you read over this rather damning article, the last sentence (above) really strikes a chord. The idea that MLMs are not about sales is uncomfortable for you, the new Manager of Operations and Member Services at the Direct Sellers Association of Canada.

You feel that a stronger, clearer response is needed to this article. The piece casts a rather long shadow on the world of MLM, and the response from the DSA has not shed enough light on that shadow. You have decided that your first task is to properly answer Flynn's article with one of your own.

You get in touch with the editorial board at *The Globe and Mail*, and they are amenable to running an opinion piece from the DSA. The paper mentions it would like to see a response based on established sales practices. Given your concern over that quote on recruitment from the original article, you decide the best focus would be on strategic prospecting. You remember how much good information can be gleaned when understanding the role of prospecting in establishing a good dialogue.

You are told to keep your opinion piece between 250 and 500 words. You are excited at the opportunity but want to go back to your notes on prospecting from your time in school. You want to determine how best to represent your field, and there needs to be multiple levels to your argument.

QUESTIONS

1. You decide to form your letter on prospecting in MLM by focusing on the trust-based sales process, where you look at steps ranging from generating sales leads to preparing for sales dialogue. What model are you using?

   a. prospecting matrix

   b. sales prospecting pyramid

   c. sales funnel

   d. prospect lead generator

2. A clear suggestion you make in your opinion piece on MLMs is that anyone who is thinking of joining an MLM should ask the organization to provide lists of previous orders to help understand why certain consumers who bought before have not bought since. You are advocating for MLMs to be more open about what?

   a. customer disclosure

   b. company records

   c. company financials

   d. corporate receipts

3. You realize that much of MLM prospecting is being done online, and it is important that your opinion piece address the power of the connected online world. What would you call this part of your argument?

   a. digital prospecting

   b. social selling

   c. digitized selling

   d. e-prospecting

CHAPTER ROLE PLAY

Strategic Prospecting and Preparing for Sales Dialogue: Prospecting and Gaining Prospect Information

BACKGROUND

Preston Adams has just completed the sales training program for the Office Equipment Division of Xerox. Adams has been assigned a territory in New Brunswick that includes the metro areas of Fredericton, Saint John, and Moncton. The company once commanded a significant market share in these markets. However, because of a problem with a previous salesperson in these markets three years ago, Xerox has not been directly working this particular region of central New Brunswick. Although a large number of Xerox machines are still in use across this territory, it has been a while since a salesperson has called on any accounts. As with any geographic area, a lot of changes have likely occurred, with existing companies moving or even going out of business and new companies opening up.

CURRENT SITUATION

Adams's sales manager, Eric Waits, is coming in two weeks to spend three days in the field with Adams calling on prospective accounts. Adams is working to develop a list of leads that he can qualify and then contact to set up the sales calls he will be making with his manager.

ROLE PLAY

Situation: Read the role play.

Characters: Preston Adams, salesperson for Xerox Business Machines Division; Jerri Spencer, office manager with purchasing responsibilities for Moncton-based McKelvey and Walters, Attorneys-at-Law.

Scene:

Location—Preston Adams's office at Xerox Business Machines Division.

Action—In the course of Adams's prospecting activities, Spencer and the McKelvey and Walters law firm have come up as a strong prospect for Xerox's new line of professional copiers. McKelvey and Walters operate a large office in Moncton that occupies most of two floors in the Planter's Bank Building and a branch office in Saint John. They were previously a customer of Xerox, but the information that Adams has obtained indicates that they are using an unspecified variety of different brands of copiers.

Role play the phone conversation between Adams and Spencer as Adams introduces himself and his company to Spencer, gathers needed information to better qualify the prospect, and asks for an appointment for an initial sales call.

6 | Planning Sales Dialogues and Presentations

In 1990, the government of Alberta formed Telus Communications to provide telephone services within the province. Since then, the organization has acquired and merged with other telephone companies to become Telus Corporation, one of Canada's largest national telecommunications companies. Telus has built its success around the notion that they "give where they live" and are dedicated to giving back to their communities to make the future friendlier for all Canadians. Their goal is to make an impact through connecting for good, which has resulted in Telus donating $1.3 billion since the year 2000, 1 million volunteer hours worked in 2018 by team members and retirees, and 2 million youth impacted annually.[1] Telus is committed to driving positive social outcomes through the power of technology and their inclusive and diverse team and customers. Diversity and inclusion are essential characteristics of their workforce, and Telus embraces different perspectives, experiences, and ways of thinking in order to deliver better insights, decisions, and solutions to their customers and community.[2] Overall, Telus's dedication to these pillars of business practice answers the question of why people want to do business with them.

Introduction

Companies like Telus are committed to gathering different types of customer information to search for insights about their customers so they can make decisions and offer solutions that best serve their customers' needs. In today's fast-changing, information-rich business world, top salespeople must be inquisitive and able to assess their own efforts when it comes to precall preparation. For example, salespeople should ask themselves if they are fully prepared in terms of what information they will need from the buyer, what they will want to convey to the buyer, what support information they will need, and what obstacles they will need to overcome. Their precall preparation must be guided by a firm objective that specifies the customer action sought as a result of the upcoming call.

Sales technology is assisting precall planning far beyond checking out the prospect's Web site. While customer Web-site searches can yield valuable information, other sources are rapidly growing in popularity. For example, LinkedIn has become a powerful tool for researching companies and individuals within those companies. Prospective buyers often seek advice on potential vendors on LinkedIn, and sales organizations are monitoring the site as part of precall preparation. InsideView.com offers an online tool that monitors LinkedIn and Twitter for relevant sales opportunities and prospect information. Google (Google.com/finance and Google alerts) and D&B Hoovers (www.hoovers.com) also offer salespeople efficient ways of preparing for sales calls.

With an abundance of information at their fingertips, salespeople have no excuse for arriving unprepared for a sales call. With most business decision makers starved for time, showing up unprepared is essentially an insult to the buyer. Top salespeople already know this,

and they would not dare insult their prospects or existing customers.[3]

LO 1 | CUSTOMER-FOCUSED SALES DIALOGUE PLANNING

 CPSA   3.2 Conduct sales presentations

Now more than ever buyers are generally well informed and have little time to waste. This means that salespeople must invest a significant amount of time in planning sales calls on prospective and existing customers so that they can communicate in a clear, credible, and interesting fashion. A **sales call** takes place when the salesperson and buyer or buyers meet in person to discuss business. This typically happens in the

> **sales call** An in-person meeting between a salesperson or sales team and one or more buyers to discuss business.

Selling in Action

Planning Sales Dialogues

Gary Walker is executive vice president of Channel Sales and Operations for CustomerCentricSelling, a global sales training firm. He urges salespeople to maximize their time with prospects and customers through strategic sales call planning. According to Mr. Walker, planning allows salespeople to focus on critical issues with the prospect and align with their key priorities. He observes that most prospects are looking for help in solving a problem or realizing a significant opportunity. To add maximum value, salespeople must be able to converse about prospects' goals, problems, and issues—not just present the features and benefits of their products. By strategically planning sales encounters, salespeople can convincingly demonstrate their situational fluency, or the ability to tailor sales conversations in terms that resonate with prospects. Mr. Walker says that customers want to do business with

salespeople who empower them. To accomplish that, salespeople must be prepared to converse about what the prospect is trying to achieve, what is preventing them from achieving it, and how the sales offering can help deliver the desired outcome. Mr. Walker says that precall planning shows the prospects that you respect their time, as time is not wasted with questions that can be answered through precall research. Planning also prevents shortcuts and carelessness. Sales call planning can become a reliable, repeatable process tailored for each individual prospect. It is easy for prospects to see how well-prepared (or not) salespeople are. As a result, Mr. Walker says, "I'd like to ask you to please prepare to win. Don't leave it to chance. Make precall preparation part of your sales process."

Source: Gary Walker, "Sales Tips: 10 Reasons Why Pre-Call Planning is Important," from the CustomerCentricSelling Sales Training Blog at http://blog.customercentricselling.com, March 14, 2017.

customer's place of business, but it may occur elsewhere, such as in the seller's place of business or at a trade show.

As defined in Chapter 1, **sales dialogue** is a business conversation between buyers and sellers that take place over time as salespeople attempt to initiate, develop, and enhance customer relationships. The term *sales conversation* is used interchangeably with sales dialogue. Some sales calls involve **sales presentations** as part of the dialogue. Sales presentations are comprehensive communications that convey multiple points designed to persuade the prospect or customer to make a purchase.

Ideally, sales presentations focus on customer value and take place only after the salesperson has completed the ADAPT process (introduced in Chapter 4). As a reminder, the ADAPT process means the salesperson has **a**ssessed the customer's situation; **d**iscovered his or her needs, buying processes, and strategic priorities; **a**ctivated the

buyer's interest in solving a problem or realizing an opportunity; helped the buyer **p**roject how value can be derived from a purchase; and then made a **t**ransition to the full sales presentation. Salespeople who attempt to make a sales presentation before building a foundation through sales dialogue risk being viewed as noncustomer-oriented and overly aggressive.

To focus on customer value and implement the trust-based selling process as discussed in Chapter 1 (refer to Figure 1.5), salespeople must have a basic understanding

© Yahoo Inc.

The importance of focusing on the customer when planning sales dialogues is reflected in the popular trade book *The Collaborative Sale* by Keith M. Eades and Timothy T. Sullivan.

sales dialogue Business conversations between buyers and sellers that occur as salespeople attempt to initiate, develop, and enhance customer relationships. Sales dialogue should be customer focused and have a clear purpose.

sales presentations Comprehensive communications that convey multiple points designed to persuade the customer to make a purchase.

of the value they and their companies can deliver to customers. Further, they must recognize that what constitutes value will typically vary from one customer to the next. Finally, as the process continues and relationships are established with customers, salespeople must work continually to increase the value their customers receive. Before, during, and after the sale, selling strategy must focus on customer needs and how the customer defines value. For additional insights on sales call planning, see Selling in Action: Planning Sales Dialogues.

To better understand the process of planning sales dialogues and presentations, we will now discuss the three most common approaches: the canned sales presentation, the written sales proposal, and organized sales communications formats. A planning template that serves as a guide for sales dialogues and comprehensive presentations will then be presented. The chapter concludes with a discussion of how to foster better sales dialogues when attempting to initiate relationships with customers.

LO 2 | SALES COMMUNICATIONS FORMATS

In planning customer encounters, salespeople must decide on a basic format, such as a canned sales presentation, a written sales proposal, or an organized sales dialogue. Exhibit 6.1 summarizes the types of communications sales professionals use. Each of these alternatives varies greatly in terms of how much customization and customer interaction is involved. A salesperson might use one or more of these formats with a particular customer. Each format has unique advantages and disadvantages. To be successful, these communications must be credible and clear. In addition, the salesperson must communicate in the right environment at an appropriate time to maximize the probability of a successful outcome.

For any of the three communications types, salespeople must plan to be as specific as possible in developing their sales message. For example, it is better to tell a prospect "This electric motor will produce 4800 RPM and requires only one hour of maintenance per week" than to say "This motor will really put out the work with only minimum maintenance."

Canned Sales Presentations

Canned sales presentations include scripted sales calls, memorized presentations, and automated presentations. The telemarketing industry relies heavily on scripted sales calls, and memorized presentations are common in trade show product demonstrations.

Exhibit 6.1
Types of Sales Communications

Canned Presentations
- These include scripted sales calls, and memorized and automated presentations.
- They can be complete and logically structured.
- The downside is that to not vary from buyer to buyer; they should be tested for effectiveness.

Written Sales Proposals
- The proposal is a complete self-contained sales presentation.
- Written proposals are often accompanied by sales calls before and after the proposal is submitted.
- Thorough customer assessment should take place before a customized proposal is written.

Organized Sales Dialogues and Presentations
- They address individual customer and different selling situations.
- They allow flexibility to adapt to buyer feedback.
- They are the most frequently used format by sales professionals.

Automated presentations often incorporate computer graphics, video, or slides to present the information to the prospect.

When done right, canned presentations are complete and logically structured. Objections and questions can be anticipated in advance, and appropriate responses can be formulated as part of the presentation. The sales message varies little from customer to customer, except that some sales scripts have "branches" or different salesperson responses based on how the customer responds. Canned presentations can be used by relatively inexperienced salespeople, and using this format might boost the confidence of some salespeople. Canned sales presentations should be tested for effectiveness, ideally with real customers, before they are implemented with the entire salesforce.

Canned sales presentations make an implicit assumption that customer needs and buying motives are essentially homogeneous. Therefore, canned presentations fail

canned sales presentation
Sales presentations that include scripted sales calls, memorized presentations, and automated presentations.

to capitalize on a key advantage of personal selling—the ability to adapt to different types of customers and various selling situations. The salesperson can only assume the buyer's need and must hope that a lively presentation of product benefits will cause the prospect to buy. The canned presentation can be effective, but is not appropriate for many situations—simply because customer opportunity to interact is minimized. During a memorized presentation, the salesperson talks 80 to 90 percent of the time, only occasionally allowing the prospect to express his or her feelings, concerns, or opinions. Canned presentations do not handle interruptions well, may be awkward to use with a broad product line, and may alienate buyers who want to participate in the interaction.

Despite its limitations, the canned sales presentation can be effective in some situations. If the product line is narrow and the salesforce is relatively inexperienced, the canned presentation may be suitable. Also, many salespeople find it effective to use a sales dialogue to introduce their company, to demonstrate the product, or for some other limited purpose.

A written sales proposal should follow a strategic sales process.

Written Sales Proposals

The second basic type of sales communication is the **written sales proposal**. The proposal is a complete self-contained sales presentation, but it is often accompanied by sales dialogues before or after the proposal is delivered. In some cases, the customer may receive a proposal and then request that the salesperson make a sales call to further explain the proposal and provide answers to questions. Alternatively, preliminary sales dialogues may lead to a sales proposal. In any event, the sales proposal should be prepared after the salesperson has made a thorough assessment of the buyer's situation as it relates to the seller's offering.

The sales proposal has long been associated with important, high-dollar-volume sales transactions. It is frequently used in competitive bidding situations and in situations involving the selection of a new supplier by the prospect. One advantage of the proposal is that the written word is usually viewed as being more credible than the spoken word. Written proposals are subject to

> Buyers expect clear, informative sales messages, and they are less tolerant of sloppy communication.

careful scrutiny with few time constraints, and specialists in the buying firm often analyze various sections of the proposal.

Sales proposal content is similar to other comprehensive sales presentations, focusing on customer needs and related benefits the seller offers. In addition, technical information, pricing data, and perhaps a timetable are included. Most proposals provide a triggering mechanism, such as a proposed contract to confirm the sale, and some specify follow-up action to be taken if the proposal is satisfactory.

With multimedia sales presentations becoming more routine, it is natural to think that written sales proposals would be declining in importance. Actually, the opposite is true. With the widespread use of multimedia, the standards for all sales communication continue to rise. Buyers expect clear, informative sales messages, and they are less tolerant of sloppy communication. Because everyone knows that word processing programs have functions to check spelling and grammar, for example, mistakes are less acceptable than ever.

Because written communication provides a permanent record of claims and intentions, salespeople should be careful not to overpromise but still maintain a positive and supportive tone. No buyer wants to read a proposal full of legal disclaimers and warnings, yet such information may be a necessary ingredient in certain written communication. As with all communication, salespeople

written sales proposal A complete self-contained sales presentation on paper, often accompanied by other verbal sales presentations before or after the proposal is delivered.

should try to give buyers the information they need to make informed decisions.

WRITING EFFECTIVE PROPOSALS

 CPSA 2.4 Communicate in writing

Whether the proposal is in response to a buyer's request for proposals (RFP) or generated to complement and strengthen a sales presentation, it is essential that the proposal be correctly written and convey the required information in an attractive manner. Professionals who specialize in the creation of sales proposals give these reasons why proposals may fail:[4]

1. Customer does not know the seller.
2. Proposal does not follow the customer-specified format.
3. Executive summary does not address customer needs.
4. Proposal uses the seller's (not the customer's) company jargon, which forces readers to interpret the message.
5. Writing is flat, technical, and without passion. A technical data dump is not effective.
6. Generic material does not match the targeted prospect, indicating a lack of customer-focused consultative selling.
7. Proposal is not convincing, and does not substantiate claims made.
8. Proposal has poor layout and glaring grammatical errors.
9. Proposal does not address key decision criteria. Don't assume what is important to the buyer—ask!
10. Proposal is vague, lacking specifics in key areas such as pricing and buyer/seller roles and responsibilities.

Clearly, developing a quality proposal takes time and effort. When beginning the proposal-writing process, it is important for the salesperson to adopt the right mindset with a key thought of "Okay, this will take some time to get the details down, but it will be worth it." To reinforce this mindset, consider the advice given in Exhibit 6.2: Tips for Creating Effective Sales Proposals.[5]

Breaking the proposal down into its primary and distinct parts can simplify the process of writing an effective proposal. Five parts common to most proposals are an executive summary, customer needs and proposed solution, seller profile, pricing and sales agreement, and an implementation section with a timetable.

Exhibit 6.2

Tips for Creating Effective Sales Proposals

- Focus on your prospect. Think like the buyer. If you were the buyer, what would you want to know before making a decision?
- Present a compelling, relevant case for your offering.
- Get to the point and make your proposal as concise as possible. Bigger is not better.
- Quantify the value you can offer so prospects can financially justify their purchase decisions.
- Present important details and make the entire proposal clear. Transparency builds trust.
- Include testimonials and endorsements when appropriate.
- Write the proposal in the customer's language. Avoid seller jargon.
- Realize that most proposals serve an educational purpose. If customers do not understand your proposal, they will reject it.
- Clearly communicate next steps and make it easy for the customer to take action, including accepting the proposal.
- Be sure communications lines are open in case the customer has questions or wants additional information.
- Allow ample time for proofreading. Sloppy proposals are completely unacceptable.

Executive Summary This summary precedes the full proposal and serves two critical functions. First, it should succinctly and clearly demonstrate the salesperson's understanding of the customer's needs and the relevance of the proposed solution. An effective summary will spell out the customer's problems, the nature of the proposed solution, and the resulting benefits to the customer. A second function of the summary is to build a desire to read the full proposal. This is important as many key members of the organization often read little more than the information provided in the summary. A question new salespeople commonly ask refers to the length of the executive summary. A good rule of thumb is that an executive summary should be limited to two typewritten pages—especially if the main body of the report is fewer than 50 pages.

Customer Needs and Proposed Solution This section is typically composed of two primary parts. First, the situation analysis should concisely explain the salesperson's understanding of the customer's situation, problems, and needs. Second, the recommended solution is presented and supported with illustrations and evidence on how the proposed solution uniquely addresses the buyer's problems and needs. The emphasis in this section should be on the benefits resulting from the solution and not on the product or service being sold. It is important that these benefits be described from the perspective of the customer. Proprietary information required in the proposal can be protected in a number of ways. The most common method is to place a confidential notice on the cover. Many technology companies ask the prospect to sign a nondisclosure agreement that is part of the overall document and, in some instances, the selling organization will even copyright the proposal.

Seller Profile This section contains information that the customer wants to know about the selling company. This section offers a succinct overview and background of the firm, but the emphasis should be on the company's capabilities. Case histories of customers for whom the company solved similar problems with similar solutions have proved to be an effective method to document and illustrate organizational capabilities and past successes.

Pricing and Sales Agreement The previous sections are designed to build the customer value of the proposed solution. Once this value has been established, the proposal should "ask for the order" by presenting pricing information and delivery options. This information is often presented in the form of a sales agreement for the buyer to sign off on and complete.

Implementation and Timetable The purpose of this section is to make it as easy as possible for the buyer to make a positive purchase decision. In effect, this section should say "if you like the proposal and want to act on it, this is what you do." There may be a contract to sign, an order form to fill out, or instructions regarding whom to call to place an order or request further information. A timetable that details a schedule of key implementation events should also be included.

Evaluating Proposals Before Submission

 2.4 Communicate in writing

In the customer's eyes, the standards for written sales proposals are high. Poor spelling and grammatical mistakes send a negative message that the seller has little regard for attention to detail. The quality of a salesperson's written documents is a surrogate for that salesperson's competence and ability as well as the capabilities and overall quality of the organization. If the proposal does not properly interpret the buyer's needs or fails to make a compelling case to justify the purchase, the odds of success are low. Although a well-written proposal is no guarantee of making the sale, a poorly written proposal will certainly reduce the probability of success.

Since the stakes are usually high when written sales proposals are used, it is a best practice to evaluate proposals carefully before they are submitted to the customer. In fact, it is a good idea to build the evaluative criteria into the proposal writing process early on, then use the criteria shown in Exhibit 6.3[6] as a final check before submitting a sales proposal.

Organized Sales Dialogues

 2.5 Conduct meetings

In most situations, the process of converting a prospect into a customer will take several sales conversations over multiple encounters. These conversations constitute an **organized sales dialogue**. For example, salespeople often speak by telephone with a qualified prospect to get an appointment for a later meeting. The second conversation with the customer typically focuses on fact finding and parallels the ADAPT process. The next step would come after the salesperson has developed a tailored solution for the customer. The salesperson may make a comprehensive sales presentation but, in this case, it is designed for dialogue with the customer throughout. To reiterate, this is not a one-way presentation or monologue—it is a sales dialogue with a high level of customer involvement. This type of comprehensive presentation is commonly called an **organized sales presentation**.

Organized sales dialogues may precede or follow other sales communications, such as a written sales proposal. Sales dialogues are much more than mere

organized sales dialogue Also known as the organized sales presentation. Unlike a canned sales presentation, an organized sales dialogue has a high level of customer involvement.

organized sales presentation A sales presentation that allows a salesperson to implement appropriate sales strategies and tactics based on customer research or information gathered during previous sales calls. Organized sales presentations feature a high-level two-way dialogue with the customer.

Exhibit 6.3

Evaluating Sales Proposals

It is a best practice to evaluate sales proposals before they are submitted to the customer. Five important dimensions for evaluating proposals are reliability, assurance, tangibles, empathy, and responsiveness.

Reliability reflects the seller's ability to identify creative and practical business solutions that will help the buyer achieve their goals and objectives.

Does the proposal

1. Present a solid business solution that meets the buyer's expectations?
2. Effectively describe the seller's offering and clearly define how it will work?
3. Describe all of the seller's fees, prices, and expenses the buyer will incur?
4. Present seller capabilities and convert them into buyer-specific financial and non-financial benefits?

Assurance increases the buyer's trust and confidence in the seller's ability to deliver successful results.

Does the proposal

1. Assure the buyer that the seller has the experience and capability required to fulfill the contract?
2. Present the seller's roles, responsibilities, and business practices to fulfill the contract?
3. Provide a schedule with clear specification of major work activities?
4. Provide customer references that are easy to verify and that demonstrate a solid track record?

Tangibles enhances and differentiates the communication of the seller's message and invites readership by its content, structure, and overall appearance.

Does the proposal

1. Focus on the customer, provide a logical flow, and have high standards for mechanics and readability?
2. Convert the intangibles into tangibles such as schedules, diagrams, graphics, or charts?
3. Effectively use appendices to control length and provide more detail for interested readers?
4. Contain an Executive Summary that condenses the entire proposal into no more than 2 to 4 pages?

Empathy reflects the seller's thorough understanding of the buyer's unique business environment, operations, organization, improvement opportunities, needs, and objectives.

Does the proposal

1. Reflect a thorough understanding of the buyer's business operations?
2. Clearly define the buyer's critical business issues or improvement opportunities?
3. Clearly define the buyer's needs for addressing critical issues or improvement opportunities?
4. Propose a product or service that satisfies the buyer's time frame and unique business needs?

Responsiveness demonstrates the seller's willingness to work closely with the buyer to understand their unique situation, present viable business solutions, and ensure achievement of promised results.

Does the proposal

1. Demonstrate the willingness to ask questions, gather information, and gain a thorough knowledge of the buyer's unique business issues or improvement opportunities?
2. Present a custom offering tailored to the customer's unique situation?
3. Offer a review between buyer and seller to answer questions and clarify issues?
4. Match the seller's consultative selling process?

Before making a comprehensive sales presentation, a salesperson will have several conversations with a potential customer.

conversation—they are a chance for the salesperson to seek information and/or action from the prospect and to explore the business reasons the prospect has for continuing the dialogue with the salesperson (e.g., solving a problem or realizing an opportunity). Feedback from the prospect is encouraged, and therefore this format is less likely to offend a participation-prone buyer.

When the situation calls for a full sales presentation, the organized sales presentation is usually favoured over both the canned presentation and the written proposal. Such an approach allows much-needed flexibility to adapt to buyer feedback and changing circumstances during the presentation. Organized presentations may also include some canned portions. For example, a salesperson for Caterpillar might show a video to illustrate the earth-moving capabilities of a bulldozer as one segment of an organized presentation. Due of its flexibility during the sales call and its ability to address various sales situations, the organized presentation is the most frequently used format for professional sales presentations.

One reality of this presentation format is that it requires a knowledgeable salesperson who can react to questions and objections from the prospect. Further, this format may extend the time horizon before a purchase decision is reached, and it is vulnerable to diversionary delay tactics by the prospect. Presumably,

> By fully participating in the dialogue, both buyer and seller have an opportunity to establish a mutually beneficial relationship.

those who make these arguments think that a canned presentation forces a purchase decision in a more expedient fashion. Overall, however, most agree that the organized presentation is ideal for most sales situations. Its flexibility allows a full exploration of customer needs and appropriate adaptive behaviour by the salesperson. By fully participating in the dialogue, both buyer and seller have an opportunity to establish a mutually beneficial relationship.

The trust-based relational selling presentation, often combining elements of need-satisfaction and consultative selling, is a popular form of an organized presentation. The first stage of the process, the need development stage, is devoted to a discussion of the buyer's needs. As seen in Figure 6.1, during this phase the buyer should be talking 60 to 70 percent of the time. The salesperson accomplishes this by using the first four stages of the ADAPT process.

The second stage of the process (need awareness) is to verify what the buyer thinks his or her needs are and to make the buyer aware of potential needs that may exist. For instance, fast-food restaurants were generally slow to recognize the need to offer more low-fat and low-carbohydrate menu items until their sales volume suffered. Others, such as Subway, gained a competitive advantage by working with their suppliers to formulate a significant number of menu alternatives for the health-conscious consumer.

A logical conclusion of the needs awareness stage is to have the prospects confirm their needs. It is a positive step when the salesperson discovers the prospect's needs, but far more effective when the prospect confirms the importance of those needs. The need-awareness stage is a good time to restate the prospect's needs and to clarify exactly what the prospect's needs are.

During the last stage of the presentations, the need-fulfillment stage, the salesperson must show how his or her product and its benefits will meet the needs of the buyer. As seen in Figure 6.1, the salesperson during the need-fulfillment stage will do more of the talking by indicating what specific product will meet the buyer's needs. The salesperson, by being a good listener early in the process, will now have a better chance to gain the buyer's interest and trust by talking about specific benefits the buyer has confirmed as being important.

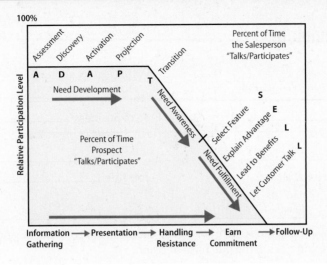

At some points in the two-way sales dialogue, the customer will do more talking; at other points, the salesperson will do more of the talking.

To engage in effective sales dialogue, salespeople should try to think like the customer and anticipate key issues that should be addressed. To reiterate a point made earlier in this chapter, researching the prospect or customer is essential in preparing for effective dialogue during organized sales presentations.

LO 3 | SALES DIALOGUE TEMPLATE

Sales dialogues are not scripted in advance as canned sales presentations are; however, salespeople should think ahead about what questions and statements to include in the conversation and be prepared to hold up their end of the conversation with an appropriate amount of detail. A **sales dialogue template** (see Exhibit 6.4) is a useful tool to ensure that all pertinent content areas are covered with each prospect. The template is flexible and can be used either to plan a comprehensive organized sales presentation or to guide sales dialogues of a more narrow scope. The template is not meant to be a script for a sales encounter, but rather an aid in planning and assembling the information required of the salesperson.

By addressing the issues noted in the template, salespeople can facilitate trust-building by demonstrating their competence and expertise, customer orientation, candour, dependability, and compatibility. It is true that trust is built through behaviour not just by planning and having good intentions. However, salespeople who are aware of what it takes to earn the customer's trust in the planning stages have a better chance of earning that trust in subsequent encounters with the customer. The sales dialogue template is organized into nine sections, each of which is discussed individually.

Section 1: Prospect Information

This section is used to record specific information on the prospect such as the company name, the key decision maker's name and job title, and the type of business. In most business-to-business situations, it is critical to know who else is involved in the buying decision and what role they play, such as gatekeeper, user, or influencer. (Refer to Chapter 3 if you need to review the buying team concept.) It is also important that the salesperson makes sure all the key players are receiving the appropriate information and getting the proper attention they deserve. A mistake salespeople often make is not identifying all the buying influencers.

> **sales dialogue template** A flexible planning tool that assists the salesperson in assembling pertinent information to be covered with the prospect.

Exhibit 6.4

Sales Dialogue Template

1. Prospect Information:

A. Company and key person information

Company Name: _____	Type of Business: _____

Key-Person Information

Prospect's Name (Key Decision Maker): _____	Job Title: _____

B. Other influences on the purchase decision: For all key people involved in the buying process, provide names, job titles, departments, and roles in the purchase decision.

Names/Job Title	Departments	Role in Purchase Decision
Add other people as necessary		

2. Customer Value Proposition: A brief statement of how you will add value to the prospect's business by meeting a need or providing an opportunity. Include a brief description of the product or service:

3. Sales Call Objective (must require customer action, such as making a purchase, supplying critical information, etc.):

4. Linking Buying Motives, Benefits, Support Information, and Reinforcement Methods: This section should address the buying motives of all persons who will be involved in the upcoming sales call.

A. *Buying motives:* What is most important to the prospect(s) in making a purchase decision? **Rational** motives include economic issues, such as quality, cost, service capabilities, and the strategic priorities of the prospect's company. **Emotional** motives include fear, status, and ego-related feelings. List all relevant buying motives in order of importance.	B. *Specific benefits matched to buying motives:* Benefits to be stressed are arranged in priority order (sequence to be followed unless prospect feedback during the presentation indicates an alternative sequence). Each benefit should correspond to one or more buying motives.	C. *Information needed to support claims for each benefit.*	D. *Where appropriate, methods for reinforcing verbal content (Audio/ visual, collateral material, illustrations, testimonials, etc.).*
1. _____	_____	_____	
Continue listing all relevant buying motives and information in columns B, C, and D.			

(Continued)

Exhibit 6.4

Sales Dialogue Template (*Continued*)

5. Current Suppliers (If Applicable) and Other Key Competitors:

Competitors	Strengths	Weaknesses
Complete for all key competitors		

6. Beginning the Sales Dialogue:

Plans for the first few minutes of the sales presentation:
Introduction, thanks, agenda agreement, then begin ADAPT as appropriate or transition into other sales dialogue or presentation:

Assessment _____

Discovery _____

Activation _____

Project _____

Transition to Presentation _____

Note: The ADAPT process may take place over several sales conversations during multiple sales calls. In other cases, it may be concluded in a single sales call, then immediately followed by a sales presentation during the same sales call.

7. Anticipating Prospect Questions and Objections, with Planned Responses:

Questions/Objections	Responses
Include a comprehensive set of questions and objections with your corresponding responses.	

8. Earning Prospect Commitment:

A preliminary plan for how the prospect will be asked for a commitment related to the sales call objective:

9. Building Value through Follow-Up Action:

Statement of follow-up action needed to ensure that the buyer–seller relationship moves in a positive direction:

Every Business Sells

Keith Collins is the CEO at xwave Solutions Ireland. His company provides a broad range of IT solutions to the Republic of Ireland (the South), working with major business and government accounts. He's been with xwave Solutions Ireland for four years.

As a salesperson, how do you provide value to your customers?

Providing value to large business and government clients goes well beyond simply offering products and services to meet their immediate IT needs. Significant value can be brought by developing a thorough understanding of the clients' industry and, more importantly, an understanding of the specific functional issues and opportunities of their organization. Stronger value is delivered and stronger partnerships are built when clients see that you are committed to gaining a better understanding of their specific short- and long-term needs and opportunities. You then become more than a salesperson.

As a salesperson, how do you provide value to your organization?

Beyond the obvious value to delivering new sources of revenue to your own organization, an effective salesperson can also bring additional types of value. Successfully bringing creative and innovative IT solutions to clients actually ensures more interesting and enjoyable work for IT specialists who are part of the solution delivery team. The energy and learning brought into the organization by these types of client solutions cannot be overstated.

What is your greatest challenge you face today as a salesperson?

In the early 2000s the Irish economy was booming and became known as the Celtic Tiger. Competition in the IT industry there was intense with a market presence by many international IT and consulting firms. The challenge this provided to a mid-sized Canadian-based IT company was finding an effective way to break through the market noise and to differentiate our solutions from those being proposed by larger firms with a global brand. Routinely xwave was competing with over 30 larger IT firms for any new piece of business.

How do you try to overcome this challenge?

We used two principal strategies to overcome this differentiation challenge. First, we limited our target clients to the four industries in which we had a proven track record of success in Canada, and in which we had strong functional knowledge—so we could speak their language more effectively than most of our competitors. Second, we were able to build many of the specific IT solutions with our teams based in Canada, which enabled more competitive pricing than those firms working in the overheated Irish economy. Using these strategies, xwave Ireland delivered a profit in its first year of operation—a major achievement given the many start-up costs in a new country.

What advice do you have for someone starting out in sales?

First, you should always look beyond the immediate sale and see the longer-term opportunities to enable the success of your clients. Second, it's important to go beyond your own technical knowledge and gain a thorough understanding of the industry dynamics and the functional issues and opportunities of your clients. This will build a mutually beneficial relationship and lead to longer-term shared success.

© Keith Collins

Every Business Sells

Taylor Young is head of business development at CoLab, a computer software company that sells enterprise SaaS for manufacturing teams. Taylor's primary focus is selling to technical leaders (managers and directors of engineering) of design and manufacturing companies in the automotive and industrial equipment industries. Working for a growing start-up, Taylor doesn't have defined sales territories, and she sells across North America with a focus in Ontario and Michigan. She's worked at CoLab for three years.

As a salesperson, how do you provide value to your customers?

I remind leads of their pain points in the early stages, guide them to the conclusion that they need to do something about it, and then facilitate conversations around what success could look like and how we could get there. Once they've become customers, I make sure our success team is set up to understand their needs intimately and I'm a readily available resource as they plan expansion.

As a salesperson, how do you provide value to your organization?

I generate revenue, and I work toward goals that drive our larger business milestones (e.g., financing rounds). I only bring on customers that we can make successful. I also filter feedback to ensure our product team is hearing the relevant information they need and not noise from poorly qualified leads. I take the information I get to hear straight from the customer, and communicate it to our team every day to make sure they're getting that value too as they make decisions about product, marketing, etc.

What is your greatest challenge you face today as a salesperson?

Turning down seemingly great opportunities that might take us away from our core objectives.

How do you try to overcome this challenge?

By regularly revisiting mission, vision, values and ensuring we're on course.

What advice do you have for someone starting out in sales?

Focus on understanding your customer's problem and their vision for success and the rest becomes a lot easier.

LO 4 | Section 2: Customer Value Proposition

6.1 Understand your company

In this section, the salesperson develops a preliminary **customer value proposition**, which is a statement of how the sales offering will add value to the prospect's business by meeting a need or providing an opportunity. Essentially, the customer value proposition summarizes the legitimate business reason for making the sales call by answering the prospect's question, "Why should I spend my time with you?" A good customer value proposition clearly states why the customer will be better off by doing business with the salesperson and his or her firm, but at this point does not try to list all of the reasons.[7]

At the planning stage, the customer value proposition is preliminary. The salesperson has good reason to believe that customer value can be enhanced by delivering on the contents of the proposition, but the true value of the proposition will be accepted or rejected by the customer as the sales process moves along. It is during this sales dialogue process that the actual customer value to be delivered will be refined and modified. This section of the template provides a point of departure for planning purposes and assumes that the value proposition is likely to be modified

> **customer value proposition**
> A statement of how the sales offering will add value to the prospect's business by meeting a need or providing an opportunity.

before the purchase decision. In writing the preliminary customer value proposition, salespeople should attempt the following:

1. Determine the primary business reasons that customers would use your offering. Key reasons include revenue generation, cost savings, customer retention, building market share, productivity gains, profitability, legal and safety compliance, and return on investment.

2. Keep the statement fairly simple so that the direction for upcoming sales dialogues is clear.

3. Choose the key benefit(s) likely to be most important to the specific customer who is the audience for this particular dialogue or presentation. (At this point, it is not necessary to list all the benefits of their offerings.)

4. Make the value proposition as specific as possible on tangible outcomes (e.g., improvements to revenues, cost containment or reduction, market share, process speed and efficiency) and/or the enhancement of the customer's strategic priority.

5. Reflect product or service dimensions that add value, whether or not the customer pays for them. For example, some companies offer delivery, installation, and training along with the purchase of their products. Added value may also accrue from what the seller's sales team provides (e.g., work in the field with a distributor's salespeople or certification training for the buyer's technicians).

6. Promise only what can be consistently delivered. Strictly speaking, a customer value proposition in the planning stage is not a guarantee, it is a belief based on the salesperson's knowledge and best judgment. As the sales process moves along, appropriate guarantees can be made.

7. Use action verbs that show a departure from the status quo such as increase, improve, cut, save, accelerate, enhance, grow, eliminate, minimize, and maximize.

8. Be as specific as possible about key metrics, including time frame, financials, and percentage targets.

9. Practise the verbal communication of the customer value proposition with people not familiar with your business. Do they understand the proposition and can they repeat it? If not, rework the proposition until it is easily recalled.

Using these points as a guide, the following is an example of a customer value proposition that could provide clear direction for planning an upcoming sales presentation or a series of sales dialogues:

"ABC Company can improve its market share by a minimum of four percentage points in a one-year period in its Vancouver and Calgary markets by implementing our customer satisfaction and retention training for its customer service personnel."

In contrast, here is an example of a poorly constructed customer value proposition:

"By adopting our customer satisfaction and retention programs, ABC Company will see a dramatic increase in its market share."

This second proposition opens the salesperson to a potential barrage of questions:

Dramatic increase in market share? What's dramatic?

We operate in 22 markets. Are you saying that we will increase market shares in all 22 markets?

What do you mean by programs? Are you referring to training programs?

In the planning stages, salespeople may or may not be fully aware of the prospect's needs and priorities—and, until they are aware of these needs and priorities, the sales dialogue should focus on the first two stages of the ADAPT process: assessing the prospect's situation and discovering his or her needs. Unless these stages are completed, the customer value proposition will not contain enough detail to be useful. Done correctly, a customer value proposition will portray the seller's company in a favourable light and give the customer reasonable expectations of the selling company. As illustrated in An Ethical Dilemma, this sometimes requires caution in communicating the customer value proposition.

Section 3: Sales Call Objective

Section 3 asks the salesperson to determine the objective for his or her sales call. Salespeople must have an objective for each sales call. Basically, sales call objectives state what salespeople want customers to do as a result of the sales call. The objectives should be specific enough to know whether or not they have been accomplished at the conclusion of the call, and they should require customer actions, such as placing an order, agreeing to participate in a test market, or supplying specific information useful to the salesperson. Many salespeople think that they have only one objective: to get an order. Other legitimate sales call objectives do exist. For instance, during an introductory call the objective may be simply to introduce the salesperson and his or her company and to gather information on the buyer's needs. Eventually, the major sales presentation objective will be to earn a commitment from the customer by making a sale, but this is not always the only objective. At the very least, the objective of any sales call should be to advance the process toward an order.

LO 5 | Section 4: Linking Buying Motives, Benefits, Support Information, and Other Reinforcement Methods

In Section 4 of the planning template, the prospect's buying motives are linked to specific benefits offered. For each benefit identified, the salesperson will also assemble the information needed to support the claims to be made in the upcoming dialogue or presentation. In some cases, verbal claims must be reinforced with audiovisual portrayal, illustrations, printed collateral material, or testimonials from satisfied customers, as appropriate to the situation.

Buying motives refer to the most important factors from the customer's perspective in making a

purchase decision. In other words, what will motivate the buyer to make a purchase? Buying motives may be rational or emotional, or a combination of both rational and emotional. **Rational buying motives** typically relate to the economics of the situation, including cost, profitability, quality, services offered, and the total value of the seller's offering that the customer perceives. **Emotional buying motives**, such as fear, the need for security, the need for status, or the need to be liked, are sometimes difficult for salespeople to uncover as prospects are generally less likely to share such motives with salespeople. In business-to-business selling, rational motives are typically the most important buying motives, but salespeople should not ignore emotional motives if they are known to exist.

In linking benefits to buying motives, benefits

buying motives A need-activated drive to search for and acquire a solution to resolve a need or problem; the most important factors from the customer's perspective in making a purchase decision.

rational buying motives Typically relate to the economics of the situation, including cost, profitability, quality, services offered, and the total value of the seller's offering as perceived by the customer.

emotional buying motives Include such motives as security, status, and the need to be liked; sometimes difficult for salespeople to uncover these motives.

should be distinguished from features. **Features** are factual statements about the characteristics of a product or service, such as "This is the lightest electrical motor in its performance category." **Benefits** describe the added value for the customer—the favourable outcome derived from a feature. For example, "The lightweight motor supports your mobile repair service strategy in that it is very portable. The ease of use allows your technicians to complete more service calls per day, thus increasing your profitability." To make such a claim about increasing profitability, the salesperson would need to gather specific information to support it. For example, in this case the claim that technicians can complete more service calls per day because the motor is easy to use might call for competitive comparisons and actual usage data or a demonstration.

Some situations may lead the salesperson to decide that a product demonstration and testimonials from satisfied customers will reinforce the spoken word. In other cases, third-party research studies or articles in trade publications might be used to reinforce oral claims. Another powerful option is material developed by the salesperson, such as a break-even chart showing how quickly the customer can recoup the investment in the new product or service. A note of caution: It is always a good idea to use these types of sales support materials sparingly—some prospects do not react positively to information overload. Chapter 7 discusses in greater detail sales tools and how they can enhance the sales effort.

Section 5: Competitive Situation

1.1 Understand the market

Understanding the competitive situation is essential in planning sales dialogues and presentations. Because buyers make competitive comparisons in their decision processes, salespeople should be prepared for it. This section of the planning template asks the salesperson to identify key competitors and to specify their strengths and weaknesses. By knowing their own product's strengths and weaknesses as well as those of their competitors, salespeople are better equipped to articulate customer value relative to their competitors. This competitive positioning is important, as most major purchase decisions are made in a highly competitive business environment. If the prospect is already buying a similar product, knowledge about the current supplier can give the salesperson critical insight into which buying motives and product attributes are likely to be affecting the buyer's decisions.

Section 6: Beginning the Sales Dialogue

Section 6 addresses the critical first few minutes of the sales call. During this period, salespeople will greet the prospect and introduce themselves, if necessary. There is typically some brief polite conversation between the salesperson and buyer as the salesperson is welcomed to the buyer's office, then both parties are usually eager to get down to business as quickly as possible.

It is recommended that the salesperson propose an agenda, to which there may or may not have been previous agreement. Once the agenda is established, the salesperson may need to gather more information to use in the sales dialogue or, depending on the situation, it could be appropriate to make a transition a sales dialogue or presentation. A typical first few minutes might sound like this:

Buyer: Come on in, Pat. I am John Jones. Nice to meet you. (*Introduction/greeting.*)

Seller: Mr. Jones, I am Pat Devlin with XYZ Company. Nice to meet you, too. I appreciate the time that you are spending with me today. (*Thanks, acknowledges importance of the buyer's time.*)

Buyer: Glad you could make it. We have had a lot of cancellations lately because of the bad weather. Did you have any problems driving over from Montreal? (*Polite conversation may last for several minutes depending on the buyer–seller relationship and on how much the buyer wants to engage in this sort of conversation.*)

Seller: Not really, it was pretty smooth today. I know you are busy, so I thought we could talk about a couple of key ways I think we can really help you build market share with your end-user market. How does that sound? (*A simple illustration of getting the buyer to agree to the agenda.*)

Buyer: Sure, let's get right to it. What do you have in mind?

Seller: Well, based on our phone call last week, I believe that our training programs for your customer service representatives can improve your customer satisfaction ratings and customer retention. I can share the details with you over the next 20 minutes or so... (*Transition to a sales dialogue or presentation based on customer needs and customer value.*)

In planning the first few minutes of the sales call, salespeople should remind themselves to be friendly and positive. They should also remain flexible in terms of their proposed agenda—customers like to have an

features Qualities or characteristics of a product or service that are designed to provide value to a buyer.

benefits The added value or favourable outcome derived from features of the product or service the seller offers.

Technology in Sales

Facilitating Team Selling with Google Apps

Major account and global sales teams must collaborate and coordinate efficiently and quickly to be effective. Technical product experts must provide their inputs, financial analysts and researchers must analyze data and make recommendations, and team leaders must finalize the entire package together prior to in-person sales calls. Google is a market leader in providing Web-enabled applications that allow communications and information sharing from mobile and stationary devices. Using these apps, sales teams can collaborate on sales proposals and presentation plans using Google Docs, which provides simultaneous content creation and real-time feedback to members of the sales team. Written content, visual designs, and videos can be stored on Google Drive.

Files can be accessed and edited on any device without using e-mail to access the files. If additional preparation, training, or strategy sessions are needed to prepare for an upcoming key account sales call, Google Hangouts can be used for virtual meetings without the travel time and costs of live meetings. If the sales call involves a formal presentation, Google Slides offers a tool for crafting key content and graphics into a compelling message. In a fast-paced, competitive marketplace, sales teams must move quickly when new opportunities arise, and collaboration through technology is increasingly popular.

Source: "Top 10 Ways to Use G Suite in Sales and Marketing," available online from Google at https://www.google.com/learning-center, May 3, 2017.

agenda but sometimes want to modify it. The salesperson should be prepared to make an adjustment on the spot. For example, in the previous dialogue, the prospect might have said, "Yes, I want to hear about your training programs for our customer service reps, but I am also interested in your thoughts on how we can build a service-based culture across our entire marketing organization." The salesperson might respond accordingly, "I would be happy to do that. In fact, let me start with an overview that shows you the big picture from a strategy and company culture perspective, then later I will show you how the customer service training piece fits into the overall strategy. How does that sound?"

In most sales situations involving one-on-one encounters with customers, salespeople would not present a formal written agenda, but instead would present a brief agenda verbally. In more formal situations that involve team selling and multiple buyers, a written agenda distributed in advance of the meeting could be appropriate. Properly presented, an agenda shows the prospect that the salesperson is prepared. It also demonstrates customer orientation by asking if the prospect has anything to add to the agenda. In addition, an agenda can provide continuity from one sales call to the next by incorporating important follow-up points from the previous sales call.

These first few minutes are critical in the trust-building process. By showing sensitivity to customer needs and opinions, and by asking questions to clarify the customer's perspective, salespeople demonstrate a customer orientation. Salespeople can demonstrate their expertise and competence by being sharp and well prepared. First impressions are crucial in all human interactions, so time spent on planning the first few minutes is a good investment on the salesperson's part. But remember that the planning template is not intended as a script. It is imperative that salespeople think logically—and from the buyer's point of view—in planning what to say after greeting the customer. When companies use team selling, precall planning by the sales teams can be facilitated by technologies that allow real-time access from multiple locations. For more on this topic, see Technology in Sales: Facilitating Team Selling with Google Apps.

Initiating Contact

When you are planning the first few minutes of the sales dialogue or presentation, there are few ironclad rules. Instead, the situation and the prospect's preferences suggest the appropriate sequence—but a few general rules do apply:

- Following an adequate introduction of the salesperson and the salesperson's company, the salesperson should use questions, careful listening, and confirmation statements to clarify and define explicit customer needs and motives as related to his or her offering.

Planning the first few minutes of a sales dialogue can help the salesperson make a positive impression and build trust.

- The salesperson should present benefits in order of importance according to the prospect's needs and motives, and these benefits may be repeated during the presentation and at the conclusion of the presentation.

- If the sales presentation is a continuation of one or more previous sales calls, the salesperson should make a quick summary of what has been agreed on in the past, moving quickly into the prospect's primary area of interest.

- As a general rule, the salesperson should not focus on pricing issues until the prospect's needs have been defined and the salesperson has shown how those needs can be addressed with the product or service being sold. After prospects fully understand how the product or service meets their needs, they can make informed judgments on price/value issues.

Obviously, the first few minutes of the sales call will be greatly influenced by previous interaction (if any) between the buyer and the salesperson. For example, if previous sales calls have established buyer needs and the buyer has agreed to a sales presentation, the first few minutes will be quite different than if this is the first sales call on this prospect. The ADAPT questioning process (refer to Chapter 4) can be used in part or whole to acquire needed information and make a transition to the sales dialogue or presentation. As a guide, the salesperson should respect the buyer's time and get to the presentation as soon as circumstances allow. The salesperson should not rush to get to the presentation and certainly should not launch into a presentation without establishing buyer needs and interest in it.

Section 7: Anticipating Questions and Objections

For reasons to be explained fully in Chapter 8, prospects will almost always have questions and objections that salespeople must be prepared to answer. In the planning stages, salespeople can prepare by asking themselves, "If I were the buyer, what would I want to be certain about before I make a purchase?" By anticipating these issues and preparing responses, salespeople can increase their chances of ultimate success.

Section 8: Earning Prospect Commitment

As sales dialogues and presentations progress, there eventually comes a critical time to ask for a customer's purchase decision. In many cases, this is an obvious point in the sales conversation, but at other times the salesperson may feel the need to probe to see if the timing is right. Earning a commitment from a customer, as discussed in Chapter 8, should be a natural step in the conversation, not a forced or high-pressure attempt by the salesperson. Although circumstances will dictate exactly when and how commitment will be sought, a preliminary action plan for seeking customer commitment should be part of the overall planning process. Most buyers expect the salesperson to seek a commitment—and, if the commitment is sought at the right time, buyers appreciate that effort from the salesperson.

Section 9: Building Value Through Follow-Up Action

Finally, the salesperson must always be looking for ways to enhance the relationship and move it in a positive direction. The salesperson should always make a note of any promises that they have made during the sales calls and especially during the proposal presentation. The buyer may ask for information that the salesperson is not prepared to give during the presentation. By taking notes, the salesperson ensures that the appropriate follow-up activities will happen.

This planning template for sales dialogues and presentations is an extremely useful tool for all salespeople, especially inexperienced salespeople. It guarantees that all the appropriate steps are covered and that all the pertinent information needed is collected. Using this template will make the task of customizing sales dialogues and presentations easier.

LO 6 | ENGAGING THE CUSTOMER

Most initial sales calls on new prospects require an appointment. Requesting an appointment accomplishes several desirable outcomes. First, the salesperson is letting the prospect know that they think the prospect's time is important. Second, there is a better chance that the salesperson will receive the undivided attention of the prospect during the sales call. Third, setting appointments is a good tool to assist the salesperson in effective time and territory management. Further, prospects may not appreciate salespeople who drop in unannounced, as their visit could be an unwelcome interruption in the prospect's busy work day. Given these realities, it is a good idea to request an appointment if there is any doubt about whether one is required.

A salesperson can request an appointment by phone, mail (including e-mail), or personal contact. Combining mail and telephone communications to seek appointments is also commonplace. Regardless of the communication vehicle used, salespeople can improve their chances of getting an appointment by following three simple directives: give the prospect a reason why an appointment should be granted; request a specific amount of time; and suggest a specific time for the appointment. These tactics recognize that prospects are busy individuals who do not spend time idly.

In giving a reason that the appointment should be granted, a well-informed salesperson can appeal to the prospect's primary buying motive as related to one of the benefits of the salesperson's offering. Be specific. For example, it is better to say that "you can realize gross margins averaging 35 percent on our product line" than "our margins are really quite attractive."

Specifying the amount of time needed to make the sales presentation alleviates some of the anxiety a busy prospect feels at the idea of spending some of his or her already scarce time. It also helps the prospect if the salesperson suggests a time and date for the sales call. It is very difficult for busy individuals to respond to a question such as, "What would be a good time for you next week?" In effect, the prospect is being asked to scan his or her entire calendar for an opening. If a suggested time and date is inconvenient, the interested prospect will typically suggest another. Once a salesperson has an appointment with the prospect and all the objectives have been established, the salesperson should send the agenda to the customer. This is a highly professional way to remind the buyer of the upcoming meeting.

STUDY TOOLS

At the back of the textbook, use tear-out cards to review key chapter information. Visit cengage.ca to purchase digital tools to help you succeed.

CENGAGE | MINDTAP

Personal Computer

☐ Gain unique perspectives on key concepts through a variety of videos and cases

☐ Increase your comprehension with online quizzes

☐ Study with existing flashcards and make your own

Mobile

☐ Stay focused and ready to study whenever it's convenient for you!

☐ Access a full, interactive ebook: online or offline

☐ Study tools that empower anytime, anywhere learning and 24/7 course access

CHAPTER CASE

NIMBLEFOOT

BACKGROUND

Nimblefoot is a manufacturer of women's running shoes that are sold through major sporting goods chain stores and specialty stores. Nimblefoot has targeted Trailrunner, a regional specialty store chain, as a potential prospect for its latest product. Nimblefoot's sales representative, Corey Whyte, hopes to replace a competitor's product in the Trailrunner stores. Corey has begun planning his upcoming sales call on Maria Tupper, head buyer at Trailrunner. At a recent trade show, Corey had a brief conversation with Maria and learned that Trailrunner's management is interested in improving the profitability of the chain. Further, Maria made it clear that Trailrunner would only be interested in high-quality products.

CURRENT SITUATION

Corey and his sales manager, Gabrielle Bellows, have been discussing the plans for the upcoming call on Trailrunner. Gabrielle asked Corey to give her a summary of Trailrunner's key buying motives and the related benefits that Nimblefoot could offer. In addition, Gabrielle wanted to review the information that would be required to support any claims made for the benefits, as well as additional ideas for how to reinforce the verbal content of Nimblefoot's sales message. Corey supplied Gabrielle with the requested information, as shown in Exhibit A. Gabrielle is now reading over Exhibit A and plans to give Corey some feedback tomorrow morning.

Exhibit A

Trailrunner's Buying Motives and Nimblefoot's Benefits

Trailrunner's Buying Motives	Related Nimblefoot Benefits	Support Information	Reinforcement of Verbal Content
Improve profitability	1. Profit margin is 6% higher than product to be replaced.	1. Cost and retail prices	1. Example income statement with and without new Nimblefoot product
	2. Nimblefoot product has significantly higher turnover rate than replacement product, thus improving total annual profitability.	2. Use historical data for existing product, projected turnover data for Nimblefoot.	2. Spreadsheet to illustrate multiplier effect of new Nimblefoot product with lower turnover rate. High-quality product
High-quality product	1. Durable synthetic material features a waterproof, breathable upper	1. Nimblefoot Web site	1. Customer interviews on Nimblefoot Web site
	2. Support around arch and extra width through the forefoot creates better shock absorption	2. Nimblefoot Web site	2. Customer interviews on Nimblefoot Web site
	3. Proprietary outsole gives best durability in high-wear areas	3. Nimblefoot Web site	3. Article from *Running World* magazine

QUESTIONS

1. 1In the role of Gabrielle Bellows, what specific comments and suggestions do you have for Corey Whyte?

2. Should a sales call objective and a customer value proposition be developed before completing the information in Exhibit A?

ROLE PLAY

Characters: Gabrielle Bellows, sales manager, and Corey Whyte, sales representative

Scene:

Location—Gabrielle Bellows's office

Action—One student plays the role of Gabrielle Bellows, and one student plays the role of Corey Whyte. Gabrielle has told Corey that she thinks it would be a good exercise to act out the presentation of the key benefits shown in section four of the template. She said to Corey "I will act like the Trailrunner buyer, and you try to convince me that your benefits are significant. Be as specific as you can."

QUESTIONS

After completing the role play, address these questions:

1. What were the strengths of Corey Whyte's performance?

2. How could Corey's performance be improved?

3. How important is sales call planning in determining sales call performance?

6 INTEGRATIVE CASE

UPFRONT AND PERSONAL

BACKGROUND

The Canadian Broadcasting Corporation (CBC) has been an ongoing concern in Canada since the middle of the Great Depression. The nationally owned broadcasting entity was created in part to try to counter the increasing American influence on media in North America.[8]

As the decades have passed so has the reach of the CBC, expanding from radio to television and then to Internet and social media. It has produced iconic shows like *Hockey Night in Canada* and has been the starting point for many Canadian actors, directors, and producers.

But the CBC is also a controversial entity. The CBC is funded by Canadian federal government grants, which represent about 60 percent of its budget.[9] The controversy with regards to the CBC often involves a debate over how much public money should be spent to support a national broadcaster.

But despite the perceived leg up received from federal funding, the CBC is still left to fend for advertising revenue from prospective companies across Canada. And the traditional way in which media companies pitch to advertisers is through something called an upfront.

Upfronts are sales presentations developed by broadcasters like CBC, Rogers, Bell, and Corus. They are usually held in Toronto around the same time period, usually in late May or early June.[10] An upfront presents to potential advertisers the upcoming schedule of programming and the myriad opportunities to find what are called "synergies" that integrate content with paid advertising. The upfronts also signal a time window where prospective advertisers have the chance to sign up for rates that are discounted.

Some media outlets question the value of upfronts, as when Rick Brace of Rogers Media explained in 2019 why Rogers did not host an upfront: "'It costs a fortune,' Rogers's Mr. Brace said. All the canapés and cocktails, putting stars on planes, venue fees and other show expenses add up…During his career, Mr. Brace has seen upfront budgets ranging from roughly $500,000 to $1.5-million for one event. He's not convinced it all results in a single ad buy that the company would not have secured anyway. 'I'd rather [cancel] than let people go,' he said. 'I'd rather … invest in programming.'"[11]

What has begun to get lost with upfronts is the fact that despite all of the glitz and glamour of shows (most bring in actors, other use pyrotechnics), upfronts are still sales presentations that need to be focused on building relationships with advertisers who will help fund a media company's aspirations.

CURRENT SITUATION

As part of the CBC sales team developing its next upfront presentation, you have been asked to build what CBC President Catherine Tait proclaimed in 2019: "A renewed commitment to growing commercial revenue. We want to be the masters of our own destiny and reinvest in more great Canadian news and programming. And you are all key to this shared future."[12]

Before developing the actual upfront presentation, Ms. Tait has asked your team to come up with your top five components for a great sales presentation. You have been asked to develop one of those components. You recall that there are many factors that go into an effective presentation, and you head off to your office to make a case for one that sticks out to you. You will need to develop your thoughts and be upfront with your idea so that your team can broadcast the best presentation possible.

QUESTIONS

1. In order to have success at the next upfront, you decide it will be vital to engage with the audience in an interactive and evolving presentation that engages the audience. Which type of sales communication do you quickly rule out?
   a. unscripted presentations   c. canned presentations
   b. adaptive presentations   d. diversified presentations

2. The organized sales dialogue, also known as the organized sales presentation, helps convert prospects into customers by being interactive and engaging. This fact-finding stage is similar to what other sales model?
   a. SIPS   c. ADAPT
   b. TIPS   d. TRIP

3. A key aspect of the next upfront for CBC will be to show clear schedules and plans for the next year in a way that differentiates the broadcaster's message from competitors. Which dimension for evaluating proposals does this best describe?
   a. reliability   c. empathy
   b. assurance   d. tangibles

CHAPTER ROLE PLAY 6

Planning Sales Dialogues and Presentations: Beats Versus Skullcandy Headphones

BACKGROUND

For this role play, students will assume one of three roles: (1) sales representative for Beats headphones; (2) sales representative for Skullcandy headphones; or (3) a buyer for an electronics retailer that is considering adding one of the two brands to its selection of headphones. Prior to the role play, all students should conduct a comparison of the features and benefits of one model of headphones from each of the two companies. To do the comparison, begin by using a search engine such as Google. Enter "Beats vs. Skullcandy" to find features and benefits of both products.

ROLE PLAY

Characters: One Beats representative, one Skullcandy representative, and a buyer for the electronics retailer.

Scene 1:

Location— The buyer's office

Action— Both sellers present their products to the buyer with a focus on explaining their product's benefits to the buyer.

After completing the role play, address the following questions:

1. Did the sellers demonstrate that they knew the difference between features and benefits?

2. Did the sellers have sufficient information to be convincing?

3. Can you suggest additional ways that the sellers could improve their sales communications?

7 | Sales Dialogue: Creating and Communicating Value

LEARNING OBJECTIVES

After completing this chapter, you should be able to

LO 1 | Describe the key characteristics of effective sales dialogue.

LO 2 | Explain how salespeople can generate feedback from buyers.

LO 3 | Discuss how salespeople use confirmed benefits to create customer value.

LO 4 | Describe how verbal support can be used to communicate value in an interesting and understandable manner.

LO 5 | Discuss how sales aids can engage and involve buyers.

LO 6 | Explain how salespeople can support product claims.

LO 7 | Discuss the special considerations involved in sales dialogue with groups.

AFTER FINISHING THIS CHAPTER GO TO THE BACK OF THE BOOK FOR CHAPTER REVIEW CARDS, AND VISIT MINDTAP FOR ACCESS TO STUDY TOOLS.

PAL Group of Companies was established in 1974 and has more than four decades of global experience. The company started in St. John's, Newfoundland, as a renowned Atlantic Canadian flight school and has evolved into PAL Group of Companies, consisting of numerous firms and offering aerospace solutions around the world. Two of the main firms in the company are PAL Airlines and PAL Aerospace. PAL Airlines has grown into one of the largest independent airlines operating in Eastern Canada. Their core services include scheduled flights, air charter, and air cargo services. They offer service to and from 24 locations throughout Eastern Canada.[1] PAL Airlines' success hinges on their promise to deliver superior safety, service, and reliability. PAL Aerospace is a Canadian-owned and -operated international aerospace and defence company with a mission to help clients solve their challenges and meet their needs with innovative custom aerospace and defence solutions. With clients around the world in Canada, Europe, the United Arab Emirates (UAE), and the Caribbean, they focus on delivering intelligence, surveillance and reconnaissance, and in-service support solutions.[2] They are recognized by governments and militaries for on-time and on-budget delivery and high reliability rates. Their teams are greatly valued and consist of highly experienced personnel with extensive backgrounds in both civilian and military aviation environments. PAL Aerospace has recently been named one of Canada's Top Employers for 2020.[3] The ability to offer comprehensive and custom solutions to their clients sets them apart from their competition and offers a unique selling point. Innovation is one of the key cornerstones of their success and the company has a rich history of innovation with many

firsts in the industry, including being the first private-sector company to use pulse compressed anti-submarine warfare radar and the first company to offer state of the art nighttime photography for maritime surveillance.[4]

Introduction

PAL's success is due in part to its ability to provide solutions to meet its customers' needs. Successful salespeople focus on creating and communicating value during sales dialogue by addressing the key issues of each buying organization. This is a difficult task because more individuals are involved in the purchasing process, buyers are more informed than in the past, and many buyers are reluctant to meet with salespeople in the early stages of the buying process. In addition, although many salespeople conduct most of their sales dialogue in personal meetings with buyers, salespeople are increasingly interacting with buyers through a variety of different technologies. More sales meetings are being conducted via Web conferencing, e-mail, and the telephone. The expansion of social selling results in more communication using social media. These technologies provide more opportunities to engage in sales dialogue, but it requires salespeople to adapt to the characteristics of each technology.

The purpose of this chapter is to examine the keys to effective sales dialogue. The chapter provides an opportunity to apply what has been learned about building trust (Chapter 2), understanding buyers (Chapter 3), and communication skills (Chapter 4). It also builds on the information gathered during the prospecting stage of the sales process (Chapter 5) and the sales dialogue template and section on "Beginning the Sales Dialogue" presented in Chapter 6. Chapter 8 expands on this chapter by addressing how to resolve buyer concerns and earn a commitment from a sales dialogue.

LO 1 | EFFECTIVE SALES DIALOGUE

3.2 Conduct sales presentations

Preparing and completing this phase of the sales process successfully has been compared to doing surgery in that it is complex and requires preparation, knowledge, and skill.[5] Prior to conducting surgery, the doctor has acquired a great deal of relevant information from a variety of sources and developed a comprehensive understanding of the patient's problems and needs. Based on this understanding of the patient's needs, the surgeon utilizes their training and skills in combination with an assortment of tools to conduct a surgical procedure unique to the individual patient's needs. Now, in the form of an effective presentation, the salesperson presents a solution that is specific and customized to the needs of the buyer, illustrates and demonstrates the benefits of the solution, and confirms the buyer's belief in and desire to obtain the benefits.

Good salespeople are very much like good surgeons in that they are serious in what they do and leave nothing to chance. They work with the prospective buyer to identify, diagnose, and clarify unsatisfied needs or problems and then show the buyer how much better the situation would be by purchasing the proposed product or service. As discussed previously, it will normally take several sales calls to complete a sales dialogue. Many firms plan for multiple sales calls in their sales process. For example, salespeople at Northwestern Mutual conduct an initial "fact finding" sales call to identify the financial situation and objectives of potential clients. Then, one or more subsequent sales calls are used to present strategies for achieving these financial objectives.

Professional selling classes often require students to role-play a sales dialogue, have sales contests within their institution, or have students competing against other schools in events such as the National Collegiate Sales Competition, National Sales Challenge, Great Northwoods Sales Warm-Up, Ball State Regional Sales Competition, and the International Collegiate Sales Competition. Each of these sales competitions requires students to conduct a complete sales dialogue within a 15- to 20-minute sales call. So, because this has been found to be an effective way for students to learn about and develop skills for

© kurhan/Shutterstock.com

Just like a mechanic diagnoses problems, salespeople must diagnose customer problems before prescribing solutions.

a sales dialogue, we will cover a complete sales dialogue in one sales call in this chapter and Chapter 8.

The keys to effective sales dialogue are presented in Exhibit 7.1. The importance of planning and practising were emphasized in Chapter 6 and are an area

Exhibit 7.1

Keys to Effective Sales Dialogue

The most effective sales dialogues

1. Are planned and practised by salespeople
2. Encourage buyer feedback
3. Focus on creating value for the buyer
4. Present value in an interesting and understandable way
5. Engage and involve the buyer
6. Support customer value through objective claims

Technology in Sales

Improving Sales Dialogue

Advances in artificial intelligence and machine learning are being transferred into technological products that can help salespeople be more successful in all types of sales dialogue. These products, offered by companies such as ClearSlide and Bigtincan, are typically called sales enablement platforms that can be integrated into CRM and e-mail systems. Salespeople can use the products when e-mailing contacts, making phone calls, conducting Web conferencing, and engaging in personal sales calls. The sales enablement platforms generally consist of a cloud-based suite of products that integrate content, communications, and insights into a guided selling process through rule-based recommendations and insights based on machine learning. They allow salespeople easy access to presentations, videos, pictures, or whatever content is most appropriate for a particular buyer. Analytics are provided to help the salesperson understand the specific interests of the buyer and to determine the most effective materials to use to communicate value more effectively to a specific buyer. Salespeople at companies such as Merck, Sacramento Kings, and the Wall Street Journal are using sales enablement platforms successfully.[6]

---

that does not receive enough attention from some salespeople. This planning and practice should focus on an organized sales dialogue and not a canned sales presentation. Salespeople who practise asking questions, getting different responses, and adapting to these responses appropriately are better prepared to be successful in a real sales dialogue. New developments in technology are becoming available to help salespeople be more successful in communicating value during sales dialogue, as presented in Technology in Sales: Improving Sales Dialogue.

LO 2 | ENCOURAGING BUYER FEEDBACK

 CPSA 3.1 Develop solutions

In a productive sales dialogue, the salesperson continually assesses and evaluates the reactions and responses of prospective buyers. The SPIN or ADAPT questioning processes are designed to get the buyer to provide feedback to specific questions the salesperson asks. During the presentation portion of a sales dialogue, the most successful salespeople encourage buyer feedback. In contrast, less successful salespeople often rush through the entire presentation from beginning to end and never stop to invite feedback from the buyer. Feedback from the prospective buyer provides the salesperson with important information measuring the climate between the salesperson and the buyer, the buyer's level of interest in the product's features and benefits, whether the salesperson has successfully responded to the buyer's concerns, and how well the presentation is progressing toward the buyer making a purchase decision.

As detailed and discussed in Chapter 4, the observant salesperson can receive a great deal of continual feedback in the form of the buyer's nonverbal cues. In addition to observing nonverbal cues, high-performing salespeople incorporate verbal probes at key points to evaluate the buyer's interest and assess the progress of the sales dialogue. These verbal probes are typically confirmatory forms of questions in search of simple "yes" or "no" responses from the buyer.

The phrases **check-backs** or **response checks** have become common names for this form of questioning—seeking feedback from the buyer. Although feedback can be sought at any point in the conversation, check-backs are commonly employed at two key points: (1) after a specific feature–benefit sequence to confirm the benefit and better assess the prospective buyer's level of interest, and (2) following

> **check-backs or response checks** Questions salespeople use throughout a sales dialogue to generate feedback from the buyer.

Exhibit 7.2

Illustrative Examples of Check-Backs

- "How does this sound to you?"

- "Does this make sense to you so far?"

- "Would this feature be useful to you in your current operations?"

- "What do you think?"

- "So is this something that would be valuable to you?"

- "Isn't that great?"

- "Do you like this colour?"

- "From your comment, it sounds as if you would want the upgraded memory. Is that correct?"

- "Does that answer your concern?"

- "Would this be an improvement over what you are doing right now?"

- "Is this what you had in mind?"

the response to an objection in order to evaluate the level to which the salesperson has handled the problem. Exhibit 7.2 provides an illustrative selection of check-back examples that salespeople indicate are typical of those they commonly use.

The effective use of check-backs offers a number of advantages. Probably the most evident is increased buyer interaction. Asking for buyer feedback helps to ensure that the dialogue remains a two-way, collaborative exchange. The effective use of response-checks also helps the salesperson evaluate the level of the buyer's understanding and keeps the salesperson on the right track. If feedback indicates a lack of understanding—or even worse, a lack of interest—on the part of a prospective buyer, the salesperson must make changes to improve alignment with the needs and expectations of the buyer. In contrast, positive feedback indicating a high level of understanding and interest on the part of the buyer would signal the salesperson to stay the course and advance the presentation toward gaining the buyer's purchase

confirmed benefits The benefits the buyer indicates are important and represent value.

commitment. A series of positive response-checks indicates that the buyer is nearing a purchase decision. The more positive affirmations a salesperson receives in relation to their response-checks, the easier the final purchase decision becomes and the more confident the prospective buyer is in having made the appropriate decision. Specific examples of check-backs within a sales dialogue will be presented at appropriate places in the remainder of this chapter.

LO 3 | CREATING CUSTOMER VALUE

 CPSA | 4.1 Close the sale

After the introductory part of a sales call, the salesperson must try to determine what the buyer considers to be of value. A salesperson can use the SPIN or ADAPT questioning strategies (discussed in Chapter 4 and included in the sales dialogue template in Chapter 6) to understand the buyer's situation and to identify needs, problems, or opportunities important to the buyer. The salesperson must ask questions, probe for details, and listen carefully to what the prospective buyer is saying. This may take more than one sales call depending on the amount of probing and clarifying that must take place to understand the prospect's needs. The salesperson's primary goal is to uncover the prospect's specific needs or problems and then focus on what products or services will solve the problem or meet the specific needs. As discussed in Chapter 6, features are the characteristics of a product and benefits are the favourable outcome from a feature or the value received by the buyer. Most products have many features and benefits, but the buyer generally is not interested in all of a product's features and benefits. **Confirmed benefits** are those benefits the buyer has indicated are of interest. A major purpose of the use of the SPIN or ADAPT questioning process is to help the salesperson identify the confirmed benefits for the buyer. Then, the salesperson presents a recommended solution by emphasizing product features that will produce the confirmed benefits the buyer desires.

Product features and confirmed benefits are linked to the buyer's specific needs in a way that generates the buyer's desire to purchase and acquire the recommended solution. The "Beginning the Sales Dialogue" section in Chapter 6 provides an effective introduction to a sales call. The sales dialogue would then transition into a stage where the salesperson identifies the confirmed benefits the buyer desires. An example of this interaction using the ADAPT questioning process is presented here.

Seller: What are you currently doing to improve your customer satisfaction ratings and customer retention?

(Assessment question)

Buyer: We are trying to do a number of things, such as improving our products, providing faster deliveries, and offering better customer service.

Seller: How are these efforts working?

(Discovery question)

Buyer: Our product and delivery improvements have been effective, but we have received a number of complaints about our customer service.

Seller: What types of customer service complaints have you received?

(Discovery question)

Buyer: Most of the complaints are that our representatives do not act professionally and cannot resolve customer issues in a timely manner. But, when I talk to our representatives, they suggest that the customers are very demanding and difficult to deal with.

Seller: What has been the impact of these customer service problems on your business?

(Activation question)

Buyer: The impact has been twofold. First, although we have not yet lost any customers, our customer satisfaction ratings have gone down, so we could lose customers in the future. Second, we have lost some of our best customer service reps because they got tired of dealing with irate customers. Losing these reps just added to the customer service problems we have been having.

Seller: So, if we could find a way to help your reps deal with difficult customers, it would improve your customer service and reduce the turnover of your reps?

(Projection question)

Buyer: That would be a big help to us.

(The seller has identified a confirmed benefit.)

Seller: Mr. Jones, have you ever provided any training to your customer service reps?

(Assessment question)

Buyer: Yes, we sent our reps to a public customer service training program a few months ago. But the reps said the program was very general and did not address the issues they face.

Seller: Do you think your reps would find a training program customized to their situation useful?

(Activation question)

Buyer: A customized program would be received well by our reps and would be valuable to them.

(The seller has identified another confirmed benefit.)

Seller: Have you ever considered online training?

(Assessment question)

Buyer: We thought about it, but many of our reps were not receptive to the idea of online training.

(The buyer has indicated that online training is NOT a confirmed benefit.)

Seller: It seems like a customized customer service training program that focused on dealing with difficult customers would improve your service to existing customers and help reduce turnover of your customer service reps. Do you think this type of training program would be valuable to your business?

(Transition question)

Buyer: I would certainly be interested in this type of program.

This sales dialogue example illustrates the value of the ADAPT questioning process to help salespeople identify confirmed benefits and transition into the presentation of a solution to solve the problems the buyer expresses. This presentation should focus on a customized training program that emphasizes dealing with difficult customers (confirmed benefits), but it should not be an online training program (benefit not confirmed). This example sales dialogue will be continued later in this chapter.

Sometimes salespeople do not focus on the confirmed benefits of the buyer and know the best product to provide the best value for the customer. However, pressure from their company or other sources can put salespeople in very difficult situations. One such situation is presented in An Ethical Dilemma. Creating and communicating value is also important in maintaining relationships with existing customers, because changes can occur in a customer's situation. For example, Match Eyewear had been doing business with a large account. This customer had made some changes in its business objectives and was ready to stop doing business with

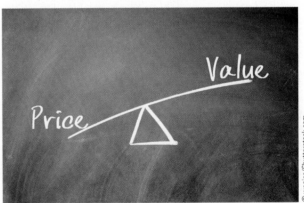

Salespeople focus on creating customer value relative to price.

Tracey Wise has been selling computer systems for just over nine years and has earned the position of senior account manager for one of the leading companies in the industry. For several months, Wise has been working with a major insurance company that is looking for an automated information system to solve the company's growing backlog of worker compensation claims. After reviewing the information from previous sales calls with the buyer, Wise and her tech-support team decided that the R740 system offered the greatest benefits to this particular customer. However, a special sales promotion provided company salespeople additional commissions and double points toward the annual sales incentive trip to Hawaii for each R800 system sold. The higher priced R800 had all the same features and capabilities of the R740 along with many more. However, few of these additional capabilities would ever be of value to the insurance company. During her last sales call, Wise explained and demonstrated the R740 and the R800. What should Tracey do?

(a) Recommend the R740 because it offers the most value to the customer.

(b) Recommend the R800 by telling the buyer that the additional features would be needed as the company grows.

(c) Present a detailed comparison of all of the features offered by the R740 and R800 and let the buyer make the decision.

© aines/Shutterstock.com

Match Eyewear. The Match Eyewear sales team found out about this and met many times with the customer. These meetings identified the new value needed by the customer. Match Eyewear addressed the new value requirements by improving its service and support offerings and communicating these changes effectively. The customer was retained and Match Eyewear used this situation to develop a stronger relationship with this customer.[7]

LO 4 | INTERESTING AND UNDERSTANDABLE SALES DIALOGUE

verbal support The use of voice characteristics, examples and anecdotes, and comparisons and analogies to make sales dialogue interesting and understandable.

voice characteristics The pitch and speed of speech, which salespeople should vary to emphasize key points.

Once confirmed benefits have been identified, the salesperson needs to present key selling points in a manner that is interesting and understandable to the buyer. The presentation should focus on the buyer and

is intended to gain and hold the buyer's attention, and to increase the buyer's understanding and retention of the information provided by the salesperson. **Verbal support** elements include voice characteristics, examples and anecdotes, and comparisons and analogies. These elements can be incorporated into stories to produce interesting and understandable sales dialogue.

Voice Characteristics

2.3 Communicate verbally

The key aspects of **voice characteristics** are the pitch and speed of speech. Varying and changing pitch on key words adds emphasis and increases impact. It is analogous to putting different colours and hues into your voice. The increased intensity and vividness grab attention, hold interest, and help the buyer remember what is said. Fluctuating the speed of speech can add emphasis and guide the buyer's attention to selected points of the presentation. Important details—especially quantitative information—should be provided at a slower, more careful pace. Less critical information can be presented at a faster pace to

Every Business Sells

Keith Stoodley is CEO, PAL Services Aircraft Maintenance LLC (United Arab Emirates), which is a subsidiary of PAL Aerospace. PAL Aerospace works in aerospace and defence, and service and manufacturing. Keith sells fixed wing intelligence, surveillance and reconnaissance aircraft and services to roughly 25 customer accounts all over the world, including the Eastern Hemisphere (Middle East, Africa, Southeast Asia, Australia-Asia including the South Pacific Island Community). He's been with PAL for 15 years, and has a 25-year long sales career.

As a salesperson, how do you provide value to your customers?

As a highly competent adviser with competency in industry and product knowledge, and superior relationship management and communication skills.

As a salesperson, how do you provide value to your organization?

In the same ways mentioned above, but also acting as an internal adviser advocating for clients' interests within my organization

What is your greatest challenge you face today as a salesperson?

Maintaining competency and currency.

How do you try to overcome this challenge?

Continuous, life-long learning of my industry, competitors, collaborators, associated technologies, cross-cultural differences, management techniques, and communication skills.

What advice do you have for someone starting out in sales?

- Focus on self-initiative
- Embrace life-long learning
- Get past "no"
- Hone your communication and relationship management skills
- Recognize that every element of the business is involved in sales in some fashion
- Understand the impact of cross-cultural differences
- Embrace feedback/criticism as an opportunity to improve

---

grab the buyer's attention and redirect their interest. Changes in volume can be used to add emphasis to an important phrase or topic, and a softer volume—almost a whisper—can build intrigue and pull the prospect into the conversation. Altering volume from loud to soft can better grab and hold the buyer's interest while simultaneously adding clarity and emphasis to increase understanding.

A salesperson can know their product inside and out, but if there is no energy and passion in their voice, the potential for making the sale will be seriously impaired. A medical salesperson talks about the importance of voice characteristics:[8]

> *Your voice is an instrument. When used wisely, varying the cadence, pitch, and speed of your voice can deliver a message that captures a buyer's attention, generates interest, and adds energy to a sales conversation. I try to speak in a very confident manner and to communicate my passion for helping buyers solve problems.*

Voice quality can be used to bring excitement and drama to the presentation by doing three things: varying the pitch, fluctuating the speed, and altering the volume.

Examples and Anecdotes

 2.3 Communicate verbally

An **example** is a brief description of a specific instance used to illustrate features and benefits. Examples may be either real or hypothetical and are used to further explain and emphasize a topic of interest. A production

> **example** A brief description of a specific instance used to illustrate features and benefits of a product or service.

Every Business Sells

Stephen Short is a charter manager at PAL Airlines. He sells commercial airline services (charters, scheduled service, cargo) and logistics management support to over 90 accounts. PAL Airlines' core commercial and charter services focus on Eastern Canada (Quebec, Maritimes, Newfoundland), with charter services to Greenland, Ontario, the Eastern US seaboard, and Western Europe. Stephen has been with PAL Airlines for six years, and has worked in sales for eight.

As a salesperson, how do you provide value to your customers?

I understand our customers' business and corresponding challenges very well. I spend a significant amount of time listening and learning about their operations and industry, which allows me to truly understand how our services will integrate with and support their company. It's important to highlight where we can provide convenience, efficiencies, or cost savings to our clients. We provide our customers with a solution—not just a service.

As a salesperson, how do you provide value to your organization?

As account managers we are the face of our organization in the regions we serve. It is critical that we remain knowledgeable with regards to new projects and emerging opportunities in these regions. We are also engaged in our communities through volunteer commitments with community organizations, including sitting on industry and charitable boards. Perhaps most importantly, our account managers are the relationship builders for our organization, creating and maintaining the public profile for PAL Airlines and acting as a convenient touchpoint for our valued corporate customers.

What is your greatest challenge you face today as a salesperson?

A challenge that we frequently encounter is related to competitive pricing. Consumers oftentimes focus on the sticker price and will overlook the combined value of the service offering.

How do you try to overcome this challenge?

An important part of overcoming competitive price considerations is ensuring open dialogue and transparency with the client. When challenged by a client with regards to price, be comfortable in acknowledging "We may not be the cheapest option available," and then follow up by taking the time to explain the value proposition to the customer. This exercise also goes a long way to build trust as it demonstrates your knowledge of your service to the client.

What advice do you have for someone starting out in sales?

1. Tune up your listening skills. Being able to listen to your customers and learn about their business is the most important tool a salesperson can have. It allows you to understand what they are really asking for and will ultimately allow you to provide them with a better solution.

2. Get involved! Get involved in industry and charitable associations that interest you. This is a meaningful way for a new salesperson to build a network and continue to learn and promote themselves and their business.

---

equipment salesperson might further explain the purpose of an infrared guidance control by using the following example:

If the feedstock coming off the main paper roll gets out of line by as little as 1.5 millimetres, the infrared guidance control will sense it and automatically make the correct adjustments. This prevents a paper jam from shutting down your package printing line and costing lost time and wasted product.

anecdote A type of example that is provided in the form of a story describing a specific incident or occurrence.

An **anecdote** is a type of example presented in the form of a story describing a specific incident or occurrence. Stories can be very effective in keeping a buyer interested and helping the buyer understand the solution a salesperson presents. The production equipment salesperson might use an anecdote such as the following:

One of my customers was having a problem with paper jams that were shutting down the firm's package printing line. Similar to your situation, there was a lot of lost production time and wasted product. We installed the infrared guidance control, which automatically adjusts the paper roll when it gets off by as little as 1.5 millimetres. This reduced paper jams, resulting in less wasted product and more production time for the customer.

A salesperson's use of examples and anecdotes keeps the buyer interested, brings clarity into the presentation, and improves the buyer's understanding and retention of what the salesperson is presenting. The use of an example and anecdote in a sales dialogue example for customer service training follows.

Seller: Customized training programs can be very effective. For example, one of our clients increased customer satisfaction ratings by 25 percent after we implemented a customized program for their reps. (*Example*) Is this the type of improvement you are looking for? (*Check-back*)

Seller: Customers of the XYZ Company were very dissatisfied with the service the firm's reps provided. We reviewed the customers' complaints, met with the customer service reps, identified the main problems, and created a specific training program to deal with the key problems. After completion of the sales training program, customer complaints decreased by 75 per cent. (*Anecdote*) What do you think about these results? (*Check-back*)

Comparisons and Analogies

2.3 Communicate verbally

A **comparison** is a statement that points out and illustrates the similarities between two points. Comparisons increase the buyer's level of interest and understanding of information. The production equipment salesperson could emphasize the value of the infrared guidance control through the use of a comparison:

You have the performance specifications of our product with infrared guidance control and the other products without this feature. As you can see, our product will automatically make adjustments to keep your package printing line running. The other products will shut your line down and require you to remove paper jams

manually before you can restart production. Our product will save you time and money compared to the other products.

A salesperson for Newell-Rubbermaid might illustrate the benefits of setting up an end-of-aisle display of special occasion containers by using the following comparison to the store manager's sales goals for the product category:

Sales data from stores similar to yours indicate that adding an end-of-aisle display for these seasonal containers will increase their sales by 35 to 40 percent during the fourth-quarter holiday season. This would certainly help you achieve—and possibly exceed—the store's goal of a 20-percent increase for this general product category.

Medical products salespeople use comparisons in their role as consultants to doctors. The salespeople will provide a direct comparison of existing products to new products that will be introduced in the near future. Doctors find these comparisons valuable and, in some cases, find the new product valuable enough to postpone non-emergency surgery until the new product is available.[9]

An **analogy** is a special and useful form of comparison that explains one thing in terms of another. Analogies are useful for explaining something complex by allowing the buyer to better visualize it in terms of something familiar that is easier to understand. The production equipment salesperson might employ an analogy to help the buyer better understand the value of infrared guidance control:

The infrared guidance control system is like a Global Positioning System (GPS) in your car. If you make a wrong turn during a trip, the GPS will automatically reroute you to get you back on the right road for your trip. If you did not have GPS in your car, you would have to stop and look at a map to determine how to get back on the right route for your trip. Our infrared guidance control system operates like a GPS for your package printing line.

The use of a comparison and analogy in our sales dialogue example is presented here.

Seller: We will incorporate your reps throughout the design and execution of our training program. This gives the reps some ownership in the program. Our competitors, in contrast, develop their programs based on what

comparison A statement that points out and illustrates the similarities between two points.

analogy A special and useful form of comparison that explains one thing in terms of another.

A GPS is a good analogy for a product that automatically corrects itself.

Exhibit 7.3

Reasons for Using Sales Aids

- Capture prospective buyer's attention.
- Generate interest in the recommended solution.
- Make presentations more persuasive.
- Increase the buyer's participation and involvement.
- Provide the opportunity for collaboration and two-way communication.
- Add clarity and enhance the prospect's understanding.
- Provide supportive evidence and proof to enhance believability.
- Augment the prospect's retention of information.
- Enhance the professional image of the salesperson and selling organization.

management tells them is important. (*Comparison*) Do you think your reps would respond well to being included in all aspects of the training program? (*Check-back*)

Seller: Developing a customized sales training program is like planning for a family vacation. Everyone in the family is likely to be more excited about the vacation if they are involved in all aspects of the planning process. (*Analogy*) What do you think about involving your reps in all aspects of the training program? (*Check-back*)

LO 5 | ENGAGING AND INVOLVING THE BUYER

CPSA | 3.2 Conduct sales presentations

Simply informing the prospect about the benefits and their value to the buyer is seldom sufficient to generate the level of interest and desire required to result in a purchase decision. To maximize the effectiveness of the sales dialogue, salespeople use various **sales aids** to engage and involve the buyer throughout the sales interaction. These sales aids also help to capture and hold the buyer's attention, boost the buyer's understanding, increase the believability of the claims, and build the buyer's retention of information (see Exhibit 7.3). Not all sales aids are suitable for all products, selling situations, or buyers. Nor should a salesperson feel the need to use each and every tool in any given sales call. A salesperson should use the sales aids

sales aids The use of printed materials, electronic materials, and product demonstrations to engage and involve buyers.

visual materials Printed materials, photographs and illustrations, and charts and graphs used as sales aids.

that will engage and involve each buyer most effectively in a particular sales dialogue. Many times, the selling organization provides these sales tools. However, experienced salespeople are quick to comment that some of their most effective sales aids are those that they developed themselves for specific prospects and selling situations.

Types of Sales Aids

Sales aids allow the salesperson to involve one or more of the buyer's senses in the presentation, help to illustrate features and confirmed benefits, and add clarity and dramatization to increase the effectiveness of a sales dialogue. The types of sales aids available to a salesperson include visual materials, electronic materials, and product demonstrations.

VISUAL MATERIALS **Visual materials** represent a variety of sales aids intended to engage and involve buyers visually. The major types of visual materials are printed materials, photographs and illustrations, and charts and graphs. Exhibit 7.4 provides salespeople with a number of tips for preparing printed materials and visuals.

Printed materials include such items as brochures, pamphlets, catalogues, articles, reprints, reports, testimonial letters, and guarantees. Well-designed printed

Exhibit 7.4

Tips for Preparing Visual Materials

- Visual materials should be kept simple.

- When possible, use phrases and let the buyer's mind complete the sentences.

- Use the same layout and format throughout to tie the presentation together.

- Check for typographical and spelling errors.

- Use colours sparingly and for functional rather than decorative purposes.

- Leave plenty of white space; do not crowd the page.

- Each visual should present only one idea.

- Try to use a maximum of seven words per line and seven lines per visual.

- Where possible, use graphics (charts and graphs) rather than tables.

- Use bullet points to emphasize key points.

- Never read the presentation directly from the visual.

- Clearly label each visual with titles and headings to guide the prospective buyer.

Printed materials are effective sales aids, often providing the customer with useful information.

materials can help the salesperson communicate, explain, and emphasize key points during a sales dialogue. They are designed to summarize important features and benefits and can be effectively used not only during the presentation but also left behind as reminder pieces for the buyer after the salesperson has left. When printed materials are left with a buyer, the salesperson's name and contact information should be clearly printed on the material or an attached business card.

Photographs and illustrations are easy to produce and relatively inexpensive. Using images allows the salesperson to present a realistic portrayal of the product or service. Many products cannot be taken into a prospective buyer's office because of their size. A well-detailed image can give the prospect an idea of the product's appearance and size. Line drawings and diagrams can show the most important details of a product. Images are most effective when they illustrate and simplify a more complex product or feature and make it easy to communicate information about size, shape, construction, and use.

Charts and graphs are useful in showing trends and illustrating relationships. As such, they can show the prospect what the problem is costing them or how a solution might work. Charts and graphs often illustrate relationships by using bars, lines, circles, or squares. For example, a salesperson for an office equipment vendor might get the cost figures associated with the buyer's use of an outside copy centre for the previous two years. The salesperson could then use this information in a comparative bar graph to better illustrate the savings possible if the buyer owned a copier. Salespeople for a leading medical technology company use a chart format to compare the features and benefits of their product versus the competitors' equipment the buyer is considering. The chart format succinctly and effectively supports statements of superiority made during the presentation.

ELECTRONIC MATERIALS

CPSA   **7.1 Leverage sales technology**

Electronic materials include all sales aids in electronic format. These span individual slides and videos to complete

electronic materials Sales aids in electronic format, such as slides, videos, or multimedia presentations.

Multimedia sales aids are being used more in sales dialogue.

multimedia presentations. As technology continues to develop, more options to use electronic materials become available to salespeople.

Salespeople today can customize graphic presentations for each buyer. Customizing and enriching presentations by using electronic multimedia can be done inexpensively and in a fairly short time. Microsoft PowerPoint, for example, allows the salesperson to build a complete, high-impact graphic presentation customized for an individual prospect quickly. The use of video has the advantage of both sound and action. These powerful multimedia presentations might include pictures of products, as well as product demonstrations and competitive comparisons. The buyer can be taken on a virtual tour of the selling organization and see the product being produced or simultaneously see and hear a personal message from the president of the selling organization as well as testimonials from satisfied customers.

David Frick, President of Success Ventures, talks about the value of electronic sales aids:

Sales aids in digital format, such as e-books, research reports, white papers, customer endorsements, case studies, infographics, press clippings, webinars, and videos, can be valuable to salespeople throughout the sales process. Much of this electronic content can be customized to be used as a sales aid in sales dialogue with a specific buyer. For example, a salesperson selling marketing services to a law firm can take a general e-book on attracting customers to a law firm and customize the title, cover, and some content to meet the confirmed benefits of the buyer. The customized e-book can then be used as a sales aid at the appropriate point in

the sales dialogue to communicate the value desired by the prospective law firm.[10]

Leading pharmaceutical companies are using electronic materials in two interesting ways. First, iPad applications (apps) have been developed by some firms to facilitate interaction between sales reps and doctors. The salesperson can use the app to visually illustrate how a drug works in the body and to respond to questions a doctor might have. Second, doctors are very busy and may not have time to interact with a salesperson during an office visit. In these cases, the sales rep can give the physician a card with a URL on it and invite the doctor to view a presentation electronically, engage in an online discussion, or participate in a live electronic presentation at a more convenient time. These and other forms of "e-detailing" are being explored by many pharmaceutical firms.[11]

PRODUCT DEMONSTRATIONS The product itself is often the most effective sales tool because it provides the prospective buyer with an opportunity for hands-on experience. When the actual product does not lend itself to being demonstrated, models can be used to represent and illustrate key features and benefits of the larger product. The value of an actual product demonstration is applicable to all types of products and services. For example, aircraft salespeople use scale models to give the buyer a detailed and realistic feel for the aircraft, which cannot be tucked into the salesperson's briefcase. Major vendors of office furniture will set up a model office so that the prospective client can experience its actual use. Pharmaceutical companies provide doctors with samples of the product for trial use with selected patients.

As detailed in Exhibit 7.5, the salesperson should make sure the product being demonstrated is typical of what is being recommended. Furthermore, it should be checked to ensure that it is in good working order before the demonstration and that setup and removal do not detract from the presentation. The last thing the salesperson wants is to have to apologize for poor appearance or inadequate performance.

It is important to customize the demonstration as close as possible to the buyer's situation, and to allow the buyer to actually use the product, if possible. Salespeople at a payroll processing firm focus on making the demonstration as realistic as possible. These salespeople conduct sales dialogue in person and electronically using Web conferencing services with individual buyers and buying teams. A software demonstration is set up to include the logo, information, and settings specific to the situation of the buyer. The salesperson can then show how each buyer need is addressed and use check-back

Exhibit 7.5

Guidelines for Product Demonstrations

- Ensure the appearance of the product is neat and clean.

- Check for problem-free operation.

- Be confident and able to demonstrate the product skillfully.

- Practise using the product before the demonstration.

- Anticipate problems and have backup or replacement parts on hand.

- Make sure that setup and knockdown are easy and quick.

questions to confirm understanding. During in-person meetings, the buyer is in fact able to use the product on a computer, as well as to try the smartphone and tablet app. This type of product demonstration is engaging and interactive, which helps the buyer understand the value offered by the salesperson's product.[12]

Sometimes it is more effective to bring the buyer to another site for a product demonstration. Toshiba Medical Systems uses this approach very successfully for buyers of computed tomography (CT) scanners and magnetic resonance imaging (MRI) systems. It conducts 20 to 40 site visits a week with potential buyers. The buyers have the opportunity to see the products in action in a clinical-like environment, and get to know the Toshiba executives. This demonstration approach has led to significant sales growth and better customer relationships for Toshiba Medical Systems.[13]

Using Sales Aids in the Presentation

Practise! Practise! Practise! Rehearsal of the presentation is the final key to conducting effective sales dialogue. Understand what features are relevant and what benefits are meaningful to the prospective buyer in terms of value to be realized. Be confident in developing and using multiple sales aids to add impact to the presentation itself. Using the SPES sequence can facilitate the effectiveness of presentation tools and sales aids: S = State selling point and introduce the sales aid; P = Present the sales aid; E = Explain the sales aid; S = Summarize.[14]

STATE THE SELLING POINT AND INTRODUCE THE SALES AID This means stating the full selling point including the feature and potential benefit and then introducing the sales aid. For instance, "To demonstrate this benefit, I would like you to take a look at this video" or "This graph summarizes the increased performance you will experience with the Honda S2000." This prepares the buyer for the visual aid and informs him or her that attention is required.

PRESENT THE SALES AID This involves presenting the sales aid to the customer and allowing a few moments for examination and familiarization before saying anything. For example, when using printed materials, place the material directly in front of the customer and allow it to be reviewed momentarily in silence. Allow the customer to review the sales aid and satisfy their natural curiosity before using it.

EXPLAIN THE SALES AID No matter how carefully a sales aid is prepared, it will not be completely obvious. The customer will not necessarily understand the significance unless the salesperson provides a brief explanation. Do not rely on a chart or graph to illustrate fully the points being supported. Similarly, a prospect might enjoy a product demonstration yet totally miss the information or experience supporting the presentation. The salesperson should point out the material information and explain how it supports their points.

> Salespeople can increase the success of a sales dialogue by using appropriate sales aids effectively.

SUMMARIZE When finished explaining the significance of the sales aid, summarize its contribution and support and remove the sales aid. If not removed, its presence can distract the prospective buyer's attention from subsequent feature and benefit points.

The use of the SPES sequence to use a sales aid in a customer service training program sales dialogue is presented here.

Seller: You mentioned earlier that your reps are not well prepared to deal with irate customers. I would like to show you a short video from a training program we developed for another firm. The video illustrates how we use role plays to help reps develop the skills to interact with irate customers effectively. (*State the selling point and introduce the sales aid*)

(The salesperson shows the video to the buyer)

Seller: Did you notice how everyone involved in the training program watched the role play carefully and was able to contribute comments to improve the interaction with the irate customer? (*Explain the sales aid*)

Buyer: The role-play exercise did get everyone involved and produced some good ideas for improvement.

Seller: Although this is just one type of exercise we employ in our training programs, the role play produced some guidelines that all reps could use to deal with irate customers more effectively. (*Summarize*) Do you think this type of exercise would be valuable to your reps? (*Check-back*)

LO 6 | SUPPORTING PRODUCT CLAIMS

As discussed earlier in this chapter, confirmed benefits answer the buyer's question, "What is in it for me?" In a similar fashion, **proof providers**, such as statistics, testimonials, and case histories, can be used to preempt the buyer from asking, "Can you prove it?" or "Who says so?" Claims of benefits and value produced and provided to the buyer need to be backed up with evidence to highlight their believability.

Statistics

3.2 Conduct sales presentations

Statistics are facts that lend believability to claims of value and benefit. When available, statistics from authoritative, third-party sources carry the highest credibility. Among others, third-party sources include independent testing organizations and labs (e.g., *Consumer Reports*,
Underwriters Laboratories of Canada), professional organizations (e.g., The Risk Management Society), research companies (e.g., PricewaterhouseCoopers), institutions (e.g., University of Toronto), and various governmental entities (e.g., Statistics

Salespeople can use independent testing organizations to support their product claims.

Canada, Industry Canada). Statistics prepared by the selling organization as well as the salesperson can also be useful in providing evidence for claims. Facts and statistics are most powerful when they fairly represent all sides to the story and are presented in printed form rather than simply stated orally. Not only does the printed word carry more credibility, but also it is convenient and can be left as a reminder to aid the prospect's retention of information.

Testimonials

Testimonials are similar to statistics, but in the form of statements from satisfied users of the selling organization's products and services. Supportive statements from current users are excellent methods to build trust and confidence. They predispose the prospective buyer to accept what the salesperson says about the benefits and value a recommended solution offers, and they reduce the prospect's perceived risk in making a purchase decision.

Written testimonials are especially effective when they are on the recommending user's letterhead and signed. However, testimonials that list customers, trade publications, trade associations, and independent rating organizations along with one-sentence comments in a presentation can also be effective. For instance:

- "The Canadian Dental Association has endorsed the new Laserlite drilling system as being safe and painless for the patient."

- "In January, *Fortune* magazine recognized CDW as the top-rated technology vendor on the basis of services provided to the buying customer."

proof providers The use of statistics, testimonials, or case histories to support product claims.

statistics Facts that lend believability to product claims and are used as proof providers.

testimonials Proof providers that are in the form of statements from satisfied users of the selling organization's products and services.

- "The *RIMS Quality Scorecard* rated Arthur J. Gallagher & Co. as the highest-rated insurance broker in North America in terms of value and service provided to its clients."

Testimonials are used extensively across industry and product/service types. To maximize their effectiveness, testimonials should be matched according to relevance and recognition to the prospective buyer. It is critical that the organization or person providing the supporting testimony be known or recognized by the prospect, above reproach, and in a position of respect.

Case Histories

Case histories are basically a testimonial in story or anecdotal form. Their added length allows more detail to be presented to further clarify an issue or better itemize the proof for a given statement. Case histories can also break the monotony of a long presentation. Like their counterpart testimonials, case histories should be used only when they clearly illustrate a particular point and are appropriate for the prospective buyer. Unrelated or tangential stories not only distract the customer but also can be a source of irritation that works against credibility building. Case histories should be short and to the point, lasting no more than a minute. They should support the presentation rather than becoming the centre of attention. Salespeople at a productivity software firm use case histories in most of their sales dialogues. Once the specific needs of the buyer are identified, the salesperson presents a solution, and then uses a case history for each need to add credibility. Each case history illustrates how they have created the value desired by the buyer for other customers. The case histories are often communicated in a story format as a way to engage the buyer more actively.[15]

The effective use of a proof provider in our customer service training program sales dialogue follows.

Buyer: I like many aspects of your approach to designing and delivering training programs. So I think your firm can develop and implement a good customer service training program for us. But I am not sure the training program will produce the increases in customer satisfaction and retention that we desire. I am concerned that my reps will take the training, like it, learn some things, but then go back to work and not do much differently. If this occurs, we have spent a lot of time and money, but not received much of a return.

Seller: I certainly understand where you are coming from, as all of my customers had similar concerns. Let me show you two letters from customers. Each is from a different industry than yours, but both are about your

Salespeople can use independent testing organizations to support their product claims.

size and both had similar customer service problems and objectives. (*Salesperson shows each letter and points to key points in each.*) Notice how this customer indicates a 25 percent increase in customer satisfaction from the training program, and this customer has calculated a 20 percent return from its investment in our training program. I think these letters provide strong evidence that our training programs can produce real business results. Do you see how our training program can help you achieve your objectives? (*Check-back*)

LO 7 | GROUP SALES DIALOGUE

Sales dialogue with groups is fairly commonplace in business-to-business selling. For example, retail chains often employ buying committees when considering the addition of new products for their stores. Hospitals use cross-functional teams comprising medical and administrative personnel to choose vendors such as food service providers. A group of marketing and upper-management people usually make the decision about which advertising agency will be chosen. Corporations often depend on representatives from several departments to make purchase decisions that affect all employees, such as the choice of insurance providers.

Interacting with groups presents special challenges and opportunities. In addition to the basic fundamentals of planning and delivering sales dialogue to individual buyers, there are additional strategies and tactics that can enhance sales dialogue with groups.

When selling to groups, salespeople can expect tough questions and should prepare accordingly. Although buyer questions are part of most sales dialogues, whether with individuals or groups, they are particularly crucial when there

case histories A testimonial in story or anecdotal form used as a proof provider.

Selling in Action

Preselling Strategies

Salespeople at a logistics company spend a lot of time preselling people from different business functions within a buying organization. The company helps manufacturing companies improve processes throughout their supply chain. The supply chain services impact many different business functions, such as warehousing, logistics, accounting, finance, and information technology. Each of these business functions has different needs and defines value in different ways. So, it is critical to identify the key concerns of each business function before conducting sales dialogue with the entire group. The typical strategy is to meet individually with someone from each buying function to determine the desired value. Sometimes it is not possible to meet with the different functions personally, so a survey or e-mails are used to get the information needed by the salesperson. This preselling approach prepares the salesperson for the group sales dialogue where the objective is to get "buy-in" from the buying group. The most successful salespeople communicate the value desired by each business function, and then summarize the total value the entire company would receive from using all of the supply chain services.[16]

---

are multiple buyers. Most buying groups are assembled to tap the individual expertise and interests of the group members. For example, a buying committee for a company's computer information system could include technical specialists; finance and accounting personnel; and representatives from production operations, logistics, management, and marketing. All of these individuals are experts and demand in-depth information to make a decision. In some situations, this calls for a sales team to address all questions adequately, while in other cases, an individual salesperson has the cross-functional expertise required to make the sale.

When selling to a group, salespeople should take every opportunity of **preselling** to individual group members before the group presentation. Preselling to individual buyers or subgroups of buyers takes place before a major sales presentation to the entire group. Buying procedures in a given company may or may not allow preselling. If it is an option, the salesperson should work with the individuals composing the buying group before presenting to the group as a whole. By doing so, the salesperson can better determine individual and group interests and motives and possibly build a positive foundation for the group presentation. Preselling can also reveal the roles of the individuals in the buying centre, as discussed in Chapter 3. Knowing who the decision maker is, along with the other roles, such as users and influencers, is crucial for success in group sales interactions. The importance of preselling is discussed in Selling in Action: Preselling Strategies.

Sales Tactics for Selling to Groups

Assuming that the salesperson or sales team has planned a comprehensive sales dialogue and done as much preselling as possible, there are some specific sales tactics that can enhance presentations to groups. Sales tactics for group presentations fall into three general categories: arrival tactics, eye contact, and communication tips for presentation delivery.

ARRIVAL TACTICS   Try to arrive at the location for the meeting before the buying group arrives. This provides an opportunity to set up and check audio-visual equipment, prepare collateral material for distribution to the group, and become familiar and comfortable with the surroundings. It also sets the stage for the salesperson to greet individuals from the buying team personally as they enter the room. In a symbolic way, it also signals territorial command, or that the salesperson is in charge of the meeting. Although the control of the meeting is typically shared with the buying group, arriving first sends a message that the salesperson is prepared to start promptly at the appointed time, thus showing respect for the buyer's time.

From the very beginning, the salesperson is hoping to connect with each individual in the group, rather than

preselling Salespeople present their product or service to individual buyers before a major sales dialogue with a group of buyers.

connecting only at the group level. By arriving first, the salesperson may have the opportunity to talk briefly with each individual. If nothing more, a friendly greeting, handshake, and introduction can help establish a rapport with individuals in the group. When not allowed to arrive first, salespeople should attempt individual introductions when joining the group. If that is not practical, salespeople must try to engage each individual through eye contact and, if appropriate, introductory remarks early in the presentation that recognize the individual interests of those present. For example, a salesperson for a food service company might begin a presentation to a hospital with the following:

> *Thank you for the opportunity to discuss our food service programs with you today. In planning for our meeting, I recognize that the dietary group is most concerned about the impact of any proposed change on the quality of patient care. Linda [the head dietician], I believe we have a program that will enhance the quality of care that your patients receive. John [the head of finance], we will also propose an efficient, cost-effective alternative . . . .*

Opening remarks such as these, when kept brief, can be most effective in building involvement with all individuals in a small group.

EYE CONTACT

2.3 Communicate verbally

For both small and large groups, establishing periodic eye contact with individuals is important. With small groups, this is easily accomplished. With larger groups, especially formal presentations in which the salesperson is standing and the group is sitting, there may be a tendency to use the so-called overhead approach. This method calls for looking just over the heads of the group, with the idea that those seated farthest from the presenter will feel included as part of the group. This method should be avoided. It might be fine for a formal speech to a large audience in a convention hall, but it is far too impersonal for groups of 10 to 25 individuals. Also avoid a rapid scanning from side-to-side. This gives the appearance of nervousness and is ineffective in connecting with individual group members. The most effective eye contact is to try to connect with each individual or small subgroups for a few seconds, moving through the entire group over the course of the presentation. Professional entertainers often use this method to connect with audience members, and salespeople can do the same.

3.2 Conduct sales presentations

When selling to groups, it is essential to make all members of the group feel that their opinions are valuable. It is also important to avoid being caught in the middle of disagreements between members of the buying group. For example, if one member likes the salesperson's proposal and another thinks it is too expensive, any resolution of this disagreement must be handled carefully. Although the salesperson may present information that resolves the issue, in some cases disagreements among group buying members may be resolved outside the meetings. It is to the salesperson's advantage if disagreements can be handled during the presentation, as it keeps the sales process moving; unresolved issues can stall the sales process. As an example of how salespeople can play a peacemaker role, consider this exchange:

Buyer A: "I really like this system and think we should install it as soon as possible."

Buyer B: "I like it too, but it is way too expensive. Is there a less expensive alternative?"

Buyer A: "Sure, but it will not do the job."

Salesperson: (*Directed to Buyer B*) "Could I add something here? I believe we have a cost-effective system and that our lease-to-purchase plan reduces the capital expenditure and allows a favourable payback period. Could we take another look at the numbers?"

The point is that salespeople must be diplomatic as a participant in discussions that might develop between members of the buying group. This sometimes means remaining silent while the discussion comes to a resolution, and sometimes it means playing an active role. There are no hard and fast rules in this area, and salespeople must simply use their best judgment to guide their actions.

In delivering group presentations, it is important to maintain contact with group members. Thus, reading or overreliance on densely worded slides should be avoided. Think of slides and other audio-visual aids as support tools, not as a "roll-and-scroll" presentation to be read to the group. Natural movement can also enhance contact with the group. Too much pacing about can be detrimental to holding the group's attention, just as remaining tethered to a laptop can detract from group communication. When possible, salespeople should stand to the left of visual aids. This way, it is easier to direct attention to the visual aids while momentarily deflecting attention away from the speaker. In this way, the salesperson becomes an unobtrusive narrator and the visual aid has maximum impact.

Body language can add to or detract from sales effectiveness in the group setting. In general, your posture should reflect an energetic, relaxed person. Conventional wisdom dictates that presenters should avoid contact with their own bodies while presenting. Salespeople who stuff their hands in their pockets, scratch their heads, or cross their arms are creating distractions to their own messages.

Handling Questions in Group Dialogue

Just as is the case with sales dialogue to individuals, questions from buyers in a group are an important part of the buyer–seller interaction that leads to a purchase decision. Salespeople should recognize that questions fill information gaps, thus allowing buyers to make better decisions. In a group setting, questions can also add a dramatic element, making the presentation more interesting for those in attendance. To the extent that it is possible, salespeople should anticipate group questions and then decide whether to address the question before it arises or wait and address the question should it arise during the presentation.

To handle questions that arise during the meeting effectively, salespeople should listen carefully and maintain eye contact with the person asking the question. Generally, it is a good idea to repeat or restate the question. Questions should be answered as succinctly and convincingly as possible. By listening carefully to the question, salespeople show respect for the person asking the question. At the same time, they are helping direct the attention of the group to the question. As the question is posed, it is important for the salesperson to maintain eye contact with the person asking the question. Again, this demonstrates respect for the person and for their right to ask questions. This may require some practice, as salespeople may be tempted to glance at sales materials or perhaps their watch when the attention is shifted to the person asking the question. To do so could insult the questioner, who may feel slighted by the lack of attention.

In many cases, it is a good idea to repeat or even restate the question. This will ensure that everyone understands the question. It also signals a shift from the individual back to the group. Additionally, it allows the salesperson to state the key issue in the question succinctly. This is often important because not all questions are well

> In answering questions during a group dialogue, salespeople should listen carefully, answer directly, and address the individual asking the question as well as the others in the group.

Salespeople need to repeat or restate questions from individuals in a group presentation.

formulated and they are sometimes accompanied by superfluous information. Consider the following dialogue:

Buyer: "You know, I have been thinking about the feasibility of matching our Brand X computers with Brand Y printers. Not too long ago, matching multiple brands would have been a disaster. Are you telling me now that Brand X computers are totally compatible with Brand Y printers?"

Seller: "You are asking whether your computers are compatible with our printers. Is that right? Yes, they are—with no special installation requirements."

When restating questions, salespeople must be careful to capture the essence of the buyer's concern accurately. Otherwise, they could be perceived as avoiding the question or trying to manipulate the buyer by putting words in their mouth. Therefore, when in doubt, it is a good practice when restating a question to seek buyer confirmation that the restated question is an accurate representation of the original question. For example, salespeople might say, "Ms. Jackson, as I understand the question, you are concerned about the effectiveness of our seasonal sales promotion programs. Is that correct?"

When you are answering questions, there are three guidelines to follow. First, a salesperson should not attempt to answer a question until they and the group members clearly understand the question. Second, salespeople should not attempt to answer questions that they are not prepared to answer. It is far better to make a note and tell the group you will get back to them with the answer than to speculate or give a weak answer. Third, salespeople should try to answer questions as directly as possible. Politicians are often accused of not answering the questions posed during press conferences, but rather steering the answer toward what they want to talk about. Salespeople will quickly lose credibility if they take a long time to get to the point in their answer. To answer convincingly, start with a "yes" or "no," then explain the exceptions to the general case. For example, saying, "Yes, that is generally the case. There are some exceptions, including . . ." is preferred to answering "Well that depends . . ." and then explaining all of the special circumstances only to conclude with "but, generally, yes, that is the case."

When answering questions, it is important to address the entire group rather than just the individual who asked the question. Otherwise, salespeople may lose the attention of other group members. When salespeople conclude their answers, they have the option of going back to the person who asked the question, continuing their presentation, or taking a question from another group member. Salespeople can rely on their common sense and experience to decide what is appropriate in a given situation.

In larger groups, it is particularly important to avoid getting locked into a question-and-answer dialogue with one person if other people are showing an interest in asking questions. Indeed, it is important to take all questions, but it is also important to spread the opportunity to ask questions around the room, coming back to those who have multiple questions until all questions are answered. If one person is a dominant force within the buying group, other group members will typically defer their questions until that person has asked all of their questions at different points in the presentation.

When selling to a group, salespeople should have a clear objective for their presentation. To get the group to take the desired action, salespeople must make a convincing case, motivate the group to take action, and make it easy for the group to take the desired action. Some of the methods for handling buyer objections and earning a commitment that will be discussed in Chapter 8 will prove useful for accomplishing these tasks.

In some cases, the group will want to deliberate and let the salesperson know of their decision at a later time. This is not uncommon, because the group may need a frank discussion without outsiders to reach a final decision. Should this occur, salespeople should be certain that the group has all the information they need or offer to provide the needed information promptly and offer to follow up within a specified time period.

The process for planning and delivering a group sales dialogue is much the same as it is for sales dialogue with individuals. By paying attention to the special considerations in this section, salespeople can build on their experience with sales interaction with individuals and engage in effective sales dialogue with groups.

STUDY TOOLS

At the back of the textbook, use tear-out cards to review key chapter information. Visit cengage.ca to purchase digital tools to help you succeed.

CENGAGE | MINDTAP

Personal Computer

- ☐ Gain unique perspectives on key concepts through a variety of videos and cases
- ☐ Increase your comprehension with online quizzes
- ☐ Study with existing flashcards and make your own

Mobile

- ☐ Stay focused and ready to study whenever it's convenient for you!
- ☐ Access a full, interactive ebook: online or offline
- ☐ Study tools that empower anytime, anywhere learning and 24/7 course access

7 CHAPTER CASE

OFFICE FURNITURE COMPANY

BACKGROUND

The Ennismore Furniture Company specializes in providing customers with office furniture solutions that are customized and designed to address productivity and aesthetic needs. It sells office furniture from the leading manufacturers, but creates value by analyzing the specific needs of each customer and then developing a customized design to meet these needs. There are several competitors in the office furniture industry, but most of them focus on low prices. Customers usually pay more for an Ennismore Furniture Company solution, but receive more value in terms of increased productivity and business effectiveness.

CURRENT SITUATION

Arnold & Associates is a small but growing accounting firm. The company plans to add more office staff and to increase the number of its accountants. This planned growth means that the firm will have to find new office space, because it will have outgrown its current location. Because it plans continued growth in the future, it is looking for a new office that will accommodate current and future growth objectives. Arnold & Associates also wants to purchase new and better furniture for its new office. You are a sales representative for the Ennismore Furniture Company and have been meeting with partner Sarah Arnold, as well as accountants and staff, at Arnold & Associates. Based on these meetings, you have identified the following office furniture needs:

1. Arnold & Associates has typically met with clients at their offices. It would like to have most client meetings in the future at its new office. This means they desire furniture that facilitates these meetings and communicates a professional and customer-friendly image.

2. Their current office furniture did not provide much storage for accountants or staff. Thus, important documents were stored at the end of a long hallway. Employees wasted a lot of time trying to retrieve important documents. Thus, they desire furniture that provides more storage for each employee.

3. Technology is changing at a rapid pace, so furniture that can be easily adapted to new technologies is very important.

4. As Arnold & Associates continues to grow, it will probably have to reorganize itself and is likely to need to adapt the physical office to different organizational arrangements. Office furniture that is adaptable to different configurations is important. You have created an office equipment design for Arnold & Associates that addresses each of the issues presented above and are preparing for a meeting with the partner, Sarah Arnold, the office manager, and a representative for the firm's accountants. You know that a competitor has already made a presentation to the same group and their offer will cost less than what you will be able to charge.

QUESTIONS

1. How will you try overcoming the lower price offer by a competitor?

2. What specific value can you offer Arnold & Associates?

3. How can you most effectively communicate the value of your proposed office equipment design?

4. What sales aids could you use to make your presentation more engaging and effective?

ROLE PLAY

Situation: Read the Ennismore Equipment Company case.

Characters: Sarah Arnold, partner; Tricia MacDonald, office manager; Jessica Attaway, accountant representative

Scene:

Location—Current Arnold & Associates office.

Action—Role-play this meeting. Be sure to address the specific needs identified earlier, to communicate effectively with each person in the meeting, and to incorporate sales aids appropriately.

After completing the role plays, address the following questions:

1. How would you evaluate the role play in terms of interesting, understandable, and engaging sales dialogue? What improvements would you recommend?

2. How well did you involve each person in the meeting? What improvements would you recommend?

3. Evaluate the effectiveness of each sales aid used. What improvements in the use of sales aids would you recommend?

INTEGRATIVE CASE

INVESTMENT AIDS

BACKGROUND

The use of sales aids is a very common occurrence in personal selling, simply due to the tangible and interactive nature of demonstrating a product. But these items have sometimes been a point of contention when it comes to legislation and taxation in Canada.

The Canada Revenue Agency defines sales aids as: "property that is a customized business form or a sample, demonstration kit, promotional or instructional item, catalogue, or other personal property that a direct seller or an ISC acquires, manufactures or produces for sale to assist in the promotion, sale or distribution of … products."[17] But there is just as important a list of what is not considered a sales aid. This includes actual products without labelling as a "tester" or "not for sale," general business books, admissions to conferences and seminars, and clothing without identified logos of the selling firm.[18]

While it is often assumed that direct sellers, such as those operating in a multilevel marketing (MLM) program, would use sales aids almost exclusively as means to create sales dialogue, there are a number of industries that also use these materials. These industries include pharmaceutical sales, insurance, and investments.

The investment industry focuses heavily on using various types of sales aids in order to help build a dialogue about products that can often be confusing and convoluted for consumers. And often the requirement is that salespeople, whether employed or independent, use the sales aids from the company.

But there is a stigma attached to the term "sales aid" in the investment community, as they began to be used to not directly sell the products in question but to shift consumers to more expensive or expansive product offerings.[19] As the term "sales aids" began to represent something of a manipulative tool, their use in sales calls started to dissipate.

One investment adviser described his experience this way: "the 'one good sales aid' he is using is his 'brain and a scrap piece of paper'… he believes his skill as a financial adviser should be to digest technical information and explain it to his clients in an accessible way."[20]

This does not mean that sales aids have gone away; it's that they have become more digital and interactive in nature. The days of only product samples, a few books, maybe some CDs are gone. One company in the investment community, Zurich, focuses almost entirely on providing salespeople with digital tools: "Zurich offers a mix of online tools and mobile apps, business protection tools, as well as technological support and thought leadership pieces."[21]

A sales director at Zurich described why digital is the way to go: "Standalone tools are dead. What advisers are looking for are tools which help them give advice and integrate into the technology they use anyway. They [want to be able to] use them as part of the process."[22] But he also notes that none of these modern aids will be useful unless they can result in face-to-face time with their customers.

CURRENT SITUATION

Canada Life Investments is an asset management company with a healthy salesforce. The company's website shows pictures of wide expanses and scenic vistas reminiscent of Canada's majestic beauty. But Canada Life Investments is based in London, England, not London, Ontario.

The company is looking to enter the Canadian market and would like someone to assess their sales aids. You can find the aids here: https://www.canadalifeinvestments.com/literature/t/sales-aids/.

You are a prospective sales employee who has been asked as part of the interview process to critique the sales aids and provide suggestions as to how best reflect the changing world of these sales dialogue enhancers. Your interview is in a few hours and you have yet to figure out what to say, so you pull out your notes from your sales class in hopes of jogging your memory. You will need to invest the next few hours in coming up with something that will impress.

QUESTIONS

1. Which of the following is NOT a reason why sales aids can maximize the effectiveness of the sales dialogue?

   a. engage and involve the buyer throughout

   b. help to capture and hold the buyer's attention

   c. provide an opportunity to upsell to different products

   d. boost the buyer's understanding

2. What is the most important advantage of using graphic presentations as a sales aid?

   a. They are more powerful than samples.

   b. They don't wear out as easily.

   c. They are customizable.

   d. They allow for greater amounts of information.

3. What is the acronym for the process to use a sales aid in a customer service training program?

   a. SPES

   b. PETS

   c. SPENT

   d. ADAPT

CHAPTER ROLE PLAY 7

Sales Dialogue: Creating and Communicating Value at Chemong Insurance and National Networks

BACKGROUND

The Chemong Insurance Company has 3,200 sales agents spread across five regions that cover all of Canada. The company is moving toward the development of a national network that would tie each of the agent offices together with the regional offices and corporate headquarters. The improved communication capability will allow all company personnel to have full access to customer records and form the core of a comprehensive customer relationship management system that is to be rolled out in 18 months.

CURRENT SITUATION

Jim Roberts is a network account specialist for National Networks, a specialist in large corporate network solutions, and has been working with the technology-buying group at Chemong Insurance for several months now. Roberts has worked through several meetings with the buying group members and has a meeting scheduled for next Wednesday to present his recommendations and demonstrate why they should select National Networks as the supplier for this sizable project. Joyce Fields (director of information systems), John Harris (comptroller and CFO), Javid Quadri (director of agent services), and Dianne Sheffield (director for customer services) will make the final decision. Roberts also knows that one other competitor will be making a presentation in hopes of landing the project. The equipment both vendors are proposing is virtually identical because of the detailed specifications that Chemong Insurance had included in the RFP. Prices are also likely to be pretty similar. The decision will most likely come down to the services each competitor includes in the proposals. Based on the information that Roberts has collected from different sources, he has come up with a comparison of customer services National Networks and the competitor offer (see the following table).

ROLE PLAY

Situation: Read the role play Background and Current Situation.

Characters: Jim Roberts—salesperson for National Networks; Joyce Fields—director of information systems for Chemong Insurance; John Harris—comptroller and CFO for

Chemong Insurance; Javid Quadri—director of agent services for Chemong Insurance; Dianne Sheffield—director for customer services for Chemong Insurance

Scene:

Location—A conference room at Chemong Insurance

Action—As described, Jim Roberts is presenting the National Networks proposal for a corporate computer network linking Chemong Insurance's corporate offices with each of its five regional offices and 3,200 sales agents out in the field.

Role play Roberts's presentation of each of the feature–benefit sets incorporating sales aids suitable for use in the group presentation.

Features	Capability of National Networks	Capability of Competitor	Benefits
Service and repair centres	175 affiliated service and repair centres across Canada	21 affiliated service and repair centres across Canada	Ensures fast and reliable repairs for hardware and software
Installation and testing	Installation and testing done by National Networks employees	Installation and testing outsourced to several different companies	Knowledge that all installations will be done the right way
Customer call centre	24 hours, 7 days per week, and staffed by National Networks employees	24 hours, 7 days per week, and staffed by an outsource commercial provider	Knowledgeable staff always available to assist Chemong Insurance employees with problems

After completing the role plays, address the following questions:

1. What other sales tools and aids might prove useful to Roberts in presenting his proposed solution to the Chemong Insurance buying team?

2. How might Roberts employ other tactics for selling to a group to increase the effectiveness of his presentation and advance the sale toward getting an order?

8 | Addressing Concerns and Earning Commitment

After completing this chapter, you should be able to

LO 1 | Explain why it is important to anticipate and overcome buyer concerns and resistance.

LO 2 | Understand why prospects raise objections.

LO 3 | Describe the five major types of sales resistance.

LO 4 | Explain how the LAARC method can be used to overcome buyer resistance.

LO 5 | Describe the recommended approaches for responding to buyer objections.

LO 6 | List and explain the earning commitment techniques that secure commitment and closing.

AFTER FINISHING THIS CHAPTER GO TO THE BACK OF THE BOOK FOR CHAPTER REVIEW CARDS, AND VISIT MINDTAP FOR ACCESS TO STUDY TOOLS.

A young mechanic's entrepreneurial spirit in 1930s Quebec sparked the creation of the company known today as Bombardier. The business started as an operation that commercially sold snowmobiles and has grown into a global leader in the transportation industry. The company is a multinational manufacturer of planes and trains, with two main divisions: aviation (headquartered in Montreal) and transportation (headquartered in Berlin). Today, their main focus lies in the aviation sector with the production of business and commercial aircraft and the provision of aerostructures and engineering services. The company has over 68,000 employees and production and engineering in 28 countries worldwide. A high-performance culture drives their dedication to commitments and a talented workforce has been built to achieve this. Employees are encouraged to develop their skills and recruited personnel are highly motivated, engaged, and resilient, all essential characteristics that fuel innovation. With the corporate goal of continuously finding better ways to bridge distances and bring people together, they strive to shape the future of mobility. Sustainability and corporate responsibility have become important pillars of the corporate structure, and as a result Bombardier has been recognized for several achievements including being listed on the 2019 Global 100 Most Sustainable Corporations in the World Index, the 2018 Clean 200 Index, and the 2018 Best 50 Corporate Citizens in Canada Index.[1] Upon the fiscal year end in 2018, Bombardier recorded revenues of $16.2 billion USD.[2]

Introduction

Bombardier can successfully deal with complex offers and extended sales cycles in part because it is adept at addressing customer concerns and maintaining commitment at every stage of the long selling process. FUSION Performance Marketing, a full-service

performance improvement company that specializes in highly creative and results-oriented incentive systems, is another example of an organization with extremely long sales cycles, ranging from three months to four or five years. For both firms, each prospective client has different challenges and objectives, requiring each to develop custom solutions specific to their clients' unique needs. In addition, because clients of both firms spend millions of dollars on their solutions, the buying decision is lengthy and challenging. Given this scenario, the opportunities for resistance are rampant and the struggle to overcome customer resistance and gain customer commitment is lengthy and arduous.

Addressing Concerns

An objection or **sales resistance** is anything the buyer says or does that slows down or stops the buying process. The salesperson's job is to uncover these objections and answer them to the prospect's or client's satisfaction. It is very difficult for a salesperson to earn commitment if there is doubt or concern on the buyer's part. Thus, the salesperson must uncover and overcome any and all objections. In doing so, the salesperson strengthens the long-term relationship and moves the sales process closer to commitment. At the very least, these concerns open dialogue between the salesperson and the prospect.

A brief discussion follows on why it is important for salespeople to anticipate and negotiate buyer concern. Following a discussion of why prospects raise objections, this chapter covers the five major types of objections. Next, different approaches to handling sales resistance are explained. Finally, techniques to earn commitment are reviewed.

sales resistance A buyer's objections to a product or service during a sales presentation.

LO 1 | ANTICIPATING AND NEGOTIATING CONCERNS AND RESISTANCE

 3.2 Conduct sales presentations

Over the years, many salesforces were taught that sales resistance was bad and would likely slow down or stop the selling process. Salespeople were also told that if they received resistance, then they had not done a good job explaining their product or service.

These notions have changed over the years to where objections are now viewed as opportunities to sell. Salespeople should be grateful for objections and always treat them as questions. The buyer is just asking for more information. It is the salesperson's job to produce the correct information to help buyers understand their concerns. Inexperienced salespeople need to learn that sales resistance is a normal, natural part of any sales conversation. The prospect that does not question price, service, warranty, and delivery concerns is probably not interested.

> Good salespeople will anticipate their buyers' concerns.

Although many salespeople fear sales resistance from their prospects or customers, it should be viewed as a normal part of the sales process. At a minimum, the salesperson has the prospect involved. The salesperson can now start to determine customer interest and measure the buyer's understanding of the problem. In some situations, a salesperson cannot overcome resistance (e.g., delivery dates do not match; technology does not fit). Under these circumstances, the successful salesperson gracefully ends the sales call while leaving open the option for further business.[3] Finally, if the sales resistance is handled correctly, the outcome can lead to customer acceptance.

LO 2 | REASONS WHY PROSPECTS RAISE OBJECTIONS

 3.2 Conduct sales presentations

There are many reasons why prospects will raise objections.

1. **The prospect wants to avoid the sales interview.** Some prospects do not want to create any more work for themselves than they already have. A sales interview takes time and buyers already have a busy schedule handling normal day-to-day tasks. Buyers may want to avoid the salesperson because they view their call as an interruption in their day. Most buyers do not have the time to see every salesperson who knocks on their door.

2. **The salesperson has failed to prospect and qualify properly.** Sometimes, poor prospects slip through the screening process. The prospect may have misunderstood the salesperson's intentions when asked for the interview. The salesperson should attempt to qualify the prospect during the sales call. For example, a computer software company used telemarketing to qualify prospects. Leads were turned over to the salesforce for in-person visits. The major product line was an inventory control package that cost $20,000. The salesperson asked the owner of the company if she had a budget for this project. The owner responded that her budget was $5,000. The salesperson gave the owner the names of a couple of inexpensive software companies, thanked the owner for her time, and moved on. The owner was not about to spend $20,000 and said so early in the sales conversation. That resistance actually helped the salesperson. What if this condition had stayed hidden for four to six weeks while the salesperson continued to call on the owner? Both the salesperson's and owner's time would have been wasted.

3. **Objecting is a matter of custom.** Many purchasing agents have a motto never to buy on the first call with a salesperson. Trust has not yet been developed and a thorough understanding of the salesperson, their company, and the products has not been created. The buyer will need most of this information to make a decision. Many buyers may say no during the first few calls to test the salesperson's persistence.

4. **The prospect resists change.** Many buyers like the way that they are currently doing business. Thus, buyers will tell the salesperson that they are satisfied with what they have now. Many prospects simply resist change because they dislike making decisions. Prospects may fear the consequences of deciding and dread disturbing the status quo. A purchase usually involves dismissing the present supplier and handling all of the arrangements (price, terms, delivery, and product specifications) to move the new supplier in smoothly. Once a buyer is comfortable with their suppliers, they will generally avoid new salespeople until a major need arises.

5. **The prospect fails to recognize a need.** The prospect may be unaware of a need, uninformed about the product or service, or content with the present situation. In any case, the lack of need creates no motivation to change suppliers. Many purchasing agents were content with their overnight mail service and were slow to recognize the fax machine as a viable solution to getting information to their customers quickly. The poor quality of the reproduced document also turned away many buyers. Only when the need for the information outweighed the aesthetics of the document did the buyers readily embrace the fax machine.

6. **The prospect lacks information.** Ultimately, all sales resistance comes back to the fact that the prospect simply lacks the information they need to make a decision comfortably. The salesperson must view this as an opportunity to put the right information in front of the buyer. Exhibit 8.1 summarizes why prospects raise objections and lists strategies for dealing with them.

Exhibit 8.1

Why Prospects Raise Objections and Strategies for Dealing with Them

- Buyer wants to avoid the sales interview.

  Strategy: Set appointments to become part of the buyer's daily routine.
- Salesperson has failed to prospect and qualify properly.

  Strategy: Ask questions to verify prospect's interest.
- Buyer will not buy on the first sales call.

  Strategy: A regular call on the prospect lets the prospect know the salesperson is serious about the relationship.
- Prospect does not want to change the current way of doing business.

  Strategy: Salesperson must help the prospect understand there is a better solution than the one the prospect is presently using.
- Prospect has failed to recognize a need.

  Strategy: Salesperson must show evidence that sparks the prospect's interest.
- Prospect lacks information on a new product or on the salesperson's company.

  Strategy: Salesperson must continually work to add value by providing useful information.

LO 3 | TYPES OF SALES RESISTANCE

 CPSA | **3.2 Conduct sales presentations**

Although there appears to be an infinite number of objections, most fall into five or six categories. Buyers use delay techniques to avoid taking immediate action. Comments such as "Give me a couple of weeks to think it over" can save the buyer the discomfort of saying no at the end of a presentation. "Your price is too high" or "I have no money" are easy ways for purchasing agents not to buy a salesperson's offering. Price is probably the most often cited objection and usually is not the most important issue. It is obvious that buyers do not buy merely based on price; if this were true, then the lowest price supplier would get all of the business and eventually be the only supplier left selling the product. "No need at this time" is another typical objection. The buyer may not be in the market to purchase at this time.

It is not unusual for salespeople to encounter product objections. Most buyers have fears associated with buying a product. The buyer may be afraid that the product will not be as reliable as the salesperson said it would. Not only do the salespeople have to demonstrate that their product will perform at the level they say it will, but they must also show how it stacks up to the competition. A competitor

"And that is what happens when we resist change."

Many salespeople fear sales resistance from their prospects or customers.

Exhibit 8.2

Types of Objections

No need	Buyer has recently purchased or does not see a need for the product category. "I am not interested at this time."
Product or service objection	Buyer may be afraid of product reliability. "I am not sure the quality of your product meets our needs." Buyer may be afraid of late deliveries, slow repairs, etc. "I am happy with my present supplier's service."
Company objection	Buyer is intensely loyal to the present supplier. "I am happy with my present supplier."
Price is too high	Buyer has a limited budget. "We have been buying from another supplier that meets our budget constraints."
Time or delay	Buyer needs time to think it over. "Get back with me in a couple of weeks."

introducing a new technology (e.g., e-commerce) may change the way a salesperson competes on a particular product line (e.g., office products).

Many buyers are constantly assessing their supplier on service (e.g., delivery, follow-up, warranties, guarantees, repairs, installation, and training). If the service is good and department heads are not complaining, the buyer is likely to stay with the status quo. Service is one variable that companies and salespeople can use to differentiate their product. Enterprise Rent-a-Car will deliver cars to the home of the renter and has made this difference a factor in its advertising. A salesperson for a wholesale distributor may make the point to a prospect that their fresh fruit, fish, and meat can be delivered daily when their competitors deliver only three times per week.

Many buyers will feel intense loyalty to their present suppliers and use this as a reason not to change. Buyers may be equally committed to the salesperson from whom they are currently buying. As a nonsupplier to the company, the salesperson must continue to call on the buyer and look for opportunities to build trust with the prospect. The salesperson may want to investigate whether the buyer has had any previous bad experience with their company that is causing the buyer not to do business with the company. Some salespeople and their buyers will not hit it

off. The salesperson has to recognize these feelings and move on if several calls do not result in an eventual sale.

At first glance, an inexperienced salesperson may be overwhelmed with the thought of how they will handle all the different types of objections buyers will raise. Salespeople need to develop skills in evaluating objections.[4] It does not take long, however, for a salesperson to learn that most objections fall into just a few categories. When preparing to buy a product or service, a prospect generally obtains information in five areas: need, product or service features, company or source, price, and timing of the buy. Objections could come from any of these areas, as shown in Exhibit 8.2.

Need Objections

Without a need, prospects have little or no reason to talk to a salesperson. If the prospect has been qualified properly, the salesperson believes the prospect has a need for the product. Many buyers have been conditioned to say automatically, "I do not need your product" (i.e., **need objection**). This may be the result of the buyer being out of budget or not having the time to look at your product or proposal. Other buyers may respond, "We are getting along just fine without your product. No one in my company is asking for your product. Call back in a few months and maybe something will change."

need objection Resistance to a product or service in which a buyer says that they do not need the product or service.

The salesperson has a tough challenge ahead if the buyer sincerely believes they have no need. It is the salesperson's job to establish a need in the buyer's mind; if the salesperson cannot do this then, logically, an objection can be expected.

Many prospects do not know they have a specific need for a product until a situation occurs that makes them aware of it (i.e., engineering calls and needs a special software package). Therefore, objections to the need require the salesperson to stimulate the need awareness of the prospect with relevant information—features and benefits that pique the prospect's interest. Exhibit 8.3 summarizes a number of the no-need objections.

Product or Service Objections

Often the product or service lacks something that the buyer wants and the salesperson cannot deliver. A competitive advantage for a large software firm (Ontario) is that it has 24-hour 800 service available to all its customers. The firm's number-one competitor offers only 8:00 a.m. to 8:00 p.m. call-in phone service. For those clients that run three shifts and need 24-hour service, the choice is easy: they buy from Ontario.

Other prospect objections could be simply emotional—the prospect does not like the way the product looks or feels (i.e., **product or service objection**). Still others have a problem with the product's performance characteristics (i.e., "I need a copier that has colour and staples in the bin"). The salesperson also must do an adequate job of fact-finding and qualifying. Many of these issues can be resolved by knowing what the prospect is looking for.

Objections toward the product centre on understanding the fit between the product and the customer's needs. The salesperson's job is to learn what product features are important to the buyer and sell those features. Products are bundles of benefits that customers seek to fit their needs.

Tying the benefits to the customer's needs helps the prospect bridge the gap from no-need to need. Exhibit 8.4 summarizes a number of product or service objections.

Company or Source Objections

Marty Reist is a manufacturer's representative for a small company in the sporting goods industry. He has to sell against many large competitors. Sales representatives from Nike, Titleist, and Reebok probably do not have to work as hard to get past the gatekeepers. Reist, in contrast, must justify his existence every day. "I have never heard of your company" (i.e., **company or source objection**) is something Reist must continually overcome.

Other buyers may be happy with their current supplier. It is not unusual for buyer–seller relationships to last 10 to 15 years and even longer. Robert Carroll, a former sales representative from Monsanto Agricultural Division, heard the following quote from many of his farmers and farm co-ops, "I'm perfectly happy with Monsanto; my crops look good. I've been buying from them for years, and they have always treated me right." This is one of the hardest objections to overcome, especially if the prospect feels genuine loyalty to their present supplier.

Professional salespeople never criticize

product or service objection Resistance to a product or service in which a buyer does not like the way the product or service looks or feels.

company or source objection Resistance to a product or service that results when a buyer has never heard of or is not familiar with the product's company.

Exhibit 8.5

Company or Source Objections

"Your company is too small to meet my needs."

"I have never heard of your company."

"Your company is too big. I will get lost in the shuffle."

"Your company is pretty new. How do I know you will be around to take care of me in the future?"

"Your company was recently in the newspaper. Are you having problems?"

their competitors. The salesperson can point out any superior features their product or service might have. They can also ask for a single order and ask for an evaluation against the present supplier.

Another form of source objection is a negative attitude a buyer might have about the salesperson's company or the poor presentation of a previous salesperson. A buyer might remember a late or damaged order the company did not properly handle. A former salesperson may have made promises to the buyer and did not follow through on them. The salesperson must investigate any and all source objections. The salesperson may uncover source problems that can be overcome with time. Exhibit 8.5 outlines typical company or source objections.

Price Objections

Most sales experts agree that price is the most common form of buyer resistance.[5] This objection has prospects saying that they cannot afford the product, the price is too high, or the product is not in their budget at this time (i.e., **price objection**). This objection may be a request for the salesperson to justify to the prospect how they can afford the product or how they can work it into their budget. Most salespeople feel the price objection is an attempt by the buyer to get the salesperson to lower their price. The salesperson must address the price objection by citing how the benefits (value) outweigh the cost. To do this, the product's value must be established before the salesperson spends time discussing price.[6] Many companies never sell as the low-cost option. Stryker

price objection Resistance to a product or service based on the price of the product being too high for the buyer.

time objection Resistance to a product or service in which a buyer puts off the decision to buy until a later date.

Medical sells hospital beds and stretchers to hospitals and emergency rooms. Stryker never offers the lowest cost. Stryker's salespeople almost always hear the price objection. First, they have to educate their prospects and customers that their products last 25 to 50 percent longer than their competitor's products. They can demonstrate with evidence their product will still be around 5 to 10 years after their competitor's has been discarded. If one of their stretchers is $1,500 more than their competitor's, they must break down the price over the entire life of the stretcher. They can actually show a savings over time. By providing the right information, Stryker can show value over the competitor's offering.

Price objections probably occur more frequently than any other type. Price objections may be used to cover the real reason for a reluctance to buy. Probing and asking questions are the salesperson's tools to get to the real reasons for a buyer's objection. Exhibit 8.6 summarizes a number of price objections.

Time Objections

Buyers use the **time objection**, or as some salespeople call it the *stalling objection*, to put off the decision to buy until a later date. Many inexperienced salespeople hear this technique and believe the prospect is going to buy in the future but not today. Some buyers use this technique to get rid of salespeople so that the buyer does not have to reject the salesperson and their sales proposal formally. Sometimes proposals are very complex and the buyer does need time to think them over. The salesperson must be sensitive to this and not push too hard to get an answer until the buyer has had adequate time to make a decision. It is acceptable for the salesperson to review the reasons to act now or soon. Waiting can have consequences (e.g., prices rise, a new

Exhibit 8.6

Price Objections

"We cannot afford it."

"I cannot afford to spend that much right now."

"That is 30 percent higher than your competitor's comparable model."

"We have a better offer from your competitor."

"I need something a lot cheaper."

"Your price is not different enough to change suppliers."

Exhibit 8.7
Time Objections

"I need time to think it over."

"Ask me again next month when you stop by."

"I am not ready to buy yet."

"I have not made up my mind."

"I do not want to commit myself until I have had a chance to talk to engineering (or any other department)."

tax begins the first of the year) and the buyer should be made aware of these. Exhibit 8.7 illustrates possible time objections.

LO 4 | USING LAARC: A PROCESS FOR NEGOTIATING BUYER RESISTANCE

CPSA 3.2 Conduct sales presentations

The term **LAARC** is an acronym for listen, acknowledge, assess, respond, and confirm and describes an effective process for salespeople to follow to overcome sales resistance. The LAARC method is a customer-oriented way to keep the sales dialogue positive. In the early days of sales, buyers and sellers were not always truthful with each other, and manipulation was the norm. Although being persuasive is necessary to be an effective sales representative, having such a singular focus can have a detrimental effect on customer rapport and relationships.[7] Salespeople who said whatever it took to get an order—who overpromised and underdelivered and misrepresented their offering—were sometimes looked on favourably by their selling organization. Professional sellers today want to keep the dialogue open and build goodwill by adding value to their proposition. By listening to buyers' concerns and negotiating through open dialogue, the seller increases the likelihood of purchase decisions being made on a favourable basis, and this leads to long-term relationships. Thus, it is the salesperson's job to communicate and demonstrate value when sales resistance arises.

Here is a description of LAARC:

- *Listen:* Salespeople should listen to what their buyers are saying. The ever-present temptation to anticipate what buyers are going to say and cut them off with a premature response should be avoided. Learning to listen is important—it is more than just being polite or professional. Buyers are trying to tell the salesperson something that they consider important.

- *Acknowledge:* As buyers complete their statements, salespeople should acknowledge that they received the message and that they appreciate and can understand the concern. Salespeople should not jump in with an instantaneous defensive response. Before responding, salespeople need a better understanding about what their buyers are saying. By politely pausing and then simply acknowledging their statement, a salesperson establishes that they are a reasonable person—a professional who appreciates other people's opinions. It also buys a salesperson precious moments for composing their thoughts and thinking of questions for the next step.

- *Assess:* This step is similar to assessment in the ADAPT process of questioning. This step in dealing with buyer resistance calls for salespeople to ask assessment questions to gain a better understanding of exactly what their buyers are saying and why they are saying it. Equipped with this information and understanding, salespeople are better able to make a meaningful response to the buyer's resistance.

- *Respond:* Based on their understanding of what and why the buyer is resisting, the salesperson can respond to the buyer's resistance. Structuring a response typically follows the method that is most appropriate for the situation. The more traditional methods of response (see Exhibit 8.8) include forestalling, direct denial, indirect denial, translation or boomerang, compensation, questioning or assessing, third-party reinforcement, feel-felt-found, and "coming to that." In An Ethical Dilemma, MaryAnne Noffke considers using one technique to handle sales resistance that should never be used by a professional salesperson.

These techniques have been used both positively and negatively. Professional salespeople use these techniques to add value to their proposal. For instance, the translation or boomerang technique can be used quite effectively if the salesperson has gathered the appropriate

> **LAARC** An acronym for listen, acknowledge, assess, respond, and confirm that describes an effective process for salespeople to follow to overcome sales resistance.

Exhibit 8.8

Techniques to Answer Concerns

Technique	How It Works	Example
Forestalling	Take care of the objection before the prospect brings it up.	Many of my customers have had a concern going into my presentation that we do not have a warranty program. Let me put this to rest: we have one-, three-, and five-year warranty programs that match our competitors. I hope this answers your concern.
Direct denial	Give a rather harsh response that the prospect is wrong.	You have heard incorrectly. We are not raising prices.
Indirect denial	Soften the blow when correcting a prospect's information.	We have heard that rumour, too—even some of our best customers asked us about it. Our senior management team has guaranteed us our prices will hold firm through the rest of the year.
Translation or boomerang	Turn a reason not to buy into a reason *to* buy.	Buyer: Your company is too small to meet our needs. Salesperson: That is just the reason you want to do business with us. Because we are smaller, you will get the individual attention you said you wanted.
Compensation	Counterbalance the objection with an offsetting benefit.	Yes, our price is higher, but you are going to get the quality you said that you needed to keep your customers happy.
Questioning or assessing	Ask the buyer assessment questions to gain a better understanding of what they are objecting to.	Your concern is price. Can you please tell me who you are comparing us with, and does that quote include any service agreement?
Third-party reinforcement	Use the opinion or data from a third-party source to help overcome the objection.	Bill Middleton from Dial Electronics had the same concern going in. Let me tell you why he is comfortable with our proposal. . . .
Feel-felt-found	Salesperson relates that others actually found their initial opinions to be unfounded.	Buyer: I do not think my customers will want to buy a product with all those features. We generally sell scaled-down models. Salesperson: I can certainly see how you feel. Lisa Richardson down the road in Brandon felt the same way when I first proposed that she go with these models. However, after she agreed to display them in the front of her store, she found that her customers started buying the models with more features—and that, in turn, provided her with larger margins. In fact, she called me less than a week later to order more!
Coming-to-that	The salesperson tells the buyer that they will be covering the objection later in the presentation.	Buyer: I have some concerns about your delivery dates. Salesperson: I am glad you brought that up. Before fully discussing our delivery, I want to go over the features that you said were important to you that will help you better understand our product. Is that okay?

An Ethical Dilemma

MaryAnne Noffke has been in sales for several years and had run into a number of difficult sales objections. She saw several orders go to her competitors because of her inability to answer these objections effectively. MaryAnne brought this issue up with her sales manager and he advised her to tell the prospect she was going to cover the concern later in the presentation. Her manager said even though she did not have an answer hopefully her prospect would forget and not bring up the objection again. How should MaryAnne handle this situation?

(a) MaryAnne should obey orders and do what her sales manager suggested.

(b) MaryAnne should tell her sales manager she is uncomfortable with his suggested tactic.

(c) MaryAnne should tell her boss she will try his advice to keep him happy, but not try it once in the field.

---

information to support their response. The buyer might state, "Your company is too big, and we might slip through the cracks as a small customer." The salesperson might respond, "That is exactly why you want to do business with us. We are larger, and we are going to be able to offer you all of the levels of expertise you said you needed. Smaller companies will not be able to do this, and you will eventually have to search for another supplier. We are one-stop shopping, and we will make sure you will not fall through the cracks." Here, the salesperson took a reason not to buy and translated it into a reason to buy. Much dialogue had to go on before this for the salesperson to be able to provide the proper information to overcome the concern. Exhibit 8.8 includes examples of how a salesperson might respond to buyer concerns in a professional manner.

- *Confirm:* After responding, the salesperson should ask confirmatory questions—response-checks to make sure that the buyer's concerns have been adequately met. Once this is confirmed, the presentation can proceed. In fact, experience indicates that this form of buyer confirmation is often a sufficient buying signal to warrant the salesperson's attempt to gain a commitment.

LO 5 | RECOMMENDED APPROACHES FOR RESPONDING TO OBJECTIONS

3.2 Conduct sales presentations

A brief description of traditional methods for responding to oxbjections follows. Exhibit 8.8 summarizes how each technique works.

Forestalling

When salespeople hear an objection arising repeatedly, they may decide to include an answer to the objection within their sales presentation before it is voiced by the prospect (i.e., **forestalling**). Marty Reist of MPRS Sales Inc. often tells his prospects he realizes he is not Nike, Titleist, or Reebok, but his size has not kept him from providing outstanding service to his customers. Reist can add a third-party testimonial to back up his statements and put his prospect's mind at ease. This technique should be used only when there is a high probability that the prospect will indeed raise the objection.[8]

Direct Denial

When using the **direct denial** technique to handle sales resistance, the salesperson is directly telling the customer that they are mistaken. Prospects may have incorrect facts or may not understand the information they have.

The prospect might say the following:

Prospect: I hear you do not offer service agreements on any of your products.

The salesperson, knowing this is not true, cannot soft-pedal their answer. In this situation, the prospect is clearly incorrect and the direct denial is the best solution.

Salesperson: I am sorry, that is not correct. We offer three- and five-year service contracts, and our warranty is also five years.

> **forestalling** A response to buyer objections in which the salesperson answers the objection during the presentation before the buyer has a chance to ask it.

> **direct denial** A response to buyer objections in which the salesperson tells the customer that they are wrong.

The important part of using the direct denial is not to humiliate or anger the prospect. The direct denial should be used sparingly, but it may be easier to use when the salesperson has a good feel for the relationship that they have with the buyer.

Indirect Denial

Sometimes it is best not to take an objection head on. The indirect approach takes on the objection, but with a softer, more tactful approach. With the **indirect denial**, the salesperson never tells the prospect directly that they are wrong. The best way to use this method is to think of it as offering sympathy with the prospect's view and still managing to correct the invalid objection of the buyer. An example follows:

Prospect: I heard that your emergency room beds are $4,000 more than your competitor's.

Salesperson: Many of our customers had a similar notion that our beds are much more expensive. The actual cost is only $1,200 higher. I have testimonials from other hospitals stating that our beds last up to five years longer. You'll actually save money.

The salesperson here tries to soften the blow with the opening sentence. Then the salesperson must correct the misconception. Techniques can be combined as the salesperson adds information from a third party to lend credibility to their statement.

Translation or Boomerang

The **translation** or **boomerang** method converts the objection into a reason that the prospect should buy. What the salesperson is trying to do is to take a reason not to buy and turn it into a reason to buy. Marty Reist of MPRS Sales Inc. offers the following advice:

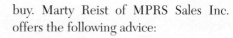
© jesadaphorn/Shutterstock.com

Whenever I hear the objection "I don't think your company is large enough to meet our service needs," I immediately come back with "that is exactly the reason you should do business with us. We are big enough to meet your service needs. In fact, you will be calling an 800 number with a larger company and you won't know who you'll get to help you. With our company, anytime you have a problem, question, or concern, you'll call me and talk to a familiar voice."

Another example using the price objection might go like this:

Buyer: "Your price appears to be high."

Salesperson: "Our high price is an advantage for you; the premium sector of the market not only gives you the highest margin but it is also the most stable sector of the market."

The goal of the translation or boomerang method is to turn an apparent deficiency into an asset or reason to buy.

Compensation

There may be a time when a salesperson has to admit that their product does have the disadvantage that the prospect has noticed. The **compensation** technique is an attempt to show the prospect that a benefit or an advantage compensates for an objection. For example, a higher product price is justified by benefits, such as better service, faster delivery, or higher performance.

A buyer may use the objection that your company's lead time is 14 days compared with 10 days for your main competitor. The salesperson's response could be: "Yes, our required lead time is 14 days, but we ship our orders completely assembled. This practically eliminates extra handling in your warehouse. My competitor's product will require assembly by your warehouse workers." With the compensation method, the objection is not denied at all—it is acknowledged and then balanced by compensating features, advantages, and benefits.

indirect denial   A response to buyer objections in which the salesperson takes a softer, more tactful approach when correcting a prospect or customer's information.

translation or **boomerang**   A response to buyer objections in which the salesperson converts the objection into a reason the prospect should buy.

compensation   A response to buyer objections in which the salesperson counterbalances the objection with an offsetting benefit.

Exhibit 8.9

Questioning (Assessing) to Overcome Sales Resistance

Example 1

Buyer:	I am not sure I am ready to act at this time.
Salesperson:	Can you tell me what is causing your hesitation?

Example 2

Buyer:	Your price seems to be a little high.
Salesperson:	Can you tell me what price you had in mind? Have other suppliers quoted you a lower price?

Example 3

Buyer:	Your delivery schedule does not work for us.
Salesperson:	To whom are you comparing me? Can you please tell me what delivery schedule will work for your company?

Questioning or Assessing

Another potentially effective way to handle buyer resistance is to convert the objection into a question. This technique calls for the salesperson to ask **questions or assess** to gain a better understanding of the precise nature of the buyer's objections. Sometimes it is difficult for the salesperson to know the exact problem. This technique is good for clarifying the real objection. This technique can also be effective in resolving the objection if the prospect is shooting from the hip and does not have a strong reason for the objection. Effective questioning and listening will lead to less sales resistance and more closes. Exhibit 8.9 illustrates the questioning method as a tool to overcome sales resistance.

Third-Party Reinforcement: Feel-Felt-Found

The **third-party reinforcement** technique uses the opinion or research of a third person or company to help overcome and reinforce the salesperson's sales points. Salespeople today can use a wide range of proof statements. Consumer reports, government reports, and independent testing agencies can all be used to back up a salesperson's statement. Secondary data such as this, or experience data from a reliable third party, could be all that is needed to turn around a skeptical prospect. A salesperson must remember that this technique will work only if the buyer believes in the third-party source that the salesperson is using.

A version of using third-party reinforcement is the feel-felt-found method. Here, the salesperson goes on to relate that others found their initial beliefs to be unfounded after they tried the product. Salespeople need to practise this method—when used in the correct sequence, it can be very effective. Again, the strength of the person and company being used as an example is critical to how much influence the reference will have on the prospect.

Coming-to-That or Postpone

Salespeople need to understand that objections may and will be made to almost everything concerning them, their products, and their company. Good salespeople anticipate these objections and develop effective answers, but sometimes it may make sense to cover an objection later in the presentation, after additional questioning and information is provided. The salesperson should evaluate how important the concern is to the prospect—and, if the objection seems to be critical to the sale, the salesperson should address it immediately.

Once the salesperson has answered all the buyer's questions and has resolved resistance issues that have come up during the presentation, the

questions or assess A response to buyer objections in which the salesperson asks the buyer assessment questions to gain a better understanding of what the buyer is objecting to.

third-party reinforcement A response to buyer objections in which the salesperson uses the opinion or data from a third-party source to help overcome the objection and reinforce the salesperson's points.

salesperson should summarize all the pertinent buying signals (i.e., fair price, acceptable delivery dates, and good service agreement).

Summarizing Solutions to Confirm Benefits

 3.1 Develop solutions

The mark of a good salesperson is the ability to listen and determine the customer's exact needs. It is not unusual for salespeople to incorporate the outstanding benefits of their product into the sales presentation. A salesperson can identify many potential benefits for each product and feature. However, it does not make sense for a salesperson to talk about potential benefits that the buyer may not need. The salesperson must determine the confirmed benefits and make these the focal point of the sales summary before asking for the business. A salesperson must be alert to the one, two, or three benefits that generate the most excitement to the buyer. The confirmed benefits of greatest interest to the buyer deserve the greatest emphasis. These benefits should be summarized in such a way that the buyer sees a direct connection in what they have been telling the salesperson over the course of the selling cycle and the proposal being offered to meet their needs. Once this is done, it is time to ask for the business.

Every Business Sells

Gerard Duggan is Vice President, eGovernment & Enterprise at Vision33, which sells enterprise software, cloud SaaS, implementation services, support services, and professional services. Gerard is responsible for approximately 100 accounts across Canada, the USA, and the UK. He has worked in sales for 26 years, 18 of them at Vision33.

As a salesperson, how do you provide value to your customers?

By articulating specifically, and pragmatically, how technology is a key part of delivering value for their own stakeholders, and ensuring our solutions are priced fairly for the value they provide to our customers. We will always ensure a solution not only meets a customer's needs from a features and functionality perspective, but also from the investment they require.

As a salesperson, how do you provide value to your organization?

A Vision33 salesperson will be a critical part of the market feedback (customers/partners/other stakeholders) that is collected and included in support of internal decision making related to product features, product and service offerings, real or perceived strengths, and opportunities and weaknesses we can address and by aligning client expectations with delivery methods.

What is your greatest challenge you face today as a salesperson?

Constantly changing/evolving technologies—keeping up to date with them and also competing with them.

How do you try to overcome this challenge?

Listening to the customer and understanding what they really need, versus the promise of a new unproven technology, typically solves most of this challenge. In addition, it is still important to keep up to date with what's coming next. Often customers will expect us to know what the latest and greatest technologies are, or are on the horizon, but they will buy current technologies because that is what their organization can successfully absorb today.

What advice do you have for someone starting out in sales?

- Accept that not all prospects are potential customers
- Spend most of your time on profitable customers that value your time and service/product offering
- Be a knowledgeable source of information inside your own company
- Know your compensation model and your sales metrics (volume, net new customers, expansion revenue, total revenue, etc.) because this model should be designed to drive behaviour and results in your organization's most strategic areas
- Speak less and listen more
- Only pitch on what you know is of value to the client
- Know your client's/prospect's business

Every Business Sells

Gina Kelly is a senior account executive at a health-care company that provides medical devices and dressings for wound care. Within her organization, she is responsible for all acute care hospitals, long-term-care facilities, and community health facilities. This amounts to roughly 23 accounts across Atlantic Canada. She has worked in sales for 25 years.

As a salesperson, how do you provide value to your customers?

I'm a consultant who's a part of the team versus a salesperson merely looking for a piece of the pie, and that's when the value happens. You spend the necessary time with your feet on the ground helping during the hard times and the good ones, suggesting solutions that may or may not be the ones you are responsible for. This allows you to become a trusted adviser to your customers and a part of their team. They know you want to help the clinician/patient achieve the best outcomes without putting your own needs (sales) first. Rolling up your sleeves and walking the talk helps to create credibility.

In addition, I provide value by having the right data to present solid clinical and economic facts. When you arm the right people with the right information, they are able to justify their choices and take that messaging to a manager or C-suite level executive and ask them to make their choices/requests actionable. You can't be afraid to have that hard discussion, and to bring up the barriers that may exist helping both sides achieve their goals. By addressing the situation in a positive and solution-based manner, all sides should win.

As a salesperson, how do you provide value to your organization?

When you develop relationships based on trust and adding value with your customers, you create immeasurable value to your company as well. You are the frontline person—you are the face of your organization and you entrench yourself by being credible, genuine, and authentic.

You have feet on the ground to uncover needs and find a solution that will answer the need while still allowing you to drive revenue and growth year over year for sustainability in the marketplace. This growth allows for the continued research and development that is needed in health care today.

What is your greatest challenge you face today as a salesperson?

Competing with the antiquated thinking that the "cheapest way is the right way." Separated health-care budgets (e.g., an O/R budget, a recovery budget, a general surgery floor budget, etc.) take away from looking at the total cost of care, from the minute a patient is ill to the day they are hopefully cured. Establishments need to look at the total cost of care, infection rates, and readmission rates.

How do you try to overcome this challenge?

Building a network of key opinion leaders in various sectors of health care has helped with this challenge. As a vendor you cannot be seen "complaining" that your product isn't selected. You have to instead seek to understand and then to educate, educate, educate. We have a plethora of clinical and economic data that supports the outcomes that health-care needs. When you give that information to the right people who have a voice higher up the chain, it is better received and acted upon.

What advice do you have for someone starting out in sales?

Uncover the need. Find what keeps the customer up at night, and what helps them meet their goals. When you can find the answer that both helps them solve their issues as well as solve yours, that win is hard to deny.

LO 6 | SECURING COMMITMENT AND CLOSING

Ultimately, a large part of most salespeople's performance evaluation is based on their ability to gain customer commitment, often called closing sales. Because of this close relationship between compensation and getting orders, traditional selling has tended to overemphasize the importance of gaining a commitment.[9] In fact, there are those who think that just about any salesperson can find a new prospect, open a sale, or take an order. These same people infer it takes a trained, motivated, and skilled professional to close a sale. They go on to say that the close is the keystone to a salesperson's success, and a good salesperson will have mastered many new ways to close the sale. This outmoded emphasis on closing skills is typical of transaction selling techniques that stress making the sales call at all costs.

Another popular but outdated suggestion to salespeople is to "close early and often." This is particularly bad advice if the prospect is not prepared to make a decision, responds negatively to a premature attempt to consummate the sale, and then (following the principles of cognitive consistency) proceeds to reinforce the prior negative position as the salesperson plugs away, firing one closing salvo after another at the beleaguered prospect. Research tells us that it will take several sales calls to make an initial sale, so it is somewhat bewildering to still encounter such tired old battle cries as "the ABCs of selling, which stand for Always Be Closing." Research based on more than 35,000 sales calls over a 12-year period suggests that an overreliance on closing techniques actually reduces the chance of making a sale.[10]

Manipulative closing gimmicks are less likely to be effective as professional buyers grow weary of the cat-and-mouse approach to selling that a surprising number of salespeople still practise. It is also surprising to find many salespeople who view their customers as combatants over whom victory is sought. Once salespeople who have adversarial, me-against-you attitudes make the sale, the customer is likely to be neglected as the salesperson rides off into the sunset in search of yet another battle with yet another lowly customer.

One time-honoured thought that does retain contemporary relevance is that "nobody likes to be sold, but everybody likes to buy." In other words, salespeople should facilitate decision making by pointing out a suggested course of action but should allow the prospect plenty of mental space within which a rational decision can be reached.[11] Taken to its logical conclusion, this means that it may be acceptable to make a sales call without asking for the order. Salespeople must be cognizant, however, of their responsibility to advance the relationship toward a profitable sale, lest they become the most dreaded of all types of salespeople—the paid conversationalist. Technology in Sales: Build Sales Pipeline the Social Way and Earn More points out that the key to closing is not necessarily generating more leads but generating and closing the right leads.

It has already been mentioned that the salesperson has taken on the expanded roles of business consultant and relationship manager, which is not consistent with pressuring customers until they give in and say yes. Fortunately,

things have changed to the point that today's professional salesperson attempts to gain commitment when the buyer is ready to buy. The salesperson should evaluate each presentation and attempt to determine the causes of its success or failure with the customer. The difference between closing and earning commitment is that commitment is more than just securing an order. Commitment signals the beginning of a long-term relationship.

Guidelines for Earning Commitment

 4.1 Close the sale

Earning commitment is the culmination of the selling process. However, it should not be viewed as a formal stage that comes only at the end of the presentation. Many salespeople fail to recognize early buyer commitment by focusing on their presentation rather than on the comments the buyer is making. **Commitment signals** are favourable statements that may be made by the buyer, such as

- "I like that size."
- "That will get the job done."
- "The price is lower than I thought it would be."
- "I did not realize you delivered every day."

These statements should be considered green lights that allow the salesperson to move the process forward. Positive statements by the buyer should start the process of determining the best time to close. Ultimately the salesperson should ask for the order when the buyer has enough information to make an informed decision. Making sure the buyer has the right information to make an intelligent decision is the main goal of a salesperson's sales presentation. Normally the earning commitment question is asked when the sales presentation is completed and all the questions and sales resistances have been successfully addressed.

Commitment may also be determined through the use of trial commitments. Throughout the presentation, it is appropriate to determine a prospect's reaction to a particular feature or product. At this time, a trial commitment is a question designed to determine a prospect's reaction without forcing the prospect to make a final "yes or no" buying decision. The trial commitment is an effort to identify how far along the prospect is in their decision making. Confirmation on the prospect's part on key features helps the salesperson determine how ready the prospect is to buy. A trial commitment can be used many times throughout a salesperson's presentation to test the buyer's level of commitment and for the salesperson to

Build Sales Pipeline the Social Way and Earn More

—Selling Power Editors

As sales professionals know, the key to closing more deals is not necessarily generating more leads but generating the right leads. These days, the best way to build a robust sales pipeline is to generate those leads using LinkedIn.

Although many people think LinkedIn is just a place to post your resume or hunt for a job, it actually represents a way to strategically build pipeline and nurture relationships. Koka Sexton, senior social marketing manager at LinkedIn, says there are two basic steps to leveraging either LinkedIn's free platform or LinkedIn's Sales navigator (http://business. linkedin.com/sales-solutions/prospecting-tool.html) for better pipeline results.

Step 1: Search LinkedIn's 300 million members and see what information is available about prospects on their profile pages. This alone can tell you a lot, and when your network is big enough, you can often request that one of your first-degree connections introduce you to a third-degree connection.

Step 2: Use LinkedIn as an engagement platform, via status updates or comments in groups, and by sharing content or responding to content posted by others. As Sexton says, these interactions add up to stronger relationships, which can help build pipeline and reduce churn.

"The more engaged you are with [buyers], the harder it is for them to break you," Sexton says. "If you engage through social media throughout the year, at year-end they know you."

Sexton predicts social selling will be the norm in five years. "We are about a year away from the tipping point, when we get to critical mass."

© AlexRoz/Shutterstock.com

https://www.sellingpower.com/2014/05/13/10342/build-sales-pipeline-the-social-way

---

gain confirmed benefits. Exhibit 8.10 summarizes both verbal and nonverbal buying signals.

Open-end questions are a good way to test a prospect's readiness to buy. A salesperson might ask during their presentation, "What do you think of our computer's larger memory capacity?" The answer to this will help direct the salesperson to their next sales points. However, many statements buyers make should be considered red lights, or formal objections. The salesperson must consider each of these objections and work to overcome them. Red light statements might include the following:

- "I am not sure that will work."

- "The price is higher than I thought it would be."

- "Your delivery schedule does not work for us."

- "I do not see the advantage of going with your proposal."

Red-light statements are commitment caution signals and must be resolved to the buyer's satisfaction before asking for a commitment. Closing early and often and

Exhibit 8.10

Favourable Buying Signals

When the prospect

- Makes a positive statement about the product
- Asks who else has bought the product
- Asks about price, delivery, installation, dates, or service
- Asks about methods of payment
- Begins to study and handle the product
- Appears more relaxed
- Begins to interact more intently with the salesperson

having a closing quota for each sales call are traditional methods that buyers do not like. In Selling in Action: Tighten Up the Use of Earning Commitment Techniques,

Selling in Action

Tighten Up the Use of Earning Commitment Techniques

Jon Young, relationship manager at Accutech Systems, has seen quite a bit of change over his 30-year sales career, especially when it comes to earning commitment. "In my early days of sales, the best salespeople were considered the best closers. Today, I know the best salespeople are the best listeners. Another trend I see is the tightening up of closing techniques. Good salespeople use only a few relationship building closing techniques. Gimmicky closing techniques will only hurt a salesperson's credibility. A summary close shows the buyer you have been listening to what the buyer has been saying. It is a logical close that brings the sales call to a conclusion. I think salespeople should ask more questions and close less. The notion of closing early and often is wrong. It should be replaced with listen early and often."

Jon Young states that it is better to replace numerous closing efforts with better listening skills. The salesperson should put himself or herself in the buyer's shoes and think about how they would like to be hammered with many closes throughout a sales presentation, particularly if a few red lights are introduced. Many times, the best method for earning commitment is simply to ask for the business. If the prospect has been qualified properly and a number of confirmed benefits have been uncovered, then naturally the next step is to ask for the business.

Techniques to Earn Commitment

CPSA | 4.2 Negotiate terms of sale

Some sales trainers will try to teach their salesforces literally hundreds of commitment techniques. One trainer recommended to his salesforce that the salespeople learn two new commitment techniques per week. Then at the end of the year, they would have more than 100 commitment techniques ready to use. Relationship managers today do not need many commitment techniques. A few good ones will suffice. Five techniques that are conducive to relationship building follow:

> **direct commitment** A selling technique in which the salesperson asks the customer directly to buy.
>
> **alternative or legitimate choice** A selling technique in which the salesperson asks the prospect to select from two or more choices during a sales presentation.

1. *Ask for the order/ direct commitment.* It is not unusual for inexperienced salespeople to lose an order simply by not asking the customer to buy. Professional buyers report that an amazing number of salespeople fear rejection. When the buyer is ready to buy, the salesperson must be prepared to ask for the buyer's commitment. The **direct commitment** technique is a straightforward request for an order. A salesperson should be confident if they have covered all the necessary features and benefits of the product and matched these with the buyer's needs. At this time, the salesperson cannot be afraid to ask "Tom, can we set up an office visit for next week?" or "Mary, I would like to have your business; if we can get the order signed today, delivery can take place early next week." Many buyers appreciate the direct approach. There is no confusion as to what the salesperson wants the buyer to do.

2. *Ask for a legitimate choice/alternative choice.* The **alternative or legitimate choice** technique asks the prospect to select from two or more choices. For example, "Will the HP 400 or the HP 600 work best for you?" An investment broker might ask their prospect, "Do you feel your budget would allow you to invest $1,000 a month or would $500 a month be better?" The theory behind this technique suggests buyers do not like to be told what to do but do like making a decision among limited choices.

3. *Provide a summary commitment.* A very effective way to gain agreement is to summarize all the major benefits the buyer has confirmed during the sales calls. Salespeople should keep track of all the important points covered in previous calls so they can emphasize them again in summary form.

   In using the summary commitment technique, a computer salesperson might say, "Of course, Tom,

Exhibit 8.11

T-Account Close

Reasons to Buy	Reasons Not to Buy
• Daily delivery schedule meets our needs	• Because of extra services
• Warranty agreement is longer than the one I have now (five years versus three years)	• Your price *is too high; I can't afford it*
• You provide a training program	
• Your service department is located in our city	

this is an important decision, so to make the best possible choice, let us go over the major concepts we have discussed. We have agreed that Thompson Computers will provide some definite advantages. First, our system will lower your computing costs; second, our system will last longer and has a better warranty, thus saving you money; and finally, your data processing people will be happier because our faster system will reduce their workload. They will get to go home earlier each evening."

The **summary commitment** is a valuable technique because it reminds prospects of all the major benefits that have been mentioned in previous sales calls.

4. *Use the T-Account or the balance sheet commitment.* The **T-account commitment** or **balance sheet commitment** is essentially a summary commitment on paper. With the T-account commitment, the sales representative takes out a sheet of paper and draws a large "T" across it. On the left-hand side, the salesperson and buyer brainstorm the reasons to buy. Here, the salesperson will list with the buyer all the positive selling points (benefits) they discussed throughout the selling process. Once this is completed, the salesperson asks the buyer for any reasons that they would not want to purchase. Visually, the left-hand side should help the buyer make their decision, as shown in Exhibit 8.11. This will not work if the weight of the reasons not to buy outweighs the reasons to buy. In the example in Exhibit 8.11, the buyer wants to act but does not have the money at this time.

5. *Use a success story commitment.* Every company has many satisfied customers. These customers started out having problems, and the sales representative helped solve these problems by recommending the product or products that matched the customer's needs. Buyers are thankful and grateful when the salesperson helps solve problems. When the salesperson relates a story about how one of their customers had a similar problem and solved it by using the salesperson's product, a reluctant buyer can be reassured that the salesperson has done this before successfully. If the salesperson decides to use the customer's name and company, then the salesperson must be sure to get permission to do so. A **success story commitment** may go something like this: Tom, thanks for sharing your copier problems with me. I had another customer you might know, Betty Brown, who had the same problem over at Thompson Electronics. We installed the CP 2000 and eliminated the problem completely. Please feel free to give Betty a call. She is very happy with our solution.

> Good salespeople are never in a hurry to earn commitment!

summary commitment A selling technique in which the salesperson summarizes all the major benefits the buyer has confirmed during the sales calls.

T-account or **balance sheet commitment** A selling technique in which a salesperson asks the prospect to brainstorm reasons on paper of why to buy and why not to buy.

success story commitment A selling technique in which a salesperson relates how one of their customers had a problem similar to the prospect's and solved it by using the salesperson's product.

Exhibit 8.12

Techniques to Earn Commitment

1. Direct commitment—Simply ask for the order.
2. Legitimate choice/alternative choice—Give the prospect a limited number of choices.
3. Summary commitment—Summarize all the confirmed benefits to which there has been agreement.
4. T-account/balance sheet commitment— Summary close on paper.
5. Success story commitment—Salesperson tells a story of a business that successfully solved a problem by buying their products.

Some companies will use the success story commitment by actually taking the prospect to a satisfied customer. The salesperson may leave the prospect alone with the satisfied customer so the two can talk confidentially. A satisfied customer can help a salesperson earn commitment by answering questions a reluctant prospect needs answered before they can purchase. Exhibit 8.12 shows a summary of relationship-building earning commitment techniques.

Probe to Earn Commitment

 4.1 Close the sale

Not every attempt to earn commitment will be successful. Successful salespeople cannot be afraid to ask a prospect why they are hesitating to make a decision. It is the salesperson's job to uncover the reason why the prospect is hesitating by asking a series of questions that reveal the key issues. For instance, a buyer may state that they are not ready to sign an order. The salesperson must ask, "Mary, there must be a reason why you are reluctant to do business with me and my company. Do you mind if I ask what it is?" The salesperson must then listen and respond accordingly. A salesperson cannot be afraid to ask why a prospect is reluctant to purchase.

Traditional Methods

Sales trainers across the nation teach hundreds of techniques to earn commitment. Exhibit 8.13 is a summary of the traditional commitment techniques. The vast majority of these are not conducive to building a strong buyer–seller relationship. As prospects become more sophisticated, most will be turned off by these techniques and they will be ineffective. An Ethical Dilemma illustrates that sometimes buyers will be put off by salespeople who use too many closes.

Research has clearly shown that buyers are open to consultative techniques of handling objections (e.g., questioning and assessing, direct denial with facts, and so on) and earning commitment (e.g., asking for the order in a straightforward manner, summarizing key benefits). However, buyers have stated that standard persuasive (traditional) tactics that have been used for years are unacceptable. They now view traditional techniques of handling objections (e.g., forestalling, postponing) and earning commitment (e.g., standing-room-only, fear) as overly aggressive and unprofessional.[12]

An Ethical Dilemma

 8.1 Act with Integrity

Ella Carnes had just left her sales meeting and was a bit uncomfortable with what she had just heard from her sales manager, Jeni Merritt, who stated for the next two weeks the sales reps were obligated to close on each and every sales call. Jeni did not think her reps were closing enough and based on their call reports they did not have a high enough closing ratio. Her only solution was they needed to try to close more often.

Ella was not sure this was going to work. What should Ella do next now that she has this direct order from her boss? How would you handle this situation?

(a) Ella should obey orders and close early and often.
(b) Ella should look for closing opportunities and close when they appear.
(c) Ella should tell her boss this is not what she learned in college.

Exhibit 8.13

Traditional Commitment Method

Method	How to Use It
standing-room-only close	This close puts a time limit on the client in an attempt to hurry the decision to close. "These prices are good only until tomorrow."
assumptive close	The salesperson assumes that an agreement has been reached. The salesperson places the order form in front of the buyer and hands him or her a pen.
fear or emotional close	The salesperson tells a story of something bad happening if the purchase is not made. "If you do not purchase this insurance and you die, your wife will have to sell the house and live on the street."
continuous yes close	This close uses the principle that saying yes gets to be a habit. The salesperson asks a number of questions, each formulated so that the prospect answers yes.
minor-points close	Seeks agreement on relatively minor (trivial) issues associated with the full order. "Do you prefer cash or charge?"

standing-room-only close A sales closing technique in which the salesperson puts a time limit on the client in an attempt to hurry the decision to close.

assumptive close A sales closing technique in which the salesperson assumes that an agreement has been reached and places the order form in front of the buyer, and hands him or her a pen.

fear or emotional close A sales closing technique in which the salesperson tells a story of something bad happening if the purchase is not made.

continuous yes close A sales closing technique that uses the principle that saying yes gets to be a habit; the salesperson asks a number of questions formulated so that the prospect answers yes.

minor-points close A sales closing technique in which the salesperson seeks agreement on relatively minor issues associated with the full order.

STUDY TOOLS

At the back of the textbook, use tear-out cards to review key chapter information. Visit cengage.ca to purchase digital tools to help you succeed.

 CENGAGE | MINDTAP

Personal Computer

☐ Gain unique perspectives on key concepts through a variety of videos and cases

☐ Increase your comprehension with online quizzes

☐ Study with existing flashcards and make your own

Mobile

☐ Stay focused and ready to study whenever it's convenient for you!

☐ Access a full, interactive ebook: online or offline

☐ Study tools that empower anytime, anywhere learning and 24/7 course access

MARTICHENKO ENGINEERING

BACKGROUND

Rob Dwhytie sells for Martichenko Engineering. He has been calling on Hudson Distributors for close to two years. Over the course of 15 calls, he has sold nothing to date. During an early call, Dwhytie had Hudson's engineers in to look over and test the quality of his products. The tests and the engineers' responses were positive. He thinks that he is extremely close to getting an order. Dwhytie knows that Hudson is happy with its present supplier, but he is aware that they have received some late deliveries. Tom Harris, Hudson's senior buyer, has given every indication that he likes Dwhytie's products and Dwhytie.

CURRENT SITUATION

During Dwhytie's most recent call, Harris told him that he'd need a couple of weeks to go over Dwhytie's proposal. Harris really didn't have any major objections during the presentation. Dwhytie knows his price, quality, and service are equal to or exceed Hudson's present supplier.

QUESTIONS

1. Harris told Dwhytie that he needed a couple of weeks to think about his proposal. How should Dwhytie handle this?

2. What should Dwhytie have done during the sales presentation when Harris told him that he needed to think it over?

3. What techniques should Dwhytie have used to overcome the forestalling tactic?

ROLE PLAY

Situation: Read Case 8; Martichenko Engineering

Characters: Rob Dwhytie, sales representative; Tom Harris, senior buyer

Scene 1:

Location—Harris's office

Action—Harris has just stated that he needs a couple of weeks to go over Dwhytie's proposal.

Role-play how Dwhytie should respond to Harris needing two weeks to think it over.

Scene 2:

Location—Harris's office

Action—Dwhytie is summarizing his product's advantages (i.e., price, quality, service).

Role-play Dwhytie's summary and his asking for the order.

Upon completion of the role play, address the following questions:

1. Why do buyers hesitate and ask for more time to think over proposals?

2. How hard should Dwhytie press to get Harris to act now?

INTEGRATIVE CASE 8

CHARGED UP

BACKGROUND

One of the most overused phrases when discussing innovation in an industry is "the future is now." But for the electric vehicles (EV) industry, it is not an exaggeration to take that statement seriously. And while there is much to admire about the advancement in technology in electric vehicles, the corresponding and complementary industries around it are faced with challenges.

At the 2020 Canadian International Auto Show, more than 40 hybrid and electric vehicles were on display. McKinsey consulting group predicts that there will be hundreds of new models of hybrid or electric vehicles between now and 2025.[13] A recent consumer poll of Canadians reported that 56 percent of respondents indicated they would be "interested" or "very interested" in purchasing an electric vehicle in the near future.[14]

However, there is still a bit of a squeak in the wheel that is the electric vehicle industry in Canada. And it can only be greased by government incentives to both car manufacturers and Canadian consumers. As of early 2020, only the federal, B.C., and Ontario governments provide rebates for purchasing an electric vehicle. And while there is no set legislation on when Canada will mandate the purchase of electric cars, the federal government has set up a hopeful date of 2030.[15]

And while sales of electric cars account for only about 2 percent of global car sales, there seems to be a worldwide push toward moving forward with an electric-only vehicle future. Governments in Europe are mandating strict legislation for the removal of the oil-reliant combustion engine vehicles. Norway will ban gas-guzzling vehicles by 2025, while France hopes to achieve this in 2040.[16]

There are significant obstacles in the way, including the high prices of EVs, battery performance, and availability. But the most challenging issue is the charging infrastructure currently in place in Canada. As *Forbes* noted recently: "It's not just the lack of public charging stations, but their clunky operation and unreliability."[17] It certainly presents a challenge not only to get consumers to buy, but also to be able to deal with concerns over the charging system that will become vital to the enjoyment and use of the EVs they purchase.

While consumers have the choice of retrofitting their homes to include an electric vehicle charger, there is still a lot of pressure on companies and government to provide the necessary infrastructure for electric vehicles, which often require more than just a charge at home.

CURRENT SITUATION

If the future of vehicles is going to be more electric, conventional gas stations are in need of a mindset change, and fast. In July 2019, the Boston Consulting Group produced a report titled "Is there a future for service stations?" The conclusions to the report were eye-opening: "To successfully adapt, fuel retailers must embrace a new mindset. Making modest changes or tweaks to the business will not suffice. Instead, companies must fundamentally rethink their business and aggressively embrace innovation and new technology. Those that boldly seize the opportunity will find themselves in a winning position. Those that do not may be left behind."[18]

You are the new local sales rep for AddÉnergie, a Quebec-based start-up that is considered one of the top producers of electric vehicle charging solutions. You have been asked to create a process for how to approach traditional gas station owners with the idea of incorporating EV charging stations into their current space.

You know very well you are going to be met with resistance. You recall a helpful model from your sales class that will help deal with the pushback you will inevitably receive. Your task is to create a one-page sheet that details the process and provides tangible tactics to clear the way for a potential sale.

QUESTIONS

1. In your one-page report you decide it is important to provide information about AddÉnergie in order to reduce what kind of objection?
   a. product
   b. service
   c. price
   d. source

2. The first stage of the LAARC model is deemed to be vital to remove customer concerns. This stage suggests resisting the urge to anticipate concerns. What is this stage called?
   a. leverage
   b. listen
   c. less talk
   d. loyalty

3. According to the LAARC method, the overarching goal of the salesperson is to listen and provide what?
   a. choice
   b. needs
   c. value
   d. options

CHAPTER ROLE PLAY   8

Addressing Concerns and Earning Commitment: ACampbell Engineering

Dan Harris has been selling for ACampbell Engineering for six months. Most of the first four months were spent in training learning ACampbell's products. He spent another two weeks learning their selling process and shadowed one of their senior reps for a couple of weeks. He has barely been in the field a month and is feeling frustrated. Dan was given a hot lead the first day in the field (Parker Distributors), and the past four weeks he has made seven calls on Parker. Dan feels he is close to getting an order from Parker. Dan knows Parker is fairly happy with their present supplier, but he is aware that they have received several late deliveries. Karen Williams, Parker's senior buyer, has given every indication that she likes ACampbell's products and Dan.

During Dan's most recent call, Williams told him she'd have to have a couple of weeks to go over his proposal. Williams really

didn't have any major objections during his presentation. Dan knows his price, quality, and service are equal to or exceed Williams's present supplier. Williams did say she wasn't looking forward to calling their present supplier to tell them about doing business with ACampbell Engineering if she decided to change.

ROLE PLAY

Location: Karen Williams's office

Action: Role play Karen Williams telling Dan Harris she needs a couple of weeks to think over his proposal. Discuss the sales resistance of forestalling Williams is using and how Dan is going to overcome the objection (use LAARC). Also, role-play Williams's concern telling her present supplier they are switching suppliers.

9 | Expanding Customer Relationships

Suncor extracts and produces oil and natural gas that is refined to heat homes, fuel vehicles, and power businesses across North America.[1] With developments coast to coast across Canada, Suncor started its operations in 1967 in one of the largest petroleum resources basins in the world: Fort McMurray, Alberta. As the fifth largest North American energy company, Suncor now has oil refineries in Alberta, Ontario, Quebec, and Colorado, and offshore developments on the east coast of Canada.[2] Today, the Canadian company employees over 12,000 people and supplies 35 percent of Colorado's gasoline and diesel fuel.[3] Suncor's dedication to innovation and technology has enabled the company to meet customer expectations and satisfaction and has focused on ensuring its products are environmentally responsible. In 2019, the company started the Forty Mile wind power project in Alberta, investing in renewable energy. To continue its promise to reduce greenhouse gas emissions, Suncor now has four wind power products and is evaluating solar energy options.[4] Continuing its commitment to meeting customer expectations, Suncor has developed a network of more than 1,500 Petro-Canada retail and wholesale outlets across the county to provide customers access to products. Suncor has always focused on value over volume, providing customers with the highest value possible per barrel. Since becoming publicly traded in 1992, the company's production has increased by 600 percent while its return on investment during that period was 5,173 percent.[5]

Introduction

Suncor's ability to foster mutually beneficial relations is seen in its ability to expand business and stakeholder networks. In traditional selling, salespeople too often thought that their job was over when they closed the sale. Once the order was obtained, they moved on to the next prospect. Any follow-up or customer service was minimal. The lifeline of an organization today is repeat business. It is important to acquire new customers, but it is critical to keep your existing customer base happy. In research involving 80,000 business customers, the number-one characteristic found to define a world-class salesperson is someone who personally manages

the customer's satisfaction by being accountable for the customer's desired results.[6] Not following up with a new customer is a shortsighted attitude toward selling, for it fails to consider the importance of developing and maintaining a customer for your company.

Research indicates that successfully retaining customers is critical for all companies' success. Salespeople's postsale service behaviours are positively related to relationship quality and share of customer business.[7] Relationship marketing efforts can lead to longer term, broader, and deeper customer relationships, which results in increases in sales, profits, and positive word of mouth.[8] Companies that invest 10 percent or more of their revenue in customer experience have greater referral rates, superior customer satisfaction scores, and better retention rates than those companies that invest less in customer experience.[9] Yet it takes only a slight decline in attention from a salesperson to lead a buyer to consider alternative suppliers.[10] Given that it is generally more expensive to acquire a new customer than to sustain a current one, salespeople should take actions to develop strong customer relationships.

A salesperson can convert new customers into highly committed lifetime customers in several ways. Examples include **building goodwill** by continually **adding value** to the product or service through appropriate follow-up, handling complaints in a timely and thoughtful manner, and processing requests for rush deliveries willingly and assuring the customer that the salesperson will do everything possible to make that request happen. However, it is just as easy for a salesperson to alienate a new customer by putting the focus on the short-term order and not the long-term activities that create a partnership. This can be done by overpromising and underdelivering, using exaggeration to get an order, and blaming everyone else for problems.

Exhibit 9.1 reviews relationship enhancers and detractors that can strengthen or destroy a relationship. To see what leading sales professionals believe it takes to make relationships work, see Exhibit 9.2.

building goodwill The process of converting new customers into lifetime customers by continually adding value to the product.

adding value The process of improving a product or service for the customer.

Exhibit 9.1

Relationship Enhancers and Detractors

Enhancers	Detractors
Focus on long term	Focus on short term
Deliver more than promised	Overpromise and/or underdeliver
Call regularly	Call sporadically
Add value	Show up only for another order
Keep communication lines open	Be unavailable to the customer
Take responsibility for problems	Lie, exaggerate, blame someone else

Relationship-oriented salespeople are creating bonds with their customers that will partially isolate them from competitive pressures or at least minimize the importance of easily altered and matched competitive variables, such as price. This chapter explains the importance of follow-up to assess customer satisfaction. Next, harnessing technology to enhance follow-up and buyer–seller relationships is covered. This is followed by a discussion of why it is the salesperson's job to take action (i.e., be proactive) before problems arise and not

Exhibit 9.2

What Makes Customer Relationships Work?

Gerhard Gschwandtner, publisher of *Selling Power*, summarizes the thoughts shared with him by 18 leading sales contributors regarding how customer relationships are formed and nurtured, and what leads to the creation of customer value:

1. Good salespeople bring positive energy to a relationship.
2. Trust hinges on the willingness to deliver on promises. Once trust is lost, relationships cannot survive.
3. A relationship's value depends on the customer's perception of value, not on the salesperson's perception of value.
4. To the customer, the top value drivers are integrity, authenticity, and consistency.
5. Effective relationship builders are willing to listen to better understand customer challenges. They ask questions that lead to consultative conversations, which open doors to greater opportunities.
6. The salesperson's courage to resolve the difficult situations customers face enhances relationships.
7. Relationships are enhanced by the salesperson's ability to communicate in compelling and creative ways.
8. Relationships demand a long-term investment.
9. There is a difference between a transaction and a relationship. Transactions create one-time value; relationships create long-term value and a stable business foundation.
10. Relationships grow through differentiation and the willingness to contribute beyond what is expected.
11. Good salespeople use smart social media strategies to enhance customer relationships. They make it their business to stay connected to customers through social media such as Twitter, Facebook, and LinkedIn.

wait for complaints (i.e., be reactive) to ensure customer satisfaction. We then discuss the importance of collaborative involvement and working to add value for the buyer. Finally, we review the value of customer service.

LO 1 | ASSESS CUSTOMER SATISFACTION

5.1 Follow-up on the sale

Keeping customers satisfied is important as it leads to customer trust and, ultimately, share of customer. Not only is customer satisfaction a significant indicator of repurchase intentions and loyalty, it serves as a point of differentiation, reduces customer defections, reduces negative word of mouth, improves customer referrals and increases the lifetime value of customers.[11] Research shows that customer satisfaction is in part affected by salespeople's reliability and responsiveness as demonstrated by returning phone calls promptly, fulfilling commitments, satisfying customer requests, and being readily available. Furthermore, salespeople who regularly, clearly, and concisely communicate product information to customers can enhance their satisfaction.[12] Such research points to the need to be diligent in following up and properly communicating with customers to build, maintain, and enhance customer relationships.

Unfortunately, many companies do a poor job understanding and satisfying their customers. Results from an annual study of business executives conducted by the Strativity Group Inc. show that most global companies (81%) are not completely dedicated to executing customer experience strategies. As a result, greater attrition rates are three times more likely for these companies—as opposed to fully committed companies, which are five times as likely to have greater referral rates.[13]

Professional salespeople view their customer base as far too valuable an asset to risk losing it through neglect. In maintaining and enhancing customer relationships, salespeople are involved in performing routine postsale follow-up activities and in enhancing the relationship as it evolves by anticipating and adapting to changes in the customer's situation, competitive forces, and other changes in the market environment. Salespeople at Hubspot, a marketing automation tool, know the value of keeping customers satisfied. After-sales support includes training on how to best use the tool, free educational webinars, and complimentary 24/7 technical support, among other things, which led them to being rated number one in customer satisfaction for marketing automation software.[14]

Furthering this notion, Darrell Beaty of Ontario Systems (a collections software company) states, "We spend too much time and effort learning about our prospects to not follow through and assess satisfaction." Figure 9.1 demonstrates the time and commitment Beaty puts in to earn an order from a prospect.[15] Beaty states, "We cannot be afraid to ask a customer, 'How are we doing?'" Keeping abreast of customers' satisfaction should go on monthly, quarterly, and yearly. Sometimes, the salesperson will not like the answers that they get from the customers. New customers generally feel special because they have received a lot of attention. Long-term customers may feel neglected because the salesperson has many new customers and cannot be as attentive as they were previously. Routine follow-up questions, such as "How are we doing?" can go a long way in letting a customer know that the salesperson cares and is willing to make sure that the customer is satisfied. In addition to salespeople asking their customers about their level of satisfaction, suppliers can use a number of means for gathering customer satisfaction information, such as observation, online (or written) surveys, focus groups, customer service feedback, monitoring social media, online communities and groups, e-mail, and Web forms. Selling in Action: Monitoring Customer Satisfaction to Improve Customer Relationships describes how one company uses customer satisfaction surveys to listen to customers.[16]

Salespeople today utilize several technologies to stay in touch with customers.

© Lissandra Melo/Shutterstock

FIG. 9.1   ONTARIO SYSTEMS CALL STRATEGY

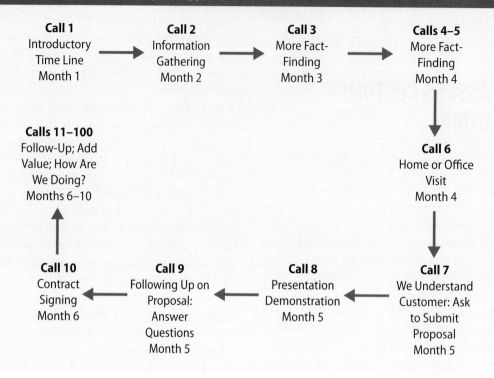

Call 1
Introductory
Time Line
Month 1

→

Call 2
Information
Gathering
Month 2

→

Call 3
More Fact-
Finding
Month 3

→

Calls 4–5
More Fact-
Finding
Month 4

↓

Call 6
Home or Office
Visit
Month 4

↓

Call 7
We Understand
Customer: Ask
to Submit
Proposal
Month 5

←

Call 8
Presentation
Demonstration
Month 5

←

Call 9
Following Up on
Proposal:
Answer
Questions
Month 5

←

Call 10
Contract
Signing
Month 6

↑

Calls 11–100
Follow-Up; Add
Value; How Are
We Doing?
Months 6–10

It takes many calls to earn commitment from a prospect. It can take months and even years to establish the trust needed to earn an order.

Selling in Action

CPSA · **5.1 Follow-up on the sale**

Monitoring Customer Satisfaction to Improve Customer Relationships

Having experienced strong growth over the past five years, Denmark-based managed IT provider Stea IT wanted to make sure its customers were still satisfied with its services. Fearing some customers may be at risk, they needed a way to monitor satisfaction levels over time. To do so, they turned to Client Heartbeat to help in developing a customer satisfaction survey. By implementing a new system where they could obtain ongoing feedback from their customers, Stea IT identified three customers that were not happy with the service levels being received. This came as a shock given that Stea had no idea there were any problems with customers. Not surprisingly, these were customers that had been acquired early during the company's formative years and had gotten neglected over time as service levels dropped due to rapid growth. Using customer feedback, Stea detected customer problems, fixed the issues, and mitigated the "at-risk" relationships. Stea credits its new focus on soliciting customer feedback with its ability to strengthen its relationships with the customers it identified as disgruntled, including one that is worth $180,000 annually. According to Ruin Tipsmark of Stea IT, "Client Heartbeat provided actionable insights into where we needed to improve our service levels that would lead to higher customer satisfaction."

LO 2 | HARNESS TECHNOLOGY TO ENHANCE FOLLOW-UP AND BUYER–SELLER RELATIONSHIPS

7.1 Leverage sales technology

Building buyer–seller relationships is easier said than done. Developing and nurturing customer relationships demands that salespeople do more than simply discover the buyer's needs and respond to them with a sales offering that resolves those needs. Relationships are formed over time through multiple buyer–seller interactions in which the seller wins the trust of the buyer. One survey found that one of the most important things buyers look for in sellers is accountability. They want someone whom they can rely on during the entire sales process and who will not abandon them after the sale is finalized.[17] According to another survey of customers, 80 percent indicated that consistent follow-up with the customer, including returning phone calls and e-mails, helps their buying process, while conversely, not focusing on after-the-sale service hindered the sale.[18]

The results of these studies emphasize the importance of effective follow-up by the salesperson. As discussed in this chapter and illustrated in Figure 9.2, effective salesperson follow-up should include specific components designed to interact with, connect with, know, and relate with customers.

- **Interact**—The salesperson acts to maximize the number of critical encounters with buyers to encourage effective dialogue and involvement between the salesperson and buyer.

- **Connect**—The salesperson maintains contact with the multiple individuals in the buying organization influencing purchase decisions and manages the various touch points the customer has in the selling organization to ensure consistency in communication.

- **Know**—The salesperson coordinates and interprets the information gathered through buyer–seller contact and collaboration to develop insight regarding the buyer's changing situation, needs, and expectations.

- **Relate**—The salesperson applies relevant understanding and insight to create value-added interactions and generate relationships between the salesperson and buyer.

Salespeople have employed a variety of technology-based sales-force automation tools to better track the increasingly complex combination of buyer–seller interactions and to manage the exchange, interpretation, and storage of diverse types of information. Among the more popular sales-force automation tools are the many competing versions of PC- and Internet-based software applications designed to record and manage customer contact information. Software applications such as Maximizer, Goldmine, and ACT!, and Internet-based applications such as Netsuite and Salesforce.com,

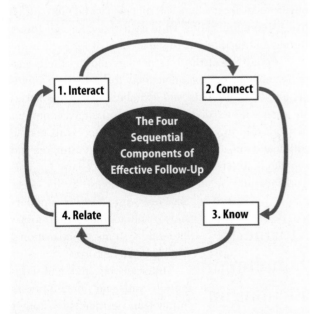

FIG. 9.2 | THE FOUR SEQUENTIAL COMPONENTS OF EFFECTIVE FOLLOW-UP

Effective salesperson follow-up should include specific components designed to interact with, connect with, know, and relate with their customers.

interact The salesperson acts to maximize the number of critical encounters with buyers to encourage effective dialogue and involvement between the salesperson and buyer.

connect The salesperson maintains contact with the multiple individuals in the buying organization who influence purchase decisions and manages the various touch points the customer has in the selling organization to ensure consistency in communication.

know The salesperson coordinates and interprets the information gathered through buyer–seller contact and collaboration to develop insight regarding the buyer's changing situation, needs, and expectations.

relate The salesperson applies relevant understanding and insight to create value-added interactions and generate relationships between the salesperson and buyer.

Technology in Sales

Building and Strengthening Relationships

Corey Vance graduated from the University of Central Missouri in May 2015 and sells for Mueller Field Operations Inc., a company that utilizes design build and field construction management capabilities to provide engineered solutions to their customers. Corey discusses how he utilizes technology to help him initiate, grow, and strengthen customer relationships. "Traditionally, customer relationships were built on a face-to-face conversation, a firm handshake, and a foundation of trust. Over time, these traditions have evolved but still hold the same core values and principles. As technology has streamlined communication and dissolved barriers in doing business internationally, it has changed the way relationships are built and procured in this new day and age.

"Technology has become an integral part in starting the relationship process, building that solid foundation, and maintaining that relationship so both parties become mutually successful. Not only are these phases of the process changing, but the amount of relationships and speed in which a relationship can be built has never been greater.

"Salespeople have instant access to a company's capabilities, financials, and historical information that helps them visualize and understand what type of relationship they can build with that potential customer or whether it is worth pursuing. Social media outlets now provide customer profiles that allow access to what the customer likes, hobbies, and information that can be used to break the ice or find something in common. Before any type of communication, salespeople can know everything about the potential customer from a mobile device anywhere in the world. I utilize the Internet, databases and social media to help me understand, communicate with, and better serve my customers, thus continuously strengthening my relationships with them."

---

enable salespeople to collect, file, and access comprehensive databases detailing information about individual buyers and buying organizations. In addition to providing explicit details about customers and the multiple individuals influencing purchasing decisions within any given account, these databases also provide an archive of the interactions and purchasing decisions taking place over time. Salespeople using these systems have found them to be invaluable in helping them track and better service their accounts to ensure and enhance customer satisfaction. By understanding every transaction and buyer–seller interaction, salespeople can be more effective in communicating with each individual customer throughout the lifetime of the account.

The advent of the Internet has allowed these customer contact management tools to be used in multi-organization intranets and extranets. An **intranet** is an organization's dedicated and proprietary computer network offering password-controlled access to people within and outside the organization (e.g., customers and suppliers). **Extranets** are proprietary computer networks created by an organization for use by the organization's customers or suppliers and linked to the organization's internal systems, informational databases, and intranet.

Internet-activated and integrated with an organization's intranet and extranets, customer contact systems are transposed to full **customer relationship management (CRM) systems**. These systems dynamically

intranet An organization's dedicated and proprietary computer network that offers password-controlled access to people within and outside the organization (e.g., customers and suppliers).

extranet Proprietary computer networks created by an organization for use by the organization's customers or suppliers and linked to the organization's internal systems, informational databases, and intranet.

customer relationship management (CRM) system A system that dynamically links buyers and sellers into a rich communication network to establish and reinforce long-term, profitable relationships.

> Relationships are formed over time through multiple buyer–seller interactions in which the seller wins the trust of the buyer.

link buyers and sellers into a rich communication network. Salespeople and buyers have immediate, 24/7 access to one another and one another's organizations. Problems can be resolved online, routine ordering procedures can be automated, and information such as product brochures and spec sheets, inventory availability, price lists, and order status can be exchanged. Salespeople can use the Web to view everything that is relevant to any account. This can include information in the organization's databases (e.g., purchasing history, credit rating) as well as pertinent information such as news stories, stock prices, and research reports from sources outside the organization (e.g., Hoover's, Standard & Poor's, etc.).

CRM systems enable salespeople to build and integrate multiple forms of customer information and create highly influential customer interactions that establish and reinforce long-term, profitable relationships. The benefits to salespeople learning to use these advanced, integrated systems effectively are self-evident. Every time a salesperson and buyer interact in a positive manner, the corresponding relationship is enriched. This enrichment translates to improved service levels, increased customer satisfaction, and enhanced revenues from loyal customers. For example, after a series of mergers and acquisitions, Honeywell Aerospace found customers telling them that it was difficult to do business with them. Two different Honeywell sales reps, for instance, might call on the same customer in the same day. After implementing a CRM system, customer satisfaction with Honeywell improved 38 percent, its on-time service request closure rate improved from 45 to 83 percent, and its sales opportunity rate improved. Moreover, Honeywell credits the CRM system with a 100 percent annual revenue improvement, from $45 million to $100 million in the sales of its after-market spare parts.[19] CRM professionals have begun syncing CRM systems with social media such as Facebook, LinkedIn, and Twitter through applications such as Faceconnector, which allow users to pull personal information into their CRM account so that they can keep up-to-date with customers' needs and concerns. CRM provider Salesforce, for instance, offers salespeople a means for listening and responding to customers across a range of social platforms, including Facebook, Twitter, and other social networks. Business outsourcing solutions provider ADP, for example, credits Salesforce for helping it to gain customer intelligence and maintain customer connections though its ability to monitor and participate in brand conversations, as well as identify pressing customer service issues.[20]

LO 3 | ENSURE CUSTOMER SATISFACTION

Exhibit 9.3 illustrates the partnership-enhancement activities and the salesperson's responsibility that goes along with them. Specific relationship-enhancement activities vary substantially from company to company but are critical to the success of building long-term relationships. Key activities include:

- Remembering the customer after the sale
- Expediting orders and monitoring installation
- Training customer personnel
- Correcting billing errors
- Remembering the customer after the sale
- Resolving complaints

Exhibit 9.3
Relationship-Enhancement Activities

Partnership-Enhancement Activities	Salesperson Responsibility
Provide useful information	• Relevant • Timely • High quality
Expedite orders/ monitor installation	• Track orders • Inform on delays • Help with installation
Train customer personnel	• Train even when contract does not call for it
Correct billing errors	• Go over all orders • Correct problem before customer recognizes it
Remember the customer after the sale	• Set up a regular call schedule • Let customer know you will be back
Resolve complaints	• Preferably prevent the need to complain • Ask customer how they want complaint resolved

FIG. 9.3   TRADITIONAL VERSUS RELATIONAL SALES PROCESS

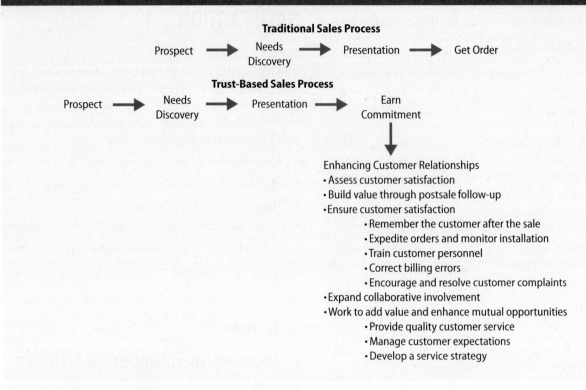

Traditional Sales Process

Prospect → Needs Discovery → Presentation → Get Order

Trust-Based Sales Process

Prospect → Needs Discovery → Presentation → Earn Commitment →

Enhancing Customer Relationships
- Assess customer satisfaction
- Build value through postsale follow-up
- Ensure customer satisfaction
  - Remember the customer after the sale
  - Expedite orders and monitor installation
  - Train customer personnel
  - Correct billing errors
  - Encourage and resolve customer complaints
- Expand collaborative involvement
- Work to add value and enhance mutual opportunities
  - Provide quality customer service
  - Manage customer expectations
  - Develop a service strategy

Traditional selling focuses on getting the order. The relational sales process indicates that many activities must take place after the sale.

Traditional selling focuses on getting the order. In a sense, the sales process was over once the order was signed. The salesperson's job was to focus on getting the next order, and it was left to others in the organization to deliver and install the product. However, the relational sales process shown in Figure 9.3 indicates that many activities must take place after the sale, and it is the salesperson's responsibility to oversee and participate in all of the follow-up activities. By being actively involved during this stage, the salesperson increases the odds that a long-term relationship will develop. Exhibit 9.4 discusses how salespeople can provide follow-up activities to increase customer satisfaction and build long-term customer relationships.

Provide Useful Information

5.1 Follow-up on the sale

Customer follow-up methods should be used to develop the relationship after the sale and to express appreciation for the purchase. Many buyers feel neglected once they place an order with a company. They were given a lot of attention before they placed the order, but after the order had been placed, the salesperson disappeared. Customers consistently cite poor service, neglect, and lack of follow-up as the primary reasons they stopped buying. At one branch office of Wallace Computer Services, there is a saying that hangs above the door: "Remember the customer between calls." This is certainly a meaningful slogan given research showing that greater interaction between the salesperson and the customer after the sale, particularly in-person or via telephone, results in a more satisfied and loyal customer who awards a larger percentage of their business to the seller.[21]

Once an economic relationship is established, the salesperson must continue to maintain open, two-way communication with the buyer and continually provide timely, relevant, high-quality information to their customers and be available to satisfy any additional needs or problems. The job of educating and satisfying the buyer never stops, and salespeople are responsible for updating customers and pointing out additional opportunities that will benefit them. Collaborative discussion becomes the

Source: Joseph Sparacino, http://blog.omega-performance.com/sites/default/files/BeyondSelling.eBook.1110.pdf, accessed on 5/9/12.

Exhibit 9.4

Building Relationships Through Follow-Up

Joseph (Joe) Sparacino, senior vice president and national sales manager for Omega Performance, who is responsible for leading his teams in sales, consulting, and service activities for client relationships across Canada, discusses activities involved in providing exquisite customer service after the sale. According to Joe, long-term relationship building can be enhanced after the sale by

- Foreseeing and planning postsale customer needs prior to completing a sale
- Developing a postsale long-term vision and strategy for ensuring customer satisfaction
- Making certain that customers are delighted with their purchase decision and think in terms of "Look what I bought" rather than "Look what they sold me"
- Planning and executing periodic postsale follow-up contacts with customers to assess their level of satisfaction
- Touching base with customers on issues or concerns discussed at the point of the initial sale
- Recalling and recognizing customer milestones
- Regularly evaluating the products and/or services customers use, and recommending new or upgraded products and/or services that better meet their needs

most effective tool when dealing with customers and their problems.

Providing information that will help customers solve their problems is a must. By providing useful information, the salesperson demonstrates a commitment to the buyer. The salesperson is expressing the notion that they are in the relationship for the long term and they value the partnership. The salesperson should remember to provide information not only to the buyer but also to the secretaries, receptionists, administrative assistants, department heads, and other influential members of the buyer's organization. If the customer believes the salesperson is sincere, listens carefully, and responds accordingly to their concerns, then an already-trusting relationship will become stronger.

Several postsale follow-up methods can be used to provide helpful information. First, however, salespeople should try to determine the customer's preferred method of receiving this information and provide it in that manner if possible. Perhaps one of the best ways to provide useful information is by a personal visit. After the sale is made, it is critical to follow up personally and make sure that the customer is completely satisfied with all the promises that have been made (e.g., delivery, installation done properly, courteous installers). This is the only strategy that provides face-to-face communication and thus affords the

salesperson the opportunity to read the customer's body language. When a salesperson takes the time to make a well-planned personal follow-up visit, they indicate to the prospect that they really care. A good salesperson will use the follow-up call to keep the customer informed of new developments in the industry, new products, or new applications. Providing this information may bring about future sales. When a salesperson makes a follow-up call, they should always have an objective for the sales call. The salesperson should be sure not to spend too much time on gossip sessions or chitchat. It is the salesperson's job to add value, not waste the customer's time. While the personal visit can be a very engaging method, perhaps its biggest weakness is that it can be time consuming.

A quick and efficient option for providing useful information after a sale is by using the telephone. The cell phone has provided salespeople with an opportunity to stay in touch with customers while on the road. A salesperson can easily make 7 to 10 phone calls per hour, and the cost is minimal. The telephone has the advantage of a two-way exchange of information and provides a mechanism for immediate feedback, although it, as well as other non-face-to-face methods of communication, does not provide the opportunity to read the customer's body language. This may be rectified in part by using technology such as Skype or Facetime, which allow two-way audio and video communication. The phone can be used to verify delivery, inform the customer of any changes (e.g., price, delivery schedule), check for problems in general, and provide new product, service, and industry insight.

Email and social media provide an efficient and cost-effective way to continuously keep in touch with customers. When getting pertinent company and buyer information, the salesperson should also get e-mail addresses. Salespeople are able to include not only text, but also sound and video to e-mail messages they send to customers. Social networking sites such as LinkedIn and Facebook allow salespeople to keep in touch with customers by posting updates, information, and feature reviews. These tools, along with Twitter, Instagram, and Snapchat, allow salespeople to have brief interactions with customers between calls to provide information, address customer concerns, and simply get to know customers on a more personal basis. Moreover, information gleaned from using social media's search features can provide salespeople with insights on industry trends, or the preferences of prospects or customers.

Finally, a handwritten thank-you card to a customer is an inexpensive and convenient form of customer follow-up. It should always be used in conjunction with the other follow-up methods. The mail can also be used to send out new promotional material, information about new products, and trade publication articles that may be of interest to customers. Periodically, a salesperson could send customers a short survey that asks "How are we doing?" Checking the customer's level of satisfaction might highlight an area of concern that the salesperson can take care of before it becomes a major problem.

Expedite Orders and Monitor Installation

 5.1 Follow-up on the sale

Generally, salespeople will set estimates on product delivery times. The salesperson must work to prevent a delay in delivery. The salesperson's job is to track the order status and inform the customers when there are delays. It is unpleasant to inform a buyer of a delay, but the information allows buyers to work around the inconvenience and plan accordingly. Waiting until the delivery date to announce a delay is inconsiderate and hurts the trust built between the salesperson and buyer.

Many problems with shipping and the delivery of an order are out of the salesperson's control. However, today's sophisticated tracking systems allow salespeople to track orders and find out what is causing the delay.

The salesperson must keep the customer up-to-date on the delivery status and any possible delays.

Monitoring order processing and after-sale activities is critical to enhancing the relationship with a customer. Customers often have done a poor job of forecasting, run short of product, and may expect their salesperson to bring their emergency to a happy conclusion. Although it is not always possible to speed up orders, the salesperson should investigate and attempt to do everything possible to help the customers. If the buyer sees concern on the salesperson's part and knows that the salesperson is attempting to help the buyer then the relationship will be strengthened, even if the order cannot be pushed through as quickly as the buyer had hoped.

Depending on the industry, salespeople generally do not help with installation. Nevertheless, some salespeople believe that it is in their best interest to supervise the installation process and to be available when customers have questions. Typically, installers do not have the same relationship with the customer and may not have the type of personality to deal with difficult situations. The salesperson can act as the buffer between the installation team and the customers.

Train Customer Personnel

 5.1 Follow-up on the sale

Companies are always looking for ways to gain a competitive advantage. Once the order is placed, traditional salespeople are happy to get their commission or bonus and move on to their next conquest. Relationship managers understand the real work begins once the order is signed. Training customer personnel may or may not be included in the price terms of the agreement. Salespeople may use this to gain the competitive edge they need. For example, instead of training only one person as stated in the sales terms, the salesperson gladly trains three people for the same price. Or, perhaps there is no mention of training in the price terms, but the salesperson takes it upon him/herself to provide the necessary training. Adding value should always be a priority with any salesperson.

When the product is technical, customer training may require the assistance of the company trainer or engineer. The salesperson still has a key role as they know the customer best and should serve as the facilitator to ensure that all the parties have been properly introduced and start off in a positive manner. The salesperson should schedule the training sessions as conveniently as possible for the customer. Customer education is an integral part of the marketing strategy of Ontario Systems Corporation, a collections software company. What separates Ontario from

Successfully training customers is a vital part in the selling process.

its competitors is its ability to provide timely training and education for all its customers. Ontario knows that service after the sale is crucial, which is why it provides an 800 telephone number for 24-hour service. Each year, Ontario strengthens its relationships with customers by providing one week of training, seminars, and goodwill at its home office. Ontario understands the importance of the team approach to providing outstanding customer service.

Correct Billing Errors

Billing errors could turn into customer complaints if not found and corrected quickly. A salesperson should go over all orders and billing records to ensure proper billing has been sent to the customer. A customer will know the salesperson has their best interests in mind if the salesperson corrects problems without being prompted by the customer. As seen in An Ethical Dilemma, it is possible that a billing error may result in an ethical dilemma.

> Complaints will never be completely eliminated by any company, but they must be addressed and resolved.

An Ethical Dilemma

CPSA

8.1 Act with integrity

Evan Celler is a sales representative for a manufacturer of windshield wipers that calls on automotive supply shops and various retail outlets. In reviewing an invoice scheduled to be submitted to one of his newest customers, he noticed a pricing error. The price should have included a quantity discount. Evan recalls mentioning the opportunity for earning quantity discounts to this customer when taking the customer's first order several months ago, but recalls not much was made of it since at that time this customer had no intent to place a large order. If Evan were to obtain this higher price, he would realize a significantly larger commission on this order. Given that this customer was relatively new, there was some question as to whether the customer would even realize he was not receiving a quantity discount. If you were Evan, what would you do?

(a) Contact my billing department and have them correct the invoice prior to sending it.

(b) Keep quiet, but if the customer questions the price, then inform the customer that billing made an error and that I will have them send out an invoice that includes the quantity discount.

(c) Take my increased commission and treat myself to a nice dinner out since I deserve it; if the customer questions the price, tell the customer that quantity discounts take effect only after a customer has been buying from our company for at least nine months, so they will be eligible for a quantity discount very soon.

Resolve Complaints and Encourage Critical Encounters

5.1 Follow-up on the sale

Complaints will never be completely eliminated by any company. Nevertheless, it is every company's hope that it can reduce the frequency of complaints. Complaints typically arise because the product did not live up to the buyer's expectations. Research shows that companies that systematically monitor, track, and address service failures, instances in which buyer expectations are not met, are rewarded with more satisfied customers and greater customer retention.[22] Buyers complain for any number of reasons: (1) late delivery, (2) wrong order sent (e.g., too many, too few), (3) product performs poorly, or (4) nobody at the salesperson's company takes the buyer's problems seriously. See Exhibit 9.5 for a more comprehensive list of complaints.

Many times, the complaint is not the fault of the salesperson (e.g., late delivery, wrong order, product performs poorly). However, this is not a concern to buyers as they expect the salesperson to resolve it. Traditional salespeople have been known to pass the blame when complaints arise. A salesperson would be better off to tackle the complaint by accepting responsibility and promptly fixing the problem. Salespeople get into trouble by overpromising what their product can do, being overly optimistic about delivery dates, and not being attentive to their customers when they do complain. Many complaints can be avoided by giving customers a reasonable expectation of what a company's product or service can do for them.

If periodic meetings are taking place between the buyer and seller after the sale, then in all probability, most of the important issues are being discussed. Salespeople must ask their buyers to be candid with them and encourage the buyer to discuss tough issues (e.g., late deliveries, damaged products), especially in areas where the salesperson's organization is providing less than satisfactory performance. Some buyers will not complain because they feel it will not do any good. Others will not complain because they feel that the salesperson should be in tune with their problems or concerns and recognize these problems on their own. If a salesperson encourages **critical encounters** and acts accordingly to defuse a situation in which the buyer's expectations have not been met, then this will help with subsequent critical encounters. If the

critical encounters Meetings in which the salesperson encourages the buyer to discuss tough issues, especially in areas in which the salesperson's organization is providing less than satisfactory performance.

Exhibit 9.5
Typical Customer Complaints

1. Late delivery
2. Damaged merchandise
3. Invoice errors
4. Out of stock—back orders
5. Shipped incorrect product
6. Shipped incorrect order size
7. Service department unresponsive
8. Product does not live up to expectations
9. Customer not informed of new developments
10. Customer's problems not taken seriously
11. Improper installation
12. Need more training
13. Price increase—no notice
14. Cannot find the salesperson when needed
15. Unreturned phone calls

salesperson does not act on these issues, then future meetings with the buyer will not uncover problem areas because the buyer is convinced nothing will be done to solve them.

Some salespeople tell the customer what they want to hear to get the order but cannot deliver on promises made. Complaints can be avoided by being truthful when presenting a product's capabilities. Providing sales support can eliminate problems with late deliveries, wrong orders being sent, and the feeling that the salesperson does not care about the customer's complaints. The following section provides an outline on how to handle customer complaints.

A PROCEDURE TO HANDLE COMPLAINTS

5.1 Follow-up on the sale

Salespeople must have an open communication line with customers and encourage feedback, either positive or negative. Some research indicates that as many as 25 percent of business customers who encounter a problem will not complain.[23] Thus, salespeople must build relationships to the point where buyers will not hesitate to speak their minds if they are unhappy with the service.

If the customer does not complain, then the salesperson does not know what needs to be fixed. When a customer does complain, the complaint should be handled quickly and with great sensitivity. One study indicates that if a company fails to deal with customers and prospects who complain, those customers will tell on average up to 10 people about their bad experience and, with e-mail and the Internet, this may turn into thousands.[24] Another study showed that when customer complaints are addressed, these customers are 30 percent more loyal than those who do not complain and 50 percent more loyal than a dissatisfied complainant—which indicates that the effort to make amends is worth it.[25] Research in consumer services suggests that satisfactory handling of customer complaints is key to customer recommendations of a firm to others.[26] A general procedure for handling customer complaints follows.

BUILD THE RELATIONSHIP TO THE POINT THAT YOUR CUSTOMERS ARE COMFORTABLE COMPLAINING

CPSA   5.1 Follow-up on the sale

Salespeople have been overheard saying to their customers, "Had I known that you were unhappy with our service, I could have fixed it." The buyer typically responds, "Well, I gave you plenty of signals. Why weren't you aware of the problems?" The buyer and salesperson must work together to develop a trust so that whenever something comes up, either person feels comfortable speaking up. Open communication channels are a must for good customer service. Salespeople cannot be afraid to ask their clients, "How are we doing?" Some companies are conducting 30-, 60-, and 90-day customer satisfaction follow-up visits after the sale. Beyond that, salespeople maintain quarterly follow-ups, even if only by phone. This at least tells customers that the salesperson is interested in them and wants to service their account well.

LISTEN CAREFULLY AND GET THE WHOLE STORY

CPSA   2.2 Practice active listening

The salesperson must listen carefully to what is being said and what is not being said. Good salespeople let the customer know that they are happy the complaint has been brought to their attention. Chances are that the customer will not complain again if they are made to feel uncomfortable with the initial complaint. The salesperson must be careful not to interrupt early in the discussion. The customer must be allowed to vent their frustration. Once the customer stops complaining, the salesperson may have to probe and ask follow-up questions to get the whole story. For instance, the buyer may not have told the salesperson

whom they talked to at the salesperson's company about the problem, and this information may be helpful to the salesperson in solving the complaint. This is a good time to show empathy. The salesperson must consider how they would feel if placed in the customer's position. Even if the customer complains in an angry tone, and it is not the salesperson's fault, the salesperson should apologize for any inconvenience and make the customer aware that they are anxious to resolve the problem and keep the buyer as a satisfied customer.

ASK CUSTOMERS HOW THEY WOULD LIKE THEIR COMPLAINT RESOLVED

CPSA   5.1 Follow-up on the sale

Many salespeople attempt to solve the complaint without understanding what the customer wants them to do. For example, a salesperson may reason that the last customer wanted a 20 percent discount to make things better. "Thus, I will offer this unhappy buyer the same thing." The salesperson may be surprised to find out the buyer wanted something totally different to resolve the problem. The salesperson cannot be afraid to ask the customer what it will take to make him or her happy. A salesperson could say something like, "Theresa, we value you and your company's business. I am sorry for the inconvenience we caused you. Can you please tell me what we can do to solve this problem and keep you as a satisfied customer?" Then, the salesperson must listen carefully. Perhaps the buyer simply wants an apology, a discount, or a substitute until the regular shipment arrives. Salespeople typically find that the customer is not demanding as much as they thought they might have been, considering the circumstances of the complaint. The solution should centre on what the customer wants and not what the salesperson thinks is appropriate. When salespeople provide customers with choice in the complaint resolution process, they are likely to increase customers' perceived control over the process and ultimately enhance customer satisfaction.[27]

GAIN AGREEMENT ON A SOLUTION

CPSA   5.1 Follow-up on the sale

Once the salesperson hears what the customer wants, they must agree on a solution. Sometimes, the salesperson can do exactly what the customer asks. Other times, the buyer may be asking for an unrealistic solution. The salesperson's focus should always be on trying to do exactly what the customer wants, if possible. When that is not possible, the salesperson's message should concentrate on what they can do for the customer and then do

Every Business Sells

Ward Avery is Managing Director at Frontier Subsea Inc., which sells engineering and technical services in the engineering and energy sector. Ward sells throughout Eastern Canada (Newfoundland) to offshore oil operating companies. He's worked in sales for seven years, all of them at Frontier Subsea Inc.

As a salesperson, how do you provide value to your customers?

Value is hard to quantify; we generally measure the value through repeat business on a continual basis with our customers. I provide value to our customers by being transparent, honest, and remaining committed to the goals (cost and schedule basis driven) that are agreed upon for each project/sale.

As a salesperson, how do you provide value to your organization?

Similar to how I provide value to our customers, I remain committed to the same approach to my organization: being transparent and approachable. Stewarding and enabling strong relationships between our customers and organization is also key.

What is your greatest challenge you face today as a salesperson?

The greatest challenge I face today is the "changing of the guard," so to speak, in that the relationships I have built up over the years with customers become eroded and/or lost as my contacts move into different roles or into different organizations.

How do you try to overcome this challenge?

Generally I try to ensure that there is some type of handover between the outgoing contact and their replacement. Often this is not possible, but it's important to start fresh and provide the same level of service through the values previously discussed.

What advice do you have for someone starting out in sales?

First, trust is not given it is only earned. By establishing the basis of transparency and honesty you can build and acquire trust with your customer base. If you have trust you have the basis of what is needed to be successful. Second, believe in what you have and what you are selling. If you don't truly believe in the product or service you can offer, then it's flawed from the start. It sounds simple, and it is.

---

it quickly.[28] The conversation might sound like, "Jim, I'm sorry for the inconvenience we caused you. Thanks for your suggestions on what we need to do to resolve the problem. Here are a couple of things we can do—which of these will work better for you?" The salesperson is telling the buyer that they cannot do exactly what the buyer asked, but the salesperson can do the following. Good salespeople always focus on the positive.

TAKE ACTION—EDUCATE THE CUSTOMER

 5.1 Follow-up on the sale

Once an agreement is reached, the salesperson must take action and solve the customer complaint in a timely fashion. The communication lines must be kept open to the customer (e.g., letting him or her know when the repair people will be arriving). Monitor complaint resolution and keep the customer up-to-date on progress. This is also a good time to convey that steps have been taken to ensure that the problem will not occur again.

If customers have unrealistic expectations of the services provided, then this would be a good time to educate them so that they will have realistic expectations. Some salespeople promise the moon to secure an order and then let the customer down when the product or service does not meet expectations. This is not the way to develop a trusting relationship.

FOLLOW THROUGH ON ALL PROMISES—ADD VALUE

 5.1 Follow-up on the sale

Whatever promises are made, good salespeople must make sure that they are kept, and this is a good time to go beyond what has been promised. Those salespeople who overdeliver what is promised will truly impress their customers and build stronger relationships faster than their competitors. By exceeding expectations and adding value, the salesperson helps ensure repeat business. Exhibit 9.6 summarizes the procedures to handle complaints.

Every Business Sells

Neil Chaulk is the VP Business Development at Solace Power Inc., which sells wireless power hardware for automotive, telecommunications, aerospace, and medical device markets. Solace Power Inc. has customers worldwide, with primary locations in the United States, Germany, Japan, Korea, France, Canada, and China. Of his 25-year career in sales, eight years have been spent at Solace Power Inc.

As a salesperson, how do you provide value to your customers?

First you have to listen so that you fully understand the "problem." The most important outcome of a sales effort is a well-educated customer who can make an informed decision. Every effort is directed at achieving that objective.

As a salesperson, how do you provide value to your organization?

Generating revenue to sustain business growth.

What is your greatest challenge you face today as a salesperson?

Lack of trained salespeople and an even bigger deficit of technically savvy salespeople.

How do you try to overcome this challenge?

We train new recruits in-house and through external expert trainers.

What advice do you have for someone starting out in sales?

Successful sales execution will come when you truly care about the success of your customer and when you take a systematic approach to sales. Outcomes are much more predictable when you are organized.

Exhibit 9.6

General Procedures for Handling Complaints

1. Build the relationship to the point that the customer is comfortable complaining.
2. Listen carefully and get the whole story.
3. Ask the customer what they would like you to do.
4. Gain agreement on a solution. Tell the customer what you can do; do not focus on what you cannot do.
5. Take action; educate the customer so they have realistic expectations.
6. Follow through on all promises. Add value.

LO 4 | EXPAND COLLABORATIVE INVOLVEMENT

 8.2 Drive results

A salesperson's goal is to work with customers who have entered into a strategic alliance with the salesperson's firm. This is done by building trust over a long time. The salesperson should always be looking for ways to take the relationship to a higher level and create a stronger bond. One way to accomplish this goal is to expand the **collaborative involvement** between the buyer's and salesperson's organizations. The salesperson may take a group of engineers along on a sales call and introduce them to the buyer's engineers. It may be possible for the engineers to work together to

> **collaborative involvement**
> A way to build on buyer–salesperson relationships in which the buyer's organization and the salesperson's organization join together to improve an offering.

enhance the product offering or perhaps provide a more customized solution. Customers often know the strengths and weaknesses of the product they use and can provide some insight into how improvements can be made.

Another example of a company's attempt to expand collaborative involvement is to host a week-long series of seminars, training sessions, and social engagements with its customers to expand the relationship. Brainstorming sessions with customers demonstrate a willingness to listen, show that the company cares, and often result in better ways to serve customers. Any time the salesperson can involve additional personnel from the buyer's company during relationship building, chances are that the relationship will become stronger.

LO 5 | WORK TO ADD VALUE AND ENHANCE MUTUAL OPPORTUNITIES

 8.2 Drive results

To build mutually satisfying relationships between buyers and sellers, professional salespeople must work toward adding value and enhancing mutual opportunities for the customer. This can be done by reducing risk through repeated displays of the seller's ability to serve the customer. By demonstrating willingness to serve the customer, the seller reduces the buyer's risk—both real and perceived. A good relationship is one that has few, if any, unpleasant surprises.

Salespeople must also establish high standards and expectations. Many relationships fail because of unmet expectations. The higher the customer's expectations the better, provided the seller can meet or exceed those expectations. Salespeople should ensure that the customer's expectations are reasonable by clearly and honestly conveying the firm's offering, and continually work to improve performance.

Finally, salespeople must monitor and take action to improve customer satisfaction. Salespeople must never let up on this. Doing so only invites competitor challenges. A good salesperson must always look for cracks in the relationship and patch them before insurmountable problems occur. All relationships require work, and taking a good customer for granted is foolish. Remember that the salesperson must continually add value to the relationship or they will run the risk of losing the customer. Exhibit 9.7 provides some suggestions for adding value by demonstrating to customers that the salesperson cares about them and appreciates their business.[29]

Exhibit 9.7

Enhancing Customer Value

1. Keep in touch with customers to pass along information and solicit customer feedback.
2. Let customers know in writing that you enjoy working with them.
3. Ask customers what can be done to make it easier on them to work with you.
4. When appropriate, refer customers to others.
5. Provide customers with leads.
6. Thank customers during the relationship, not only after the sale has been made.
7. Offer advice for improving customers' operations.
8. Pass along useful articles or ideas.
9. If possible, lend a helping hand (e.g., one sales manager has been known to assist customers in their booths at trade shows).
10. Recommend customers for awards or news stories.
11. Be candid in providing opinions.
12. Come to the defence of customers who are criticized.
13. Quickly address customer problems.
14. Demonstrate reliability by promptly (the day it is received) responding to customer communication.
15. Provide customers with reports, survey results, and articles free of charge.
16. Be proactive, rather than reactive, when dealing with customers. Take the initiative to do what is right or necessary before being asked.
17. Keep your word. If circumstances dictate otherwise, then quickly explain yourself.
18. Show respect by not getting "too friendly" with customers.

Provide Quality Customer Service

All salespeople are looking for a competitive edge to help them differentiate their products in the eyes of customers. Many of the products that a salesperson sells have essentially the same features and benefits as those of competitors. Chris Crabtree of Lanier once said, "A copier is a copier, is a copier. There is just no difference between what I have to offer and my competitors. We all charge about the same price. In fact, I can match any price my competitor puts on the table. That leaves only one attribute for me to differentiate on—service."

More and more companies are turning to **service quality** as a strategy to acquire and maintain customers. A salesperson must be able to convince a customer that service is important, demonstrate service quality, and then maintain a high level of service over an extended period of time.

The problem is that every salesperson claims to provide outstanding service. The goal today is not to meet customer expectations but to exceed them. Salespeople will rarely be given a second chance to prove that they provide outstanding service if they do not get it right the first time. A sign in a small-town business reads,

Service is advertised . . .

Service is talked about . . .

But the only time service really counts . . .

Is when it is delivered . . .

And we promise your experience with us will be outstanding.

Customers do not care about slogans and service claims until something happens to them. This is called a moment of truth. Each salesperson experiences daily moments of truth—brief moments that occur whenever a customer comes into contact with a salesperson, the training staff, installers, field engineers, or service personnel and has an opportunity to form an impression. These moments of truth are when the customer will determine if promises are being kept by the sales organization, and whether the salesperson truly cares about the customer or is simply an order getter.

There are four benefits of service enthusiasm that allow the sales organization to gain an advantage over its competitors. First, reputation is an important part of any organization's ability to attract and keep new customers. Reputation allows a salesperson to distinguish himself or herself from the competition. A solid reputation indicates that the salesperson cares and will help him or her establish loyal relationships with customers. Reputations take a long time to establish and only one negative event to destroy.

Second, by providing good customer service the first time, an organization makes the profit that it needs to stay in business. Whenever mistakes are made (e.g., wrong order, short order delivered), service personnel have to sort out the problem and fix it. The result could lead to a lost customer. In any event, it does not take long to go into the red when people have to be added to fix problems. Efficient operations, cost savings, and doing things right the first time increase the chances for increased profits.

The third benefit of service enthusiasm is convenience. It is critically important to put the customer's convenience first. For example, most customers are uncomfortable complaining. Thus, a salesperson must make it easy for their customers to discuss problems or complaints. Since customers can be reluctant to complain, the salesperson must be vigilant in asking customers to express their problems or concerns. Building a strong, trusting relationship with open communication will make it easier for customers to voice their concerns. Furthermore, to be convenient, salespeople must be readily accessible to customers. This involves using technology (e.g., cell phone, e-mail) to stay accessible, quickly acknowledging customer requests, and then responding in an appropriate and expedient manner. When it comes to servicing customers, salespeople often must accommodate customers' schedules rather than their own. Naturally, this may pose some inconvenience to the salesperson, but customer needs must be considered first.

Salespeople must design user-friendly feedback systems. Periodically inquiring about customer satisfaction can greatly enhance a customer's feelings toward a salesperson and their organization. Ontario Systems (http://www.ontariosystems.com) provides a Client Resource Centre as one of its links on its website. Clients can easily get up-to-date information on product support, training, industry links, and discussion lists. Ontario Systems is always looking for ways to provide more services to its clients.

Finally, service enthusiasm goes hand in hand with spirit. A customer can be turned onto an organization by meeting many caring "can-do" people. The spirit must start with an enthusiastic, service-minded corporate culture. The salesperson, sales manager, field engineer, installer, and customer service representative must all have the same service enthusiasm to generate the benefits of service enthusiasm. That is why the salesperson must monitor and coordinate all the people who have access to the account to ensure that good customer service is taking place.

The most difficult aspect of customer service is the potential for inconsistency. For instance, field engineer A, who has a great understanding of service enthusiasm, may be called into an account early in the week. The customer is very impressed. Three weeks later, the customer calls for help again. Field engineer A is out on another account, and field engineer B, who has little or no service skills, is sent out on the next call. Field engineer B is

service quality Meeting and/ or exceeding customer service expectations.

good at fixing the problem but has a hard time relating to customers; in fact, he is downright cold! As a result of this unevenness, the customer's level of satisfaction decreases.

The inconsistency of customer service is a problem for every sales organization. By understanding the benefits of service enthusiasm and the rewards of proper spirit, the sales organization can ensure consistency and exceed customer expectations.

Customer Expectations

A salesperson must meet the needs of their customers. At a minimum, customers expect a warm and friendly salesperson. Buyers have enough things going on during their day that it would not be a plus to have to deal with a surly salesperson. Warmth and friendliness are the building blocks of a successful relationship.

Reliability is another attribute that buyers look for in choosing a salesperson with whom to do business. Customers must have the confidence that the expected service will be delivered accurately, consistently, and dependably. Helpfulness and assistance are two more variables that buyers expect when working with a salesperson. Will the customer be able to find their salesperson when they need to do so? Can the salesperson provide the speed and promptness needed by the customer? The salesperson can solve this issue by developing a regular call routine so that the customer knows when to expect the salesperson. Customers also want to deal with salespeople in whom they have confidence and trust will always do what is right for them (i.e., assurance). As such, salespeople must be trustworthy. Furthermore, salespeople must pay attention to detail as customers expect accuracy from them, particularly as it pertains to product or service orders. Other customer expectations include follow-through as promised; empathy; and resolution of complaints, mistakes, or defects. The customer must know that if anything goes wrong, the salesperson will move in quickly and solve the problem. Ultimately, the customer is looking for someone who is personally accountable for their desired results.[30] Exhibit 9.8 summarizes what customers expect from their salesperson.

service strategy A plan in which a salesperson identifies their business and customers and what the customers want and what is important to them.

communication A two-way flow of information between the salesperson and the customer.

Develop a Service Strategy

Salespeople can calculate the lifetime value of their customers. For example,

Hershey Foods Corporation knows exactly how much candy it has sold at the Walmart in Muncie, Indiana. It is easy for Hershey to calculate the loss if any customer decides to replace it. It is imperative for Hershey to provide the service level that each of its customers demands. Less than quality service can lead to the loss of a customer.

Developing a **service strategy** allows a salesperson to plan their actions for each customer. A service strategy asks a salesperson to identify their business and customers and what the customers want and what is important to them. The salesperson also has to determine how their customers' needs and perceptions are changing. The salesperson cannot be afraid to ask how the customers rate them in terms of their expectations. What does the salesperson's company do best, and what can the organization do better? The salesperson, ultimately, must determine how to position their company in the market to differentiate its products and services. All this must be done while directing efforts against the competitors. Exhibit 9.9 is an example of a checklist for developing a service strategy.

Customer Service Dimensions

There are three dimensions of customer service, with **communication** being the most important. Most problems arise because the customer was not informed of a change in plans (e.g., late delivery, price increase). Salespeople are extremely busy and many times do not have the time to communicate with all their customers.

Exhibit 9.9

Checklist for Developing a Service Strategy

Questions a salesperson must ask when developing a service strategy:

- What is our business?
- Who are our customers?
- What do our customers want, and what is important to them?
- How are our customers' needs and perceptions changing?
- How are social, economic, and political factors affecting current and future customer needs and our ability to respond to them? How are competitors responding to these factors?
- How do customers rate us in terms of their expectations?
- For what are we best known?
- What do we do best?
- What can we do better?
- How can we position ourselves in the market to differentiate our services?

Communication tools such as e-mail can be used to quickly do mass communication to inform customers of these changes. Over time, the telephone and personal visits can be used to confirm that the customers are aware of the changes.

Another customer service dimension is **resilience**. Resilience is the ability of a salesperson to get knocked down several times a day by a customer's verbal assault (i.e., complaint) and get right back up with a smile and ask for more. A salesperson cannot lose their cool just because a customer does. A tired salesperson must treat late-afternoon, difficult customers the same way that they would treat a dilemma at the day's beginning. They must both be treated well. Finally, **service motivation** is another important customer service dimension. Salespeople must be motivated to find time each day to deal with difficult customers and problems that exist. Ignoring these activities will not make them go away. Working diligently on behalf of the customer indicates to him or her that the salesperson truly cares about the partnership. If a salesperson has a complaint from a customer and gladly fixes it, the customer becomes a more committed customer.

resilience The ability of a salesperson to get knocked down several times a day by a customer's verbal assault (i.e., complaint) and get right back up with a smile and ask for more.

service motivation The desire of a salesperson to service customers each day.

STUDY TOOLS

At the back of the textbook, use tear-out cards to review key chapter information. Visit cengage.ca to purchase digital tools to help you succeed.

CENGAGE | MINDTAP

Personal Computer

- ☐ Gain unique perspectives on key concepts through a variety of videos and cases
- ☐ Increase your comprehension with online quizzes
- ☐ Study with existing flashcards and make your own

Mobile

- ☐ Stay focused and ready to study whenever it's convenient for you!
- ☐ Access a full, interactive ebook: online or offline
- ☐ Study tools that empower anytime, anywhere learning and 24/7 course access

NATURALLY BEAUTIFUL INC.

BACKGROUND

Naturally Beautiful Inc. is a maker and marketer of organic cosmetics. Its cosmetics are formulated from all-natural organic ingredients. Although the company currently serves primarily the higher-end market, distributing through upscale department stores and boutiques, it would like to expand its distribution channels. It is currently developing an organic line to sell through outlets such as drug store chains and discount retailers. Long-term plans include expanding internationally, first to the United States and Mexico, and eventually to Western Europe and beyond. Sales are strong and continue to rise. The company gives much of the credit for its success to its salesforce, which has done a great job expanding into new outlets while establishing and maintaining strong customer relationships. Heather Aunaturale, a nontraditional student, was hired as a sales representative by Naturally Beautiful out of college approximately ten months ago. Since being hired she has had a good deal of success, landing several new accounts. In fact, if she can land a few more accounts by the end of the rapidly approaching fiscal year, she will exceed her quota and achieve a hefty bonus. Heather is counting on this bonus because she has planned a big family trip and does not want to let her family down.

CURRENT SITUATION

Lately, Heather has heard various concerns from several of her customers. For instance, the other day she received a voice mail from Rick at Beauty Boutique, a recently acquired customer whose order was missing a few items. Heather figured that shipping must have inadvertently omitted the items and that Rick could give them a call to get it fixed. She figured that it was not her fault; Rick still had product to sell and she certainly did not have time to mess with this. Similarly, she received a text from Kim at Devine's department store indicating that an expected delivery was late. Again, Heather figured she could not do anything about the delivery. She texted Kim to tell her to contact the shipping department at Naturally Beautiful about the matter. Heather also received a second e-mail from Sarah at Cosmetics Unlimited:

> Dear Heather,
> A few weeks ago you promised you would return to train our beauty consultants on your newest product line. Our consultants need to fully understand the benefits of this new product and how it is to be applied so that they can best serve our customers. As you know, we take great pride in providing the highest quality products and services to our customer base. We discussed this when you offered me your line. Although we like your line, if we are unable to offer our customers top-shelf service with your brand then we may have to look elsewhere.
>
> Sincerely,
>
> Sarah

Heather recalls telling Sarah that she would conduct training for her sales consultants but has been so busy working to get new accounts that she put it on the back burner. Heather was not sure that she could put Sarah off much longer, but felt it would be in her best interest to write her back and stall her for at least a couple more weeks. By then, she thought, she might have exceeded her quota.

To Heather, these incidents were minor customer issues, not even problems. In her opinion, they were nothing more than "needy" customers. As far as she was concerned, she was delivering a great product at a great price. Besides, she had more sales to make and nobody was going to help her if she came up short on providing that great family vacation she promised.

QUESTIONS

1. For each of the concerns expressed by Heather's customers in the case, explain an alternative means for handling the concern.

2. What are the potential long-run implications of how Heather is handling her current customers?

3. What types of activities can Heather do after acquiring an account to enhance customer value and ensure long-term customer relationships?

ROLE PLAY

Situation: Read the Naturally Beautiful Inc. case

Characters: Heather Aunaturale, sales representative for Naturally Beautiful; Rick, customer at Beauty Boutique; Kim, customer at Devine's department store; Sarah, customer at Cosmetics Unlimited

Scene: Employing a more personal touch, Heather contacts each customer and takes appropriate action to ensure customer satisfaction. Role-play these conversations.

COMPLAINT RESOLUTION

BACKGROUND

When perusing top brands worldwide, it is not often that Canadian companies can crack the top 100, let alone a top 50 or 10. There are Canadian success stories like Lululemon and Tim Hortons, but those firms are just not large enough to garner the brand equity and international reputation required to become a recognized company and brand.

The exception to this rule lies in a group called the Big Six. The six are: Royal Bank of Canada (RBC), Toronto Dominion Bank (TD Bank), Scotiabank, Bank of Montreal, Canadian Imperial Bank of Commerce (CIBC), and National Bank of Canada. This is the group of banks in Canada that do crack the top company lists. In a list of top Canadian brands from late 2019, five out of the top six banks were in the top 10, with three of the Big Six occupying spots in the top 4.[31]

But another list the Big Six sits atop is one each bank might not want to be on: a list of companies that handle complaints poorly. The Financial Consumer Agency of Canada (FCAC) released a report in February 2020 specifically focused on "Bank Complaint Handling Procedures."[32] The results of the report were not flattering to the Big Six.

While the banks were effective at dealing with smaller complaints, which could be handled by frontline staff, they were less effective when complaints escalated. Without consistent or clear processes, the large banks in Canada were allowing escalated complaints to linger for up to seven months.[33] The guidelines provided by the FCAC had a cap of 90 days to deal with complaints. Even at 90 days, the Canadian standard for handling complaints falls far behind countries like England and Australia.

In looking for the culprit in the system, CBC News was able to distill it down to this: "The review found banks' procedures for handling complaints objectively 'are inadequate,' noting the same frontline staff who deal with them 'are under pressure to make sales and control costs, and these pressures may influence their decision to reimburse the customer.'"[34]

The inclusion of the word "sales" is another indictment on the pressures of sales and how it can often clash with trying to provide strong customer service. Forbes magazine highlighted the challenges with sales and customer satisfaction: "Losing focus on customer satisfaction and getting tunnel vision about performance is a real issue. Salesforce found that although 66 percent of sales teams use customer satisfaction as a key performance indicator, 66 percent of teams also measure their performance by tracking whether their team's quota was met."[35]

When quotas are given primary importance, consumers, companies, and entire industries can suffer. And while the Big Six banks own close to a monopoly on banking services in Canada, there has been an uptick in alternatives such as credit unions and online-only financial institutions.

CURRENT SITUATION

The FCAC report made it clear that changes need to be made in regard to complaints and major Canadian banks. While stronger policies and complaint handling procedures seemed logical, it was the third suggestion that stood out. There is a need for actual training programs for staff at the Big Six banks that relates directly on how to handle complaints.

The Canadian Bankers Association (CBA) speaks for banks in Canada and responded to the FCAC by saying: "providing an effective mechanism for resolving differences is a longstanding priority for banks in Canada."[36] The CBA has reached out to your school to ask for guidance from aspiring sales professionals, and would like to include an academic model that will help inform the new training programs for complaints. The focus is on creating a guide for frontline sales staff at Canadian banks. You eagerly volunteer yourself to be part of this, and need to put together a few slides that will make up your proposal.

QUESTIONS

1. In order to gain customer trust and create a partnership, you suggest that CBA focus on converting customers by offering something of value each time they interact

with a banking customer. You are advocating for what relationship enhancer?

a. building loyalty

b. value creation

c. establishing connection

d. building goodwill

2. When looking at resolving complaints, you recommend to the CBA that the banks create systems that eliminate the need for the complaint in the first place. Beyond that, what is another key to resolving complaints?

a. deciding on terms of compensation

b. interact three times as a minimum

c. determine the complainant's needs

d. ask how the customer would like it to be resolved

3. If bank customers hear about studies like this, they might be more likely avoid complaining in the future if they think nothing will be done. What can you encourage salespeople to do in this situation?

a. confront the customer

b. build strong transaction capital

c. encourage critical encounters

d. bring potential solutions to the customer

CHAPTER ROLE PLAY   9

Expanding Customer Relationships:
Midwest Live Bait & Tackle, LLC

BACKGROUND

Midwest Live Bait & Tackle, LLC, located in Haliburton, Ontario, is a regional wholesaler of live bait and tackle to bait shops and service stations around Haliburton, Bracebridge, and Huntsville. Known for its high-quality live bait, reasonably priced tackle, and good customer service, the company has been able to maintain a steady market share over the years. Its five salespeople have been primarily responsible for selling and servicing the company's current accounts. This involves making sure that customers have bait and tackle when needed, assisting them with merchandising and pricing, and ensuring their complete satisfaction. Wanting to retire, the owner recently sold the business. The new owner was very ambitious and had big plans for expanding the company's market share. He felt that the quickest and most efficient way to move in that direction was to have his current salespeople actively pursue new accounts. Thus, he mandated new customer quotas, compensated salespeople for achieving targeted growth goals, and threatened their jobs if minimal new account requirements were not met.

CURRENT SITUATION

Don Laton has been a sales representative for Midwest for over five years. Until the new ownership, he enjoyed his job very much and made a good living doing it. With his fourth child on the way, a poor economy, and a tight job market, Don did not want to jeopardize his position with the company and reluctantly went along with the new changes. However, he was very concerned with how much time prospecting for new business was taking. He felt it may be endangering his current customer relationships. What follows are excerpts from a recent conversation with Jeff Carp, a very significant customer, especially considering he sold bait and tackle out of his service station convenience store and was contemplating opening a couple more locations:

Jeff:	Don, I've been having some problems recently with the minnows you've supplied for me. Some loss is typical, but lately the loss percentage has increased. What's going on here?
Don:	I don't know Jeff. None of my other customers are having problems with their minnows. You're making sure that you don't add chlorinated water when replenishing your minnow holding tanks, aren't you?
Jeff:	Of course! I recently refurbished my tanks and added a new oxygen system. Maybe that has something to do with the increasing loss. Could you check it out and see what you think?
Don:	Just let me know how many minnows you think you lost and I'll see what I can do.
Jeff:	Okay, but since this has been going on for the last couple of weeks I was just hoping you might be able to give me your thoughts on my new system. By the way, that new line of fishing poles doesn't seem to be moving very well. How are they moving for your other customers?
Don:	I haven't heard much about those, so I guess they are moving okay.
Jeff:	Do you have any ideas on how I might improve my merchandising so I can move more of them? Perhaps my price point is too high. What do you think?
Don:	I'm really busy today Jeff. I have several stops yet to make and I need to call on a couple of new prospects in the area.
Jeff:	You're not planning to supply my competition down the street, are you?
Don:	I don't know Jeff. I've got to make a living, too, you know.
Jeff:	Last week you promised to bring by some of those new plastic cricket containers you were telling me about. Did you bring any of those for me to examine?
Don:	Oh no, those completely slipped my mind.

Jeff:	Hmm. Well, certainly you brought me the crayfish you promised me last week. I've had customers coming in every day asking for them. Also, how about those waterdogs we talked about? I've been getting some requests for those.
Don:	I should have told you sooner, but our usual crayfish supplier is having difficulty getting us as many crayfish as we need. I know you wanted 500 but I think I can give you 100. I thought we'd have the waterdogs by now, at least that is what I was told. We're still waiting.
Jeff:	Don, I'm beginning to wonder how much you value my business. If you can't take care of me any longer, maybe I need to look for someone who can.
Don:	I've been under a lot of pressure lately to get more done in the same amount of time. My new boss is driving me nuts! I definitely want your business.

Don needed to hurry off to meet with a new prospect. He didn't have time to preview some of the new spinner baits his company was now carrying.

ROLE PLAY

Characters: Don, sales rep; Jeff, service station owner

Action: Role-play the meeting between Don and Jeff. This time have Don handle the situation (i.e., respond) as a sales rep who takes customer complaints seriously and cares about providing great customer service.

10 | Adding Value: Self-Leadership and Teamwork

Prince Edward Island (PEI) is Canada's smallest province, with 1.4 million acres of total land area.[1] Farms represent a significant portion of the province, accounting for 42.5 percent of this total area. Combined, the agriculture, forestry, and fishing sectors employ 8.9 percent of the workforce in the province, and 3.6 percent of the provincial population lives on farms.[2] PEI's farms are primarily focused on growing crops and raising livestock. The major sectors include potatoes, grains and oilseeds, fruits, vegetables, organic products, beef and dairy, hogs, and poultry. Twenty percent of cropland in PEI is devoted to the growth of potatoes, one of their most popular crops. PEI has Canada's largest share of potato acreage and their potatoes are not only sold in Canada and the United States but exported abroad as well. The total value of international exports of PEI potatoes from 2014 to 2018 ranged from $288 CAD to $415 million CAD.[3] The industry is a culmination of hard work and dedication and requires self-leadership and teamwork across an intertwined network of families, communities, and organizations within the province of PEI. The Department of Agriculture and Land within the provincial government is a source of support for the industry and they have set up numerous programs that aim to provide resources to assist in promotion and awareness, growth, and future prosperity of the agriculture industry in the province. Some of these programs include the Agri-Food Growth Program (to build and enhance local markets), the Agri-Food Promotion Program (to increase awareness and demand), the Agriculture Research and Innovation Program (support for farm-level research and innovation projects), and the Future Farmer Program (support new farmers to start profitable and sustainable farm businesses).[4]

Introduction

The success of Prince Edward Island's natural resources sector begins with the dedicated farmers, fishers, and foresters who have specialized expertise and something to sell. They rely on their own initiatives, available and relevant information, and support networks for their products and services to reach the final customer. What makes some of these individuals more successful than others? When observing the actions of a person who has truly mastered the skills of their profession, we think the person's actions come naturally. However, closer consideration will most often reveal that these seemingly innate and natural abilities are actually the result of years of fervent and purposeful planning, combined with many hours of practice over a period of years. This is true for successful farmers, world-class surgeons, sports stars, leading educators,

top attorneys—and yes, even high-performance salespeople. Good salespeople are consciously developed and intentionally supported, not born. They are the result of purposeful and conscious self-leadership based on using factual data that enables goal setting, strategically developing selling plans to achieve those goals, monitoring the resulting sales performance, and continuously revising those plans based on the dynamics of selling situations and interim results. Toward the objective of *developing* strong salespeople, this chapter builds on the process of self-leadership to generate a framework for developing and enhancing selling skills and abilities.

First, setting effective selling goals and objectives is discussed and integrated with methods for territory analysis and account classification. This is followed by a discussion of how the objectives and information from the territory and account analysis become inputs for generating and implementing effective multilevel sales

Like the skills and abilities of an athlete, the skills and abilities required for success in selling are the result of purposeful planning and many hours of practice.

planning. The importance of assessing performance results and level of goal attainment is also reviewed. Wrapping up the chapter is an examination of teamwork as a vehicle for expanding the capabilities of an individual salesperson, increasing customer value, and creating sustainable competitive advantage for salespeople.

LO 1 | EFFECTIVE SELF-LEADERSHIP

CPSA   8.2 Drive results

How often have you said or thought to yourself, "I just don't have enough time to get everything done?" In reality,

self-leadership The process of doing the right things and doing them well.

most people do not need more time. Rather, they need to prioritize the time they have. There are only so many hours in a day, and highly effective salespeople know that they can never have enough quality selling time. To maximize their selling time, these high performers have developed strong self-leadership skills and treat time as a valuable, irreplaceable resource and invest it wisely where it will accomplish the most good.

Self-leadership—a critical requirement for success in any career—has been described as doing the right things and doing them well. It is not simply the amount of effort that determines an achievement, but rather how well that effort is honed and aligned with our goals. In selling, this is often restated as selling smarter rather than selling harder. That is, before expending valuable time and resources, salespeople must establish priorities in the form of objectives. Then, and only then, do they implement the strategic plan that has been specifically developed to achieve their objectives in the light of the available resources and market potential that exist within the territory. Self-leadership translates to a process of first deciding what is to be accomplished and then putting into motion the proper plan designed to achieve those objectives.

The process of self-leadership is composed of five sequential stages. First, goals and objectives must be set that properly reflect what is important and what is to be accomplished. This is followed by an analysis of the territory and classification of accounts. Next, with goals in place and accounts classified, strategic plans designed to achieve the objectives through proper allocation of resources and effort are implemented. The next stage maximizes the effectiveness of allocated resources through the process of tapping technology and automation to expand resource capabilities. Finally, assessment activities are conducted to evaluate performance and goal attainment and to assess possible changes in plans and strategies. The nature of the sequential interrelationships among these five stages is illustrated in Figure 10.1.

FIG. 10.1 FIVE SEQUENTIAL STAGES OF SELF-LEADERSHIP

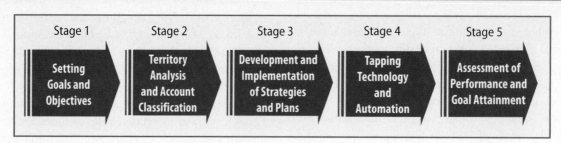

Stage 1	Stage 2	Stage 3	Stage 4	Stage 5
Setting Goals and Objectives	Territory Analysis and Account Classification	Development and Implementation of Strategies and Plans	Tapping Technology and Automation	Assessment of Performance and Goal Attainment

Self-leadership is a process of first deciding what is to be accomplished and then setting into motion the proper plan to achieve the desired objectives.

Selling in Action

Importance of Sales Call Planning to Drive Selling Success

Jaime Anderson, Senior Vice President of Marketing at SAP, underscores the importance of thorough planning and preparation prior to making contact with prospects and buyers.

Buyers are becoming more and more immune and even intolerant of inefficient sales contacts and activities. According to the What's the Future of Sales report by SAP, business buyers now receive an average of 64 to 107 approaches by salespeople over the course of a week. As a result, buyers across the globe are feeling hounded by the sales community and becoming less tolerant and less trusting of salespeople who come in too hard or without sufficient information and preparation. Aggressive salespeople (48%) and salespeople who lack relevant

knowledge (46 percent) are the biggest frustrations with salespeople. As a result, buyers block calls and avoid initial sales advances.

Anderson emphasizes that "B2B buyers are time-challenged, they don't want the dog and pony show. They don't want the dance. They just want the salesperson to be informed and to understand where they are and what they need at that point." Today's buyers have less time and patience for meandering or scripted and inflexible sales processes. Instead, they demand relevant and focused sales interactions that can only occur as the result of significant research, planning, and preparation in advance of any sales contact.

Stage One: Setting Goals and Objectives

 1.2 Conduct sales planning

Establishing priorities by setting **goals and objectives** is the key to effective self-leadership. This first stage of self-leadership has been appropriately referred to as "beginning with the end in mind."[5] First of all, if a salesperson does not understand what is important, how does that salesperson know what to focus on? Further, if a salesperson does not understand what they are setting out to accomplish, how could that salesperson know where to begin, how to proceed, or even which plan is best for getting there? Finally, without clear goals, how could salespeople know when the objective has been achieved? Without clear goals and objectives, it is very natural to drift from task to task and typically focus on minor and less-productive tasks, as they are the easiest to complete.

The result of this natural drift is poor sales performance and frustration. The positive impact of planning ahead and establishing priorities is further evidenced by the experiences of Jaime Anderson, Senior Vice President at SAP, in Selling in Action: Importance of Sales Call Planning to Drive Selling Success.

What Makes a Good Goal?

 1.2 Conduct sales planning

Although goals and objectives might best be described as desired outcomes, these two words carry specific meaning. *Desired* implies that it is something worthy of working toward and expending resources to reach. *Outcome* connotes

goals and objectives The things a salesperson sets out to accomplish.

Exhibit 10.1

Required Characteristics of Goals and Objectives

Effective Goals and Objectives Must Possess Three Fundamental Characteristics:

- Goals should be realistic, yet challenging.
- Goals should be specific and quantifiable.
- Goals should be time specific.

that it is a specific result or effect resulting from certain activities or behaviours—something that can be described and pointed out. As illustrated in Exhibit 10.1, properly developed goals share three key characteristics: (1) realistic, yet challenging, (2) specific and quantifiable, and (3) time specific.

- *Realistic, Yet Challenging*—Goals should be realistic and reachable. When set beyond what is possible, goals cease to motivate and often become a disincentive to performance. At the same time, goals should be challenging. If goals are continually set at a level that is too easy to reach, performance tends to regress to the lower standard. Goals that are challenging tend to be more motivating than goals that are easily achieved.

- *Specific and Quantifiable*—Without specificity, goals become ambiguous and have no clear meaning. For instance, the goal of having the top territory in the district could be interpreted in many ways. Does top territory translate to having the largest increase in sales, having the fewest number of customer defections, having the highest customer satisfaction scores, having the smallest number of price discounts, or possibly having the largest reduction in travel expenses? Without specificity, the goal becomes a moving target, and it is difficult to know where to apply effort. In a similar fashion, goals should be quantifiable—that is, they should be measurable. The goal of increasing sales is certainly commendable, but how might it be judged as having been accomplished? Is a 1

personal goals A salesperson's individual desired accomplishment, such as achieving a desired annual income over a specific period.

percent increase sufficient or is 12 percent more in line with expectations? If a 12 percent increase is the expectation, then the goal should be a 12 percent increase in sales—a quantifiable and measurable outcome that can be objectively measured and assessed.

- *Time Specific*—Stating a specific time line is the third requirement of goals and objectives. A goal of achieving a 12 percent increase in sales by December 31 is much more appealing than simply stating that the goal is to increase sales by 12 percent. Associating time lines with goals establishes a deadline for planning purposes and provides motivation by instilling a sense of urgency for taking action.

LO 2 | WORKING WITH DIFFERENT LEVELS AND TYPES OF GOALS

CPSA | 8.4 Engage in continuous learning

For maximum effectiveness, salespeople establish goals at four different levels: personal goals, territory goals, account goals, and sales call goals. Although each level requires different types of effort and produces different outcomes, each of the levels is interrelated and interdependent on the others. These interrelationships and dependencies are illustrated in Exhibit 10.2. A salesperson's **personal goals** might include achieving a $70,000 annual

Exhibit 10.2

Four Interdependent Levels of Salesperson Objectives

Personal goal—desired annual income	$ 70,000
Is dependent on annual territory sales goal (11% commission on sales)	$ 636,364
Is dependent on annual account sales goal (19 equally sized accounts)	$ 33,493
Is dependent on sales call goal (each account is called on twice a month)	$ 1,396

income during the current year ending December 31. If the salesperson receives a commission of 11 percent on sales, this personal goal is directly related to and dependent on achieving the **territory goal** of selling $636,364 in products across the territory in the same time period. Assuming 19 equally sized accounts compose the territory, the territory goal is dependent on achieving the **account goal** of an average of $33,493 in products sold to each account during the year. Considering that each account is called on twice every month, a **sales call goal** of $1,396 in sales per call is required to achieve the account goal. As illustrated in this example, each higher level goal is ultimately dependent on the salesperson setting and achieving lower level, specific goals for each and every sales call.

Although illustrative of the interdependence among different levels of goals, the previous example is admittedly simplistic in its exclusive use of goals based on sales volume. In reality, there are many different types of goals that a salesperson might effectively use. Exhibit 10.3 illustrates examples of common sales goals.

Stage Two: Territory Analysis and Account Classification

 CPSA 1.2 Conduct sales planning

Territory analysis and classification of accounts, the second stage of self-leadership, is all about finding the customers and prospects who are most likely to buy. Who are they, and where are they located? What and why do they buy? How much and how often do they purchase? Who has the authority to buy, and who can influence the purchase decision? What is the probability of selling

territory goal A salesperson's desire to sell a certain amount of product within an area or territory to achieve personal goals.

account goal A salesperson's desire to sell a certain amount of product to one customer or account to achieve territory and personal goals.

sales call goal A salesperson's desire to sell a certain amount of product per each sales call to achieve account, territory, and personal goals.

territory analysis The process of surveying an area to determine customers and prospects who are most likely to buy.

Exhibit 10.3
Common Types of Sales Goals

• Financial goals	Income, financial security
• Career advancement goals	Work in chosen field, advancement
• Personal development goals	Education, training, relationships outside work
• Sales volume goals	Dollar sales, unit sales, number of orders, aggregates or by groups
• Sales call activity goals	Calls made, calls/day, calls/account, presentations made
• Sales expense goals	Total expenses, by category, percentage of sales
• Profitability goals	Gross profits, contribution margin, returns and discounts
• Market share	Total share of potential market, peer group comparisons
• Share of account	Share of customer's purchases
• Ancillary activity goals	Required reports turned in, training conducted, service calls made
• Customer retention goals	Number of accounts lost, complaints received, lost account ratios
• New account goals	Number of new accounts
• Customer service goals	Customer goodwill generation, level of satisfaction, receivables collected
• Conversion goals	Ratio of number of sales to number of calls made

to this account? What is the potential share of account that might be gained?

Many sources offer intelligence that will assist the salesperson in answering these questions, and the information boom on the Internet makes accessing this information easier than ever before. In addition to numerous supplier directories available on the Web, commercial business information suppliers, such as *Canadian Trade Index*, Scott's Directories, Standard & Poor's, and *Canadian Key Business Directory*, offer easy-to-use databases that are fully searchable by company, industry, and geographic location. Salespeople can also access individual company Web sites, trade directories, professional association membership listings, and commercial mailing list providers. Personal observation, discussions with other selling professionals, and company sales records are also excellent sources for gaining valuable information.

Much of this information can be plotted to develop detailed territory maps and pinpoint pockets of existing and potential business. In addition, understanding the territory at the individual account level provides the input required for account classification.

> It is common for salespeople to find 80 to 90 percent of their sales potential generated by 10 to 20 percent of their accounts.

LO 3 | ACCOUNT CLASSIFICATION

 1.2 Conduct sales planning

Account classification places existing customers and prospects into categories based on their sales potential and assists salespeople in prioritizing accounts for call planning and time allocation purposes. During the process of account classification, it is common for salespeople to find that 80 to 90 percent of their sales potential is generated by 10 to 20 percent of the total accounts. Consequently, the results of account classification can guide salespeople in more efficient allocation of time, effort, and resources while simultaneously enabling them to be more effective in achieving sales goals. Two commonly used methods for classifying accounts are single-factor analysis and portfolio analysis.

Single-Factor Analysis

Single-factor analysis, also referred to as ABC analysis, is the simplest and most often used method for classifying accounts. As the name suggests, accounts are analyzed on the basis of one single factor—typically the level of sales potential. On the basis of sales potential, the accounts are placed into three or four categories denoted by letters of the alphabet, A, B, C, and D.

Accounts with the highest potential are traditionally sorted into category A, whereas those with medium potential go into B, and so on. All accounts in the same category receive equal selling effort. For example, A accounts may be called on every two weeks, B accounts every four to six weeks, and C accounts might receive a personal sales call once a year and be serviced by the seller's telemarketing team during the interim. Single-factor classification schemas used by three different sales organizations are summarized in Exhibit 10.4.

The simplicity of single-factor analysis is a prime contributor to its popularity for use by field salespeople. It is straightforward and requires no statistical analysis or data manipulation. Although this lack of complexity is appealing, its ability to use only one factor for analyzing and classifying accounts is also a significant limitation. Sales potential is certainly an important input in allocating selling effort, but other factors should also be considered. Possible other factors of interest are the selling company's competitive strength in each account, the account's need for additional attention and effort, profitability of the account, and amount of competitive pressure on the account.

Portfolio Analysis

 1.2 Conduct sales planning

Also referred to as two-factor analysis, the **portfolio analysis** method attempts to overcome the weakness of single-factor analysis by allowing two factors to be considered simultaneously. Each account is examined on the basis of the two specified factors and sorted into the proper segment of a matrix. This matrix is typically divided into four cells, and accounts are placed into the

account classification The process of placing existing customers and prospects into categories based on their potential as a customer.

single-factor analysis A method for analyzing accounts that is based on one single factor, typically the level of sales potential.

portfolio analysis A method for analyzing accounts that allows two factors to be considered simultaneously.

Exhibit 10.4

Different Single-Factor Account Analysis Schema Used by Different Companies

Class of Account	Schema One: InquisLogic Inc.	Schema Two: Web Resource Associates, LLC	Schema Three Federal Metal Products
A Accounts	Accounts with highest potential (the 20% that do or could account for 80% of sales) Annual number of calls = 24	Accounts with highest potential (the 20% that do or could account for 80% of sales) Annual number of calls = 52	High volume current customers (the 20% that currently account for 80% of sales volume) Annual number of calls = 48
B Accounts	Medium potential accounts (the 80% that account for 20% of sales volume) Annual number of calls = 12	Accounts with moderate sales potential but who are regular and reliable customers Annual number of calls = 24	Accounts with high potential but who are not current customers Annual number of calls = 12
C Accounts	Accounts with the least sales potential Annual number of calls = 4	Lower sales potential accounts Annual number of calls = 8	Medium potential accounts that are current customers Annual number of calls = 12
D Accounts	None. This schema only uses 3 classes of accounts	Accounts that cost more in time and energy than they produce in sales or profits Annual number of calls = 0	Accounts with medium potential but who are not current customers Annual number of calls = 6

proper classification cell on the basis of their individual ratings ("high" and "low" or "strong" and "weak") on each factor of interest. Cell location denotes the overall attractiveness of the different accounts and serves as a guide for the salesperson's allocation of resources and effort. Typically, each account in the same cell will receive the same amount of selling effort.

Exhibit 10.5 details the account characteristics and suggested selling effort allocations for a typical portfolio analysis incorporating the factors of (1) account opportunity and (2) seller's competitive position.[6] Account opportunity takes into consideration the buyer's level of need for and ability to purchase the seller's products, along with financial stability and growth prospects. Competitive position denotes the relationship between the account and the seller and includes such variables as the seller's share of account, competitive pressure, and the key decision maker's attitude toward the seller. Accounts sorted into Segment One are high on opportunity, exhibit strong competitive positions, and should receive the highest level of selling effort. Accounts falling into Segment Two are high on opportunity but

weak on competitive position. These accounts should receive a high level of attention to strengthen the seller's competitive position. Segment Three contains the 80 to 90 percent of accounts doing 10 to 20 percent of the seller's volume. These accounts are loyal and regular customers (high on competitive position) but offer weak opportunity.

Strategically, these accounts should receive a lower investment of selling effort designed to maintain the seller's current competitive position. Accounts sorted into Segment Four are considered unattractive and allocated minimal selling effort as they are characterized by low opportunity and weak competitive position. Within the past several years, many sellers have been successful in servicing Segment Three and Four accounts outside the personal selling channel by using alternatives, such as telemarketing, direct mail, the Internet, and proprietary extranets.

Portfolio analysis offers the advantages of enhanced flexibility and ability to incorporate multiple variables for analyzing and sorting accounts. Reflecting these strong points, the use of portfolio analysis is gaining in popularity.

Exhibit 10.5

Portfolio/Two-Factor Account Analysis and Selling Strategies

	Competitive Position	
	Strong	**Weak**
Account Opportunity — High	**Segment One** **Level of Attractiveness** Accounts are very attractive because they offer high opportunity and the seller has a strong competitive position. **Selling Effort Strategy** Accounts should receive a heavy investment of effort and resources to take advantage of high opportunity and maintain/improve competitive position. **Exemplary Sales Call Strategy = 36 calls/yr**	**Segment Two** **Level of Attractiveness** Accounts are potentially attractive because of high opportunity, but the seller currently has weak competitive position. **Selling Effort Strategy** Where it is possible to strengthen the seller's competitive position, a heavy investment of selling effort should be applied. **Exemplary Sales Call Strategy = 24 calls/yr**
Account Opportunity — Low	**Segment Three** **Level of Attractiveness** Accounts are moderately attractive because of the seller having a fairly strong competitive position. However, future opportunity is low. **Selling Effort Strategy** Accounts should receive a moderately heavy level of selling effort that is sufficient to maintain current competitive position. **Exemplary Sales Call Strategy = 12 calls/yr**	**Segment Four** **Level of Attractiveness** Accounts are very unattractive. They offer low opportunity and the seller has weak competitive position. **Selling Effort Strategy** Accounts should receive minimal personal selling effort. Alternatives such as telemarketing, direct mail, and Internet, should be explored. **Exemplary Sales Call Strategy = 6 calls/yr**

Stage Three: Development and Implementation of Strategies and Plans

 1.2 Conduct sales planning

Stage One provides the salesperson with the guidelines of what is important and the goals to be accomplished at the levels of individual sales calls, accounts, and the overall territory. Stage Two identifies and establishes the priority and potential of each account in the territory, along with the relative location of each account. Top salespeople do not stop there! They use this information to develop strategies and plans that will guide them toward achieving their goals by applying their available resources in a deliberate and organized fashion that effectively cultivates and harvests the potential sales available in the territory.

sales planning The process of scheduling activities that can be used as a map for achieving objectives.

Establishing and Implementing Selling Tasks and Activity Plans

 1.2 Conduct sales planning

When properly executed, **sales planning** results in a schedule of activities that can be used as a map for achieving objectives. First, start with the big picture—a long-term plan spanning the next 6 to 12 months. This big picture highlights commitments and deadlines and facilitates setting up the activities required to meet those commitments and deadlines. In turn, the longer-range plans provide the basis for shorter time frame plans and selling activities. The salesperson planning program at

Federal Metal Products (FMP) offers a good overview and prototype of effective salesperson planning.

FMP, a middle market supplier of metal production components, trains its salespeople to prepare and submit annual territory plans and budgets by November 15 each year. With that recurring deadline marked on their schedules, FMP salespeople work backward on their calendars to establish key checkpoints for their planning activities. This establishes a timeline to guide and assist salespeople in making the submission deadline.

If salespeople project that it will take four weeks to assemble and draft their territory sales plan, they work back four weeks from the November 15 date and establish October 15 as the date to begin assembling their data and building their plans. How long will it take to collect the needed data properly? Six weeks? If so, their schedule should reflect beginning that activity by September 1.

Sales plans should take into consideration scheduled meetings and training sessions, holidays, trade shows, and vacation time. Plans should also contain periodic checkpoints for assessing progress toward goals. A salesperson's objective of $750,000 in sales for the year equates to a goal averaging $62,500 in sales every month. Accordingly, the long-term master plan should include monthly checkpoints to compare the schedule versus actual performance data. Is performance on course, ahead, or lagging behind? If not on schedule, the corresponding and more detailed weekly plans should be revised to reflect salespeople's strategies for getting back on course.

Salespeople at FMP develop weekly plans from their longer-term annual plan. These shorter term plans detail the selling-related activities to be accomplished that week. To create a weekly plan, first identify the priorities that must be accomplished to stay on schedule. Then, for each of these priorities, detail the associated activities and schedule the time that it will take for completion. What areas of the territory will you focus on? What accounts will be called on, and what is the objective for each call? What are the best times to call for appointments? Are there account preferences as to what days and

An effective plan works like a map, showing the way from where you are to where you want to go—your objective.

times they work with salespeople? How much time must be allowed for travel, waiting, and working with each account? What products will be featured? What information and materials will be needed?

In turn, the priorities and activities identified in the weekly plan should become the points of focus for the daily plan. Days that end on a successful note begin with a thorough and written schedule detailing tasks and priorities for that day and the activities that must be carried out to achieve them.

The optimum schedule emphasizes tasks and activities that will make the greatest sales impact—working with customers. As illustrated by the FMP's "Daily Sales Plan Worksheet" shown in Exhibit 10.6, daily plans should detail the amount of time projected for each scheduled task and activity. To maximize the effectiveness of daily sales plans, salespeople should adhere to two guiding principles.

- *Do them, and do them in writing.* Written plans are better developed and provide more motivation and commitment for salespeople to carry them through to completion. Furthermore, written plans help to ensure that priority items do not fall through the cracks because something was forgotten.

- *Keep it current and flexible.* Make a new daily plan every day. Try as we might, things do not always go as planned. Consequently, changes may be needed, and uncompleted priorities or activities from one day may have to be carried over to the next.

Exhibit 10.6

Example of a Typical Daily Sales Plan Worksheet

Federal Metal Products
Daily Sales Plan Worksheet
Salesperson: Shiv Manchanda   **Day:** Friday   **Date:** 8/29

Time	Task or Priority	Activity	People Involved	Time Needed	Goal/ Anticipated Results	Notes and Comments
8:30 A.M.	Set appointments	Phone calls	Jill Attaway Digital Systems	10 min	Appointment for next week	Requested that I come by
	"	"	Bart Waits Enterprise One	10 min	"	
	"	"	Kerri Williams Flo-Forms	10 min	"	Will be placing order in 3 weeks
9:00 A.M.	"	"	Marilyn Henry InQuisLogic	10 min	Clarify service problem	Send info to engineering
10:30 A.M.	Demonstrate new bearing line	Sales call	Mike Humphreys ICOM	60 min	Info gathering	Currently buying from Gem Rollers
12 NOON	Get order commitment	Sales call— Lunch	Jack Kessler MDQG	120 min	$12,000 order	Gem submitted proposal 8/20
3:00 P.M.	Take sample of proposed line	Sales call	Aimee Williams MOCO, Inc	60 min	$15,200 order	Ready to buy, wants to see pdct. sample
4:30 P.M.	Check on delivery	Service call	Ron Meier Web Resources	50 min	Delight the customer	First time to buy from us!
6:00 P.M.	Complete paperwork	Submit call reports		45 min		
7:00 P.M.	Prepare daily schedule	Planning		45 min		

LO 4 | ESTABLISHING TERRITORY ROUTING PLANS

 CPSA   **1.2 Conduct sales planning**

Territory routing plans incorporate information developed in the territory analysis and account classification stage to minimize the encroachment of unproductive travel time on time that could be better spent working with customers. Good routing plans minimize the backtracking and crisscrossing that would otherwise occur and allow the salesperson to use time more efficiently.

Knowing how many calls can be made each day, the required call frequency for each account classification, and the relative geographic location of and distance between accounts, a salesperson can plot different routing strategies and decide on the optimal plan. Many sales professionals continue to use the traditional coloured map pins and felt-tip markers on a wall map.

FIG. 10.2 STRAIGHT-LINE ROUTE PATTERN

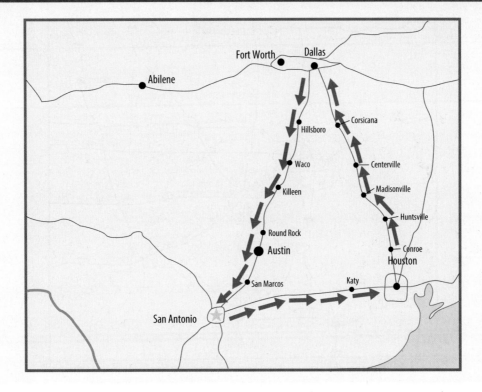

Straight-line territory routes make calls across the territory in one direction and then change direction to work back to the starting point.

However, a variety of easy-to-use and affordable computer and mobile device applications that plot optimal routing plans are available and are growing in popularity. Optimized routing plans correspond to one of five common patterns: straight line, cloverleaf, circular, leapfrog, and major city.

STRAIGHT-LINE ROUTING PLANS With a **straight-line routing plan**, salespeople start from their offices and make calls in one direction until they reach the end of the territory. As illustrated in Figure 10.2, at that point they change direction and continue to make calls on a straight line following the new vector. This continues until the salesperson returns to the office location. The straight-line pattern works best when accounts are located in clusters that are some distance from one another.

CLOVERLEAF ROUTING PLANS The **cloverleaf routing plan** pattern is best used when accounts are concentrated in different parts of the territory. On each trip, the salesperson works a different part of the territory and travels in a circular loop back to the starting point. An example of the cloverleaf routing plan is depicted in Figure 10.3. Each loop could

take a day, a week, or longer to complete. A new loop is covered on each trip until the entire territory has been covered.

CIRCULAR ROUTING PLANS **Circular routing plans** begin at the office and move in an expanding pattern of concentric circles that spiral across the territory. Figure 10.4 traces an exemplary circular routing plan working from an office in Dallas. This method works best when accounts are evenly dispersed throughout the territory.

LEAPFROG ROUTING PLANS The **leapfrog routing plan** is best applied when the territory is large and accounts

straight-line routing plan
A territory routing plan in which salespeople start from their offices and make calls in one direction until they reach the end of the territory.

cloverleaf routing plan
A territory routing plan in which the salesperson works a different part of the territory and travels in a circular loop back to the starting point.

circular routing plan A territory routing plan in which the salesperson begins at the office and moves in an expanding pattern of concentric circles that spiral across the territory.

leapfrog routing plan A territory routing plan in which, beginning in one cluster, the salesperson works each of the accounts at that location and then jumps to the next cluster.

FIG. 10.3 CLOVERLEAF ROUTE PATTERN

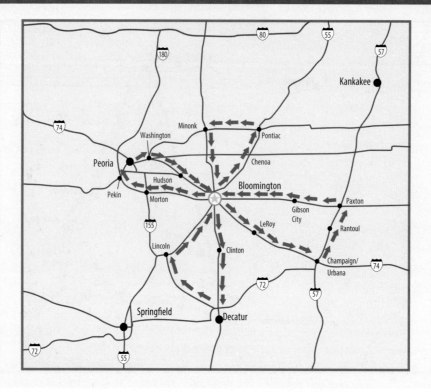

Cloverleaf territory routes work different parts of the territory in a series of circular loops.

FIG. 10.4 CIRCULAR ROUTE PATTERN

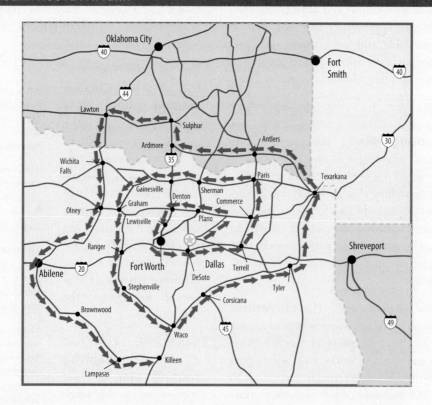

Circular territory routes cover the territory in a series of concentric circles spiraling across the territory.

FIG. 10.5 | LEAPFROG ROUTE PATTERN

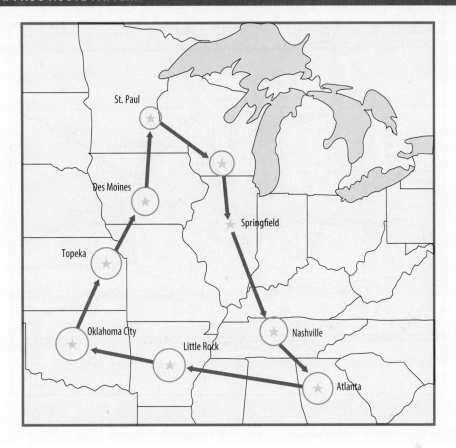

Cloverleaf territory routes work different parts of the territory in a series of circular loops.

are clustered into several widely dispersed groups. Beginning in one cluster, the salesperson works each of the accounts at that location and then jumps to the next cluster. As shown in Figure 10.5, this continues until the last cluster has been worked and the salesperson jumps back to the office or home. When the distance between clusters is great, the salesperson will typically make the jumps by flying.

MAJOR CITY ROUTING PLANS When the territory is composed of a major metropolitan area, the territory is split into a series of geometric shapes reflecting each one's concentration and pattern of accounts. Figure 10.6 depicts a typical **major city routing plan**. Downtown areas are typically highly concentrated with locations controlled by a grid of city blocks and streets. Consequently, the downtown segment is typically a small square or rectangular area allowing accounts to be worked in a straight-line fashion street by street. Outlying areas are placed in evenly balanced triangles or pie-shaped quadrants, with one quadrant being covered at a time in either a straight-line or cloverleaf pattern.

LO 5 | STAGE FOUR: TAPPING TECHNOLOGY AND AUTOMATION

 CPSA   7.1 Leverage sales technology

Selling technology and automation tools are here to stay and are being transformed from neat toys to necessary tools. Properly applied, selling technology spurs and creates creativity and innovation, streamlines all aspects of the selling process, generates new and improved selling opportunities, facilitates cross-functional teaming and intraorganizational communication, and enhances communication and follow-up with

major city routing plan
A territory routing plan used when the territory is composed of a major metropolitan area and the territory is split into a series of geometric shapes reflecting each one's concentration and pattern of accounts.

selling technology and automation Tools that streamline the selling process, generate improved selling opportunities, facilitate cross-functional teaming and intraorganizational communication, and enhance communication and follow-up with customers.

FIG. 10.6 MAJOR CITY ROUTE PATTERN

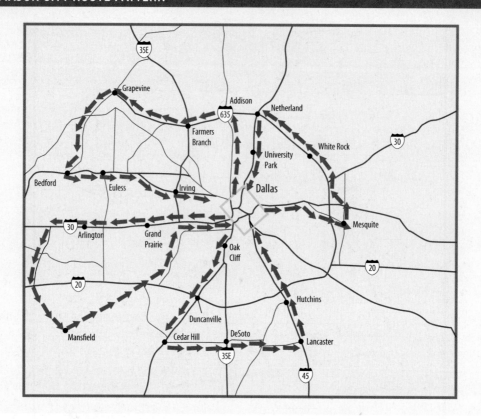

Major city territory routing patterns work downtown on a basis of street grids and work outlying areas by using a cloverleaf or straight-line pattern.

customers. In summary, tapping the proper selling technologies and salesforce automation tools allows salespeople to expand their available resources for enhanced selling performance and outcomes. Kirsten Halverson, Customer Development Associate for Kimberly-Clark, discusses the importance of using data analysis and visualization technologies in order to leverage the multiple sources of big data to better understand the customer and competitive landscape in Technology in Sales: Using Data Analytics to Drive Business.

Salespeople, sales managers, and customers are unanimous in their agreement that the best salespeople are those who stay up with changes and developments in technologies with selling applications. With a multitude of rapidly changing and evolving technology choices, salespeople not only must master the technology itself but also must understand when and where it can be applied most effectively. Exemplary selling technologies being used by today's salespeople include the following tools.

Mobile Sales Technologies

At the centre of virtually every selling technology is some form of mobile computing technology. Choices include desktops, notebooks, laptops, tablets, and smartphones. With the ever-expanding availability of broadband and wireless connectivity, today's salesperson is always in touch with customers, with sales support, and with sales data and information. For immediate immersion into the high-tech side of selling, simply walk through the waiting areas of any major airport. Salespeople can be seen entering customer orders, generating reports, and submitting proposals by using standard word-processing packages and even customized online electronic forms. Others are analyzing customer accounts by using spreadsheet applications and query-based business intelligence programs that access and analyze a database according to the questions the user wishes to have answered. Several will be observed reviewing and updating customer files by using one of the many mobile and highly capable

Technology in Sales

Using Data Analytics to Drive Business

Kirsten Halverson graduated from Illinois State University in May 2016 and is a Customer Development Associate for Kimberly-Clark. Based in Boston, Kirsten's key areas of involvement are in category analytics and customer relationship management within the adult and feminine care brands. Kirsten talks about how what she learned in her sales classes provided her a head start in earning customer trust and building customer relationships.

"As Customer Development Associate, I focus on building business with our existing accounts through securing new and additional distribution for product innovations and extensions, developing and tracking yearly account-based promotional plans, and working with shopper loyalty and consumption data. The heart of our trust-based selling model is a focus on data analytics to better understand the customer landscape and provide valuable insight for our customers in terms of shopper trends and sales opportunities anchored with solid ROI outcomes for the customer.

"Working with customers, our data analytics are primarily based on Excel spreadsheets and Tableau visualization charts and dashboards. These programs are mobile and tablet-based, which facilitates using them in field-based customer presentations. They are also easy to use and allow combining data from multiple sources—such as internal account performance data as well as commercial data vendors such as Nielsen and RSI providing sales trends, shopper loyalty information, and consumption reports. It is all about utilizing data to point out shopper needs and opportunities and clearly linking them to our innovative product solutions to enable our customers to grow their businesses and revenues.

"Our number one goal is to become the thought-leader and indispensable partner for our customers. We achieve that through the use of data analytics to discover and illustrate areas of opportunity that result in win–win outcomes. My sales classes emphasized the consultative selling approach and how to utilize actual data in the sales call to build trust by bringing new ideas and illustrating opportunities for the customer to grow their revenues. Those learning experiences were well aligned with the sales model here at Kimberly-Clark and equipped me to move up the learning curve faster."

contact management/customer relationship management (CRM) software applications. These user-friendly programs provide salespeople with a convenient option to catalogue, search, and access comprehensive information regarding individual customers. Looking closer, numerous salespeople will be revising and polishing graphics and presentations with software such as Power-Point, Tableau, Keynote, Prezi, Flash, and Open Office Impress. Still others will be checking and responding to e-mail, submitting electronic reports, accessing online territory route maps, and using scheduling programs to set up the next day's call plans.

Salesperson Customer Relationship Management (CRM)

Effective customer relationships generate customer loyalty and the revenue increases critical for sustained performance. Toward meeting this challenge, companies of all sizes are deploying customer relationship management (CRM) applications and strategies that integrate multiple communication and customer contact channels—including the Web, e-mail, call centres, and social media applications in order to maximize customer interactions. However, detailed customer information is of little use if a salesperson cannot access it when they need it—such as during a sales call in a customer's office. Sales professionals often work outside the office and need up-to-date information while in the field. Being able to access and offer the right information to customers at the right point in the sales cycle enables salespeople to increase sales dramatically while simultaneously increasing customer satisfaction and loyalty. **Mobile salesperson CRM solutions**, such as Salesforce.com, Microsoft Dynamics, SAP,

mobile salesperson CRM solutions Wireless broadband applications that enable users to view, create, and modify data on any Internet-capable devices, such as smartphones, netbooks, and laptops.

and Saleslogix, are the key to accessing this information from the field and provide remote access to data, such as contacts, customer information, leads, reports, price lists, inventory levels, and opportunity forecasting. Mobile CRM applications use wireless broadband access to enable users instantly to view, create, and modify data on any Internet-capable device, such as smartphones, tablets and pads, netbooks and laptops. This handheld access to valuable account information allows a salesperson to tap into the same sales, marketing, and customer service data they have access to in the office—without having to leave the field. Mobile CRM is rapidly becoming a critical requirement for effectively competing in today's fast-paced selling environment and increasing customer expectations in terms of customized levels of service.

Deal Analytics

Deal analytics is the descriptive name given to a new set of "smart" tools in the area of salesforce automation that are proving especially useful for salespeople. These analytical tools use mobile CRM systems to access and analyze data on past customer behaviour, cross-selling opportunities, and demographics to identify areas of opportunity and high interest to a customer. Salespeople also use deal analytics tools to access and compare competitive information, such as pricing and bundled offers, which can result in more effective proposals and negotiations.

The Internet, Intranets, and Extranets

Accessing the Internet instantly networks a salesperson with the world: customers, information sources, other salespeople, sales management, and others. More importantly, the Internet puts the salesperson into contact with their customer-community and support networks from anywhere in the world, 24 hours a day, seven days a week. Going beyond the convenience of e-mail, many sales organizations are setting up intranets and extranets—secure and proprietary organizational Web sites that are protected by passwords and security authorizations. Intranets are networks within the organization that use the Internet or commercial channels to provide direct links between company units and individuals. Extranets are a special form of intranet that is still for proprietary and restricted use but links to specific suppliers and customers to allow them controlled and secure access to the organization's network to facilitate communication and exchange.

These secure Web sites become instant organizational intranets used for communication, training, videoconferencing, Web-conferencing, and secure data interchange. Using such Web-enabled intranets, Diamond Equipment Corporation's salespeople can link to the latest product information and spec sheets, obtain updated inventory and production numbers, download company information, and print customized proposals for customer presentations from anywhere in the world. CDW provides each of their major accounts with a customized extranet that gives the customer access to CDW on a 24-hour-a-day, seven-day-a-week basis. Buyers can track orders online, download product and technical specifications, access customer support technicians, check prices and availability of products, and even place orders for next-day delivery. Rather than spending time travelling to customers' offices, Windy City Wire's salespeople deliver their sales presentations by combining teleconferences and Web presentations using WebEx. The use of Internet- and intranet-based technologies shortens the sales cycle by allowing sales meetings and presentations to be created and delivered in less time than traditional face-to-face processes would take. If a salesperson can save just 10 minutes a day by using Web-based presentation libraries and online product and pricing information, they will gain an additional week's worth of productivity over the course of a year. However, as illustrated by the situation described in An Ethical Dilemma, the adoption and roll-out of advanced technologies often presents some challenges along the way.

High-Tech Sales Support Offices

Organizations that have salesforces widely dispersed geographically or travelling across multiple regions of the nation or world have found it advantageous to establish **high-tech sales support offices** at multiple locations. Both resident and nonresident salespeople use these offices to access a wider range of selling technology than could be easily carried on a tablet or laptop computer. These offices also provide points of access to the various networks, intranets, and extranets the organization maintains. IBM maintains such high-tech offices as these at its installations around the world. An IBM

deal analytics "Smart" salesforce automation tools that analyze data on past customer behaviour, cross-selling opportunities, and demographics to identify areas of opportunity and high customer interest.

high-tech sales support offices Offices set up at multiple locations where salespeople can access a wider range of selling technology than could be easily carried on a notebook or laptop computer.

An Ethical Dilemma

 CPSA   8.1 Act with integrity

Janice is an account manager for Timaru Solutions and is responsible for selling the company's hardware and application-based technology solutions throughout the Greater Toronto Area. Embracing the collaborative selling approach, Timaru utilizes an extensive and highly interactive Internet-based extranet system to stay close to its customers and ahead of the competition. Timaru's extranet system allows customers to access product, service, and account information 24/7. Because the extranet allows customers to access proprietary information including order status, product availability, pricing, and even order entry and transactions, access is controlled through a secure password authentication process. Access is granted only to well-established, major customers. Janice has just learned that a technology buyer at Advanced Energy Partners, one of Janice's key accounts, has shared their extranet access codes with the salesperson for Timaru's main competitor. Apparently the competitor wanted access to Timaru's pricing structure so they could undercut the prices and acquire some of Timaru's major customers.

What should Janice do?

(a) Inform her sales manager so that Timaru can change their pricing as a result of the breach in security.

(b) Deactivate the Advanced Energy Partners codes for accessing Timaru's extranet so the competitor can no longer access the information.

(c) Provide the Advanced Energy Partners purchasing department with new access codes, remind them that the codes are proprietary, and use the breach of trust as an opportunity to enhance the Timaru–Advanced Energy Partners relationship.

---

representative in Montreal might find himself working as part of a team on a project in Saint John. While in Saint John, the representative has access to the same technology and support as was available in Montreal. Full access is available to company networks, customer accounts, communication links, and software applications. Consequently, convenience and productive time are maximized for the benefit of all parties.

Stage Five: Assessment of Performance and Goal Attainment

 CPSA   1.2 Conduct sales planning

A critical, and often overlooked, stage in the process of self-leadership is the periodic assessment of progress. Although certainly important, this stage should involve more than a simple check at the end of the period to determine whether goals were achieved. Assessment checkpoints should be built into plans at progressive points in time to encourage and facilitate the evaluation of a salesperson's progress. These frequent comparisons of actual performance with periodic checkpoints allow time to consider revisions or modifications before it is too late to make a difference. In addition to assessing progress, evaluation should also consider what is working well and what could be improved. This knowledge and understanding can be used to guide modifications in the various plans, tasks, and activities that populate the different stages of self-leadership to further enhance future success and performance.

Periodic performance assessments should be built into plans so as to encourage evaluation of progress and identify areas of improvement.

LO 6 | INCREASING CUSTOMER VALUE THROUGH TEAMWORK

CPSA   **8.3 Work as part of a team**

Excellent customer service is taking on a key role in competitive business strategy, and as customer expectations and needs continue to grow in complexity, selling organizations are finding that they can no longer depend solely on salespeople as the exclusive arbiter of customer satisfaction. Teamwork, both inside the organization and with customers, is being emphasized as the key to customer focus and sales performance.

Internal Partnerships and Teams

The practices and experiences of top-ranked selling organizations, as well as considerable sales research, support the emphasis on teamwork as a key to long-term selling success. The results from three studies of more than 200 companies that employ some 25,000 salespeople supported the belief that cooperating as a team player was critical for success in selling.[7] Similar results have been found in other studies that examine what business-to-business buyers expect from suppliers. In two studies incorporating 6,708 customer evaluations of vendor performance and customer satisfaction in the financial services industry, the suppliers' performance in building internal and external partnerships was found to be the key driver of customer satisfaction.[8]

Building **external relationships** is the focal point of contemporary selling techniques and reflects the ongoing paradigm shift in today's salesforces. This emphasis on building *external* customer relationships could overshadow the critical role of building *internal*, close-working relationships with other individuals in their own company. The importance of these **internal relationships** would seem to be logical, as a salesperson's success depends on the degree of support they receive from others in the various functional areas of the organization. Ultimately, the salesperson owns the responsibility for customer relationships, but the strength of those customer relationships depends on the joint efforts and resources contributed by multiple individuals across the selling organization.

Account managers at Contour Plastics Corporation have full responsibility for bringing together individuals from functional departments across the organization to work as a sales team dedicated to selling and providing presale and post-sale services to a specific account. As needed, team members will incorporate research chemists, application specialists, production engineers, and logistics specialists. Coordinated by the salesperson, each team member contributes their special expertise toward maximizing the understanding of the customer's situation and needs, and then working together to create a unique, value-added solution that few, if any, competitors can equal.

Teamwork results in a synergy that produces greater outcomes and results for all parties than would be possible with multiple individuals acting independently. Consequently, it is important that salespeople also develop the ability to sell internally as they represent their customers to the selling organization and give recognition to the important role others play in winning, keeping, and growing customer accounts.

James Champy, chairman of consulting for Perot Systems, notes that customers are expecting and receiving better service and product options than ever, and he characterizes the role of the salesperson as having been transformed to that of a trusted adviser.[9]

In this adviser role, the salesperson works with customers to develop a mutual understanding of the customer's situation, needs, possibilities, and expectations. On the basis of this information, the salesperson assembles a team of individuals, experts from across the selling organization, who work together to create a product response that will deliver more unique customer value than the competitors' offerings. In delivering this unique and added value for customers, salespeople often find themselves working with other individuals in sales, marketing, design and manufacturing, administrative support, shipping, and customer service.

Sales Partnerships

Within the sales department, salespeople often team with other salespeople to gain the strengths and expertise required for a specific selling situation or customer. Partnerships with sales managers and other sales executives are also important in winning support for developing innovative responses to customer needs. XL Capital is a global leader in alternative risk transfer products, financial risk management, and surplus lines of commercial property and casualty insurance. Selling to Fortune 500 and Fortune 1000 customers, XL Capital's salespeople (customer business unit managers)

external relationships
Relationships salespeople build with customers outside the organization and working environment.

internal relationships
Relationships salespeople have with other individuals in their own company.

specialize along customer and industry lines. It is common for XL's salespeople to work together in teams to bring together the experience and expertise required to work with customers whose businesses span a large number of different industries.

Marketing Partnerships

Teaming with individuals in the marketing department is critical for salespeople in generating integrated solutions for customers over the long term. Marketing is responsible for developing organizational marketing strategies that serve as guidelines for the salesforce. Using information gathered in the field by the salesforce, marketing also assists in the generation of new market offerings in response to changing customer needs and requests. Marketing can also be a valuable partner for salespeople in accessing information and developing sales proposals.

At Pocahontas Foods, a top-10 institutional food broker with nationwide operations, account managers regularly work with members of the marketing department to communicate changes in customer needs and activities of competitors. This collaborative partnership allows Pocahontas to continue bringing innovative product offerings to the marketplace that are designed around the inputs from their salespeople.

Design and Manufacturing Partnerships

Salespeople often find themselves selling ideas for product designs and changes in manufacturing schedules to meet the needs of customers. When individuals from design, manufacturing, and sales work as a team, performance and delivery commitments are more likely to be met and customer satisfaction further enhanced. Wallace works to maintain its industry leadership in business forms and systems by aggressively nurturing a companywide culture emphasizing customer orientation and support. As part of their training, salespeople actually work in production facilities to understand what has to be done to meet product design and delivery requirements that the salespeople might commit to in the field. By-products of this cross-training come about in the form of one-to-one personal relationships between salespeople and production staff. In the case of complex

> Salesperson effectiveness in building internal and external partnerships is a key driver of customer satisfaction.

customer needs or special delivery needs, these relationships become invaluable.

Administrative Support Partnerships

Salespeople work with others from administrative support functions, such as management, finance and credit, billing, and information systems. Like sales, each of these functional units has certain goals and objectives that translate to policies and procedures that govern their own activities and affect operations throughout the organization—including sales. Customer needs are served best when salespeople have worked to establish effective relationships within these units and all parties work together for the mutual good of the organization and customer. Jim Gavic, account manager for Cross Canada Trucking, manages a territory stretching from the industrial sector of Calgary east to Halifax. Gavic credits his close relationships with individuals in the company's finance and credit department for making 20 percent of his annual sales. By working together, they were able to establish special billing terms for several of his larger accounts. If finance and credit had simply enforced Cross Canada's standard terms, these customers would have been lost to a competitor with more flexible credit policies.

Shipping and Transportation Partnerships

Salespeople periodically find themselves facing an urgent customer need that requires special handling of an order. Perhaps it is an expedited shipment for immediate delivery or the processing and shipping of an interim order of less than economical size. Whatever the need, it will affect other shipments getting out on time and could even increase the department's operating costs. Curtis James, territory manager for General Electric Appliances, found sales going better than usual at a new store opening in Winnipeg. To keep the customer from being caught short, he hand-carried a fill-in order to the GE district office, walked it through credit approval, hand-delivered the shipping order to the warehouse, and helped load the truck. Teamwork enabled Curtis to accomplish in less than a day what normally would have taken 8 to 10 days. It takes a team effort to work through exceptions such as these, and it is common to find the salesperson actually helping to make it happen by pulling orders, packing boxes, and even helping to load the truck.

Customer Service Partnerships

Teamwork between sales and customer service can create a synergy that has a broad-based impact that can translate to higher customer satisfaction, higher rates of customer retention, and increased sales performance. On the one hand, customer service personnel, such as call centre operators and service technicians, often have more extensive contact with customers than the account representatives. As such, they can serve as an early warning system for salespeople and provide valuable information regarding customer complaints, problems, developing needs, and changes that they encounter through customer contacts. As a salesperson for Southwestern School Supply, Cap Williams regularly checks in and visits with the company's customer service personnel to keep abreast of contacts that they might have with any of his customers. The information he receives allows him to get ahead of any possible customer problems, provide an uncanny level of after-sale support that continues to mystify upper management, and helps secure his consistent receipt of Top Salesperson of the Year Award year after year. When salespeople such as Williams act on the information provided by customer service to advance customer relationships and increase sales, customer service personnel will also be further inclined to work together to benefit the team. On the other hand, salespeople often assist customer service personnel by working directly with customers to address problems before they become complaints and provide instruction and training to assist customers in using the products sold.

LO 7 | BUILDING TEAMWORK SKILLS

CPSA | 8.3 Work as part of a team

Effective teams do not form by default. Nor can a team be effective in producing synergistic benefits solely because it is called a team. Like customer relationships, internal relationships are built on reciprocal trust. The salesperson who arbitrarily and repeatedly

teamwork skills Skills salespeople must learn to build internal partnerships that translate into increased sales and organizational performance.

asks for special production runs, extensions to customers' lines of credit, expedited shipments, or special attention from customer service is simply asking for quick fixes. These quick fixes serve the objectives of the customer and salesperson but often work against the objectives of the functional unit and the organization as a whole.

Synergistic teamwork requires a commitment on the part of all parties to look for and work for win-win solutions. However, in the rush to take care of a customer, it is all too easy for salespeople to fall into a win-lose orientation. It is not that they want anyone to lose, but rather that they get what they want. This win orientation is most common in everyday negotiation—in which people think and act in terms of accomplishing their own goals and leave it to others to attain theirs. As illustrated in Figure 10.7, optimum solutions develop from a team orientation based on the philosophy of win-win alternatives.[10] In turn, this can happen only when there are high levels of mutual trust and communication: "Not your way, not my way, but a better way."

In his bestselling book on personal development, Stephen Covey offers six keys to developing synergistic relationships and teams.[11] These are the six **teamwork skills** that salespeople must learn and sincerely apply in their process of building internal partnerships that translate to increased sales and organizational performance.

- *Understanding the Other Individuals*—Fully understanding and considering the other individuals in the partnership is necessary to know what is important to them. What is important to them must also be important to the salesperson if the partnership is to grow and be effective. This means that salespeople must take time to learn the objectives of other functional areas and consider how those needs and requests might affect the salesperson's goals and objectives.

- *Attending to the Little Things*—The little kindnesses and courtesies are often small in size and great in importance. In building relationships, the little things are the big things. Properly attended to and nurtured, they enhance the interrelationships. At the same time, if they are neglected or misused, they can destroy the relationship very quickly.

- *Keeping Commitments*—We all build our hopes and plans around the promises and commitments of others. When a commitment is not kept, disappointment and problems result. As a result, credibility and trust suffer major damage that is always difficult, and often impossible, to repair. However, consistency in keeping commitments builds and solidifies trust-based relationships.

Every Business Sells

Greg Owen is the founder and chief experience creator at WeGo Tour Experiences, a travel tour operator. WeGo Tour Experiences sells personalized and customized group travel and learning experiences where customers explore, experience, and create a story to share. Greg sells across North America, with expansion to Europe and Southeast Asia on the horizon. He has an over 20-year-long sales career, and has worked for five years at WeGo Tour Experiences.

As a salesperson, how do you provide value to your customers?

By listening to what customers are looking for in a travel experience, by providing them with our advice and knowledge to create an excellent experience for them, and by focusing on executing the experience very well.

As a salesperson, how do you provide value to your organization?

By being curious and continually learning about possible travel experiences we can offer to our customers, by talking with our customers so that we can understand their needs, and by working with our team to push for excellence in delivering for our customers.

What is your greatest challenge you face today as a salesperson?

Getting in front of possible customers and demonstrating we can meet their needs. Our products are experiences and customers have lots of choices. The sales lead time can be 6 to 24 months from planning to delivery.

How do you try to overcome this challenge?

We put the customer first, designing and delivering experiences that we ourselves want to take. We are always building networks, using word of mouth, face-to-face meetings and events, and selective direct lead generation and advertising including social media to raise awareness of our experiences and our expertise. We are very focused on delivering an excellent customer experience. It is high-touch.

What advice do you have for someone starting out in sales?

Listen to the customers. Be personable, persistent, and seek to understand what they want and need. Listening is the number one skill; listen more than you talk. Then make sure you know your products. Focus on building the relationship and trust. Follow up what you say you will do. Be creative, always starting with a "yes" when looking at opportunities, and be willing to stretch. And sometimes it is important to say "no, we are not the right people for the job." Above all, to quote Steve Jobs: "Customers don't measure you on how hard you tried. They measure you on what you deliver." We live by that.

- *Clarifying Expectations*—The root cause of most relational difficulties can be found in ambiguous expectations regarding roles and goals—exactly where are we going and who is responsible for what? Investing the time up front to clarify expectations regarding goals and roles can save even more time down the road when misunderstandings become compounded and turn into goal conflicts and breakdowns in communication.

- *Showing Personal Integrity*—Demonstrating personal integrity generates trust, whereas a lack of integrity can quickly undermine the best of teamwork orientations. People can seek to understand others, carry through on the little things, keep commitments, and clarify expectations, but still fail to build trust by being inwardly duplicitous and pursuing a personal agenda. Be honest, open, and treat everyone by the same set of principles.

- *Apologizing Sincerely When a Mistake Is Made*—It is one thing to make a mistake. It is another thing not to admit it. People forgive mistakes. What is harder to forgive are the ill intentions and motives justifying any attempt to cover up. "If you are going to bow, bow low." The apology must be perceived as sincere and not simply as automated lip-service response.

FIG. 10.7 RELATIONSHIP OF OPTIMIZED SOLUTIONS, TRUST, AND COOPERATION

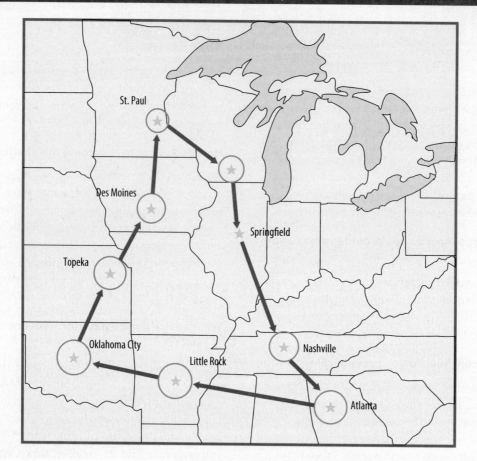

Optimum buyer–seller solutions result from a team orientation and require high levels of mutual trust and mutual cooperation. (Excerpt from The 7 Habits of Highly Effective People © 2004 Stephen R. Covey. The Time Management Matrix phrase and model are trademarks of Franklin Covey Co., http://www.franklincovey.com. Used with permission. All rights reserved.)

STUDY TOOLS

At the back of the textbook, use tear-out cards to review key chapter information. Visit cengage.ca to purchase digital tools to help you succeed.

CENGAGE | MINDTAP

Personal Computer

☐ Gain unique perspectives on key concepts through a variety of videos and cases

☐ Increase your comprehension with online quizzes

☐ Study with existing flashcards and make your own

Mobile

☐ Stay focused and ready to study whenever it's convenient for you!

☐ Access a full, interactive ebook: online or offline

☐ Study tools that empower anytime, anywhere learning and 24/7 course access

CHAPTER CASE 10

UNIVERSAL CONTROL CORP.

BACKGROUND

Universal Control Corp. is a leading supplier for process control systems and equipment used in a wide variety of production and distribution applications. You have taken a sales representative job with Universal and, having just completed training, been given a territory of your own. Your district manager has provided you with a list of accounts as well as several boxes of notes and files that had been assembled and used by your predecessor. These are the accounts currently buying your products. You are expected to build these accounts and add new accounts to the list as you increase your territory's sales performance. You have summarized the account information into the summary set of account profiles, which is provided following the Questions.

QUESTIONS

1. Develop a portfolio classification of accounts and assess the allocation of sales calls your predecessor made over the past year.

2. What problems do you find with the previous allocation of calls on these accounts?

3. Based on your account classification analysis, suggest a new sales call allocation strategy that would make better use of your time in the territory.

ROLE PLAY

Situation: Read the case.

Characters: Zack Hanna, salesperson for Universal Control Corp.; Gage Waits, district sales manager and Hanna's immediate supervisor

Scene:

Location—Gage Waits's office at Universal Control Corp.

Action—Zack has just been assigned this territory and has completed an analysis of sales and customer files to profile the individual accounts and sales call allocation strategies used by the previous salesperson in the territory. Based on this information, Hanna has developed information responding to each of the three questions following the Universal Control Corp. case materials. This information includes a new sales call

allocation strategy. Hanna is meeting with his sales manager to explain his new sales call allocation plan.

As Hanna, answer the three questions previously listed. Using this information, role-play your interaction with your sales manager, Gage Waits, as you discuss and explain (1) your analysis of the previous salesperson's sales call allocation and (2) your new plans and how they will increase the effectiveness and efficiency of your selling efforts in this territory.

Account Name	Account Opportunity	Competitive Position	Annual Number of Sales Calls Last Year
Mueller Distribution	High	Low	30
Tri-State Specialties	Low	High	20
Birkey Paper Co.	Low	High	26
Normal Supply	Low	Low	12
Darnell Aggregate Products	Low	High	21
Reinhart Chemicals	High	High	26
ACCO Manufacturing	Low	High	23
Tri-State Manufacturing	High	Low	28
Ideal Engineering	Low	Low	11
Terracon	High	High	25
Lowry Foods	High	Low	26
SCS Industrial	High	High	27
Lowell Services	Low	High	18
Bowles and Sons	Low	High	21
Canada Foundry	High	Low	22
Hewitt & Associates	Low	Low	16
Bright Metals Inc.	High	High	22
Decatur Extrusions	Low	Low	14
King Chemicals	Low	High	22
Bear's Steel Corp.	Low	High	20
Hoffman Pharmaceuticals	High	Low	20
Barlow & Clark Systems	Low	High	18

After completing the role play, address the following questions:

1. How might Hanna's sales allocation plan be different if he had used single-factor analysis (ABC analysis) instead of portfolio analysis?

2. Develop a sales call allocation plan using single-factor analysis. Compare the results of Hanna's portfolio analysis with the results of your single-factor analysis. Where and how are they different?

3. How might those differences translate to increased selling effectiveness and efficiency?

INTEGRATIVE CASE 10

ATTITUDE ADJUSTMENT

BACKGROUND

Fleet Owner is a Web site that serves executives in commercial trucking. In 2017, they published an article titled "Good Sales Is a Matter of Knowledge, Skills and Attitude," where they distinguished among the three the qualities of a good salesperson. To be a competent salesperson, you need the following:

- "Knowledge: What to do or information, understanding or skills gained from experience or education.

- Skills: How to do it or the ability to do something that comes from training, experience and practice.

- Attitude: Want to do it."[12]

According to this article, there are three components to competency: knowledge, skills, and attitude. First you need to understand the material (gain knowledge), then you need to be able to show that understanding (skills), and you must have the right mindset in order to achieve competency (attitude).[13]

You are already familiar with the competencies created by the CPSA, and competencies are being used extensively in education around the world by organizations like the Organisation for Economic Co-operation and Development (OECD). The concept has become part of the DNA of the organization, as it strives to help form the global citizenry of tomorrow.[14]

The sales competency laid out in the article above shows the importance of all three aspects, but it places a special emphasis on attitude. "Attitude is developed by major events that shape one's thinking and by discovering new facts. Attitude can be changed through increasing the use of positive language, and by being aware of negative 'habits of thought.'"[15]

These habits of thought often are developed by blindly adhering to the way things have always been done. And, as the article concludes, "During the hiring process, test for attitude and once you have hired someone reward behaviors that align with your sales goals."

CURRENT SITUATION

As you come to the end of your course, and are now a sales expert, you are tasked with creating a mini course outline of your own. This course outline should be based on the concept of competencies: knowledge, skills, and attitude. This chapter has provided plenty of knowledge and examples of the skills required to be a successful salesperson.

But where you will stand out with your mini course is the inclusion of attitude. The term "attitude" has been defined already in this case, and you can use that as the basis for your work; you can also research other definitions of "attitude."

The way you organize this mini course is up to you, but to create your course outline you should cover (at minimum) material from this chapter. Your time to go from student to teacher is now—be sure to set yourself some high standards so you can give yourself a much-deserved A+.

QUESTIONS

1. As a first part of your mini course, you decide to discuss a critical requirement for success in any career. This requirement involves doing things right and doing them well. What is this referred to as?

    a. self-leadership

    b. self-starter

    c. competency

    d. skills base

2. Which of the following is NOT a key teamwork skill addressed in this chapter?

    a. understanding other individuals

    b. attending to the little things

    c. writing out sales aspirations

    d. showing personal integrity

3. Of the five stages to self-leadership described in this chapter, you decide you will isolate the first stage and make it a separate lesson for your mini course. This stage is called:

    a. implementation plans

    b. setting goals and expectations

    c. territory analysis

    d. assessment and evaluation

10 CHAPTER ROLE PLAY

Adding Value: Self-Leadership and Teamwork: Payroll Pro

BACKGROUND

You are a senior-level account manager for Payroll Pro, an industry leader providing automated payroll processing and related record keeping for medium to large businesses having 15 or more employees. Your primary selling responsibilities centre on new account development and working with existing accounts to increase share of account by selling them expanded employment applications and services as their business needs evolve and grow. The day-to-day account management and servicing activities are handled by your dedicated Customer Solutions Team—service representatives who work closely with both you and with customers through the phone and Internet to provide the personal touch and frequent follow-up necessary to assure everything is working as expected and to enhance long-term relationships with customers.

Recent feedback from a number of key accounts has pointed out that the level of service provided by your Customer Solutions Team has become inconsistent and all too often falls below the level of service you have committed to and which your customers expect. As a result, several customers

have left and gone with competitive service providers. Rather than acquiring new accounts, you are spending much of your time working to patch over the service shortcomings and working to win back the accounts who have defected to the competition. Not only are you losing business, but your own reputation—as well as the reputation of the company—is beginning to suffer in the marketplace.

ROLE PLAY

In discussing these problems with your sales manager, it was decided that you would meet with your dedicated Customer Solutions Team in order to discuss and find a workable solution to the problems.

Role-play how you would approach and initiate a positive discussion with the members of the customer service team that would generate improved experiences and outcomes for your customers and Payroll Pro. Remember to employ Covey's six teamwork skills discussed in this chapter.

1

1. Sun Life Financial, "Q4'18 Results Fact Sheet," https://cdn.sunlife.com/static/Global/Investors/Financial%20results%20and%20reports/Quarterly%20reports/pa_e_Q418_Fact_Sheet.pdf, accessed February 25, 2020.

2. Sun Life Financial, "Who We Are," https://www.sunlife.ca/ca/About+us/Who+we+are?vgnLocale=en_CA, accessed February 25, 2020.

3. Sun Life Financial, "Canadian Group Annuity Sales Exceed $3 Billion for the First Time," https://www.sunlife.ca/Canada/DBSolutions/News+and+insights/Media/2018/Canadian+group+annuity+sales+exceed+3+billion+for+the+first+time?vgnLocale=en_CA, accessed February 25, 2020.

4. Andris Zoltners, P. K. Sinha, and Sally E. Lorimer, "How More Accessible Information Is Forcing B2B Sales to Adapt," from the *Harvard Business Review*, online at https://hbr.org, January 6, 2016; and Pete Caputa, "Top Salespeople Are More Likely to Use These Tools Than the Rest of You," from HubSpot's Sales Blog, online at https://blog.hubspot.com, June 15, 2016.

5. Jon M. Hawes, Anne K. Rich, and Scott Widmier, "Assessing the Development of the Sales Profession," *Journal of Personal Selling & Sales Management* 24 (Winter 2004): 27–38.

6. Thomas Wotruba, "The Evolution of Selling," *Journal of Personal Selling & Sales Management* (Summer 1991): 1–12; Jon M. Hawes, Anne K. Rich, and Scott Widmier, "Assessing the Development of the Sales Profession," *Journal of Personal Selling & Sales Management* 24 (Winter 2004): 27–38; synthesized from Eli Jones, Steven P. Brown, Andris A. Zoltners, and Barton A. Weitz, "The Changing Environment of Selling and Sales Management," *Journal of Personal Selling & Sales Management* 25 (Spring 2005): 105–111; William C. Moncrief and Greg W. Marshall, "The Evolution of the Seven Steps of Selling," *Industrial Marketing Management* 34 (January 2005): 13–22; Raymond W. LaForge, Thomas N. Ingram, and David W. Cravens, "Strategic Alignment for Sales Organization Transformation," *Journal of Strategic Marketing* (June–August 2009): 199–219; Jagdish N. Sheth and Arun Sharma, "The Impact of the Product to Service Shift in Industrial Markets and the Evolution of the Sales Organization," *Industrial Marketing Management* 37 (May 2008): 260–269.

7. "America's 500 Largest Sales Forces," *Selling Power* (June 2019): 40–56.

8. Joel Le Bon, *Competitive Intelligence and the Sales Force* (New York: Business Expert Press, 2014).

9. To learn more about what customers expect from salespeople, see Tom Atkinson and Ron Koprowski, "Sales Reps' Biggest Mistakes," *Harvard Business Review* 84 (July–August 2006): 20; Philip Kreindler and Gopal Raj Guru, "What B2B Customers Really Expect," *Harvard Business Review* 84 (July–August 2006): 22–24.

10. Robert F. Gwinner, "Base Theory in the Formulation of Sales Strategy," *MSU Business Topics* (Autumn 1968): 37.

11. James Buck, "Open-Ended Sales Questions: How to Get Your Prospect Talking," from the IMPACT Sales Training Blog published by The Brooks Group, May 6, 2015.

12. For more discussion of consultative selling, see Mack Hanan, *Consultative Selling*, 8th ed. (New York: American Management Association, 2011); Kevin J. Corcoran, Laura K. Petersen, Daniel B. Baitch, and Mark F. Barrett, *High Performance Sales Organizations* (Chicago: Irwin, 1995): 44; and Jonathan Farrington, "Strategic Selling—All Three Roles Defined," http://www.superperformance.com/strategicsell.php, accessed August 12, 2011.

13. Yellow Pages, "Yellow Pages Group, 2010," http://www.ypg.com/en/, January 3, 2010; Mark Marone and Seleste Lunsford, *Strategies That Win Sales* (Chicago, IL: Dearborn Trade Publishing, 2005): 83.

14. E. Robert Dwyer, Paul Schurr, and Sejo Oh, "Developing Buyer–Seller Relationships," *Journal of Marketing* (April 1987): 11–27; Jon M. Hawes, Kenneth E. Mast, and John E. Swan, "Trust Earning Perceptions of Sellers and Buyers," *Journal of Personal Selling & Sales Management* 9 (Spring 1989): 1; Gary K. Hunter and William D. Perreault, "Making Sales Technology Effective," *Journal of Marketing* 71 (January 2007): 16–34.

15. Thomas N. Ingram and Charles H. Schwepker, Jr., "Perceptions of Salespeople: Implications for Sales Managers and Sales Trainers," *Journal of Marketing Management* 2 (Fall/Winter 1992–1993): 1–8.

16. Katherine B. Hartman, "Television and Movie Representations of Salespeople: Beyond Willie Loman," *Journal of Personal Selling & Sales Management* 26 (Summer 2006): 283–292.

17. Thomas N. Ingram, "Relationship Selling: Moving from Rhetoric to Reality," *Mid-American Journal of Business* 11 (Spring 1996): 5–12.

18. Emin Babakus, David W. Cravens, Ken Grant, Thomas N. Ingram, and Raymond W. LaForge, "Removing Salesforce Performance Hurdles," *Journal of Business and Industrial Marketing* 9, no. 3 (1994): 19–29.

19. See Herbert M. Greenberg and Jeanne Greenberg, *What It Takes to Succeed in Sales* (Homewood, IL: Dow-Jones Irwin, 1990).

20. James M. Comer and Alan J. Dubinsky, *Managing the Successful Sales Force* (Lexington, MA: D.C. Heath and Co., 1985): 5; Steven P. Brown, Thomas W. Leigh, and J. Martin Haygood, "Salesperson Performance and Job Attitudes," in *The Marketing Manager's Handbook*, 3rd ed., eds. Sidney J. Levy, George R. Frerichs, and Howard L. Gordon (Chicago: The Dartnell Corporation, 1994): 107.

21. Babakus et al., "Removing Salesforce Performance Hurdles," 19; Greg W. Marshall, Daniel J. Goebel, and William C. Moncrief, "Hiring for Success at the Buyer–Seller Interface," *Journal of Business Research* 56 (April 2003): 247–255.

22. Rosann L. Spiro and Barton A. Weitz, "Adaptive Selling: Conceptualization, Measurement, and Nomological Validity," *Journal of Marketing Research* 27 (February 1990): 61.

23. Marshall et al., "Hiring for Success," 251.

24. Kevin J. Corcoran, Laura K. Petersen, Daniel B. Baitch, and Mark F. Barrett, *High Performance Sales Organizations* (Chicago: Irwin Professional Publishing, 1995): 77.

25. Marshall et al., "Hiring for Success," 251.

26. Arun Sharma and Rajnandini Pillai, "Customers' Decision-Making Styles and Their Preference for Sales Strategies: Conceptual Examination and an Empirical Study," *Journal of Personal Selling & Sales Management* 16 (Winter 1996): 21.

27. Victoria D. Bush, Gregory M. Rose, Faye Gilbert, and Thomas N. Ingram, "Managing Culturally Diverse Buyer–Seller Relationships: The Role of Intercultural Disposition and Adaptive Selling Behavior in Developing Intercultural Communication Competence," *Journal of the Academy of Marketing Science* 29, no. 4 (Fall 2001): 391–404.

28. Gabriel R. Gonzalez, K. Douglas Hoffman, and Thomas N. Ingram, "Improving Relationship Selling Through Failure Analysis and Recovery Efforts: A Framework and Call to Action," *Journal of Personal Selling & Sales Management* 25 (Winter 2005): 57–66.

29. "Summary Report for 41-4011.00—Sales Representatives, Wholesale and Manufacturing, Technical and Scientific Products," http://www.onetonline.org/link/summary/41-4011.00, accessed August 16, 2011; and Jennifer Salopek, "The Power of the Pyramid," *T + D* (May 2009): 70–75.

30. Randstad, "The Tech Brain Drain and Talent Shortage in Canada," https://www.randstad.ca/employers/workplace-insights/job-market-in-canada/the-tech-brain-drain-and-talent-shortage-in-canada/, accessed March 12, 2020.

31. Ryan Holmes, "The Huge Job Opportunity in Canadian Tech (That No One Is Talking About)," https://business.financialpost.com/entrepreneur/the-huge-job-opportunity-in-canadian-tech-that-no-one-is-talking-about, last updated April 19, 2018.

32. Laziridis Institute. "Laurier's Lazaridis Institute Collaborates with Deloitte and TMX Group to Support Growth of Canadian Tech Firms," https://lazaridismba.ca/lauriers-lazaridis-institute-collaborates-with-deloitte-and-tmx-group-to-support-growth-of-canadian-tech-firms/, accessed March 12, 2020.

2

1. McCain, "Our Company," https://mccain.ca/en/our-company, accessed February 25, 2020.

2. McCain, "Our Business and Brands," https://www.mccain.com/about-us/our-business-brands/, accessed February 25, 2020.

3. McCain, "The All Smiles Blog: McCain Foods—Canada's Best Managed Companies Platinum Member," https://mccain.ca/en/blog/canadas-best-managed-companies, accessed March 2, 2020.

4. McCain, "Media Assets," https://www.mccain.com/information-centre/media-assets/, accessed February 25, 2020.

5. Sherry Kilgus, "Building Trust into High Level Alliances," *NAMA Journal* 34 (Winter 1998).

6. John Andy Wood, James S. Boles, Wesley Johnston, and Danny Bellenger, "Buyers' Trust of the Salesperson: An Item-Level Meta-Analysis," *JPSSM* 28, no. 3 (Summer 2008): 263–283.

7. Michael Ahearne, Ron Jelinck, and Eli Jones, "Examining the Effect of Salesperson Service Behavior in a Competitive Context," *Journal of Academy of Marketing Science* 35 (2007): 603–616.

8. John Andy Wood et al., "Buyers' Trust of the Salesperson."

9. S. Newell, J. Belonax, M. McCardle, and R. Plank. "The Effect of Personal Relationship and Consultative Task Behaviors on Buyer Perceptions of Salesperson Trust, Expertise, and Loyalty," *Journal of Marketing Theory and Practice* (December 8, 2014): 307–316.

10. John E. Swan and Johannah Jones Nolan, "Gaining Customer Trust: A Conceptual Guide for the Salesperson," *Journal of Personal Selling & Sales Management* 5, no. 2 (November 1985): 39.

11. Robert F. Dwyer, Paul H. Schurr, and Sejo Oh, "Developing Buyer–Seller Relationships," *Journal of Marketing* 51 (April 1987): 11.

12. Lubomira Radoilska, "Trustfulness and Business," *Journal of Business Ethics* 79 (2008): 21–28.

13. This was the concluding point of the symposium on trust held by the National Account Management Association at Wake Forest University, September 24–26, 1997.

14. R. Agnihotri and M. Krush, "Salesperson Empathy, Ethical Behaviors, and Sales Performance: The Moderating Role of Trust in One's Manager," *Journal of Personal Selling & Sales Management* (February 13, 2015): 164–174.

15. Kevin Bradford and Barton Weitz, "Salespersons' Management of Conflicts in Buyer–Seller Relationships," *JPSSM* 29, no. 1 (Winter 2009): 25–42.

16. C. Bateman and Sean Valentine, "The Impact of Salesperson Customer Orientation on the Evaluation of a Salesperson's Ethical Treatment, Trust in the Salesperson, and Intentions to Purchase," *Journal of Personal Selling & Sales Management* (February 18, 2015): 125–142.

17. Robert Petersen, "Consultative Selling: A Qualitative Look at the Salesperson Credibility Requirements," *AMA Educator Proceeding Enhancing Knowledge Development in Marketing* 8 (1997): 224.

18. *Ibid*.

19. Interview with Gary Schliessman, Gary Schliessman and Associates, January 26, 2009.

20. Gerhard Gschwandtner, "Lies and Deception in Selling: How to Tell When Customers or Prospects Are Lying to You," *Selling Power* 15, no. 9 (2010).

21. Sergio Roman and Salvador Ruiz, "Relationship Outcomes of Perceived Ethical Sales Behavior: The Customer's Perspective," *Journal of Business Research* 58 (2005): 439–445; Douglas B. Grisaffe and Fernando Jaramillo, "Toward Higher Levels of Ethics: Preliminary Evidence of Positive Outcomes," *Journal of Personal Selling & Sales Management* 27, no. 4 (2007): 355–371.

22. Reprinted by permission of Sales & Marketing Executives International, Inc. (http://www.smei. org). "SMEI Certified Professional Salesperson" and "SCPS" are registered trademarks of Sales & Marketing Executives International, Inc.

23. *Ibid*.

24. Thomas Ingram, Scott Inks, and Lee Mabie, *Sales and Marketing Executive Certification Study Guide* (Memphis, TN: Marketing Executive International, 1994).

25. Nigel F. Piercy and Nikala Lane, "Ethical and Moral Dilemmas Associated with Strategic Relationships between Business-to-Business Buyers and Sellers," *Journal of Business Ethics* 72 (2007): 87–102; Thomas N. Ingram, Raymond W. LaForge, and Charles H. Schwepker, Jr. "Salesperson Ethical Decision Making: The Impact of Sales Leadership and Sales Management Control Strategies," *Journal of Personal Selling & Sales Management* 27, no. 4 (2007): 301–324.

26. Interview with John Huff, Shering-Plough, November 15, 2004.

27. Nicholas McClaren, "The Personal Selling and Sales Management Ethics Research: Managerial Implications and Research Directions from a Comprehensive Literature Review of the Empirical Literature," *Journal of Business Ethics*, 112 (2013): 101–125.

28. Christine Ro, "The Jobs Where Liars Excel," *BBC*, last updated June 25, 2019, https://www.bbc.com/worklife /article/20190625-the-jobs-where-liars-excel.

29. Aja Frost, "Only 3% of People Think Salespeople Possess This Crucial Character Trait," HubSpot, https://blog.hubspot.com/sales /salespeople-perception-problem, last updated July 28, 2017.

30. John Irwin, "'Barbarians at the Gate' Threaten the Traditional Sales Model," *Automotive News Canada*, https://canada.autonews.com/canada-congress-barbarians-gate-threaten-traditional -sales-model, last updated February 17, 2020.

31. *Ibid*.

32. John Irwin, "AutoCanada Says It Will Close Two 'Loss-Generating' Dealerships in U.S.," *Automotive News Canada*, https://canada.autonews. com/retail/autocanada-says-it-will-close-two-loss -generating-dealerships-us, last updated November 8, 2019.

3

1. Empire Company Limited, "About Us," https://www.empireco.ca/en/about-us/, accessed February 28, 2020.

2. Sobeys, "Our History," https://corporate.sobeys. com/history/, accessed February 28, 2020.

3. Sobeys, "Our Company and Our Purpose," https://corporate.sobeys.com/our-purpose/, accessed February 28, 2020.

4. Jakki Mohr and John R. Nevin, "Communication Strategies in Marketing Channels: A Theoretical Perspective," *Journal of Marketing* (October 1990): 36–51.

5. Alan S. Khade and Nathan Lovaas, "Improving Supply Chain Performance: A Case of Walmart's Logistics," *International Journal of Business Strategy* 9 (2009): 157–164; Alexander Harsono, "How Walmart Enhances Supply Chain Management with CPFR Initiatives," http://www. academia.edu/9437177/How_Walmart_Enhances _Supply_Chain _Management_With_CPFR _Initiatives, accessed January 25, 2017.

6. Howard Stevens and Theodore Kinni, *Achieve Sales Excellence* (Avon, MA: Platinum Press, 2007).

7. Adapted from Jagdish N. Sheth, Bahwari Mittal, and Bruce I. Newman, *Customer Behavior: Consumer Behavior and Beyond* (Fort Worth, TX: The Dryden Press, 1999); Jagdish N. Sheth, Bruce I. Newman, and Barbara L. Gross, *Consumption Values and Market Choice: Theory and Application* (Cincinnati, OH: South-Western Publishing Co., 1991).

8. Content Marketing Institute, "B2B Content Marketing," http://contentmarketinginstitute.com /wpcontent/uploads/2016/09/2017_B2B_Research _FINAL.pdf, accessed January 27, 2017.

9. Bixby Cooper, Cornelia Drodge, and Patricia Daughtery, "How Buyers and Operations Personnel Evaluate Service," *Industrial Marketing Management* (February 1991): 81–85.

10. Howard Stevens and Theodore Kinni, *Achieve Sales Excellence* (Avon, MA: Platinum Press, 2007).

11. Adapted from Michael A. Humphreys and Michael R. Williams, "Exploring the Relative Effects of Salesperson Interpersonal Process Attributes and Technical Product Attributes on Customer Satisfaction," *Journal of Personal Selling & Sales Management* 16 (Summer 1996): 47–58; Michael A. Humphreys, Michael R. Williams, and Ronald L. Meier, "Leveraging the Total Market Offering in the Agile Enterprise," *ASQ Quality Management Journal* 5 (1997): 60–74.

12. Stevens and Kinni, *Achieve Sales Excellence*.

13. http://www.123edi.com/edi-examples-101.asp, accessed January 27, 2017.

14. D. W. Merrill and R. H. Reid, *Personal Styles and Effective Performance* (Radnor, PA: Chilton Book Company, 1981).

15. Reprinted by permission of Growmark, Inc.

16. Wesley J. Johnston and Thomas V. Bonoma, "The Buying Center: Structure and Interaction Patterns," *Journal of Marketing* (Summer 1981): 143–156.

17. "Customers: The Future of B-to-B Customer Experience 2020," http://www.walkerinfo.com /knowledge-center/webcasts/docs/Walker-Insights -Webcast-Customers-2020.pdf, accessed January 30, 2017.

18. "Customers: The Future of B-to-B Customer Experience 2020," http://www.walkerinfo.com /knowledge-center/webcasts/docs/Walker-Insights -Webcast-Customers-2020.pdf, accessed January 30, 2017.

19. "Building Better Relationships at Dell," https://www.lattice-engines.com/wp-content /uploads/2015/03/LAT-CaseStudy_Dell-Web.pdf, accessed April 1, 2015; Rachel King, "How Dell Predicts Which Customers Are Most Likely to Buy," *The Wall Street Journal*, December 5, 2012.

20. http://www.rstrain.com/customer-stories/cisco/, accessed February 1, 2017.

21. Robert McGarvey, "All About Us," *Selling Power* 30 (November/December, 2010): 48–52.

22. Jonathan Bacon, "B2B Brands Shift Focus to Customer Experience," https://www. marketingweek.com/2016/02/04/b2b-brands-shift -focus-to-customer–experience/, accessed February 8, 2017.

23. Stevens and Kinni, *Achieve Sales Excellence*.

24. Emma Bedford, "Canadian Retail Sales of Meat Substitutes 2015–2022," *Statistia*, https:// www.statista.com/statistics/981282/meat-substitute -sales-canada/, last updated November 14, 2019.

25. Rebecca Harris, "More Than Half of Canadians Eat Meat Alternatives: Mintel," *Canadian Grocer*, http://www.canadiangrocer.com/research/more -than-half-of-canadians-eat-meat-alternatives -mintel-79934, last updated April 13, 2018.

26. Maple Leaf Foods, "Carbon Strategy," https:// www.mapleleaffoods.com/sustainability/carbon -strategy/, last updated November 9, 2019.

27. Josh Rubin, "It Didn't Work for Tim Hortons— Will Beyond Meat Be a Starbucks Success at

Canadian Stores?" *Toronto Star*, https://www
.thestar.com/business/2020/02/26/fake-meat-and
-a-latte-starbucks-adds-beyond-meat-to-canadian
-stores.html, last updated February 26, 2020.

28. Kat Thompson, "This New Wendy's Burger Is
Made with Plant-Based 'Meat,'" *Thrillist*, https://
www.thrillist.com/news/nation/wendys-plantiful-
burger-plant-based, last updated February 28, 2020.

4

1. WestJet, "About Us," https://www.westjet.com
/en-ca/about-us/index, accessed February 28, 2020.

2. WestJet, "History," https://www.westjet.com
/en-ca/about-us/history, accessed February 28,
2020.

3. Odgers Berndtson, "The Four Values Powering
WestJet's Take-off," https://www.odgersberndtson.
com/en-ca/insights/the-four-values-powering
-westjets-take-off, June 18, 2019, accessed
February 28, 2020.

4. WestJet, "About Us," https://www.westjet.com
/en-ca/about-us/index, accessed February 28, 2020.

5. WestJet, "Awards," https://www.westjet.com
/en-ca/about-us/history/awards, accessed
February 28, 2020.

6. Al Simon, Sandler Training, Simon Inc.
"Hearing versus Listening," *Sales and Marketing
Management's SMM*, May 23, 2011. Reprinted with
permission.

7. Neil Rackham, *Spin Selling* (New York: McGraw
Hill, 1998).

8. Thomas Ingram, Tubs Scott, and Lee Mabie,
Certification Study Guide (New York: Sales and
Marketing Executives International, 1994): 44–46.

9. Jerry Acuff and Wally Wood, *The Relationship
Edge in Business* (Hoboken, NJ: John Wiley &
Sons, Inc., 2004): 149–150; Geoffrey James, "How
to Build Customer Relationships—An Interview
with Jerry Acuff," *Selling Power* (March 2006):
43–46.

10. T. N. Ingram, C. Schwepker Jr., and D. Huston,
"Why Salespeople Fail," *Industrial Marketing
Management* 21 (1992): 225–230.

11. R. P. Ramsey and R. S. Sohi, "Listening to Your
Customers: The Impact of Perceived Salesperson
Listening Behavior on Relationship Outcomes,"
Journal of the Academy of Marketing Science 25
(Spring 1997): 127–137.

12. L. Barker, *Listening Behavior* (Englewood
Cliffs, NJ: Prentice Hall, 1971): 30–32.

13. S. B. Castleberry and C. D. Shepherd,
"Effective Interpersonal Listening and Personal
Selling," *Journal of Marketing Theory and Practice*
7/1 (Winter 1999): 30–39.

14. From *Effective Listening: Key to Your Success*
by L. K. Steil, L. L. Barker, and K. W. Watson:
21. Reprinted by permission of The McGraw-Hill
Companies.

15. Ramsey and Sohi, "Listening to Your
Customers."

16. *Ibid*.

17. J. C. Mowen and M. Minor, *Consumer
Behavior* (New York: Macmillan Publishing Co.,
1997).

18. H. A. Taute, R. S. Heiser, and D. N. McArthur,
"The Effect of Nonverbal Signals on Student Role-
Play Evaluations," *Journal of Marketing Education*
33 (April 2011): 28–40; J. S. Seiter, H. W. Weger,
Jr., A. Jensen, and H. J. Kinzer, "The Role of
Background Behavior in Televised Debates," *The
Journal of Social Psychology* 150 (May 2010):
278–300; G. P. Thomas, "The Influence of Processing

Conversational Information on Inference, Argument
Elaboration, and Memory," *Journal of Consumer
Research* 19 (June 1992): 83–92.

19. R. A. Avila, T. N. Ingram, R. W. LaForge, and
M. R. Williams, *The Professional Selling Skills
Workbook* (Fort Worth, TX: The Dryden Press,
1996): 83; H. A. Taute, R. S. Heiser, and D. N.
McArthur, "The Effect of Nonverbal Signals
on Student Role-Play Evaluations," *Journal of
Marketing Education* 33 (April 2011): 28–40; J. S.
Seiter, H.W. Weger, Jr., A. Jensen, and H. J. Kinzer,
"The Role of Background Behavior in Televised
Debates," *The Journal of Social Psychology* 150
(May 2010): 278–300.

20. Adapted from R. M. Rozelle, D. Druckman,
and J. C. Baxter, "Nonverbal Communication,"
in *A Hand-book of Communication Skills*, ed. O.
Hargie (London: Croom and Helm 1986): 59–94;
T. Alessandra and R. Barrera, *Collaborative
Selling* (New York: John Wiley & Sons, Inc.,
1993): 121–122; H. A. Taute, R. S. Heiser, and
D. N. McArthur, "The Effect of Nonverbal Signals
on Student Role-play Evaluations," *Journal of
Marketing Education* 33 (April 2011): 28–40; J. S.
Seiter, H. W. Weger, Jr., A. Jensen, and H. J. Kinzer,
"The Role of Background Behavior in Televised
Debates," *The Journal of Social Psychology* 150
(May 2010): 278–300.

21. Canadian Professional Sales Association,
"Government of Canada Partners with Canadian
Professional Sales Association to Address Sales
Force Skills Gap," Cision, https://www.newswire.ca
/news-releases/government-of-canada-partners
-with-canadian-professional-sales-association-to
-address-sales-force-skills-gap-697671541.html, last
updated October 18, 2018.

22. *Ibid*.

23. Canadian Professional Sales Association,
"Competency Framework," https://www.cpsa.com/
professional-certification/competency-framework,
last updated October 18, 2018.

24. Canadian Professional Sales Association, "Sales
Professional Competency Framework (PDF),"
p. 13, https://www.cpsa.com/docs/default-source
/hosted-documents/competency-framework_f1
_web.pdf?sfvrsn=2.

25. Canadian Professional Sales Association, "Sales
Professional Competency Framework (PDF)," p. 18.

5

1. True North Sports and Entertainment,
"History," https://www.tnse.com/our-company
/history/, accessed February 28, 2020.

2. Forbes, "The Business of Hockey: Winnipeg
Jets," https://www.forbes.com/teams/winnipeg
-jets/#6834a39539e3, accessed February 28, 2020.

3. True North Youth Foundation, "About Us,"
https://www.truenorthyouthfoundation.com
/about-us/, accessed February 28, 2020.

4. Kenneth Le Meunier-FitzHugh and Leslie
Caroline Le Meunier-FitzHugh, *Creating Effective
Sales and Marketing Relationships* (New York:
Business Expert Press, 2015): 33; Laurence Minsky
and Keith A. Quesenberry, "How B2B Sales Can
Benefit from Social Selling," hbr.org (November 10,
2016): 1–6.

5. Introduction adapted from Henry Canaday,
"The Same Team," *Selling Power* (January/February
2011): 51–52.

6. Tim Riesterer, "Is the 57% Statistic an Urban
Legend?" salesandmarketing.com (January 26,
2017): 1–2; Nicholas Toman, Brent Adamson, and
Cristina Gomez, "The New Sales Imperative,"

Harvard Business Review (March-April 2017):
119–125.

7. Minsky and Quesenberry, "How B2B Sales Can
Benefit from Social Selling."

8. Vanessa DiMauro, "Social Selling: Let's Get a
Few Things Straight," socialmediatoday.com
(May 5, 2016): 1–5.

9. Paul Nolan, "Taming the Technology Tornado,"
salesandmarketing.com (June 27, 2016): 1–2.

10. Paul Nolan, "Get Social or Get Left Behind,"
salesandmarketing.com (January 14, 2017): 1–2;
Minsky and Quesenberry, "How B2B Sales Can
Benefit from Social Selling."

11. Heather Clancy, "Social Selling Success Isn't
Limited to Millennials," fortune.com (May 9, 2016):
1–3.

12. Minsky and Quesenberry, "How B2B Sales Can
Benefit from Social Selling."

13. Clancy, "Social Selling Success Isn't Limited to
Millennials."

14. Author interview with Gwen Tranguillo,
Hershey Chocolate, U.S.A.

15. Bernie Borges, "Integrating Social Selling
Process and Technology Is the Key to Optimal
Results," socialmediatoday.com (July 27, 2016): 1–7;
Irfan Ahmad, "The State of Social Selling in 2016,"
social/mediatoday.com (December 17, 2015): 1–6.

16. Michael Labate, Kirsten Boileau, and Phil
Lurie, "Three Ways Salespeople at SAP Are
Winning with Social Selling," Selling Power Blog
(April 3, 2017): 1–3.

17. Lain Chroust Ehmann, "Sales Up! Why
Reports Selling Is a Dying Profession Are Widely
Exaggerated," *Selling Power* (January/February
2011): 40–44.

18. *Ibid*.

19. J. B. Oldroyd, K. McElheran, and D.
Elkington, "The Short Life of Sales Leads,"
Harvard Business Review (March 2011): 28.

20. E. A. Sullivan, "A Worthwhile Investment,"
Marketing News (December 30, 2009): 10–11.

21. Selling Power Editors, "Maximize Web Leads,
Virtually," *Selling Power* (February 2017): 5.

22. Author interview with Tom Raisor,
Northwestern Mutual.

23. Author interview with Brittany Morriston,
Consolidated Electrical Distributors.

24. H. Canaday, "In Transition," *Selling Power*
(May/June 2011): 39–41.

25. H. Baldwin, "Big Change @ Big Pharma,"
Selling Power (May/June 2011): 29–32.

26. H. Canaday, "In Transition," *Selling Power*
(May/June 2011): 39–41.

27. H. Baldwin, "Big Change @ Big Pharma,"
Selling Power (May/June 2011): 29–32.

28. "Free and Low-Cost Customer Relationship
Management (CRM) Solutions for Your Business,"
https://www.bdc.ca/en/articles-tools/technology
/free-low-cost-applications/pages/crm-solutions
-free-low-cost-options.aspx, accessed February 5,
2020.

29. "Salesforce to Invest $2 Billion in Its Canadian
Business Over Five Years," https://www.newswire.
ca/news-releases/salesforce-to-invest-2-billion-in
-its-canadian-business-over-five-years-673375623.
html, February 8, 2018, accessed February 5, 2020.

30. Ellie Flynn. "Multilevel Marketing Sells a
Dream. Don't Buy It," *The Globe and Mail*,
https://www.theglobeandmail.com/opinion/article
-multilevel-marketing-sells-a-dream-dont-buy-it/,
last updated August 30, 2019.

31. *Ibid*.

32. *Ibid.*

33. Peter Maddox, "DSA Canada Responds to Globe & Mail Article," Direct Sellers Association, https://www.dsa.ca/dsa-canada-responds-to-globe -mail-article/, September 7, 2019.

34. Ellie Flynn, "Multilevel Marketing Sells a Dream."

35. *Ibid.*

6

1. Telus, "About Us," https://www.telus.com /en/about/company-overview/community -investment?linktype=ge-meganav, accessed March 2, 2020.

2. Telus, "Company Overview," https://www.telus .com/en/about/company-overview, accessed March 2, 2020.

3. Mike Schultz, "Sales Call Planning: What to Know Before Every Sales Call," from the RAIN Group blog at https://rainsalestraining.com, May 25, 2017; Mark Magnacca, "Why Salespeople Must Become More Than Order Takers," for the Selling Power blog at https:/ /selling power.com, April 27, 2016; and Rikke Friis Dam, "How to Prepare for a Successful Sales Call," from the Interaction Design Foundation Web site, https://www.interaction- design.org, December 16, 2016.

4. Felice Philip Vedrrecchia, "How to Write a Sales Proposal," online Entrepreneur's Resource Center of the Edward Lowe Foundation, http:// edwardlowe.org/digital-library, accessed April 23, 2017; Jim McCarthy, 29 Reasons Why Government Contract Proposals Fail," Artillery Marketing online, https://www.artillerymarketing.com, May 10, 2017; and Dave Decker, "Most Common Sales Proposal Mistakes," from the Carew International Sales Excellence blog at https://www .carew.com, accessed October 20, 2016.

5. For more tips on writing effective sales proposals, see Scott Stiver, "Tips for Writing a Better Proposal," from the Carew International Sales Excellence blog at https://www.carew. com, October 27, 2016; Dhruv Patel, "10 Tips to Create an Effective Sales Proposal," from the Sales Handy blog at https://www.saleshandy.com, August 10, 2016; and Mikata Mikado, "5 Ways to Create Sales Proposals That Close Deals," from The Center for Sales Strategy blog at http://www .thecenterforsalesstrategy.com, September 26, 2016.

6. Adapted from Bob Kantin, "Sales Proposal RATER," available from http://www.salesproposals .com, May 9, 2017.

7. For more discussion of customer value propositions, see Jill Konrath, "Value Proposition Generator," available at http://www.jillkonrath .com, accessed April 3, 2017; Gregory Ciotti, "Writing Value Propositions That Work," from the Help Scout blog at https://www.helpscpout.net/ blog, April 21, 2016; and Laura Lake, "How to Develop Your Value Proposition," from The Balance Web site at https://www.thebalance, December 19, 2016.

8. CBC, "Through the Years," https://cbc.radio -canada.ca/en/your-public-broadcaster/history, accessed March 12, 2020.

9. Ross A. Eamon, "CBC/Radio-Canada," *The Canadian Encyclopedia*, https://www .thecanadianencyclopedia.ca/en/article/canadian -broadcasting-corporation, last updated June 24, 2015.

10. Amber Dowling, "Canadian Upfronts: Programming Execs on Acquisition Strategies," *Variety*, https://variety.com/2019/tv/features /canadian-upfronts-2019-programming-acquisition -trends-interview-1203237981/, June 10, 2019.

11. Susan Krashinsky Robertson, "'It Doesn't Fit Our Market': Are TV Upfronts Behind the Times?" *The Globe and Mail*, https://www.theglobeandmail. com/business/article-are-upfronts-behind-the -times/, last updated June 9, 2019.

12. Simon Houpt, "CBC Pitches Advertisers in Push to Save Commercial Revenues, Pre-empt Election Funding Fight," *The Globe and Mail*, https://www.theglobeandmail.com/arts/television /article-cbc-pitches-advertisers-in-push-to-save -commercial-revenues-pre-empt/, last updated May 30, 2019.

7

1. PAL Airlines, "Where We Fly," https://www .palairlines.ca/en/fly-pal/where-we-fly/, accessed March 13, 2020.

2. PAL Aerospace, "PAL Companies," https:// palaerospace.com/en/about-us/pal-companies, accessed March 13, 2020.

3. Canada's Top 100, "Provincial Aerospace Ltd./ PAL," https://reviews.canadastop100.com/top -employer-provincial-aerospace#, accessed March 13, 2020.

4. PAL Aerospace, "Global Leaders in Aerospace + Defence Solutions," https://palaerospace .squarespace.com/homepage#home, accessed March 13, 2020.

5. Adapted from Brian Tracy, *Advanced Selling Strategies* (New York: Simon & Schuster, 1995): 302.

6. Henry Canaday, "Engage in Sales," *Selling Power* (March 2015): 29; www.clearslide.com, www.bigtincan.com.

7. Wright Wiley, "Eye-to-Eye Selling," *Selling Power* (May/June 2011): 27.

8. Author interview with Chris Pursell, DRE Medical.

9. Geoffrey James, "Lifesaving Sales," *Selling Power* (June 2009): 40–43.

10. Author interview with David Frick, Success Ventures.

11. Heather Baldwin, "Big Change @ Big Pharma," *Selling Power* (May/June 2011): 29–32

12. Author interview with Nick George, Advanced Payroll Systems.

13. Sharon Yoon, "A Site for Satisfied Eyes," *Sales & Marketing Management* (September/ October 2008): 10.

14. Adapted from Mary Ann Oberhaus, Sharon Ratliffe, and Vernon Stauble, *Professional Selling: A Relationship Approach* (Fort Worth, TX: The Dryden Press, 1995): 410–12.

15. Author interview with Sara Ames, Aspect Software.

16. Author interview with Todd Harrett, Northern Continental Logistics.

17. Canada Revenue Agency, "Direct Seller's Sales Aids," https://www.canada.ca/en/revenue -agency/services/forms-publications/publications /gi-023/harmonized-sales-tax-british-columbia-new -housing-rebate.html, August 2010.

18. *Ibid.*

19. Carmen Reichman, "Death of a Sales Aid: How Advisers Interact with the Clients of Today," *Professional Advisor*, https://www .professionaladviser.com/feature/2392027/death -sales-aid-advisers-interact-clients, January 30, 2015.

20. *Ibid.*

21. *Ibid.*

22. *Ibid.*

8

1. Bombardier, "Sustainability at Bombardier," https://www.bombardier.com/en/sustainability.html, accessed March 2, 2020.

2. Bombardier, "About Us," https://www .bombardier.com/en/about-us.html, accessed March 2, 2020.

3. Marc Diener, "Don't Know When to Cut Your Losses and Leave the Negotiating Table? Look for These Telltale Signs," *Entrepreneur Magazine*, August 2003, http://www.entrepreneur.com /magazine/entrepreneur/2003/august/63334.html, accessed July 26, 2011.

4. Brad Huisken, "Saving the Sale: Objections, Rejections and Getting to Yes," *JCK* (January 2003): 62–63.

5. Tom Reilly, "Why Do You Cut Prices?" *Industrial Distribution* (June 2003): 72.

6. Robert Menard, "'Cost' Is About More Than the Price," *Selling* (July 2003): 9.

7. Kim Sydow Campbell and Lenita Davis, "The Sociolinguistic Basis of Managing Rapport When Overcoming Buying Objections," *Journal of Business Communication* (January 2006): 43–66.

8. Salespeople can forestall known concerns, but they should not bring up issues that are not even a problem with a particular prospect. Thus, the need for good precall information gathering becomes obvious. See "Think Like a Consumer to Make Buying from a Cinch," *Selling* (November 2004): 8.

9. Mark Borkowski, "How to Succeed in Closing Deals, without Closing," *Canadian Electronics* 19 (May 2004): 6.

10. Neil Rackham, *Spin Selling* (New York: McGraw-Hill, 1988): 19–51.

11. Joan Leotta, "Effortless Closing," *Selling Power* (October 2001): 28–31.

12. Susan Del Vecchio, James Zemanek, Roger McIntyre, and Reid Claxton, "Updating the Adaptive Selling Behaviors: Tactics to Keep and Tactics to Discard," *Journal of Marketing Management* 20 (2004): 859–875.

13. Ian Bickis, "Electric Vehicle Options Grow, But Automakers Still Unclear If Canadians Will Buy Them," *Global News*, https://globalnews.ca /news/6586084/electric-vehicle-profitability -canada/, February 23, 2020.

14. *Ibid.*

15. *Ibid.*

16. Michael J. Coren, "Nine Countries Say They'll Ban Internal Combustion Engines. So Far, It's Just Words," Quartz, https://qz.com/1341155 /nine-countries-say-they-will-ban-internal- combustion-engines-none-have-a-law-to-do-so/, accessed August 7, 2018.

17. Neil Winton, "Electric Car Charging Hassle Will Spur Buyer Resistance," *Forbes*, https://www.forbes.com/sites /neilwinton/2019/06/27/electric-car-charging -hassle-will-spur-buyer-resistance/#f5711d5772a3, June 27, 2019.

18. Mirko Rubeis et al., Boston Consulting Group, "Is There a Future for Service Stations?" https:// www.bcg.com/en-gb/publications/2019/service -stations-future.aspx, accessed July 12, 2019.

9

1. Suncor, "Products & Services," https://www.suncor.com/en-ca/about-us/products-and-services, accessed March 6, 2020.

2. Suncor, "History," https://www.suncor.com/en-ca/about-us/history, accessed March 6, 2020.

3. Suncor, "Shell and ExxonMobil," https://www.suncor.com/en-ca/about-us/products-and-services/shell-and-exxonmobil, accessed March 6, 2020.

4. Suncor, "Products & Services."

5. Suncor, "Business Overview," https://www.suncor.com/en-ca/investor-centre/business-overview, accessed March 6, 2020.

6. Howard Stevens and Theodore Kinni, *Achieve Sales Excellence* (Avon, MA: Platinum Press, 2007).

7. Michael Ahearne, Ronald Jelinek, and Eli Jones, "Examining the Effects of Salesperson Service Behavior in a Competitive Context," *Journal of the Academy of Marketing Science* 35 (December 2007), 603–616.

8. Robert W. Palmatier, Srinath Gopalakrishna, and Mark B. Houston, "Returns on Business-to-Business Relationship Marketing Investments: Strategies for Leveraging Profits," *Marketing Science* 25 (September–October 2006): 477–493.

9. Strativity Group, "The 2014 Customer Experience in Action Study," http://strativity.com/wp-content/uploads/2014/03/CEM-Benchmark-Study-2014-Executive-Summary.pdf, accessed February 10, 2017.

10. John Taschek, "How to Avoid a CRM Failure," eWeek 18, no. 40 (October 15, 2001): 31.

11. Ross Beard, "Why Customer Satisfaction Is Important (6 Reasons)," January 2014, http://blog.clientheartbeat.com/why-customer-satisfaction-is-important/, accessed February 22, 2017.

12. Ahearne, Jelinek, and Jones, "Examining the Effect of Salesperson Service Behavior in a Competitive Context."

13. Katie Kazmierczak, "Strativity Releases Benchmark Survey Results—81% of Global Companies Are Not Committed to Customer Experience," http://strativity.com/customer-experience-benchmarkstudy-release-2014/, accessed February 10, 2017.

14. Ross Beard, "5 Examples of How Customer Satisfaction Can Be Used as a Point of Differentiation," January 2014, http://blog.clientheartbeat.com/customersatisfaction-point-of-differentiation/, accessed February 22, 2017.

15. Interview with Darrell Beaty, Ontario Systems Corporation, February 29, 2000.

16. "How Stea IT Saved an $180,000 Contract by Using Client Heartbeat," https://www.clientheartbeat.com/customers/steait/, accessed March 3, 2017.

17. Christine Galea, "What Customers Really Want," *Sales & Marketing Management* 158 (May 2006): 11.

18. Ken Dooley, "Why Customers Buy & Why They Don't: The Latest Research Reveals…," http://www.customerexperienceinsight.com/why-customers-buy-why-they-dont/, accessed October 3, 2015; Geoffrey James, "10 Things Every Customer Wants," http://www.inc.com/geoffrey-james/10-things-every-customer-wants.html, accessed October 3, 2015.

19. "Advance CRM Solutions," *Personal Selling Power* (January/February 2007): 96–99.

20. "ADP Reps Make Every Moment a Selling Moment with Salesforce," http://www.salesforce.com/customer-success-stories/ADP/, accessed February 24, 2017.

21. Stevens and Kinni, *Achieve Sales Excellence.*

22. Gabriel Gonzalez, Douglas Hoffman, Thomas Ingram, and Raymond LaForge, "Sales Organization Recovery Management and Relationship Selling: A Conceptual Model and Empirical Test," *Journal of Personal Selling & Sales Management* 30 (Summer 2010): 223–237.

23. Eileen McDargh, "Provide Great Service," *Sales & Service Excellence* 10 (June 2010): 10.

24. John Werner, "Customer Complaints: A Gift in Disguise," *ASQ Six Sigma Forum Magazine* (May 2013): 28–30.

25. *Ibid.*

26. Sandra Rothenberger, Dhruv Grewal, and Gopalkrishnan R. Iyer, "Understanding the Role of Complaint Handling on Customer Loyalty in Service Relationships," *Journal of Relationship Marketing* 7, no. 4 (2008): 359–376.

27. Chia-Chi Chang, "When Service Fails: The Role of the Salesperson and the Customer," *Psychology & Marketing* 23 (March 2006): 203–224.

28. Robert D. Ramsey, "How to Handle Customer Complaints," *American Salesman* 55 (June 2010): 25–30.

29. John Graham, "Well, Thanks!" *Selling Power* 31 (March/April 2011): 12–15.

30. Stevens and Kinni, *Achieve Sales Excellence.*

31. Kantar Canada Inc. "Banks Lead First BrandZ™ Top 40 Most Valuable Canadian Brands Ranking." *Cision*, https://www.newswire.ca/news-releases/banks-lead-first-brandz-tm-top-40-most-valuable-canadian-brands-ranking-840261962.html, October 30, 2019.

32. Financial Consumer Agency of Canada, Industry Review: Bank Complaint Handling Procedures, https://www.canada.ca/en/financial-consumer-agency/programs/research/banks-complaints-handling-procedures.html, last updated February 19, 2020.

33. Yvonne Colbert, "Banks Do Little to Help Consumers Resolve Their Complaints, Review Finds," *CBC News*, https://www.cbc.ca/news/canada/nova-scotia/banks-customers-complaints-processes-1.5468539, accessed February 19, 2020.

34. *Ibid.*

35. Ghani, Moe. "How to Make the Sale by Focusing on the Customer," *Forbes*, https://www.forbes.com/sites/forbesfinancecouncil/2019/12/20/how-to-make-the-sale-by-focusing-on-the-customer/#3942ac8413c0, accessed December 20, 2019.

36. Yvonne Colbert, "Banks Do Little to Help Consumers Resolve Their Complaints, Review Finds."

10

1. Prince Edward Island, "Agriculture on PEI," https://www.princeedwardisland.ca/en/information/agriculture-and-land/agriculture-on-pei, accessed March 6, 2020.

2. *Ibid.*

3. *Ibid.*

4. Prince Edward Island, "Supports and Services," https://www.princeedwardisland.ca/en/topic/supports-and-services, accessed March 6, 2020.

5. S. R. Covey, *The 7 Habits of Highly Effective People* (New York: Simon & Schuster, 2004).

6. T. Ingram, R. W. LaForge, R. Avila, C. H. Schwepker Jr., and M. R. Williams, *Sales Management: Analysis and Decision Making*, 9th ed. (New York: Routledge, 2015).

7. E. Babakus, D. W. Cravens, K. Grant, T. N. Ingram, and R W. LaForge, "Removing Salesforce Performance Hurdles," *Journal of Business and Industrial Marketing* 9, no. 3 (1994): 19–29.

8. J. Attaway, M. Williams, and M. Griffin, *The Rims-QIC Quality Scorecard* (Nashville, TN: The Quality Insurance Congress, 1998, 1999).

9. James Champy, "Selling to Tomorrow's Customer," *Sales & Marketing Management* (March 1999): 28.

10. Covey, *The 7 Habits of Highly Effective People.* Used with permission.

11. *Ibid.*

12. Jane Clark, "Good Sales Is a Matter of Knowledge, Skills and Attitude," *Fleet Owner*, https://www.fleetowner.com/industry-perspectives/ideaxchange/article/21701565/good-sales-is-a-matter-of-knowledge-skills-and-attitude, accessed December 4, 2017.

13. Quinones, M.A., and Ehrenstein, A. (1997), *Training for a Rapidly Changing Workplace: Applications of Psychological Research*, Washington, D.C.: American Psychological Association, p. 154.

14. Transformative Competencies—Organisation for Economic Co-operation and Development (n.d.), retrieved from https://www.oecd.org/education/2030-project/teaching-and-learning/learning/transformative-competencies/

15. Jane Clark, "Good Sales Is a Matter of Knowledge, Skills and Attitude."

CHAPTER SUMMARY

LO 1

Define personal selling and describe its unique characteristics as a marketing communications tool. Personal selling, an important part of marketing, relies heavily on interpersonal interactions between buyers and sellers to initiate, develop, and enhance customer relationships. The interpersonal communications dimension sets personal selling apart from other marketing communications, such as advertising and sales promotion. Personal selling is also distinguished from direct marketing and electronic marketing in that salespeople are talking with buyers before, during, and after the sale. This allows a high degree of immediate customer's feedback, which becomes a strong advantage of personal selling over most other forms of marketing communications.

LO 2

Distinguish between transaction-focused traditional selling and trust-based relationship selling, with the latter focusing on customer value and sales dialogue. As summarized in Exhibit 1.2, trust-based selling focuses more on the customer than does transaction-focused selling. The salesperson will act as a consultant to the customer in trust-based selling, whereas in transaction-based selling the salesperson concentrates more on making sales calls and on closing sales. There is far more emphasis on postsales follow-up with relationship selling than with transaction selling, and salespeople must have a broader range of skills to practise relationship selling. Rather than pitching products to customers, trust-based selling focuses on establishing sales dialogue with customers, and salespeople not only communicate customer value but also help create and deliver customer value.

LO 3

Describe the emphasis on sales professionalism. The business environment is becoming more complex, competition is intensifying, and buyer expectations are increasing. These factors are creating more focus on sales professionalism in progressive sales organizations. Sales professionalism requires truthful, nonmanipulative tactics to satisfy the long-term needs of both the customer and the selling firm. To improve sales professionalism, salespeople can embrace high ethical standards, participate in professional organizations, and work from a continually evolving knowledge base.

LO 4

Explain the contributions of personal selling to society, business firms, and customers. Salespeople contribute to society by acting as stimuli in the economic process and by assisting in the diffusion of innovation. They contribute to their employers by producing revenue,

GLOSSARY TERMS

personal selling An important part of marketing that relies heavily on interpersonal interactions between buyers and sellers to initiate, develop, and enhance customer relationships.

trust-based relationship selling A form of personal selling that requires that salespeople earn customer trust and that their selling strategy meets customer needs and contributes to the creation, communication, and delivery of customer value.

customer value Customers' perception of what they get for what they have to give up; for example, benefits from buying a product in exchange for money paid.

sales dialogue Business conversations between buyers and sellers that occur as salespeople attempt to initiate, develop, and enhance customer relationships. Sales dialogue should be customer focused and have a clear purpose.

sales professionalism A customer-oriented approach that uses truthful, nonmanipulative tactics to satisfy the long-term needs of both the customer and the selling firm.

economic stimuli Something that stimulates or incites activity in the economy.

diffusion of innovation The process whereby new products, services, and ideas are distributed to the members of society.

revenue producers A role fulfilled by salespeople that brings in revenue or income to a firm or company.

adaptive selling The ability of salespeople to alter their sales messages and behaviours during a sales presentation or as they encounter different sales situations and different customers.

stimulus-response selling An approach to selling in which the key idea is that various stimuli can elicit predictable responses from customers. Salespeople furnish the stimuli from a repertoire of words and actions designed to produce the desired response.

CHAPTER REVIEW 1

GLOSSARY TERMS

continued affirmation An example of stimulus-response selling in which a series of questions or statements furnished by the salesperson is designed to condition the prospective buyer to answering yes time after time, until, it is hoped, they will be inclined to say yes to the entire sales proposition.

mental states selling An approach to personal selling that assumes that the buying process for most buyers is essentially identical and that buyers can be led through certain mental states, or steps, in the buying process; also called the formula approach.

need satisfaction selling An approach to selling based on the notion that the customer is buying to satisfy a particular need or set of needs.

problem-solving selling An extension of need satisfaction selling that goes beyond identifying needs to developing alternative solutions for satisfying these needs.

consultative selling The process of helping customers reach their strategic goals by using the products, services, and expertise of the sales organization.

strategic orchestrator A role the salesperson plays in consultative selling in which they arrange the use of the sales organization's resources in an effort to satisfy the customer.

business consultant A role the salesperson plays in consultative selling in which they use internal and external (outside the sales organization) sources to become an expert on the customer's business. This role also involves educating customers on the sales firm's products and how these products compare with competitive offerings.

long-term ally A role the salesperson plays in consultative selling in which they support the customer, even when an immediate sale is not expected.

sales process A series of interrelated steps beginning with locating qualified prospective customers. From there, the salesperson plans the sales presentation, makes an appointment to

performing research and feedback activities, and composing a pool of future managers. They contribute to customers by providing timely knowledge to assist in solving problems.

LO 5

Discuss five alternative approaches to personal selling. Alternative approaches to personal selling include stimulus-response, mental states, need satisfaction, problem solving, and the consultative approach. Stimulus-response selling often uses the same sales presentation for all customers. The mental states approach prescribes that the salesperson leads the buyer through stages in the buying process. Need satisfaction selling focuses on relating benefits of the seller's products or services to the buyer's particular situation. Problem-solving selling extends need satisfaction by concentrating on various alternatives available to the buyer. Consultative selling focuses on helping customers achieve strategic goals, not just meeting needs or solving problems.

LO 6

Understand the sales process as a series of interrelated steps.
As presented in Figure 1.5, the sales process involves initiating, developing, and enhancing customer relationships. Salespeople must possess certain attributes to earn the trust of their customers and be able to adapt their selling strategies to different situations. Throughout the sales process, salespeople should focus on customer value, first by understanding what customer value is to the customer and then by working to create, communicate, and continually increase that value. Salespeople initiate customer relationships through strategic prospecting, assessing the prospect's situation, planning value-based sales dialogue, and activating the buying process. Relationships are then further developed through engaging prospects in a true dialogue to earn commitment from those prospects. Salespeople enhance customer relationships by following up after the sale, taking a leadership role, and sometimes working as part of a team to increase constantly the value received by the customer. The details of the sales process are covered in Chapters 5 through 10 in this book.

FIG. 1.5 TRUST-BASED SALES PROCESS

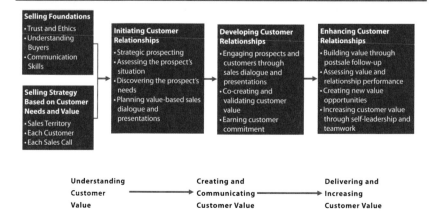

LO 7

Understand the characteristics of sales careers and the skills and qualifications necessary for success in sales careers. Sales careers offer relatively good job security and reasonable opportunities for advancement. Salespeople get immediate job feedback which makes their jobs stimulating, challenging, and interesting. On a daily basis, salespeople are immersed in a dynamic environment with high levels of job variety, thus boredom is rarely an issue. Sales careers have long been associated with independence of action, although sales managers are now monitoring sales activities more closely to improve sales productivity. Sales compensation is tied closely to job performance, especially if commissions and bonuses are part of the pay package. We discuss six types of sales jobs in this chapter: sales support, new business, existing business, inside sales (nonretail), direct-to-consumer, and combination sales jobs. The skills needed for success will depend somewhat on the specific sales job. Among the most important qualifications for sales success are communications skills, a service orientation, problem solving, motivation and taking initiative, dependability, integrity, and adaptability.

inside sales Nonretail salespeople who remain in their employer's place of business while dealing with customers.

combination sales job A sales job in which the salesperson performs multiple types of sales jobs within the framework of a single position.

empathy The ability to see things as others would see them; salespeople with empathy are better able to adapt to various sales situations and adjust to customer feedback.

ego drive An indication of the degree of determination a person has to achieve goals and overcome obstacles in striving for success.

ego strength The degree to which a person is able to achieve an approximation of inner drives.

self-efficacy The strong belief that success will occur on the job.

interpersonal communication skills Skills that include listening and questioning.

enthusiasm A strong feeling of excitement. Salespeople should have an enthusiastic attitude in a general sense and a specific enthusiasm for selling.

service motivation A strong desire to provide service to the customer. Service motivation comes from desiring the approval of others.

see the customer, completes the sale, and performs postsale activities.

missionary salespeople A category of sales support personnel who are not typically involved in the direct solicitation of purchase orders. Their primary roles are disseminating information, stimulating the sales effort to convert prospects into customers, and reinforcing customer relationships.

detailer A category of sales support personnel in the pharmaceutical industry working at the physician level to furnish valuable information regarding the capabilities and limitations of medications in an attempt to get the physician to prescribe their product.

technical support salespeople Technical specialists who may assist in design and specification processes, installation of equipment, training of the customer's employees, and follow-up technical service.

pioneers Salespeople who are constantly involved with either new products, new customers, or both. Their task requires creative selling and the ability to counter the resistance to change that will likely be present in prospective customers.

order-getters Also called hunters, these salespeople actively seek orders, usually in a highly competitive environment.

order-takers Also called farmers, these salespeople specialize in maintaining existing business.

CHAPTER REVIEW 1

NOTES

_____
_____
_____
_____
_____
_____
_____
_____
_____
_____
_____
_____
_____
_____
_____
_____
_____
_____
_____
_____
_____
_____
_____
_____

CHAPTER SUMMARY

LO 1

Explain what trust is. Trust is when an industry buyer believes that they can rely on what the salesperson says or promises to do in a situation where the buyer is dependent on the salesperson's honesty and reliability. One of the keys to a long-term relationship with any client is to create a basis of trust between the sales representative and the client organization.

The *trust* described here goes beyond the typical transaction-oriented trust schema. Many issues—such as, Will the product arrive as promised? Will the right product actually be in stock and be shipped on time? Will the invoice contain the agreed-on price? Can the salesperson be found if something goes wrong?—are only preliminary concerns. In relationship selling, trust is based on a larger set of factors due to the expanded intimacy and longer-term nature of the relationship. The intimacy of this relationship will result in both parties sharing information that could be damaging if leaked or used against the other partner.

LO 2

Understand why trust is important. In today's increasingly competitive marketplace, buyers typically find themselves inundated with choices regarding both products and suppliers. Buyers are demanding unique solutions to their problems, which are customized on the basis of their specific needs. This shift toward relationship selling has altered both the roles played by salespeople and the activities and skills they exercise in carrying out these roles—the selling process itself. Today's more contemporary selling process is embedded within the relationship marketing paradigm. As such, it emphasizes the initiation and nurturing of long-term buyer–seller relationships based on mutual trust and value-added benefits. The level of problem-solving activity common to relationship selling requires deliberate and purposeful collaboration between both parties. These joint efforts are directed at creating unique solutions based on an enhanced knowledge and understanding of the customer's needs and the supplier's capabilities so that both parties derive mutual benefits.

LO 3

Understand how to earn trust. Buyers are constantly asking themselves whether the salesperson truly cares about them. Salespeople can answer this question for the buyer through trust-building activities. Trust can be earned by demonstrating expertise, dependability, candour, customer orientation, competence, and compatibility.

LO 4

Explain how knowledge bases help build trust and relationships. Salespeople do not have much time to make a first impression. If a salesperson can demonstrate competitive knowledge and expertise in the buyer's industry, company, marketplace, and so on, then the buyer will more likely be willing to listen. The salesperson must bring valued experience to the buyer.

GLOSSARY TERMS

trust The extent of the buyer's confidence that they can rely on the salesperson's integrity.

openness Completely free from concealment; exposed to general view or knowledge.

honesty Fairness and straightforwardness of conduct.

confidentiality The state of being entrusted with information from a buyer that cannot be shared.

security The quality of being free from danger.

reliability Consistency of a salesperson over time to do what is right.

fairness Impartiality and honesty.

expertise The ability, knowledge, and resources to meet customer expectations.

contributions Something given to improve a situation or state for a buyer.

dependability Predictability of a person's actions.

predictability A salesperson's behaviour that can be foretold on the basis of observation or experience by a buyer.

candour Honesty of the spoken word.

customer orientation The act of salespeople placing as much emphasis on the customer's interests as their own.

compatibility and likeability A salesperson's commonalities with other individuals.

competitor knowledge Knowledge of a competitor's strengths and weaknesses in the market.

CHAPTER REVIEW 2

GLOSSARY TERMS

product knowledge Detailed information on the manufacture of a product and knowing whether the company has up-to-date production methods.

service issues Concerns of the buyer that the salesperson should address.

promotion knowledge Knowledge tools salespeople must possess to explain their firm's promotional programs.

price knowledge Knowledge tools salespeople must have about pricing policies in order to quote prices and offer discounts on products.

market knowledge Information salespeople must have if larger companies break their customers into distinct markets; salespeople must be familiar with these markets to tailor their sales presentations.

customer knowledge Information about customers that is gathered over time and from very different sources that helps the salesperson determine customer needs to better serve them.

technology knowledge Information salespeople must have about the latest technology.

ethics The right and wrong conduct of individuals and institutions of which they are a part.

price fixing Agreements between sellers to prevent or unduly lessen competition or to unreasonably enhance the price of a product by selling at a fixed price.

bid rigging An agreement in which competitors agree in advance who will win a bid based on the tenders submitted.

price discrimination Knowingly and systematically selling the same goods or services at different prices to different buyers.

LO 5

Understand sales ethics and legal implications. Salespeople are constantly involved with ethical issues. A sales manager might encourage their salesforce to pad their expense account in lieu of a raise. A salesperson might sell a product or service to a customer that the buyer does not need. A salesperson might exaggerate the benefits of a product to get a sale. The list can go on and on. How a salesperson handles these situations will go a long way in determining the salesperson's credibility. One wrong decision can end a salesperson's career.

Three of the more popular areas of unethical behaviour are deceptive practices, illegal activities, and noncustomer-oriented behaviour.

- *Deceptive practices*: Salespeople giving answers they do not know to be right, exaggerating product benefits, and withholding information may appear only to shade the truth, but when it causes harm to the buyer the salesperson has jeopardized future dealings with the buyer.

- *Illegal activities*: Misuse of company assets has been a long-standing problem for many sales organizations. Using the company car for personal use, charging expenses that did not occur, and selling samples for income are examples of misusing company assets. Some of these violations discovered by company probing also constitute violations of Canada Revenue Agency (CRA) law and are offences that could lead to jail time or heavy fines.

- *Noncustomer-oriented behaviour*: Most buyers will not buy from salespeople who are pushy and practise the hard sell. Too much is at stake to fall for the fast-talking, high-pressure salesperson.

predatory pricing A firm or an individual deliberately sets prices to incur losses for a long time to eliminate a competitor or to inhibit competition in the expectation that the firm or individual will later be able to recoup its losses by charging prices above competitive levels.

bait and switch selling Firms or individuals advertise products at bargain prices that they do not have available in reasonable quantities and try to sell more expensive products instead.

pyramid selling Fees or commissions paid not on the basis of product sales but on the recruitment of others to make sales.

express warranty A way a salesperson can create product liabilities by giving a product warranty or guarantee that obligates the selling organization even if the salesperson does not intend to give the warranty.

misrepresentation False claim(s) made by a salesperson.

negligence False claim(s) made by a salesperson about the product or service they are trying to sell.

basis of the bargain When a buyer relies on the seller's statements in making a purchase decision.

CHAPTER SUMMARY

LO 1

Categorize the primary types of buyers. Buyers are classified according to the unique buying situations that influence their needs, motivations, and buying behaviour. The most common categorization splits buyers into either consumer markets or business markets. Consumers purchase goods and services for their own use or consumption, whereas members of the business market acquire goods and services to use as inputs into manufacturing, for use in doing business, or for resale. Business markets are further divided into firms, institutions, and governments.

LO 2

Discuss the distinguishing characteristics of business markets. Among the more common distinguishing characteristics are consolidation, which has resulted in buyers being fewer in number but larger in size; demand that is derived from the sale of consumer goods; more volatile demand levels; professional buyers; multiple buying influences from a team of buyers; and increased interdependence and relationships between buyers and sellers.

LO 3

List the different steps in the business-to-business buying process. This process involves (1) recognition of the problem or need, (2) determination of the characteristics of the item and the quantity needed, (3) description of the characteristics of the item and quantity needed, (4) search for and qualification of potential sources, (5) acquisition and analysis of proposals, (6) evaluation of proposals and selection of suppliers, (7) selection of an order routine, and (8) giving of performance feedback and evaluation.

LO 4

Discuss the different types of buyer needs. Salespeople are better able to generate and demonstrate value-added solutions by understanding different types of buyer needs. The five general types of buyer needs are described as follows:

- *Situational needs*—Needs that are related to, or possibly the result of, the buyer's specific environment, time, and place.

- *Functional needs*—The need for a specific core task or function to be performed—the need for a sales offering to do what it is supposed to do.

- *Social needs*—The need for acceptance from and association with others—a desire to belong to some reference group.

- *Psychological needs*—The desire for feelings of assurance and risk reduction, as well as positive emotions and feelings such as success, joy, excitement, and stimulation.

- *Knowledge needs*—The desire for personal development and need for information and knowledge to increase thought and understanding as to how and why things happen.

GLOSSARY TERMS

consumer market A market in which consumers purchase goods and services for their use or consumption.

business market A market composed of firms, institutions, and governments that acquire goods and services to use as inputs into their own manufacturing process, for use in their day-to-day operations, or for resale to their own customers.

derived demand Demand in business markets that is closely associated with the demand for consumer goods.

acceleration principle When demand increases (or decreases) in the consumer market, the business market reacts by accelerating the buildup (or reduction) of inventories and increasing (or decreasing) plant capacity.

supply chain management The strategic coordination and integration of purchasing with other functions within the buying organization as well as external organizations.

desired states A state of being based on what the buyer desires.

actual states A buyer's actual state of being.

needs gap A perceived difference between a buyer's desired and actual state of being.

situational needs The needs that are contingent on, and often a result of, conditions related to the specific environment, time, and place.

functional needs The need for a specific core task or function to be performed.

social needs The need for acceptance from and association with others.

psychological needs The desire for feelings of assurance and risk reduction, as well as positive emotions and feelings, such as success, joy, excitement, and stimulation.

knowledge needs The desire for personal development, information, and knowledge to increase thought and

CHAPTER REVIEW 3

GLOSSARY TERMS

understanding as to how and why things happen.

content marketing A form of marketing that involves creating and distributing valuable, relevant, and consistent content to attract and retain buyers.

request for proposals (RFPs) A form created by firms and distributed to qualified potential suppliers that helps suppliers develop and submit proposals to provide products as specified by the firm.

multiattribute model A procedure for evaluating suppliers and products that incorporates weighted averages across desired characteristics.

competitive depositioning Providing information to create a more accurate picture of a competitor's attributes or qualities.

two-factor model of evaluation A postpurchase evaluation process buyers use that evaluates a product purchase by using functional and psychological attributes.

functional attributes The features and characteristics that are related to what the product actually does or is expected to do.

must-have attributes Features of the core product that the customer takes for granted.

psychological attributes A category of product characteristics that refers to how things are carried out and done between the buyer and seller.

delighter attributes The augmented features included in the total market offering that go beyond the buyer's expectations and have a significant positive impact on customer satisfaction.

straight rebuy decision A purchase decision resulting from an ongoing purchasing relationship with a supplier.

electronic data interchange (EDI) Transfer of data electronically between two computer systems.

new task decision A purchase decision that occurs when a buyer is purchasing a product or service for the first time.

modified rebuy decision A purchase decision that occurs when a buyer has experience in purchasing a

LO 5

Describe how buyers evaluate suppliers and alternative sales offerings by using the multiattribute model of evaluation. Using the multiattribute model, buyers establish the attributes they perceive as important and evaluate the degree to which each of the specified attributes is present (or how well each performs) in a proposed solution. Each evaluation is then multiplied by the attribute's relative level of importance to calculate a weighted average for each attribute. These weighted averages are then totalled to derive an overall score for each supplier or product being compared. The product or supplier having the highest score is favoured for the purchase.

LO 6

Explain the two-factor model that buyers use to evaluate the performance of sales offerings and develop satisfaction. The two-factor model is a special type of multiattribute model in which further analysis of the multiple characteristics results in two primary groupings of factors: functional attributes and psychological attributes. Functional attributes are the more tangible characteristics of a market offering whereas the psychological attributes are primarily composed of the interpersonal behaviours and activities between the buyer and seller. The psychological attributes have been repeatedly found to have higher levels of influence than functional attributes on customer satisfaction and repeat purchase.

LO 7

Explain the different types of purchasing decisions.

- *Straight rebuy*—Comparable with a routine repurchase in which nothing has changed, the straight rebuy is often the result of past experience and satisfaction, with buyers purchasing the same products from the same sources. Needs have been predetermined, with specifications already established. Buyers allocate little, if any, time or resources to this form of purchase decision, and the primary emphasis is on continued satisfactory performance.

- *Modified rebuy*—The buyer has some level of experience with the product but is interested in acquiring additional information regarding alternative products and suppliers. The modified rebuy typically occurs as the result of changing conditions or needs. Perhaps the buyer wants to consider new suppliers for current purchase needs or new products offered by existing suppliers.

- *New task*—New task decisions occur when a buyer is purchasing a product or service for the first time. With no experience or knowledge on which to rely, buyers undertake an extensive purchase decision and search for information designed to identify and compare alternative solutions. Reflecting the extensive nature of this type of purchase decision, multiple members of the buying centre or group are usually involved. As a result, the salesperson often works with several different individuals rather than a single buyer.

LO 8

Describe the four communication styles and how salespeople must adapt their own styles to maximize communication. Based on high and low levels of two personal traits, assertiveness and responsiveness, communication styles can be categorized into four primary types:

- Amiables are high on responsiveness and low on assertiveness.

- Expressives are defined as high on both responsiveness and assertiveness.

- Drivers are low on responsiveness but high on assertiveness.
- Analyticals are characterized as low on assertiveness as well as responsiveness.

Mismatched styles between a seller and a buyer can be dysfunctional in terms of effective collaboration and present significant barriers for information exchange and relationship building. Differences in styles manifest themselves in the form of differences in preferred priorities (relationships versus task orientation) and favoured pace (fast versus slow) of information exchange, socialization, and decision making. To minimize potential communication difficulties stemming from mismatched styles, salespeople should flex their personal styles to better fit the preferred priorities and pace of the buyer.

LO 9

Explain the concept of buying teams and specify the different member roles. In the more complex modified rebuy and new task purchasing situations, purchase decisions typically involve the joint decisions of multiple participants working together as a buying team. Team members bring the expertise and knowledge from different functional departments within the buying organization. Team members may also change as the purchase decision changes. Team members are described by their roles within the team: initiators, influencers, users, deciders, purchasers, and gatekeepers.

LO 10

Understand means for engaging customers. To ensure that today's customers are fully engaged, selling organizations are focusing on the customer experience, turning to information technology, providing buyers with timely and relevant information, and adding value to buyer–seller relationships through various means.

product in the past but is interested in acquiring additional information regarding alternative products and/or suppliers.

assertiveness The degree to which a person holds opinions about issues and attempts to dominate or control situations by directing the thoughts and actions of others.

responsiveness The level of feelings and sociability an individual openly displays.

amiables Individuals who are high on responsiveness, low on assertiveness, prefer to belong to groups, and are interested in others.

expressives Individuals who are high on both responsiveness and assertiveness, are animated and communicative, and value building close relationships with others.

drivers Individuals who are low on responsiveness, high on assertiveness, and detached from relationships.

analyticals Individuals who are low on responsiveness and assertiveness, and are analytical, meticulous, and disciplined in everything they do.

buying teams Teams of individuals in organizations that use the expertise and multiple buying influences of people from different departments throughout the organization.

initiators Individuals within an organization who identify a need.

influencers Individuals within an organization who guide the decision process by making recommendations and expressing preferences.

users Individuals within an organization who will actually use the product being purchased.

deciders Individuals within an organization who have the ultimate responsibility of determining which product or service will be purchased.

purchasers Organizational members who negotiate final terms of the purchase and execute the actual purchase.

gatekeepers Members of an organization who are in a position to control the flow of information to and between vendors and other buying centre members.

outsource To give to a supplier certain activities that were previously performed by the buying organization.

CHAPTER REVIEW 3

NOTES

CHAPTER REVIEW 4
Communication Skills

CHAPTER SUMMARY

LO 1

Explain the importance of collaborative, two-way communication in trust-based selling. The two-way exchange inherent in collaborative communication facilitates accurate and mutual understanding of the objectives, problems, needs, and capabilities of each of the parties. As a result, solutions can be generated that provide mutual benefits to all participants. This would not be possible without collaboration, and one party would benefit at the expense of the other. Although this might be good for the "winning" party, the disadvantaged party would be less inclined to continue doing business and would seek out other business partners.

LO 2

Explain the primary types of questions and how they are applied in selling. Questions can be typed into two categories according to (1) the amount of information and specificity desired and (2) the strategic purpose of the question.

- Questions typed by the amount of information and specificity desired include open-end questions, closed-end questions, and dichotomous questions. *Open-end questions* encourage the customer to respond freely and provide more expansive information. They are used to probe for descriptive information. *Closed-end questions* limit responses to one or two words and are used to confirm or clarify information. *Dichotomous questions* request the buyer to choose between specified alternatives.

- Questions typed by their strategic purpose include questions for (1) probing, (2) evaluative, (3) tactical, and (4) reactive purposes. *Probing questions* penetrate beneath surface information to provide useful details. *Evaluative questions* uncover how the buyer feels about something. *Tactical questions* are used to shift the topic of discussion. *Reactive questions* respond to information provided by the other party and ask for additional details about that information.

LO 3

Illustrate the diverse roles and uses of strategic questioning in trust-based selling. Questions are used to elicit detailed information about a buyer's situation, needs, and expectations while also providing a logical guide promoting sequential thought. Effective questioning facilitates both the buyer's and the seller's understanding of a problem and proposed solutions. Questioning can also test the buyer's interest and increase their cognitive involvement and participation in the selling process. Questions can also be used to redirect, regain, or hold the buyer's attention subtly and strategically.

LO 4

Identify and describe the five steps of the ADAPT questioning sequence for effective fact finding and needs discovery. The five steps are assessment questions, discovery questions, activation questions, projection questions, and transition questions.

GLOSSARY TERMS

trust-based sales communication Talking *with* rather than *at* the customer. A collaborative and two-way form of communication that allows buyers and sellers to develop a better understanding of the need situation and work together to cocreate the best response for resolving the customer's needs.

open-end questions Questions designed to let the customer respond freely; the customer is not limited to one- or two-word answers but is encouraged to disclose personal or business information.

closed-end questions Questions designed to limit the customer's responses to one or two words.

dichotomous questions A directive form of questioning; these questions ask the customer to choose from two or more options.

probing questions Questions designed to penetrate below generalized or superficial information to elicit more articulate and precise details for use in needs discovery and solution identification.

evaluative questions Questions that use the open- and closed-end question formats to gain confirmation and to uncover attitudes, opinions, and preferences the prospect holds.

tactical questions Questions used to shift or redirect the topic of discussion when the discussion gets off course or when a line of questioning proves to be of little interest or value.

reactive questions Questions that refer to or directly result from information the other party previously provided.

SPIN A questioning system that sequences four types of questions designed to uncover a buyer's current situation and inherent problems, enhance the buyer's understanding of the consequences and implications of those problems, and lead to the proposed solution.

situation questions One of the four types of questions in the SPIN questioning system used early in the sales call that provides salespeople with leads to develop the buyer's needs and expectations fully.

problem questions One of the four types of questions in the SPIN questioning system that follows the more general situation questions to further probe for specific difficulties, developing problems, and areas of dissatisfaction that might be positively addressed by the salesperson's proposed sales offering.

implication questions One of the four types of questions in the SPIN questioning system that follows and is related to the information flowing from problem questions; they are used to assist the buyer in thinking about the potential consequences of the problem and understanding the urgency of resolving the problem in a way that motivates him or her to seek a solution.

need-payoff questions One of the four types of questions in the SPIN questioning system that is based on the implications of a problem; they are used to propose a solution and develop commitment from the buyer.

ADAPT A questioning system that uses a logic-based funnelling sequence of questions, beginning with broad and generalized inquiries designed to identify and assess the buyer's situation.

assessment questions One of the five stages of questions in the ADAPT questioning system that do not seek conclusions but rather should address the buyer's company and operations, goals and objectives, market trends and customers, current suppliers, and even the buyer as an individual.

discovery questions One of the five stages of questions in the ADAPT questioning system that follows up on the assessment questions; they

- *Assessment questions are broad, general, nonthreatening questions designed to spark conversation.* Assessment questions elicit factual information about the customer's current situation that can provide a basis for further exploration and probing.

- *Discovery questions probe for details needed to identify and understand a buyer's problems and needs.* The buyer's interpretations, perceptions, feelings, and opinions are sought in regard to their needs, wants, dissatisfactions, and expectations.

- *Activation questions help the customer evaluate the negative impact of an implied need.* The objective is to "activate" interest in solving discovered problems by helping the customer gain insight into the true consequences of the problem.

- *Projection questions encourage the buyer's decision making by "projecting" what it would be like if the problems or needs did not exist.* They switch the focus from problems to benefits—the payoff for taking action and investing in a solution—and allow the buyer to establish the perceived value of solving the problem or need.

- *Transition questions smooth the transition to a subsequent phase in the selling process.* They are typically closed end and evaluative in format and strive to confirm the buyer's desire to seek a solution and move forward with the buying/selling process.

LO 5

Discuss the four sequential steps for effective active listening.

- *Sensing* is the first activity in active listening and involves receiving the message. Sensing is more than just hearing the message and requires concentration and practice.

- *Interpreting*. After sensing the message, it must be interpreted in terms of what the sender actually meant. In addition to meanings of words and symbols, the experiences, knowledge, and attitudes of the sender should also be considered.

- *Evaluating*. Effective communication requires the receiver to decide whether or not they agree with the sender's message. This requires evaluating the results from the interpretation stage to sort fact from opinion and emotion.

- *Responding*. Collaborative communication requires listeners to provide feedback to the other party. Responses take the form of paraphrasing the sender's message, answering questions, or asking questions to gain additional details and clarification.

LO 6

Discuss the superiority of pictures over words for explaining concepts and enhancing comprehension. Pictures are more memorable than words. Using descriptive words to "draw" mental pictures can enhance understanding as they are more easily recalled than abstract words and symbols. Understanding and recall can be aided by providing illustrative analogies or stories to emphasize a key point and bring it alive in the buyer's mind. Rather than abstract words that convey only a broad general understanding, utilize words and phrases that convey concrete and detailed meaning. Concrete expressions provide the receiver with greater information and are less likely to be misunderstood than their abstract counterparts.

LO 7

Describe and interpret the different forms of nonverbal communication. Nonverbal behaviours are made up of the various movements and utterances that people use. These can be conscious or unconscious and include eye movement and facial expressions; placement and movements of hands, arms, head, and legs as well as body orientation; the amount of space maintained between individuals; and variations in vocal characteristics. Sensing and interpreting groups or clusters of nonverbal cues can provide a reliable indicator of the underlying message and intent. Evidence shows that nonverbal behaviours carry 50 percent or more of the meaning conveyed in the process of interpersonal communication.

should drill down and probe for further details needed to develop, clarify, and understand the nature of the buyer's problems fully.

activation questions One of the five stages of questions in the ADAPT questioning system used to activate the customer's interest in solving discovered problems by helping him or her gain insight into the true ramifications of the problem and to realize that what may initially seem to be of little consequence is, in fact, of significant consequence.

projection questions One of the five stages of questions in the ADAPT questioning system used to encourage and help the buyer project what it would be like without the problems that have been previously "discovered" and "activated."

transition questions One of the five stages of questions in the ADAPT questioning system used to smooth the transition from needs discovery into the presentation and demonstration of the proposed solution's features and benefits.

social listening An informal mode of listening that can be associated with day-to-day conversation and entertainment.

serious listening A form of listening that is associated with events or topics in which it is important to sort through, interpret, understand, and respond to received messages.

active listening The cognitive process of actively sensing, interpreting, evaluating, and responding to the verbal and nonverbal messages of current or potential customers.

SIER A model that depicts active listening as a hierarchical, four-step sequence of sensing, interpreting, evaluating, and responding.

nonverbal communication The conscious and unconscious reactions, movements, and utterances that people use in addition to the words and symbols associated with language.

proxemics The personal distance that individuals prefer to keep between themselves and other individuals; an important element of nonverbal communication.

nonverbal clusters Groups of related nonverbal expressions, gestures, and movements that can be interpreted to better understand the true message being communicated.

CHAPTER REVIEW 4

NOTES

CHAPTER SUMMARY

LO 1

Discuss why prospecting is an important and challenging task for salespeople. Prospecting is important because market changes could cause current customers to buy less, customers could go out of business or be acquired by other firms, or business could be lost to competitors. Salespeople often fear rejection, and prospective buyers may be difficult to contact because they have never heard of a salesperson's firm, do not have the time to spend with all potential new suppliers, are somewhat shielded by gatekeepers trained to limit access, and are not relying on salespeople to provide information early in their buying process.

LO 2

Explain strategic prospecting and each stage in the strategic prospecting process. Strategic prospecting is a process for identifying the best sales opportunities. The strategic prospecting process consists of generating sales leads, determining sales prospects, prioritizing sales prospects, and preparing for sales dialogue.

FIG. 5.1 SALES FUNNEL

Generating Sales Leads

↓ Qualifying Sales Leads

Determining Sales Prospects

Prioritizing Sales Prospects

Preparing for Sales Dialogue

Remaining Stages in the Trust-Based Sales Process

GLOSSARY TERMS

strategic prospecting A process designed to identify, qualify, and prioritize sales opportunities, whether they represent potential new customers or opportunities to generate additional business from existing customers.

sales funnel or **pipeline** A representation of the trust-based sales process and strategic sales prospecting process in the form of a funnel.

sales leads or **suspects** Organizations or individuals who might possibly purchase the product or service a salesperson offers.

qualifying sales leads The salesperson's act of searching out, collecting, and analyzing information to determine the likelihood of the lead being a good candidate for making a sale.

sales prospect An individual or organization that has a need for the product or service, has the budget or financial resources to purchase the product or service, and has the authority to make the purchase decision.

ideal customer profile The characteristics of a firm's best customers or the perfect customer.

social selling Leveraging social media to identify, understand, engage, and network with prospects to develop relationships.

cold calling Contacting a sales lead unannounced and with little or no information about the lead.

referral A name of a company or person given to the salesperson as a lead by a customer or even a prospect who did not buy at this time.

introduction A variation of a referral in which, in addition to requesting the names of prospects, the salesperson asks the prospect or customer to prepare a note or letter of introduction that can be sent to the potential customer.

centres of influence Well-known and influential people who can help a salesperson prospect and gain leads.

CHAPTER REVIEW 5
GLOSSARY TERMS

noncompeting salespeople Salespeople selling noncompeting products.

electronic networking Using Web sites designed to help salespeople identify and gather information about prospects.

company records Information about customers in a company database.

advertising inquiries Sales leads generated from company advertising efforts.

inbound telemarketing A way to locate prospects in which the prospect calls the company to get information.

outbound telemarketing A way to locate prospects in which the salesperson contacts the prospect by telephone.

trade shows Events at which companies purchase space and set up booths that clearly identify each company and its offerings and that are staffed with salespeople who demonstrate the products and answer questions.

seminars A presentation salespeople give to generate leads and provide information to prospective customers who are invited to the seminar by direct mail, word of mouth, or advertising on local television or radio.

directories Electronic or print sources that provide contact and other information about many different companies or individuals.

lead management services Lists of targeted businesses or individuals with detailed contact and other information, as well as e-mail, direct mail, telephone, and Web-based marketing services to connect with targeted leads.

strategic prospecting plan A salesperson's plan for gathering qualified prospects.

tracking system Part of the strategic prospecting plan that records comprehensive information about the prospect, traces the prospecting methods used, and chronologically archives outcomes from any contacts with the prospect.

LO 3

Describe the major prospecting methods and give examples of each method. Salespeople should use different prospecting methods. The major prospecting methods are cold canvassing (cold calling, referrals, and introductions), networking (centres of influence, noncompeting salespeople, and social selling and social media), company sources (company records, advertising inquiries, telephone inquiries, trade shows, and seminars), and commercial sources (directories and lead management services).

LO 4

Explain the important components of a strategic prospecting plan. A strategic prospecting plan consists of setting specific goals for the numbers of prospects to be identified, a regular schedule for prospecting activities, a tracking system to keep records of prospecting activities, an evaluation system to assess prospecting progress, and a positive and confident attitude. .

LO 5

Discuss the types of information salespeople need to prepare for sales dialogue. Salespeople must gather information about the prospect that will be used to help formulate the sales presentation. The buyer's needs, motives, and details about the buyer's situation should be determined. The more a salesperson knows about the buyer, the better chance they will have to meet the buyer's needs and eventually earn the commitment.

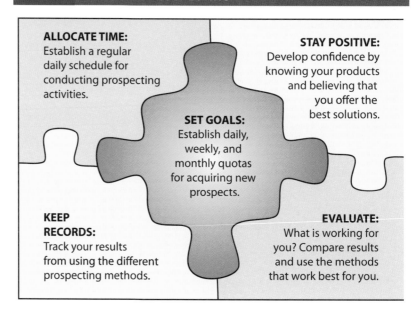

FIG. 5.2   PROSPECTING PLANS ARE THE FOUNDATION FOR EFFECTIVE PROSPECTING

ALLOCATE TIME: Establish a regular daily schedule for conducting prospecting activities.

STAY POSITIVE: Develop confidence by knowing your products and believing that you offer the best solutions.

SET GOALS: Establish daily, weekly, and monthly quotas for acquiring new prospects.

KEEP RECORDS: Track your results from using the different prospecting methods.

EVALUATE: What is working for you? Compare results and use the methods that work best for you.

CHAPTER SUMMARY

LO 1

Explain why it is essential to focus on the customer when planning sales calls. Buyers are well informed and have little time to waste on unproductive conversations with salespeople. To optimize the time spent on sale calls, salespeople should focus on customer needs and how the customer defines value. Customers differ in how they define value, and salespeople must understand each customer's concept of value so that they can establish sales dialogues that are clear, credible, and interesting.

LO 2

Understand alternative ways of communicating with prospects and customers through canned sales presentations, written sales proposals, and organized sales dialogues and presentations. Canned sales presentations include scripted sales calls, memorized presentations, and automated presentations. Effective canned presentations have usually been tested with real customers before an entire salesforce uses them. Canned sales presentations can be complete and logically structured. Objections are anticipated in advance, and appropriate responses can be formulated as part of the presentation. A written sales proposal is a complete, self-contained sales presentation. A sales proposal should be prepared after the salesperson has made a thorough assessment of the buyer's situation as it relates to the seller's offering. An organized sales dialogue, which could include a comprehensive sales presentation, is tailored to the prospect's particular situation and needs. It is a flexible format that allows for maximum input and feedback from the prospect. Sales dialogues and organized sales presentations (sometimes referred to as sales conversations) can take place over multiple sales calls before a purchase decision is made.

LO 3

Discuss the nine components of the sales dialogue template that can be used for planning an organized sales dialogue or an organized sales presentation. The sales dialogue template consists of nine sections: (1) prospect information; (2) customer value proposition; (3) sales call objective; (4) situation and needs analysis—linking buying motives, benefits, support information, and other reinforcement methods; (5) competitive situation; (6) beginning the sales dialogue; (7) anticipating questions and objections; (8) earning prospect commitment; and (9) building value through follow-up action. This template should not be used to develop a rigid script for a sales call. It is properly used to help the salespeople ensure that they are prepared to discuss all pertinent content with the customer.

GLOSSARY TERMS

sales call An in-person meeting between a salesperson or sales team and one or more buyers to discuss business.

sales dialogue Business conversations between buyers and sellers that occur as salespeople attempt to initiate, develop, and enhance customer relationships. Sales dialogue should be customer focused and have a clear purpose.

sales presentations Comprehensive communications that convey multiple points designed to persuade the customer to make a purchase.

canned sales presentation Sales presentations that include scripted sales calls, memorized presentations, and automated presentations.

written sales proposal A complete self-contained sales presentation on paper, often accompanied by other verbal sales presentations before or after the proposal is delivered.

organized sales dialogue Also known as the organized sales presentation. Unlike a canned sales presentation, an organized sales dialogue has a high level of customer involvement.

organized sales presentation A sales presentation that allows a salesperson to implement appropriate sales strategies and tactics based on customer research or information gathered during previous sales calls. Organized sales presentations feature a high-level two-way dialogue with the customer.

sales dialogue template A flexible planning tool that assists the salesperson in assembling pertinent information to be covered with the prospect.

CHAPTER REVIEW 6

GLOSSARY TERMS

customer value proposition A statement of how the sales offering will add value to the prospect's business by meeting a need or providing an opportunity.

buying motives A need-activated drive to search for and acquire a solution to resolve a need or problem; the most important factors from the customer's perspective in making a purchase decision.

rational buying motives Typically relate to the economics of the situation, including cost, profitability, quality, services offered, and the total value of the seller's offering as perceived by the customer.

emotional buying motives Include such motives as security, status, and the need to be liked; sometimes difficult for salespeople to uncover these motives.

features Qualities or characteristics of a product or service that are designed to provide value to a buyer.

benefits The added value or favourable outcome derived from features of the product or service the seller offers.

LO 4

Explain how to write a customer's value proposition statement. A customer value statement should be simple so that it provides a clear direction for upcoming sales dialogues. Salespeople should not attempt to include all their benefits in a value proposition statement—rather, they should choose the key benefits that are likely to be most important to the specific customer. The value proposition should be as specific as possible, on listing tangible outcomes, such as revenue improvement, cost containment or reduction gain in market share, process speed and efficiency, or the enhancement of a customer's strategic priority. Value proposition statements should promise only what can be consistently delivered. Strictly speaking, a customer value proposition in the planning stage is not a guarantee; it is a belief based on the salesperson's knowledge and best judgment. As the sales process moves along, appropriate guarantees can be made.

LO 5

Link buying motives to benefits of the seller's offering, support claims made for benefits, and reinforce verbal claims made. Organized sales dialogues and organized sales presentations should focus on the most important motives for a given buyer. Benefits must be linked to both rational and emotional motives, and supporting information must be given for each claim made about a benefit. In some cases, the claim needs support beyond the spoken word (e.g., through audio-visual content, printed collateral material, third-party research studies, or testimonials from satisfied customers).

LO 6

Engage the customer by setting appointments. Salespeople customarily set an appointment, at least for their initial sales calls on new prospects. Appointments may be arranged by telephone, e-mail, or a combination of phone and mail and should include a request for a specific time and date, as well as the amount of time being requested for the sales call. Salespeople have a better chance of securing an appointment if they are prepared to give the customer a good reason for spending time with them.

CHAPTER REVIEW 7
Sales Dialogue: Creating and Communicating Value

CHAPTER SUMMARY

LO 1
Describe the key characteristics of effective sales dialogue. The most effective sales dialogues are planned and practised by salespeople, encourage buyer feedback, focus on creating value for the buyer, present value in an interesting and understandable manner, engage and involve the buyer, and support customer value through objective claims.

LO 2
Explain how salespeople can generate feedback from buyers. Salespeople can generate feedback from buyers by paying attention to nonverbal cues from the buyer and using check-backs or response checks to get the buyer to respond to what the salesperson has said throughout the sales dialogue.

© kurhan/Shutterstock.com

Just like a mechanic diagnoses problems, salespeople must diagnose customer problems before prescribing solutions.

GLOSSARY TERMS

check-backs or response checks Questions salespeople use throughout a sales dialogue to generate feedback from the buyer.

confirmed benefits The benefits the buyer indicates are important and represent value.

verbal support The use of voice characteristics, examples and anecdotes, and comparisons and analogies to make sales dialogue interesting and understandable.

voice characteristics The pitch and speed of speech, which salespeople should vary to emphasize key points.

example A brief description of a specific instance used to illustrate features and benefits of a product or service.

anecdote A type of example that is provided in the form of a story describing a specific incident or occurrence.

comparison A statement that points out and illustrates the similarities between two points.

analogy A special and useful form of comparison that explains one thing in terms of another.

sales aids The use of printed materials, electronic materials, and product demonstrations to engage and involve buyers.

visual materials Printed materials, photographs and illustrations, and charts and graphs used as sales aids.

electronic materials Sales aids in electronic format, such as slides, videos, or multimedia presentations.

proof providers The use of statistics, testimonials, or case histories to support product claims.

statistics Facts that lend believability to product claims and are used as proof providers.

CHAPTER REVIEW 7

GLOSSARY TERMS

testimonials Proof providers that are in the form of statements from satisfied users of the selling organization's products and services.

case histories A testimonial in story or anecdotal form used as a proof provider.

preselling Salespeople present their product or service to individual buyers before a major sales dialogue with a group of buyers.

LO 3

Discuss how salespeople use confirmed benefits to create customer value. Salespeople can use the ADAPT or SPIN questioning process to interact with the buyer and determine what the buyer considers to be value. The salesperson then focuses on these confirmed benefits during the remainder of a sales dialogue.

LO 4

Describe how verbal support can be used to communicate value in an interesting and understandable manner. Salespeople need to communicate value in an interesting and understandable manner. This can be accomplished by varying the pitch and speed of speech, using examples and anecdotes, and including comparisons and analogies.

LO 5

Discuss how sales aids can engage and involve buyers. Sales aids are various tools salespeople can use to engage and involve buyers, generate interest and attention, and be more persuasive. Visual materials, electronic materials, and product demonstrations are the major categories of sales aids. It is important for salespeople to select the appropriate sales aids, but also to use them effectively. The SPES sequence of stating the selling point and introducing the sales aid, presenting the sales aid, explaining the sales aid, and summarizing can help salespeople use sales aids successfully.

LO 6

Explain how salespeople can support product claims. Salespeople need to be able to support the claims they make concerning their products. Proof providers, such as statistics, testimonials, and case histories, represent the major approaches for supporting product claims.

LO 7

Discuss the special considerations involved in sales dialogue with groups. Sales dialogues with individual buyers and with groups have many similarities and several important differences. Salespeople interacting with a group of buyers need to address their arrival tactics, how to handle questions, the proper use of eye contact, and how to communicate most effectively to the group and to individuals within the group.

CHAPTER SUMMARY

LO 1

Explain why it is important to anticipate and overcome buyer concerns and resistance. During the early years of selling, salespeople looked at sales resistance as a negative that was a likely indication their buyer was not going to buy. This notion has changed over the years, and now objections are viewed as opportunities to sell. Salespeople should be grateful for objections and always treat them as indications that the prospect needs more information; if the salesperson provides the correct information, they are moving closer to gaining the sale.

LO 2

Understand why prospects raise objections. Some prospects are happy with their present suppliers and want to avoid the sales interview. In other instances, the salesperson has failed to qualify the prospect properly. A prospect who has recently purchased a product is probably not in the market for another. Sometimes, prospects simply lack information on the salesperson's product category, and they are uncomfortable making a decision.

> ## Exhibit 8.2
>
> ## Types of Objections

No need	Buyer has recently purchased or does not see a need for the product category.
	"I am not interested at this time."
Product or service objection	Buyer may be afraid of product reliability.
	"I am not sure the quality of your product meets our needs."
	Buyer may be afraid of late deliveries, slow repairs, etc.
	"I am happy with my present supplier's service."
Company objection	Buyer is intensely loyal to the present supplier.
	"I am happy with my present supplier."
Price is too high	Buyer has a limited budget.
	"We have been buying from another supplier that meets our budget constraints."
Time or delay	Buyer needs time to think it over.
	"Get back with me in a couple of weeks."

GLOSSARY TERMS

sales resistance A buyer's objections to a product or service during a sales presentation.

need objection Resistance to a product or service in which a buyer says that they do not need the product or service.

product or service objection Resistance to a product or service in which a buyer does not like the way the product or service looks or feels.

company or source objection Resistance to a product or service that results when a buyer has never heard of or is not familiar with the product's company.

price objection Resistance to a product or service based on the price of the product being too high for the buyer.

time objection Resistance to a product or service in which a buyer puts off the decision to buy until a later date.

LAARC An acronym for listen, acknowledge, assess, respond, and confirm that describes an effective process for salespeople to follow to overcome sales resistance.

forestalling A response to buyer objections in which the salesperson answers the objection during the presentation before the buyer has a chance to ask it.

direct denial A response to buyer objections in which the salesperson tells the customer that they are wrong.

indirect denial A response to buyer objections in which the salesperson takes a softer, more tactful approach when correcting a prospect or customer's information.

translation or **boomerang** A response to buyer objections in which the salesperson converts the objection into a reason the prospect should buy.

compensation A response to buyer objections in which the salesperson counterbalances the objection with an offsetting benefit.

questions or assess A response to buyer objections in which the salesperson asks the buyer assessment questions to gain a better understanding of what the buyer is objecting to.

third-party reinforcement A response to buyer objections in which the salesperson uses the opinion or data from a third-party source to help overcome the objection and reinforce the salesperson's points.

commitment signals Favourable statements a buyer makes during a sales presentation that signal buyer commitment.

direct commitment A selling technique in which the salesperson asks the customer directly to buy.

alternative or legitimate choice A selling technique in which the salesperson asks the prospect to select from two or more choices during a sales presentation.

summary commitment A selling technique in which the salesperson summarizes all the major benefits the buyer has confirmed during the sales calls.

T-account or **balance sheet commitment** A selling technique in which a salesperson asks the prospect to brainstorm reasons on paper of why to buy and why not to buy.

success story commitment A selling technique in which a salesperson relates how one of their customers had a problem similar to the prospect's and solved it by using the salesperson's product.

standing-room-only close A sales closing technique in which the salesperson puts a time limit on the client in an attempt to hurry the decision to close.

assumptive close A sales closing technique in which the salesperson assumes that an agreement has been reached, places the order form in front of the buyer, and hands him or her a pen.

fear or emotional close A sales closing technique in which the salesperson tells a story of something unfavourable if the purchase is not made.

continuous yes close A sales closing technique that uses the principle that saying yes gets to be a habit; the salesperson asks a number of questions formulated so that the prospect answers yes.

minor-points close A sales closing technique in which the salesperson seeks agreement on relatively minor issues associated with the full order.

LO 3

Describe the five major types of sales resistance. Typically, objections include the following: "I don't need your product," "Your product is not a good fit," "I don't know your company," "Your price is too high," and "This is a bad time to buy."

LO 4

Explain how the LAARC method can be used to overcome buyer resistance. LAARC allows the salesperson to listen carefully to what the buyer is saying. It allows the salesperson to better understand the buyer's objections. After this careful analysis, the salesperson can then respond. The buyer feels that the salesperson is responding to their specific concern rather than giving a prepared answer.

LO 5

Describe the recommended approaches for responding to buyer objections. Salespeople have a number of traditional techniques at their disposal to handle resistance. Some of the more popular techniques include forestalling, or answering the objection before the prospect brings it up; direct denial; indirect denial, which softens the answer; translation or boomerang, which means to turn a reason not to buy into a reason to buy; compensation, or offsetting the objection with superior benefits; questions, which are used to uncover the buyer's concerns; and third-party reinforcements, which use the opinion or research of others to substantiate claims.

LO 6

List and explain the earning commitment techniques that secure commitment and closing. Many techniques can be used to earn commitment. Most are gimmicky in nature and reinforce the notion of traditional selling. Successful relationship-building techniques include the summary commitment, the success story commitment, and the direct commitment or ask for the order.

CHAPTER SUMMARY

LO 1
Explain how to follow up to assess customer satisfaction.
Salespeople cannot be afraid to ask their customers, "How are we doing?" Periodic follow-up is critical to long-term sales success. New customers generally feel special because they have received a lot of attention from the salesperson. Long-standing customers may feel neglected because the sales rep has many new customers and cannot be as attentive as they were previously. Routine follow-up to assess "How are we doing?" can go a long way in letting a customer know that the salesperson cares and is willing to make sure that they are satisfied.

LO 2
Explain how to harness technology to enhance follow-up and buyer–seller relationships. Effective salesperson follow-up should include specific components designed to interact, connect, know, and relate with their customers.

- *Interact*: The salesperson maximizes the number of critical encounters with buyers to encourage effective dialogue and involvement between the salesperson and the buyer.

- *Connect*: The salesperson maintains contact with multiple individuals in the buying organization who influence purchase decisions and manages the various touch points the customer has in the selling organization to ensure consistency in communication.

- *Know*: The salesperson coordinates and interprets the information gathered through buyer–seller contact and collaboration to develop insight regarding the buyer's changing situation, needs, and expectations.

- *Relate*: The salesperson applies relevant understanding and insight to create value-added interactions and develop relationships between the salesperson and buyer.

Salespeople have employed a variety of technology-based salesforce automation tools to better track increasingly complex buyer–seller interactions and to manage the exchange, interpretation, and storage of diverse types of information. Among the more popular salesforce automation tools are the many competing versions of PC– and Internet-based software applications designed to record and manage customer contact information. PC–based software applications such as Maximizer, Goldmine, and ACT!, and Internet-based applications such as Netsuite and Salesforce.com enable salespeople to collect, file, and access comprehensive databases detailing information about individual buyers and buying organizations.

GLOSSARY TERMS

building goodwill The process of converting new customers into lifetime customers by continually adding value to the product.

adding value The process of improving a product or service for the customer.

interact The salesperson acts to maximize the number of critical encounters with buyers to encourage effective dialogue and involvement between the salesperson and buyer.

connect The salesperson maintains contact with the multiple individuals in the buying organization who influence purchase decisions and manages the various touch points the customer has in the selling organization to ensure consistency in communication.

know The salesperson coordinates and interprets the information gathered through buyer–seller contact and collaboration to develop insight regarding the buyer's changing situation, needs, and expectations.

relate The salesperson applies relevant understanding and insight to create value-added interactions and generate relationships between the salesperson and buyer.

intranet An organization's dedicated and proprietary computer network that offers password-controlled access to people within and outside the organization (e.g., customers and suppliers).

extranet Proprietary computer networks created by an organization for use by the organization's customers or suppliers and linked to the organization's internal systems, informational databases, and intranet.

CHAPTER REVIEW 9

GLOSSARY TERMS

customer relationship management (CRM) system A system that dynamically links buyers and sellers into a rich communication network to establish and reinforce long-term, profitable relationships.

critical encounters Meetings in which the salesperson encourages the buyer to discuss tough issues, especially in areas in which the salesperson's organization is providing less than satisfactory performance.

collaborative involvement A way to build on buyer–salesperson relationships in which the buyer's organization and the salesperson's organization join together to improve an offering.

service quality Meeting and/ or exceeding customer service expectations.

service strategy A plan in which a salesperson identifies their business and customers and what the customers want and what is important to them.

communication A two-way flow of information between the salesperson and the customer.

resilience The ability of a salesperson to get knocked down several times a day by a customer's verbal assault (i.e., complaint) and get right back up with a smile and ask for more.

service motivation The desire of a salesperson to service customers each day.

LO 3

Discuss how to take action to ensure customer satisfaction.
Salespeople must follow up on specific relationship-enhancement activities such as:

- Providing useful information to their customers
- Expediting orders and monitoring a successful installation
- Training customer personnel
- Correcting billing errors
- Remembering the customer after the sale
- Resolving complaints in a timely manner

LO 4

Discuss how to expand collaborative involvement. The easiest way to expand collaborative involvement is to get more people involved in the relationship from both the buyer's and the seller's firms.

LO 5

Explain how to add value and enhance mutual opportunities. The salesperson can enhance mutual opportunities by reducing risk for the buyer through repeated displays of outstanding customer service. The salesperson can also demonstrate a willingness to serve the customer over extended periods of time. The buyer needs to experience a readiness on the seller's part to go to bat for the buyer when things get tough.

CHAPTER SUMMARY

LO 1

Explain the five sequential stages of self-leadership. As a process, self-leadership is composed of five sequential stages. First, goals and objectives must be set that properly reflect what is important and what is to be accomplished. In turn, an analysis of the territory and classification of accounts is conducted to better understand the territory potential and prioritize accounts according to revenue-producing possibilities. With goals in place and accounts prioritized, the third stage develops corresponding strategic plans designed to achieve sales goals through proper allocation of resources and effort. The next stage maximizes the effectiveness of allocated resources by incorporating technology and salesforce automation to expand salesperson resource capabilities. Finally, assessment activities are conducted to evaluate performance and goal attainment and to assess possible changes in plans and strategies.

LO 2

Identify the four levels of sales goals and explain their interrelationships. Salespeople must establish the following four different levels of goals to maximize sales effectiveness:

1. Personal goals: what one wants to accomplish relative to oneself.

2. Sales call goals: the priorities to be accomplished during a specific call

3. Account goals: the objectives for each individual account

4. Territory goals: what is to be accomplished for the overall territory

    Each level requires different types of effort and produces different outcomes, and each of the levels is interrelated with and interdependent on the others. Ultimately, each higher level goal is dependent on the salesperson setting and achieving the specific goals for each lower level.

LO 3

Describe techniques for account classification. There are two basic methods of classifying accounts. In ascending order of complexity, these methods are single-factor analysis and portfolio analysis (also referred to as two-factor analysis).

- *Single-factor analysis:* Also referred to as ABC analysis, this is the simplest and most often-used method for classifying accounts. Accounts are analyzed on the basis of one single factor—typically the level of sales potential—and placed into either three or four categories denoted by letters of the alphabet: A, B, C, and D. All accounts in the same category receive equal selling effort.

- *Portfolio analysis (two-factor analysis):* This classification method allows two factors to be considered simultaneously. Each account is examined on the basis of the two factors selected for analysis and sorted into the proper segment of a matrix. This matrix is typically divided into four cells, with accounts placed into the proper classification cell on the basis of their

GLOSSARY TERMS

self-leadership The process of doing the right things and doing them well.

goals and objectives The things a salesperson sets out to accomplish.

personal goals A salesperson's individual desired accomplishment, such as achieving a desired annual income over a specific period.

territory goal A salesperson's desire to sell a certain amount of product within an area or territory to achieve personal goals.

account goal A salesperson's desire to sell a certain amount of product to one customer or account to achieve territory and personal goals.

sales call goal A salesperson's desire to sell a certain amount of product per each sales call to achieve account, territory, and personal goals.

territory analysis The process of surveying an area to determine customers and prospects who are most likely to buy.

account classification The process of placing existing customers and prospects into categories based on their potential as a customer.

single-factor analysis A method for analyzing accounts that is based on one single factor, typically the level of sales potential.

portfolio analysis A method for analyzing accounts that allows two factors to be considered simultaneously.

sales planning The process of scheduling activities that can be used as a map for achieving objectives.

CHAPTER REVIEW 10

GLOSSARY TERMS

straight-line routing plan A territory routing plan in which salespeople start from their offices and make calls in one direction until they reach the end of the territory.

cloverleaf routing plan A territory routing plan in which the salesperson works a different part of the territory and travels in a circular loop back to the starting point.

circular routing plan A territory routing plan in which the salesperson begins at the office and moves in an expanding pattern of concentric circles that spiral across the territory.

leapfrog routing plan A territory routing plan in which, beginning in one cluster, the salesperson works each of the accounts at that location and then jumps to the next cluster.

major city routing plan A territory routing plan used when the territory is composed of a major metropolitan area and the territory is split into a series of geometric shapes reflecting each one's concentration and pattern of accounts.

selling technology and automation Tools that streamline the selling process, generate improved selling opportunities, facilitate cross-functional teaming and intraorganizational communication, and enhance communication and follow-up with customers.

mobile salesperson CRM solutions Wireless broadband applications that enable users to view, create, and modify data on any Internet-capable devices, such as smartphones, netbooks, and laptops.

individual ratings (high and low or strong and weak) on each of the two factors. Accounts in the same cell share a common level of attractiveness as a customer and will receive the same amount of selling effort.

LO 4

Understand the application of different territory routing techniques. Territory routing plans incorporate information developed in the territory analysis and account classification to minimize unproductive travel time that could be better spent working with customers. Good routing plans minimize the backtracking and crisscrossing that would otherwise occur. Routing plans correspond to one of five common patterns.

- *Straight line*—With a straight-line plan, salespeople start from their offices and make calls in one direction until they reach the end of the territory. At that point, they change direction and continue to make calls on a straight line on the new vector.

- *Cloverleaf*—Using the cloverleaf pattern, a salesperson works a different part of the territory and travels in a circular loop back to the starting point. Each loop could take a day, a week, or longer to complete. A new loop is covered on each trip until the entire territory has been covered.

- *Circular*—Circular patterns begin at the office and move in an expanding pattern of concentric circles that spiral across the territory. This method works best when accounts are evenly dispersed throughout the territory.

- *Leapfrog*—When the territory is exceptionally large and accounts are clustered into several widely dispersed groups, the leapfrog routing methodology is most efficient. Beginning in one cluster, the salesperson works each of the accounts at that location and then jumps (often by flying) to the next cluster. This continues until the last cluster has been worked and the salesperson jumps back to the office or home.

- *Major city*—Downtown areas are typically highly concentrated with locations organized by a grid of city blocks and streets. Consequently, the downtown segment is typically a small square or rectangular area allowing accounts to be worked in a straight-line fashion street by street. Outlying areas are placed in evenly balanced triangles or pie-shaped quadrants, with one quadrant being covered at a time in either a straight-line or cloverleaf pattern.

LO 5

Interpret the usefulness of different types of selling technology and automation. Properly applied, selling technology spurs creativity and innovation, streamlines the selling process, generates new selling opportunities, facilitates communication, and enhances customer follow-up. Salespeople not only must master the technology itself but also must understand when and where it can be applied most effectively. Today's selling technologies provide the production tools for generating reports, proposals, and graphic-enhanced presentations. Spreadsheet applications and database applications facilitate the analysis of customer accounts and searching for information needed by customers. Contact management software enables the salesperson to gather and organize account information and schedule calls. Access to the Internet and World Wide Web provide salespeople with access to an assortment of public and corporate networks that enable them to communicate, research, and access company information and training from anywhere in the world. Mobile devices and customized applications put salespeople in touch with customers, the home office, and even the family while traveling cross-country or just walking across the parking lot to make a customer call. Voice mail and texting applications avoid the previous restrictions of time and place that accompanied the requirement to make personal contact. Messages can now be left and received 24 hours a day and seven days a week. High-tech sales support offices provide geographically dispersed salespeople with a common standard of computing technology, access to software applications, and portals to organizational networks at offices around the world. Wherever they may be working, they have the tools and capabilities identical to those available to them in their home offices.

LO 6

Describe increasing customer value through artwork. With increasing customer expectations and growing complexity of selling situations, teamwork has become critical for maximizing customer focus and sales performance. Teamwork results in synergies that produce greater outcomes and results for all parties than would be possible with multiple individuals acting independently of one another. Highly effective sales professionals work with customers to develop a mutual understanding of the customer's situation, needs, possibilities, and expectations. Based on that mutual understanding, the salesperson assembles a team of individuals—experts from across the selling organization—who work together in creating a product response that delivers more unique customer value than competitors' offerings. In delivering this unique and added value for customers, salespeople often find themselves working with other individuals in sales, marketing, design and manufacturing, administrative support, shipping, and customer service. Teamwork is built on reciprocal trust enhanced through six teamwork skills: (1) Understanding the other individuals; (2) Attending to the little things; (3) Keeping commitments; (4) Clarifying expectations; and (5) Showing personal integrity; and (6) Apologizing sincerely when a mistake is made.

LO 7

Identify the six skills for building internal relationships and teams.

1 *Understanding the other individuals*—Fully understanding and considering the other individuals in the partnership is necessary to know what is important to them. What is important to them must also be important to the salesperson if the partnership is to grow and be effective.

2 *Attending to the little things*—The little kindnesses and courtesies are small in size, but great in importance. Properly attended to and nurtured, they enhance the interrelationships. However, when neglected or misused, they can destroy the relationship very quickly.

3 *Keeping commitments*—We build hopes and plans around the promises and commitments made to us by others. When a commitment is not kept, disappointment and problems result and credibility and trust suffer major damage that will be difficult or impossible to repair.

4 *Clarifying expectations*—The root cause of most relational difficulties can be found in ambiguous expectations regarding roles and goals. By clarifying goals and priorities as well as who is responsible for different activities up front, the hurt feelings, disappointments, and lost time resulting from misunderstandings and conflict can be prevented.

5 *Showing personal integrity*—Demonstrating personal integrity generates trust. Be honest, open, and treat everyone by the same set of principles.

6 *Apologizing sincerely when a mistake is made*—It is one thing to make a mistake. It is another thing to not admit it. People forgive mistakes, but ill intentions and cover-ups can destroy trust.

CHAPTER REVIEW 10
GLOSSARY TERMS

deal analytics "Smart" salesforce automation tools that analyze data on past customer behaviour, cross-selling opportunities, and demographics to identify areas of opportunity and high customer interest.

high-tech sales support offices Offices set up at multiple locations where salespeople can access a wider range of selling technology than could be easily carried on a notebook or laptop computer.

external relationships Relationships salespeople build with customers outside the organization and working environment.

internal relationships Relationships salespeople have with other individuals in their own company.

teamwork skills Skills salespeople must learn to build internal partnerships that translate into increased sales and organizational performance.

CHAPTER REVIEW 10

INTRODUCTION

The National Copier Company (NCC) sells a variety of copiers to small and medium-sized businesses. NCC has been in business for five years and has been growing at a steady pace. NCC differentiates itself from other copier companies by customizing its products to meet the specific needs of each customer and by providing excellent customer service. The company's salesforce plays a key role in creating value and managing customer relationships.

Brenda Smith has been an NCC salesperson for the past three years. She has steadily improved her sales performance during her time with NCC, and now she is in the top 25 percent of all NCC sales representatives as measured by two key metrics: overall sales volume and customer satisfaction. Brenda has been especially successful with small professional firms, such as attorneys, architects, accountants, and medical professionals. She is excited to begin her fourth year with NCC and has established challenging goals to increase sales from existing customers and to generate new customers.

Brenda recently met with Jin Tan, her sales manager, and was quite excited about the upcoming year. Jin had told Brenda that she was progressing toward a possible promotion into sales training if she had another good year in her sales position. In addition, Jin gave Brenda this feedback: "Brenda, I think you are doing a fine job with your customers, but I would like to see you become more of a consultative salesperson in the coming year. I would also like for you to sharpen your group communications skills, as that will be important if you are promoted into sales training. We will talk about the specifics more as the year goes along. Meanwhile, thanks for your results to date and good luck with the upcoming year."

QUESTIONS

1. Brenda had been thinking about Jin Tan's feedback that directed her to become more of a consultative salesperson. In thinking about her own selling approaches, she knew that she had been concentrating on the needs satisfaction and problem-solving approaches. What must Brenda do to become a more consultative salesperson?

2. Three months later, Brenda was having mixed results with the consultative selling approach. She was finding that some of her customers just wanted the convenience of having a copier in their offices and did not seem eager to discuss their strategic goals. She was beginning to wonder about the consultative selling model, thinking it was not such a good idea after all. What recommendations do you have for Brenda?

3. A month before the annual meeting for all NCC sales representatives, Jin Tan told Brenda, "For the upcoming meeting, I want you to prepare a 10-minute

presentation about the pros and cons of the basic selling approaches that we use at NCC compared with our competitors." NCC's sales training program advocated the use of needs satisfaction, problem-solving, and consultative selling. Many of NCC's key competitors used the same approaches. However, some of the toughest competitors used stimulus-response and mental states (AIDA) approaches. This latter category of competitors often stressed lower prices and used telemarketing instead of field sales representatives in selling their products. Put yourself in Brenda's role and prepare the presentation requested by Jin Tan.

4. Early in the year, Jin Tan told Brenda that her efforts were needed to gain more exposure for NCC's university recruiting program: "Brenda, I want you to be part of a two-person team to help with recruiting on two university campuses in your territory. The other team member will be an experienced recruiter who had sales experience before moving into recruiting. The two of you should seek out opportunities as guest speakers for classes and student organizations. Your role will be to talk about how sales can be a great place to start a career and for some, a great career path. Think about the future of selling and what it takes to be successful and share your thoughts with students." Acting as Brenda, make note of ten key points you would like to make about the future of professional selling and what it takes to be successful.

NOTES

_____

_____

_____

_____

_____

_____

_____

_____

_____

_____

_____

_____

Building Trust and Sales Ethics: Developing Trust and Mutual Respect with Clients

BUILDING TRUST

Because the National Copier Company (NCC) has been in business for only five years, Brenda Smith is concerned that most of her competitors are older than she is. The prospective customers she has been calling on state they know they can count on her competitors because they have a long track record. As NCC expands into new markets some of her prospects are not familiar with her company. One prospective customer, who works for one of the most prestigious and largest medical offices (30 doctors) in the area, told her he has been buying copiers from the same company for more than 25 years. He also told her his sales representative for the company has been calling on him for more than seven years, and he knows that when he calls on his copier supplier for advice he can count on him for a solid recommendation. Brenda realizes these are going to be tough accounts to crack.

Brenda does have an advantage because of the high quality of NCC products. In a recent trade publication, NCC's copiers tied for first in the industry on ratings of copier quality and dependability. NCC was also given a high rating for service. Brenda has had this information for two weeks now and has brought it up in conversations with her prospective customers without much success. To make matters worse, one of her competitors must have started rumours about NCC. In the past month, she has heard the following rumours:

"NCC is going out of business because of financial troubles."

"NCC has missed several delivery deadlines with customers."

"NCC's copiers have a software glitch that cannot be corrected."

"NCC has cut its service staff."

Brenda knows these rumours are not true, but prospects might believe them. At a recent sales meeting, Brenda's manager suggested that their competitors must be getting nervous about NCC's success, causing them to start such vicious rumours.

Brenda is sitting at her desk trying to figure out what to do next and she is not exactly sure how to proceed.

QUESTIONS

1. What would you recommend Brenda do to handle the challenges she faces?
2. Brenda appears to have an advantage with her products and services. Develop a plan for Brenda to build trust in NCC with prospective customers.

3. What do you recommend Brenda do to compete effectively against competitors that have a long and successful track record?

4. How should Brenda go about handling the rumour mill?

NOTES

_____

_____

_____

_____

_____

_____

_____

_____

_____

_____

_____

_____

_____

_____

_____

_____

_____

_____

_____

_____

UNDERSTANDING TOM PENDERS

It was Monday afternoon and Brenda Smith was very excited. She had just got off the phone with Tom Penders, the administrator in charge of a large medical office in her territory. After an introductory letter and several follow-up phone calls, Tom Penders had finally agreed to meet with Brenda next Friday to discuss the possibility of replacing his organization's old copiers, as well as adding new copiers to keep pace with his organization's rapid growth. The primary purpose of the meeting was for Tom to learn more about the National Copier Company (NCC) and its products and for Brenda to learn more about Tom's company and its specific needs.

When Brenda arrived about 10 minutes early for her meeting with Tom Penders at the medical offices on Friday, she was greeted by a receptionist who asked her to be seated. Ten minutes passed and Brenda was promptly shown to Tom's office. Brenda couldn't help but notice how organized Tom's office was. It appeared to Brenda that Tom was a man of detail. First, Tom explained that the medical offices housed more than 30 doctors specializing in a variety of fields. They occupied two floors and were planning to expand to the vacant third floor in the near future. Currently, they were organized into five divisions with an office professional assigned to approximately six doctors for each division. Each division ran its own office with a separate copier and administrative facilities. Tom also had an assistant and a copier. After giving his overview, Tom provided Brenda with an opportunity to ask questions. After that, Tom systematically went down a list of questions he had about NCC, its products, and Brenda herself. Following this, Tom had his assistant take Brenda on a tour of the facility so she could overview their processes. Before leaving, Tom agreed to meet with Brenda in two weeks.

Based on her conversation with Tom, Brenda did not find Tom to be a particularly personable individual. In fact, she found him to be somewhat cool and aloof, deliberate both in his communication and his actions. Yet Tom was willing to learn how NCC could help his medical office. Although Brenda preferred communicating with someone more personable and open, such as herself, she was determined to find a way to win Tom's business.

QUESTIONS

1. What type of communication style do you believe that Tom exhibits? What are the characteristics of this communication style?

2. Based on your understanding of Tom's communication style, outline a plan for selling to Tom Penders.

3. Identify other members of Tom Penders' organization that may play a role in the buying decision and explain the role they might play. How should Brenda handle these individuals?

4. Explain the types of buyer needs that will be most important in this selling situation.

NOTES

_____

_____

_____

_____

_____

_____

_____

_____

_____

_____

_____

_____

_____

_____

_____

_____

_____

_____

CHAPTER CONTINUING CASE · 4
Communication Skills

SHARPENING THE SELLING TOOLS

Brenda Smith is working in the office this morning preparing for tomorrow's sales call with Gage Waits, managing partner, and Tanisha Autry, operations manager, at Energy-Based Funds LLC. Energy-Based Funds is a major investment banking organization specializing in managing and marketing a variety of energy-based mutual funds. The company operates throughout Canada and employs 175 people, with offices occupying the top three floors of a major office building in the heart of the financial district. For the past several years, Energy-Based Funds has been leasing and purchasing office equipment from Altima Systems, one of Brenda's biggest competitors. Brenda has been working her network to get a chance to begin a sales dialogue with Energy-Based Funds and she finally has an appointment with the main players on the purchasing team: Gage and Tanisha.

Brenda knows that planning is a key part of success in selling and is diligently working on her strategy and plans in preparation for tomorrow's sales call with Gage and Tanisha at Energy-Based Funds. According to the sales call plan that Brenda is developing, the purpose of this initial meeting is twofold: (1) to discover more about Energy-Based Funds' current operations, their future plans, and the nature of their use of and needs for copiers; (2) to begin acquainting Gage and Tanisha with NCC and the value they can provide Energy-Based Funds. At this point in her sales call plan, Brenda is considering the different pieces of information she needs to get from the dialogue and what questions she might use to elicit that information from Gage and Tanisha.

QUESTIONS

1. Based on the purpose of probing questions explained in your text, explain how Brenda should use probing types of questions in her initial sales dialogue with Gage and Tanisha at Energy-Based Funds. Consider the types of information Brenda needs and develop several illustrative examples of probing questions Brenda might use.

2. Evaluative questions are also effective in sales conversations. Explain the purpose of evaluative questions and how Brenda might effectively use them in this initial sales call. Provide several illustrative examples of evaluative questions Brenda could use.

3. The ADAPT questioning system is a logic-based sequence of questions designed for effective fact-finding and gaining information about a buyer's situation. Develop a series of ADAPT questions that Brenda might use in her sales call to develop the information she needs regarding Energy-Based Funds, their operations, and their needs for copiers.

4. What recommendations would you give Brenda regarding nonverbal communication and how she might use it for more effective communication in this sales call?

NOTES

_____

_____

_____

_____

_____

_____

_____

_____

_____

_____

_____

_____

_____

_____

_____

_____

_____

_____

_____

_____

_____

_____

FISHING FOR NEW CUSTOMERS

Brenda Smith has been very successful at getting existing customers to upgrade or purchase new copiers during the past two months. She is, however, disappointed in her efforts to get new customers. To add more new customers, Brenda has been spending a great deal of time prospecting. These efforts have produced a large number of leads. Once she generates a lead, she contacts the firm and tries to set up an appointment. Unfortunately, most of these leads are not interested in talking about copiers and are not willing to schedule a meeting with her. This has been so frustrating that she decided to make several cold calls this week to see if this would be a good way to get to meet with prospective customers. The cold calls were also not very successful and were extremely time consuming. Brenda did finally get a few leads to agree to meet with her, but these appointments were not very productive. The leads were typically satisfied with the copiers they were using and were not interested in learning about NCC copiers.

Jin Tan, her sales manager, accompanied her on a recent sales call to a lead. After the sales call, Jin expressed his disappointment that they had really wasted their time with this meeting. Jin then asked Brenda about her prospecting process because it was clear that she was not identifying and spending her time with the best sales opportunities. Her approach was not working well and was taking a lot of time. If she continued doing the same things, Brenda was not likely to generate many new customers and might lose some existing customers because she was spending too much of her time prospecting.

Brenda realizes that she must improve her prospecting process, but she is not sure exactly how to proceed.

QUESTIONS

1. What is Brenda doing wrong? What would you recommend Brenda do to improve her prospecting efforts?

2. Explain the strategic prospecting process to Brenda and discuss how she can implement it.

3. What secondary lead sources would you recommend Brenda use to identify the best attorneys, architects, accountants, and medical professionals as prospects?

4. What specific types of information should Brenda obtain before contacting a qualified prospect?

5. How could Brenda use social selling to improve her strategic prospecting?

NOTES

CHAPTER CONTINUING CASE

Planning Sales Dialogues and Presentations

CUSTOM PRODUCT, CUSTOM PRESENTATION

During the past three months, Brenda had improved her prospecting process. She was identifying more prospects that represented better sales opportunities. Brenda knew that it was important to plan her sales calls in advance to maximize the time she spent in face-to-face selling. In this selling environment, most customers were not interested in all of the features of Brenda's products. Brenda had to determine what was important to each customer, and customize her presentations accordingly. Further, she had to clearly communicate the benefits of her products, and not overwhelm potential buyers with too much technical language. Assume that Brenda has an appointment with EFP, a nonprofit organization that raises money to promote environmentally friendly practices such as recycling. The organization uses e-mail, Web-based communications, and direct mail campaigns to reach potential donors. EFP is currently using an older-generation copy machine that frequently needs maintenance. When EFP needs high-quality colour copies, they rely on a local company to produce the copies. This works fairly well, although sometimes there are delays in getting the copies back from the local copy shop. EFP has a fax machine. Although it is rarely used, EFP's management has told Brenda that a fax capability is important for communicating with some clients. Currently, EFP does not have a good way of scanning documents. This is a big problem, as using scanned documents in client e-mails is increasingly preferred. Given these circumstances, Brenda believes that EFP could benefit from a multifunction printer. A multifunction printer consolidates the functionality of a printer, copier, scanner, and fax machine into one machine. EFP has agreed to consider a multifunction printer, but their management is concerned about cost and the reliance on a single machine if there are breakdowns.

QUESTIONS

1. Using an Internet search engine such as Google, find the general benefits of multifunction printers. You might enter "benefits of multifunction printers" in the search engine, or examine data from copier providers such as Ricoh, Canon, or Xerox to find these benefits. List five to six potential benefits of a digital copier to EFP.

2. From the listing developed in question 1, select three benefits. For each benefit, write a sentence or two that Brenda might use to communicate these benefits during her sales call with EFP.

3. For the three benefits identified in question 2, describe what information Brenda should have on hand when she makes the sales call on the EFP buyer. Also describe how this information would be best

communicated—that is, what support materials will Brenda need to enhance her verbal communications?

4. Assume that the buyer acknowledges interest in at least two of the benefits identified in question 2. Write a realistic buyer–seller dialogue of Brenda's interaction with the EFP buyer concerning these benefits.

NOTES

_____

_____

_____

_____

_____

_____

_____

_____

_____

_____

_____

_____

_____

_____

_____

_____

_____

_____

_____

_____

_____

CHAPTER CONTINUING CASE

Sales Dialogue: Creating and Communicating Value

UP FOR THE CHALLENGE

Brenda has a meeting today with the office manager at the law firm Arseneau and Wilson (A&W). A&W is a local law firm with five attorneys and one main office. During her initial telephone conversation, the office manager indicated that the firm was reasonably satisfied with their current copiers but that he was always looking for ways to increase office productivity. He also mentioned that he was a little concerned that the firm was paying for many copier features that were not really used. The law firm needed to make a lot of legal-sized copies and be able to collate and staple them. There was little need for other "bells and whistles." It was also important that a copier was dependable because the law firm made many copies each day. When the copier did break down, fast service was needed to get it repaired as soon as possible.

The office manager had some familiarity with NCC products and was eager to talk to Brenda. However, he made it clear that any decision to switch to NCC copiers would require that Brenda also meet with the attorneys and office personnel to get their approval. If Brenda convinced him that NCC copiers would increase office productivity at the law firm, he would be glad to set up a meeting for her with the attorneys and office personnel.

Brenda is excited about this opportunity. She knows that NCC copiers are very dependable and that NCC provides exceptional service. She can also offer the law firm a copier with the specific features A&W desires.

QUESTIONS

1. Prepare the sales dialogue Brenda might employ and use an anecdote to communicate the dependability of NCC copiers to the office manager.

2. Brenda will not be able to demonstrate a copier during this sales call. Describe the types of sales aids she should use to show the buyer an NCC copier with the exact features they desire.

3. How can Brenda best use statistics and testimonials to support the excellent service provided by NCC?

4. Brenda did a terrific job in her sales call with the office manager. He is interested in NCC copiers and has scheduled a meeting for Brenda with the five attorneys and the office personnel. Discuss the major things Brenda should do during her sales call to this group.

CHAPTER CONTINUING CASE 7

CHAPTER CONTINUING CASE

8

Addressing Concerns and Earning Commitment

HANDLING SALES RESISTANCE

Brenda recently returned from a two-week training session that focused on how to handle sales resistance and how to earn commitment. Brenda has become quite familiar with the ADAPT questioning system and knows she must use assessment questions to allow the buyer to describe their present situation. She has also developed a pretty good set of discovery questions that helps her identify the buyer's needs and problems. Her challenge has been what to do with this information. Whenever Brenda attempts to use features and benefits to make her case, she encounters myriad objections. Brenda knows she has great products and service, but she has not been able to communicate this effectively to her prospects.

The objection she hears most often is, "I've never heard of your company. How long have you been in business?" If that is not bad enough, she heard the following objections in just one morning:

> "I'm not sure I am ready to buy at this time. I'll need to think it over."

> "Your company is pretty new. How do I know you'll be around to take care of me in the future?"

> "Your price is a little higher than I thought it would be."

> "Your company was recently in the news. Are you having problems?"

> "I think your company is too small to meet our needs."

Brenda hears most of these objections right after she attempts to earn a commitment. She is now getting a little reluctant about asking her prospects for the order.

Brenda is sitting at her desk trying to figure out what to do next. She is not sure how to proceed.

QUESTIONS

1. What would you recommend Brenda do to handle the challenges she faces?

2. Brenda appears to have an advantage with her products and services. Develop a plan for Brenda to overcome the sales resistance she is receiving.

3. Use the LAARC process to develop a suggested dialogue Brenda can use to address one of the major types of resistance she is receiving.

4. What can Brenda do in the future to encounter less sales resistance when she asks for the order?

NOTES

THE DISGRUNTLED CUSTOMER

It was 8:30 a.m. Friday morning when Brenda received the voice mail. It was Susan Swanson, owner of a small architecture firm, who Brenda had acquired as a customer nearly three months ago. "I'm finished with you all," she barked. "Come get my copier. I want my money back! This blasted machine you sold me keeps jamming. I was billed for extra toner that I never received. You promised me training, and I have yet to see any. And this machine is much slower than I thought it would be. I don't see how your company stays in business. I knew I should have gone with Xerox!"

It's true, Brenda had told Susan that she would provide training on how to use some of the advanced features of the copier. She had neglected to get back to Susan and since she had not heard from Susan she assumed Susan no longer desired the training. As for the paper jams, Brenda found this to be unusual. NCC carried high-quality copiers and she could not imagine what might be wrong. She was sure she had told Susan the specific type of paper to use for her application. However, using the wrong paper could lead to more frequent paper jams. But why hadn't Susan said anything to her about this sooner? As for the extra toner, Brenda recalls that Susan did order it and later contacted her to let her know that she had not received it. Brenda then contacted NCC's shipping department who said they would ship Susan the product. Brenda just assumed that it had been shipped. As for the speed of the machine, Brenda was certain its output was per specifications as equipment at NCC must pass strict quality control measures. Perhaps Susan simply misunderstood the machine's capabilities. *Wow*, Brenda thought, *now what am I going to do?*

QUESTIONS

1. How should Brenda handle this complaint?

2. What could Brenda have done to avoid this incident?

3. What steps can Brenda take to do a better job of maintaining open, two-way communication with Susan?

4. Assuming that Brenda can retain Susan as a customer, how can she add value to her relationship with Susan's firm?

MANAGING AND CLASSIFYING ACCOUNTS

Brenda's planning and extra effort in servicing and developing her accounts continue to produce increasing levels of profitable business for NCC. Her methodical approach to identifying new prospects and building repeat business within her existing accounts has been observed by her sales manager as well as the regional vice president of sales. As a result of Brenda's consistent performance, she has been given the opportunity to expand her current list of accounts by taking over part of the account list of a retiring salesperson and integrating them into an expanded territory. Brenda is working through the account information files for each of these added accounts and has summarized the information into the following table.

Account Name	Account Opportunity	Competitive Position	Annual Number of Sales Calls (Last Year)
Maggie Mae Foods	Low	High	23
C³ Industries	High	Low	28
Trinity Engineering	High	High	28
Britecon Animations	High	High	22
Lost Lake Foods	High	Low	26
Attaway Global Consulting	High	High	24
Waits and Sons	Low	High	21
Reidell Business Services	High	High	26
Ferrell & Associates	Low	Low	16
Biale Beverage Corp	High	High	18
Captain Charlie's Travel	High	Low	23
Cole Pharmaceuticals	High	Low	20
PuddleJumper Aviation	Low	High	18
Tri-Power Investment Services	Low	Low	18
Ballou Resin & Plastics	Low	Low	14
Tri-Chem Customer Products	Low	High	20
Guardian Products	High	High	25
Bartlesville Specialties	Low	High	26

CHAPTER CONTINUING CASE 10

1. Develop a portfolio classification of Brenda's 18 new accounts. What is your assessment of the allocation of sales calls made by Brenda's predecessor over the previous year?

2. What specific suggestions would you make in terms of sales call allocation strategy for Brenda to make better use of available selling time in calling on these new accounts?

3. Develop a classification of these 18 accounts by using the single-factor analysis method. How do these results differ from the results from the portfolio analysis?

4. How might the differences between the single-factor analysis and the portfolio classification translate to increased selling effectiveness and efficiency for Brenda?

NOTES

_____

_____

_____

_____

_____

_____

_____

_____

_____

_____

_____

_____

_____

_____

_____

_____